THE HU

THE TEMPLE OF GOD;

OR,

THE PHILOSOPHY OF SOCIOLOGY,

BY

VICTORIA CLAFLIN WOODHULL

(MRS. JOHN BIDDULPH MARTIN)

AND

TENNESSEE C. CLAFLIN

(LADY COOK),

Together with other Essays. &c., &c.

ALSO

PRESS NOTICES

OF

EXTEMPORANEOUS LECTURES DELIVERED THROUGHOUT AMERICA AND ENGLAND

FROM

1869 TO 1882.

"PEOPLE IN EARNEST HAVE NO TIME TO WASTE IN PATCHING FIGLEAVES FOR THE NAKED TRUTH."—*James Russell Lowell.*

1890.

"The author of a great reformation is always unpopular in his own age. He generally passes his life in disquiet and danger. It is therefore for the interest of the human race that the memory of such men should be had in reverence, and that they should be supported against the scorn and hatred of their contemporaries by the hope of leaving a great and imperishable name. To go on the forlorn hope of truth is a service of peril—who will undertake it, if it be not also a service of honour? It is easy enough, after the ramparts are carried, to find men to plant the flag on the highest tower. The difficulty is to find men who are ready to go first into the breach."—*Lord Macaulay*.

"The noblest works of human genius have been produced in times of tumult, when every man was his own master, and all things were open to all. Homer, Dante, and Milton appeared in such times, and add Virgil.

"Man is the creation of circumstances. Free, he has the qualities of a freeman: enslaved, those of a slave.

"It would lessen very much the severity with which men judge of each other, if they would but trace effects to their causes, and observe the progress of things in the moral as accurately as in the physical world.

"We should always remember that wherever justice is ill-administered the injured *will* redress themselves, that nations are naturally patient and longsuffering, and seldom rise in rebellion till they are so degraded by a bad Government as to be almost incapable of a good one."

PREFACE.

FROM 1869 to 1877 I addressed myself to my countrymen, and yet more to my countrywomen, throughout the
length and breadth of America in the character of a public
lecturer. The topics with which I dealt were mainly two:
the one political, the other social. The question of Female
Suffrage, and of woman's political rights under the Constitution of the United States, was then, and still is, of
interest to many; the question of raising society, through
woman, to a higher standard of morals should be of
supreme moment to all.

During this career of publicity, my views were subjected to the free criticism of a free press; but travelling
as I did fast and far, by no means all of the opinions of the
newspapers ever came under my eyes: fewer still have survived the vicissitudes of the years that have since elapsed.
I have gathered together in the following pages those
that remain, as a record, fragmentary though it be, of work

that was carried on through much abuse and misrepresentation to a triumphant conclusion.

But I trust that some record of my work other than the ephemeral approbation of the press may yet remain, and that of those who listened to me in the years that are past many may bear witness by a higher aim in life, and a purer standard of morals, that my labour was not in vain.

VICTORIA C. (WOODHULL) MARTIN.

17, HYDE PARK GATE, LONDON, ENGLAND.

CONTENTS.

	PAGE
THE GARDEN OF EDEN; OR, THE PARADISE LOST AND FOUND	1
THE ARGUMENT FOR WOMAN'S ELECTORAL RIGHTS ...	59
THE CONSTITUTION OF THE UNITED STATES	67
MANIFESTO (Reprinted from the *New York Herald*, April 2nd, 1870)	86
MEMORIAL TO CONGRESS	90
FURTHER ARGUMENT IN SUPPORT OF THE MEMORIAL ...	93
REPORT OF THE COMMITTEE	106
MINORITY REPORT OF THE COMMITTEE	113
CONSTITUTIONAL EQUALITY. A Lecture delivered at Washington, February 16th, 1871	145
THE XIVTH AND XVTH AMENDMENTS TO THE CONSTITUTION OF THE UNITED STATES. A Speech delivered before the National Woman's Suffrage Convention, May 11th, 1871	176
A NEW POLITICAL PARTY AND A NEW POLITICAL PLATFORM. A Paper read at the Woman's Suffrage Convention, May 12th, 1871	184
A REVIEW OF THE NEW DOCTRINE OF STATE RIGHTS. A Speech delivered before the National Woman's Suffrage Association, January 10th, 1872	190
THE REVIEW OF A CENTURY; OR, THE FRUIT OF FIVE THOUSAND YEARS. A Lecture delivered at Boston, October 22nd, 1876	229
PRESS NOTICES	269
MISCELLANEA	589

NOTE.—The plates contained in this volume are reproductions of illustrations that appeared in contemporary newspapers.

THE GARDEN OF EDEN.

THE GARDEN OF EDEN;

OR,

THE PARADISE LOST AND FOUND.

INTRODUCTION.

MOST of the ideas which permeate our social, religious, and political institutions of to-day arise from misconceptions of the human body. These institutions which are the outcome of civilization define laws to regulate and control the actions of *human beings ;* and yet, the proper understanding of the growth and development of man individually was, and is, considered of secondary importance in adjusting these laws. My philosophy has been on the lines of Aristotle, who said, " The *nature* of everything is best seen in its smallest portions." My efforts were for the individual or ontogenic development of humanity as the only basis upon which to frame any laws—that by understanding and giving the proper attention to this the *quality* of the whole must of necessity ultimately reach a higher standard. And as the influence of woman is vital, no advance could be made until the co-operation of woman was properly understood and insisted upon as essential to any ideal society, to any true realization of religion, to any perfect government. Active not passive aid is what I demanded from woman. She must be appreciated as the architect of the human race. Men are what their mothers make them. Their intelligence or ignorance has the power to teach them to revere or desecrate womanhood. Night after night throughout the United States I pleaded for the intellectual emancipation and the redemption of womanhood from sexual slavery—insisting that social evils could only be eliminated by making your daughters the peers of your sons—that the greatness of a nation depends upon its mothers. I denounced as criminal the ignorant marriages which were filling the world with their hereditary consequences of woe, shame, and every manner of crime. The theme of my public work was that I would make it a criminal offence to allow persons to marry in ignorance of parental responsibility. I realized that the Bible was little understood, but had in it the germ of a great and divine truth—that is the redemption of the body. A part of this truth regarding the "Garden of Eden," &c., I gave in my extemporaneous lectures. It was afterwards put into consecutive biblical articles and pamphlets. I did not then give the whole truth with which my soul had become illuminated; for I knew the fulness of time was not yet. I considered the work I was then doing as a necessary part of the evolution of thought—as initiatory to my reformatory work. In a book that I am at present writing, it is my intention to give the entire truth of all Bibles, which was only partially understood by primeval religious sects through their ignorance of the phenomena of life.

V. C. W. M.,

17, Hyde Park Gate, London.

—— — ——

"BUT IN THE DAYS OF THE VOICE OF THE SEVENTH ANGEL, WHEN HE SHALL BEGIN TO SOUND, THE MYSTERY OF GOD SHALL BE FINISHED."

Revelation x. 7.

CHAPTER II.

THUS the heavens and the earth were finished, and all the host of them.

2 And on the seventh day God ended his work which he had made; and he rested on the seventh day from all his work which he had made.

3 And God blessed the seventh day, and sanctified it: because that in it he had rested from all his work which God created and made.

4 ¶ These *are* the generations of the heavens and of the earth when they were created, in the day that the LORD God made the earth and the heavens,

5 And every plant of the field before it was in the earth and every herb of the field before it grew; for the LORD God had not caused it to rain upon the earth, and *there was* not a man to till the ground.

6 But there went up a mist from the earth, and watered the whole face of the ground.

7 And the LORD God formed man *of* the dust of the ground, and breathed into his nostrils the breath of life; and man became a living soul.

8 ¶ And the LORD God planted a garden eastward in Eden; and there he put the man whom he had formed.

9 And out of the ground made the LORD God to grow every tree that is pleasant to the sight, and good for food; the tree of life also in the midst of the garden, and the tree of knowledge of good and evil.

10 And a river went out of Eden to water the garden; and from thence it was parted, and became into four heads.

11 The name of the first *is* Pison: that *is* it which compasseth the whole land of Havilah, where *there is* gold;

12 And the gold of that land *is* good: there *is* bdellium and the onyx stone.

13 And the name of the second river *is* Gihon: the same *is* it that compasseth the whole land of Ethiopia.

14 And the name of the third river *is* Hiddekel: that *is* it which goeth toward the east of Assyria. And the fourth river *is* Euphrates.

15 And the LORD God took the man, and put him into the garden of Eden to dress it and to keep it.

16 And the LORD God commanded the man, saying, Of every tree of the garden thou mayest freely eat:

17 But of the tree of the knowledge of good and evil, thou shalt not eat of it: for in the day that thou eatest thereof thou shalt surely die.

18 ¶ And the LORD God said, *It is* not good that the man should be alone; I will make him an help meet for him.

19 And out of the ground the LORD God formed every beast of the field, and every fowl of the air; and brought *them* unto Adam to see what he would call them; and whatsoever Adam called every living creature, that *was* the name thereof.

20 And Adam gave names to all cattle, and to the fowl of the air, and to every beast of the field; but for Adam there was not found an help meet for him.

21 And the LORD God caused a deep sleep to fall upon Adam, and he slept: and he took one of his ribs, and closed up the flesh instead thereof:

22 And the rib, which the LORD God had taken from man, made he a woman, and brought her unto the man.

23 And Adam said, This *is* now bone of my bones, and flesh of my flesh: she shall be called Woman, because she was taken out of Man.

24 Therefore shall a man leave his father and his mother, and shall cleave unto his wife: and they shall be one flesh.

25 And they were both naked, the man and his wife, and were not ashamed.

CHAPTER III.

Now the serpent was more subtle than any beast of the field which the LORD God had made. And he said unto the woman, Yea, hath God said, Ye shall not eat of every tree of the garden?

2 And the woman said unto the serpent: We may eat of the fruit of the trees of the garden:

3 But of the fruit of the tree which *is* in the midst of the garden, God hath said, Ye shall not eat of it, neither shall ye touch it, lest ye die:

4 And the serpent said unto the woman, Ye shall not surely die:

5 For God doth know that in the day ye eat thereof, then your eyes shall be opened, and ye shall be as gods, knowing good and evil.

6 And when the woman saw that the tree *was* good for food, and that it *was* pleasant to the eyes, and a tree to be desired to make *one* wise, she took of the fruit thereof, and did eat; and gave also unto her husband with her, and he did eat.

7 And the eyes of them both were opened, and they knew that they *were* naked: and they sewed fig leaves together, and made themselves aprons.

8 And they heard the voice of the LORD God walking in the garden in the cool of the day: and Adam and his wife hid themselves from the presence of the LORD God amongst the trees of the garden.

9 And the LORD God called unto Adam, and said unto him Where *art* thou?

10 And he said, I heard thy voice in the garden, and I was afraid, because I *was* naked; and I hid myself.

11 And he said, Who told thee that thou *wast* naked? Hast thou eaten of the tree, whereof I commanded thee that thou shouldest not eat?

12 And the man said, The woman whom thou gavest *to be* with me, she gave me of the tree, and I did eat.

13 And the LORD God said unto the woman, What *is* this *that* thou hast done? And the woman said, The serpent beguiled me, and I did eat.

14 And the LORD God said unto the serpent, Because thou has done this, thou *art* cursed above all cattle, and above every

beast of the field: upon thy belly shalt thou go, and dust shalt thou eat all the days of thy life:

15 And I will put enmity between thee and the woman, and between thy seed and her seed; it shall bruise thy head, and thou shalt bruise his heel.

16 Unto the woman he said, I will greatly multiply thy sorrow and thy conception; in sorrow thou shalt bring forth children; and thy desire *shall be* to thy husband, and he shall rule over thee.

17 And unto Adam he said, Because thou hast hearkened unto the voice of thy wife, and hast eaten of the tree, of which I commanded thee, saying, Thou shalt not eat of it: cursed *is* the ground for thy sake; in sorrow shalt thou eat *of* it all the days of thy life;

18 Thorns also and thistles shall it bring forth to thee; and thou shalt eat the herb of the field:

19 In the sweat of thy face shalt thou eat bread, till thou return unto the ground; for out of it wast thou taken: for dust thou *art*, and unto dust shalt thou return.

20 And Adam called his wife's name Eve; because she was the mother of all living.

21 Unto Adam also, and to his wife, did the LORD God make coats of skins, and clothed them.

22 ¶ And the LORD God said, Behold, the man is become as one of us, to know good and evil: and now, lest he put forth his hand, and take also of the tree of life, and eat, and live for ever;

23 Therefore the LORD God sent him forth from the garden of Eden, to till the ground from whence he was taken.

24 So he drove out the man; and he placed at the east of the garden of Eden cherubims, and a flaming sword which turned every way, to keep the way of the tree of life.

--- --- --- ---

I take up this book and call your attention to it. You perhaps will say, "Oh, that is the old Bible, worn threadbare long ago. We do not wish to be fed with its dry husks. We want living food and drink." Well, that is what I am going to give you.

Yes! it is an old book, a very old book. There are very few books extant that can compare with it, on the score of age, at least. Some parts of it were written over three thousand years ago; and all of it more than eighteen hundred years ago. Yes! an old book. And yet everybody seems to have one about the house. What is the matter with the old book? Why do people cling to it with such tenacity? Can any of those who have laid it on the shelf as worthless answer these questions? Why do they not burn it, so that it shall no longer cumber the house? This was a mystery to me for many years; but it is so no longer. I know the reason for its hold upon the people. It contains that, though clad in mystery, which acts upon the soul like a potent spell; like a magnet, which it is indeed. Had it no value, or had its value been wholly extracted; were there no truth in it unrevealed, it had long since ceased to exert any influence whatever over anybody. Books that are exhausted of their truth by its being transferred to the minds of the people, lose their force and die. And this is the reason that I ask you to search its hidden mystery with me; to cast aside preconceived ideas of its meaning; to commence to read it as if it were for the first time.

Religion and science admit that there was an original cause which set up in matter the motion that ultimated in man. The latter examines into the various works that preceded his appearance, and discovers that he came as a result of them all; indeed, that, except they had first existed, he could never have lived; that the omission of a single progressive step in the creative plan would have defeated the work. But science goes further than this. It not only asserts that man was the last link in a long chain of development, but it also maintains that, when the creation once began, there was no power residing anywhere that could have interposed its edicts to stay the progress, or defeat the final production of man; that he was a necessary product of creation, as fruit is of the tree, and that all the

designs and purposes of the moving power were contained in and
exhausted by his creation ; that is, that as a fruit of the creative
plan, man was the highest possibility of the universe.

Religious theory, in inquiring into the creation of man, has
pursued the method precisely the reverse of this. Having found
man on the earth, it assumes that he was a special creation ; that
is, that God, having purposed in Himself that He would create
man, set Himself about to prepare a place in which he was to
live ; the earth, formed according to the account in Genesis,
being that place. I say that this is the theory of religionists ;
but it is by no means certain that their account of the creation
justifies any such conclusion. The biblical account of the
creation is an allegorical picture of it, which, in detail, is
strikingly in harmony with the real truth. "In the beginning
God created the heavens and the earth, and the earth was without form, and void." There were light and darkness—day and
night. There were the divisions into water and land ; the
vegetation, fish, fowl, beast, and man; and next, the rest from
labour. In so few words, who could make a clearer statement
of what we know about the creation of the earth than this ?

We must remember that the Bible does not pretend to be a
scientific book at all. It deals altogether with the inspirational
or spirit side of the universe. St. Paul informs us that the God
of the Bible "is a spirit." At least the translators have made
him state it thus; but it is not exactly as he wrote it, although
in the end it has the same significance, since if God is a spirit, a
spirit is also God. The original Greek of this, which is what
Paul meant to say, and did say, and which is the truth,
religiously and scientifically also, is *Pneuma Theos*—Pneuma
meaning spirit, and Theos God. According to St. Paul, then,
spirit is God, and according to science, the life that is in the
world is its creative cause; so both agree in their fundamental
propositions, however much the priestcraft of the world may
have attempted to twist St. Paul into accordance with their

ideas of the personal character of God, and in placing God first
in the declaration, instead of making spirit the predominant
idea. The biblical Creator, then, as defined by the Apostle, is
spirit : "And the Spirit of God moved upon the face of the
waters" (Genesis i. 2), which was the beginning of creation.
The fact, stated scientifically, would be : And the power (or the
spirit) resident in matter, caused it to move, and by this motion
the earth began to assume form and to be an independent existence, revolving upon its own axis as a planet, and around the sun
as its centre.

But I do not purpose to enter into a detailed discussion of the
relations which the Bible creation bears to the demonstrations of
geology and astronomy. I desire to show merely that the Bible
Creator, God, is not at all incompatible with the power which
science is compelled to admit as having been the creative cause
of all things.

If we take the Darwinian theory and endeavour to find where
and how man came, we are led necessarily to a time when there
was nothing existing higher than that type of animal by which
man is connected with the brute creation, and through which he
came to be man. Man is an animal ; but he is something more
as well. He knows good and evil, and this is to be more than an
animal. There was a time, however, when man did not know
good and evil. It was then that the form—the human man—
was in existence ; and it is easy to conceive that the whole face
of the earth may have been occupied by human beings who were
nothing more than animals, as it is now occupied by them being
more than animals. These were the male and female whom
God created according to the first chapter of Genesis. It does
not mean at all that they were a single male and female. They
were not Adam and Eve then. They were simply male and
female man, or Adam ; for in chapter v. verse 2, we are told,
"Male and female created he them and called *their* name
Adam ;" that is, the human animals that inhabited the earth
were called Adam.

Now, this is precisely the condition in which science informs us that man, at one time, must have been. 'He was not created at one and the same time, physically, mentally, and morally; he may have lived for ages in this animal condition. Of this, Moses tells us nothing in his history of the creation. But as there were immense periods of time—days—between the various epochs of the creation of which he tells us nothing, we must remember that with God there are no divisions of time, for all time is eternity. But there came a point in time when male and female man had developed to the condition in which the gleams of reason began to light up the horizon of the intellect, as the first rays of the morning sun lights the tallest mountains which reflect them into the valleys below.

It was at this time that the Lord God " planted a garden eastward in Eden," in which he put the man whom he had formed " to dress it and to keep it." It is sufficient here to say that it consisted of the ground that was cursed by reason of the sin that Adam and Eve committed. Nor is it essential to the argument, at this time, to consider whether this ground—this garden—was a single one, or whether there was more than one, scattered here and there among male and female men.

The probability is, however, that these names refer to *conditions* and not to individuals. Indeed, it may as well be said now, as later, that the Bible is not a history of individuals and nations at all, but rather the condition and development of universal man, sometimes, perhaps often, using historical facts by which to typify them, but for all that, intended to refer to the *interior* instead of the exterior progress of man; that is, the Bible relates to the building and progress of God's holy temple.

It is upon the consequences of the fall of man, which is therein set forth, that the necessity for a plan of redemption rests. Take away the first three chapters of Genesis and the superstructure of orthodox religion would topple and fall. So, then, it becomes necessary, since Christians have made them vital, to inquire into what these chapters mean—to inquire what was the

Garden of Eden, there so graphically set forth—whether a spot of ground situated somewhere on the surface of the earth, or something altogether different—something, perhaps, that it may seldom or never have been suspected of being, and yet something that the language of these chapters plainly states it to have been; or, as may prove to be the exact truth, something other than which it is impossible to derive from the language in which the description is clothed. *For instance, if the various parts of a thing be described as parts, when the parts are put together, that which they form must be the real thing which was in the mind of its relator.* Therefore, if when we shall take the several things described by Moses and put them together, they shall be found to constitute something widely different from a spot of ground on the surface of the earth, why then we shall be forced to conclude that it was not such a spot that Moses had in view when he wrote the second chapter of Genesis; and therefore, also, that the Garden of Eden must be sought elsewhere than in a geographical location.

Indeed, I do not hesitate to say here at the outset, knowing full well the responsibility of the assertion, that I can demonstrate to you—to any minister or number of ministers—to all the theologians everywhere—that there is not a shadow of reason contained in the language used for concluding that the Garden of Eden ever was a geographical locality; but, on the contrary, without resorting to anything outside of the Bible—without any words of my own—I can show, beyond the possibility of cavil, and to the satisfaction of all who will give me their attention, that the Garden of Eden is something altogether different from a vegetable patch, or a fruit or flower garden; aye, more definite than this still—that I can demonstrate, so that there can be no manner of question about it, just what this garden was, and what it still is, with its cherubim and flaming sword defending the approach to its sacred precincts. Nor, as I said, will I go outside of the Bible to do all this, so that, when it shall be done, none can say that I have cited any irrelevant matter or any questionable authority.

The Bible has seldom, if ever—certainly never by professing Christians—been searched with the view to discover any new truth that might not be in harmony with their preconceived ideas as to what the truth ought to be; that is to say, it has never been searched fearlessly of what the truth might prove to be. The seal of mystery that is visible all over the face of the Bible, and that is clearly set forth in words within itself, has never been broken, nor the veil penetrated which hides its real significance from the minds of the people; while the attempts that have been made to interpret this significance have had their origin in a desire to verify some already entertained idea.

To want the truth for the sake of the truth—to want the truth, let it be what it may and lead where it may—has had, so far, no conspicuous following in the world, or at least so few that, practically, it may be said that there has never been any desire for the truth for its own sake. When the truth has appeared to be in antagonism with the cherished conceits of the people, they have shut their eyes and closed their hearts against it, and blocked up all avenues for its approach to them. One of the best evidences that the full truth is soon to dawn upon the world, lies in the fact that there are now a few persons who want the truth for its own sake, and who will follow it wherever it may lead them.

For one I want the truth, the whole truth; and I will proclaim it, no matter if it be opposed to every vestige of organization extant—political, social, religious! No matter if it be revolutionary to every time-honoured institution in existence! Let creeds fall if they will; let churches topple if they must; let anarchy even reign temporarily if it cannot be avoided, but let us for once in the world have the simple, plain truth; and let us welcome it because it is the truth, and not because it may or may not be in accord with popular notions and opinions.

But now to the Garden of Eden: In the second chapter of Genesis, beginning at the 8th verse, and, for the present, ending with the 14th verse, we read thus:—

8 "And the Lord God planted a garden eastward in Eden; and there he put the man whom he had formed.

10 "And a river went out of Eden to water the garden; and from thence it was parted, and became into four heads.

11 "And the name of the first river *is* Pison: that *is* it which compasseth the whole land of Havilah, where *there is* gold; there *is* bdellium and the onyx stone.

12 "And the gold of that land is good.

13 "And the name of the second river *is* Gihon: the same *is* it that compasseth the whole land of Ethiopia.

14 "And the name of the third river *is* Hiddekel; that *is* it which goeth toward the east of Assyria. And the fourth river *is* Euphrates."

These six verses comprise the physical description of the garden, and it is upon them that the structure, now to be taken in pieces and examined, rests. For a moment let us look at the language in its literal sense and see whether in this way it appears as if it were probable even that it may be true. "And the Lord God planted a garden eastward in Eden." Bible geographers and commentators say that the locality of the garden is lost, and they do not pretend to tell where Eden is, or was, to say nothing about a particular spot in Eden where the garden was planted. It is supposed that Eden was somewhere in Asia; in fact, somewhere in the neighbourhood of Jerusalem, the holy city. If they who say so knew how nearly they have hit upon the truth without knowing what the truth is, the ministers would indeed be astonished. But where is eastward in Eden? Since the best informed Christian geographers can give no help to aid us in the search which we propose to make for this famous garden, we might as well conclude that it is anywhere else in the world as to conclude that it is in Asia.

But an astute person suggests that it must have been in Western Asia, because the rivers named as being in the garden are there. Yes! There were some rivers, and there were some countries in which they were situated, and yet we are coolly informed that the garden is lost, as if it were a matter of only the slightest moment. But will Christians assert, with the expectation that it will be believed, that the location of the four rivers and of the countries in which they were located, are lost with the garden. To say that the garden is lost is virtually to say just that. The four rivers are enumerated specifically, to wit: the Pison, the Gihon, the Hiddekel, and the Euphrates. Are these rivers lost and also the countries Havilah, Ethiopia, and Assyria—all well known geographical terms? If they are not, how does it happen that the garden can be lost? There seems to be something very strange about all this.

And as the allegory continues, when the Lord God had expelled Adam from the garden, we are informed that he "placed at the east of the garden Cherubims [*the Cherubims, the eyes; and the flaming sword, the tongue*], and a flaming sword which turned every way to keep the way of the tree of life." Is it not proper also to inquire after these sentries of the Lord God? What has become of them, and the tree of life that they were set to guard? If they were set "at the east of the garden," and the garden was in Western Asia, why are they not to be found somewhere now? If I were anxious about the consistency of my theology, I should send off a Livingstone at once to hunt up this garden, fearing lest my religion might go to keep company with the garden upon which it is founded. I will venture the opinion that anyone who should start upon that journey, would have a more difficult task than discovering the sources of the Nile, or the North Pole, has proved to be.

But what about that tree of life which was in the midst of the garden? What has become of that? Is that lost also? Is that perished? and if so, are there any more in the world? The Lord God expelled Adam from the garden "lest he should put forth his hand and take of the tree of life, and eat and live for ever." It seems that this kind of tree was not very common then, at least in that part of the world. If they are common in any part, I have never heard of them. If there were any in existence, it is my opinion that two cherubims and one flaming sword would afford them but poor protection against the ravages of a people who cling to life with the tenacity with which most of the people exhibit, not excepting that portion which believes itself safe from the uncomfortable regions of the other world, and who should most desire to die.

Thousands of the wisest men of Oriental nations have searched Asia over and over, and have failed to find a single tree of life anywhere. Has the logic of this fact ever had its legitimate weight in the consideration of this matter? I think not. The generality of people have never thought upon this subject at all, or about anything else connected with their religion.

In the second chapter of Genesis we are told all about the countries in which the garden was located, and the rivers that bounded it. From what I have already said, however, it is understood that I do not believe in this garden as commonly understood; nor do I believe that so important a spot as this garden is claimed to be, should be summarily given up as lost. The most important clue is the course of one of the rivers of this garden. Let us follow it to its source; for, in the tenth verse, it says, "And a river went out of Eden to water the garden; and from thence it was parted, and became into four heads;" that is to say, it gave off four branches. Let us see which of the four rivers we shall select as the basis of operations, and on which to make the ascent to find the place where it divides from the main river. The first river, as we have seen, is called Pison. As we can find no geographical mention of this river, we shall be obliged to omit Pison. The next in order is the Gihon. We are told (2 Chronicles xxxii. 30) that King Hezekiah turned the upper water-course of Gihon so that it should run by the City of David. That ought to be definite; but we fear, if we were to go to the City of David to-day, we should find the river in the same condition as the garden itself which it once watered—that its location is lost. So we must also pass the Gihon, and turn to the next, which is Hiddekel. Though both Moses and Daniel said that this river was in Assyria, we can find no geographical mention made of its locality anywhere; therefore we shall be obliged to dismiss this with the others, and have recourse to the last one, which is the Euphrates. We all know where the Euphrates river is located, and if we can reach its banks, and follow up its course, we must, as a matter of necessity, find its source; and in finding it, find also the greater river Pison, from which it divides. Having done this, all the other rivers also will be discovered. There can be no mistaking the place, since it was at that point where the great river divided into four heads. When we arrive at this place, we shall be, at least, near the garden.

But, alas for our hopes! We wander along the banks of the beautiful Euphrates, from its mouth to its source, and find no place where it divides from another river; but, on the contrary, discover a number flowing into its ever-increasing stream. And now we cross to the opposite shore, and again from the Persian Gulf to the mountains of Armenia, seek the desired spot, but still are doomed to disappointment. If this be the river Moses describes, then his description is not true. The Euphrates river does not divide from any other river, but has its own source, as other rivers have their sources. So our last hope from the rivers is gone. We must dismiss the Euphrates as well as the Pison, the Gihon, and the Hiddekel.

Let us not, however, be altogether discouraged by our repeated failures with the rivers. The object in view is too important to be hastily abandoned. We have not yet exhausted our means of discovery. So, with heavy hearts, we will turn our backs upon the rivers, and seek elsewhere, hoping for better success. Since we cannot find the garden through the medium of its rivers, perhaps, if we reverse the process, we may be able to hunt up the rivers by seeking for them in the countries in which Moses said they were located. The river Pison, so he informs us, is the name of the first of the four rivers into which the great river divides, and "that it compasseth the whole land of Havilah." Now, certainly, we ought to be able to find the river Pison, for Havilah is a district of country on the Red Sea, in Arabia, south-east of Sanaa. Referring to the map of this portion of the earth, we readily find the land called Havilah. But what is this? It is not an island at all. Moses said that it was compassed—that is, encircled—by the river Pison, and that should make it an island. But there is no river that runs about this Havilah. Indeed, there is not any river in this land that is laid down on the maps. Moreover, we find from the conformation of this land that it is a physical impossibility for a stream of water to compass it. The western part of Havilah rests upon the Red Sea, where no river could ever have run. So it cannot be said that there might have been a river there in the time of Moses, which has since disappeared. He must have been very much mistaken, or else the land of Havilah, to which he referred, is something quite apart from geographical land; and yet Moses is most explicit, since he says that the ground of this land was cursed.

Having failed with Havilah, we will go on to the next. "And the name of the second river is Gihon," says Moses, " the same is it that compasseth the whole land of Ethiopia." Now, Ethiopia is a large country—a very large country—and Moses says that the whole land was compassed by this river Gihon; a river that should encircle the whole of this land of Ethiopia must be no less than three thousand miles in length. It were impossible to lose such a river as this; hence, if it ever had an existence anywhere, it must be now in existence somewhere. Besides it must have been a still larger river even than this from which so large a one could have been given off. But what is this that

2 *

we find? Ethiopia is a vast domain, situated in the very heart of Africa, with mountains on the north, mountains on the east, mountains everywhere. If the second chapter of Genesis is geography, Moses must have meant to have said there were mountains instead of a river compassing the whole land of Ethiopia, or else his Ethiopia was some country other than the one which we have under consideration, and one of which there is nothing known in our day save what Moses tells us.

We will now re-cross the Red Sea into Asia, and go through the land of Assyria, looking for the river Hiddekel, which Moses says is there. Turning again to the maps, we also again fail to find such a river as Hiddekel there set down, and we run through the geographies fruitlessly. As far as our investigations have been pushed, we can find two places only in all the books where this river is mentioned, and these occur in the text, and in Daniel x. 4. This is the river on the banks of which Daniel had the most remarkable vision recorded in the Old Testament; and it rises into the greatest significance by reason of the character of that vision. Where should this river be? Bible geographers endeavour to account for the discrepancies between the Bible and the geographies by saying that it is supposed that this river Hiddekel was the one now known as the Tigris. To be sure the Tigris runs with a swift current as did the Hiddekel; but it is not in the right place, nor does it run in the right direction. The maps show that the river Tigris instead of running "to the east of Assyria," runs southward into the Persian Gulf. Nor do the maps discover any river running to the east of Assyria which may be taken for the river Hiddekel of the Bible. So we shall have to abandon the search for the Garden of Eden. We have exhausted the rivers, and the countries also, in which Moses set it down as being located.

Although we have not discovered the garden, we have found all the countries named by Moses. If the Garden of Eden really consisted of all of these countries, and for some reason, now unknown, their rivers cannot be discovered, it must have been a very large garden—almost as large as the half of North America. But we have stumbled upon one rather singular fact that needs to be explained: We know that the river Euphrates is in Turkey in Asia. Then how does it happen that another river, which has its source in the same river from which it is said to divide, is in Ethiopia, in Africa—which is separated from both Assyria and Havilah by the Red Sea? How does the river Gihon find its way across the Red Sea into Ethiopia to compass the whole of that land? Failing to explain this, however, an attempt perhaps will be made to clear it away upon the well-known hypothesis, that with God all things are possible; and consequently, that it was possible for Him to construct a river that could run under the Red Sea to get into Ethiopia; and a garden made up of large countries, widely separated each from the other, and still be altogether in one place, with a single tree in its midst; to watch and guard which, cherubims and a flaming sword were set at the east of the garden, a distance of not less than three thousand miles from its western limits.

But why dwell longer upon this mass, geographically considered, of physical impossibilities and absurdities. Any school boy of twelve years of age who should read the description of this garden and not discover that it has no geographical significance whatever, ought to be reprimanded for his stupidity. Nevertheless, learned Divines have written and preached for ages over this mythical garden just as if it ever had a geographical existence, and never suspected that what they were writing and talking about was all a fable, simply incredible.

Geography must have been interdicted in the schools where they were educated; or else the theological spectacles must have been so highly coloured by authority that they could not perceive that the geography of the Bible and that of the face of the earth ought to agree somewhat, which in this case it does not at all.

Do you not begin to see how preposterous and impossible, how

contradictory and absurd, it is even to pretend to think that the
Garden of Eden is a geographical locality? I challenge any
clergyman—all clergymen—to impeach the truth, force, or application which I shall make of a single one of the rivers and
countries of this famous garden. And I call upon them, failing
to do it, to lay this whole fable open to their people as I have
laid it open to you. Will they do so? If they care more for
their theology than they do for the truth, No! But if they love
the truth better than they do their theology, Yes!

But was there not a Garden of Eden! I think some will query
in their minds. Or is this thing a bare-faced fraud upon the
credulity of a simple people? Oh, yes!—There was a Garden
of Eden. It is not at all a fraud. The fraud has been in the
preachers, who would not look into the Bible with sufficient
reason to discover a most palpable absurdity. There is where
the fraud lies, and there it will, sooner or later, come to rest. I
do not say that they have done this intentionally. I say only
that they have done it; and the responsibility for having misled
the people, year after year for centuries, rests with them. They
have been the blind leading the blind; and they have both fallen
into the ditch of deception.

It was necessary, before there could be a successful search to
find the Garden of Eden, to clear away the last vestige of
possibility upon which to conceive that it might have been a
geographical locality. Have I not made it clear to you all that
it was not? If I have, then we are ready to look without bias
or prejudice in other directions to find it—for there was a Garden
of Eden.

As introductory to this part of my subject, it is proper to say
that the general misunderstanding of the real meaning of the
Bible can be easily explained. The proper names have been translated from the original languages, arbitrarily, and mingled with the
common usage of the new languages, in such a way as to deprive
them of their original significance, unless we are familiar with

the meaning of the words from which they were translated.
The term Eden is a good example. If we are ignorant of the
meaning of Eden, in the original language, its use signifies to us
that there was a garden which bore this name simply for a
designation. But if we were to use the meaning of the word,
in the place of the word itself, then we should get at the
meaning of the one who gave this designation to the garden.
The failure to translate the Bible after this rule is one reason
for its still being veiled in mystery; and this fact will become
still more evident when it is remembered that, in early times,
names were given to persons and things, not merely that they
might have a name, but to embody their chief characteristics.

So, then, the first step to be taken is to inquire into the
significance of the names that the rivers and countries of the
Garden of Eden bear. I cannot explain better what I mean by
this than by quoting St. Paul on this very subject. In his letter
to the Galatians, beginning at the 22nd verse of the 4th chapter,
he says :—

"For it is written, that Abraham had two sons; the one by a bondwoman,
the other by a freewoman. But he who was of the bondwoman was born
after the flesh; but he who was of the freewoman was by promise. Which
things are an allegory: for these are the two covenants; the one from the
Mount Sinai, which is Agar. For this Agar is Mount Sinai in Arabia, and
answereth to Jerusalem, which is now in bondage with her children."

Now, suppose that Paul had not entered into any explanation
about this story regarding Abraham. Of course we should
have been left to suppose, conjecturing after the manner of the
suppositions about the Garden of Eden, that Abraham really
had these two children as described; and so he did. But Paul
says it is an allegory; meaning that they represented all
children born under both covenants; those of the first being
children of bondage—that is, born in sin—and those of the latter
being free-born, or born free from sin. This is still more evident
when the last verse quoted is interpreted. Jerusalem always

means woman, and to get the meaning of the verse it should be read thus: For this Agar is Mount Sinai in Arabia, and answereth to "*woman*," who is in bondage with her children. The succeeding verse demonstrates this clearly, since it reads: "But Jerusalem [woman, remember], which is above, is free, which is the mother of us all." The interpretation of the meaning of the words used in the description of the Garden of Eden will make equally as wonderful transformations of the apparent meaning as are made by Paul in this allegorical story about Abraham.

It is now generally admitted that the account of the creation contained in the first chapter of Genesis is wholly allegorical. Having admitted so much, it would be preposterous to not also conclude that the allegory extends into the second chapter, and includes the Garden of Eden. If the first chapter refers to the creation of the physical universe, it is not too much to say that it is a wonderfully correct picture of the manner in which the world was evolved. If we apply the same statement to the second chapter, then we are ready to inquire what the subject is which this allegorical picture represents.

First in the allegory is the name of the garden, then its rivers, and lastly the countries through which they run. Passing, for the time, the name of the garden, we will begin by inquiring into the rivers. The name of the first is Pison; that of the second is Gihon; and that of the third is Hiddekel; and that of the fourth is Euphrates. These were the names of all the rivers mentioned as being in the garden. Turning to Cruden's Concordance, quarto edition, there will be found what is called "An alphabetical table of the proper names in the Old and New Testaments, together with their meaning or signification in the original languages." That is what we want. And the study of it will convince everybody of what and where the Garden of Eden is, and make it clear why its locality has been lost, as superficial students of the Bible say it has.

In that learned work we read thus: "Pison—changing or doubling, or extension of the mouth."

"Gihon—The Valley of Grace, or breast, or impetuous." In other authorities this word is held to mean "Bursting forth as from a fountain, or from the womb."

"Hiddekel—a sharp voice or sound;" other authorities say, "Swift, which refers to the swiftness of the current."

"Euphrates—that makes fruitful or grows." Now we may inquire into the meaning of the names of the countries in which these rivers were situated.

"Havilah—that suffers pain, that brings forth."

"Ethiopia—Blackness—[Darkness]—heat, burning."

Assyria is the country of, and signifies Ashur, "One that is happy," which would make the meaning of Assyria to be, the land of the happy; or the land in which the happy dwell.

And the whole of these rivers and countries combined form the Garden of Eden, which, as we learn, means: "Pleasure or delight." So, the Garden of Eden into which the Lord God put the man whom he had formed, "to dress it and to keep it," was the garden situated in the land of pleasure or delight. Remember that these words are not mine, but that I quote them from that acknowledged authority, Cruden's Concordance.

It will be necessary to give the meaning of one more word before entering upon the application of the meaning of these words, and that is "East." The direction of east is always to the light, let the light be of whatsoever kind—physical, mental, or moral. Toward the west means going, following, or looking after the receding light. These are astrologic terms, and were taken from the ancient magi, who derived them from the sun. When the light of the sun is looked for as coming, it is toward the east that the eye is turned, because it always comes from that direction; but when we look toward the west to observe it, it is to see the departing light which precedes darkness. So, east, in our investigations, means toward or into the light. We look, allegorically, to the east when we seek a new light or a new truth. The Star in the East, which stood over the place where "the young child lay," was the new spiritual light that came by Him into the world. The same meaning attaches to the word east wherever it appears in the Bible.

"And the Lord God planted a garden eastward in Eden, and there he put the man whom he had formed." The signification of these words would make the text read thus: "And the Lord God planted a garden in pleasure or delight, the fruit of which was to be, or was, a new revelation in, or a new light to, the world."

"And a river went out of Eden to water the garden, and from thence it was parted and became into four heads. The name of the first river was Pison; that is, it which compasseth the whole land of Havilah, where there is gold." If this language be transposed into the signification of its words it would read thus: "And a river went out of the garden in which there is pleasure or delight, which river watered, fed, and drained the garden; and to water, feed, and drain the garden it was divided into four channels. The first of these new rivers, and the main one in which all the others found their sources, was the extension of the mouth; and as this river ran onward in its course, compassing or encircling that which suffers pain and brings forth fruit, the character of its waters was constantly changing by reason of its giving food and receiving refuse from the land through which it ran; and in this land there were things of great value, besides the bdellium and the onyx-stone."

This is the full meaning of the 10th, 11th, and 12th verses of the second chapter. The 13th verse reads thus: "And the name of the second river is Gihon; the same is it that compasseth the whole land of Ethiopia." This, transposed into its signification, would read thus: "And the second river of the garden bursts forth as a fountain, or from the womb, from the valley of grace, in which valley it flows in darkness and in heat."

The first clause of the 14th verse reads thus : "And the name of the third river is Hiddekel; that is it which goeth toward the east of Assyria." The translation of this, into its signification, would be as follows : "The third river of the garden runs with a swift current and a sharp sound into the light. Furthermore, this river, being in that part of the land known as Mesopotamia, which, interpreted, means 'in the midst of the rivers,' is surrounded by the other rivers of the garden, and is, therefore, situated in their midst."

The last sentence of the 14th verse is : "And the fourth river is Euphrates." The rendering of this, according to the significance of this word, would be this : "And the fourth river is that one which makes the garden fruitful; that is, in which the garden yields its fruit."

Summing up the signification of the several rivers and countries, we have, first, the river that is the extension of the mouth, which, changing the character of its waters as it flows, encircles the whole of that which suffers pain and brings forth ; second, a river that bursts forth from the valley of grace, which is in darkness, and where there is heat; third, a river that runs with a swift current and a sharp sound to the light, in front of the happy land; and fourth, a river that makes the garden fruitful.

The meaning of this summary is too evident to be escaped. The signification of these rivers is descriptive of the functions and of the various physical facts and capacities of the garden ; they inform us how that garden is fed with new, and how drained of refuse or old and worn-out matter ; they set forth the method by which the garden is made productive. Can there be anything more added to point the application with greater directness and force, save to designate the garden by the name by which it is now commonly known ?

This Garden of Eden is a very much despised place ; and if I were not to prepare the way, and guard every word I utter about it with the most scrupulous care, some of you might be so very innocent (by innocence, you must know, I mean that kind which comes of ignorance), or so modest (by modesty, you must know, I mean that kind which is born of conscious corruption, and which blushes at everything, and thus unwittingly proclaims its own shame)—I repeat that, if I were to approach the culmination too abruptly, such innocence and such modesty as that of which I speak, should there happen to be any present, might be too severely shocked.

At the outset, I must ask you to remember that it is out of the most despised spots of the earth that the greatest blessings spring; that it is out of the most obnoxious truths that the forces are developed which move the people heavenward fastest. It is the same old question, "Can there any good thing come out of Nazareth?" It should also be remembered that Jesus was conceived at the most despised of all the places of Galilee. The Jews could not believe that a Saviour of any kind could come from such a source. The promulgators of the new truths have ever been, and probably ever will be, Nazarenes; that is, will be the despised people of the world—though the meaning of that term in the original language is, "consecrated or set apart." It was in this sense that Jesus was a Nazarene. It was in this sense that the prophets were able to foretell that he would be a Nazarene. They knew that he would be set apart to do the greatest work of the ages, and therefore that, at first, he would be despised by the great of this world. Therefore, when we shall find the Garden of Eden, we may expect that it will be among the most despised, ignored, and ostracized of all the despised things of the world.

Lo, here—or, Lo, there—is Christ! is the cry of the world, which is always looking in the wrong direction for Him. Jesus said, "The Kingdom of God is within you." Suppose we find that the Garden of Eden is also within you? If the human body be a place worthy to be, and indeed is, the Kingdom of

God, it cannot be sacrilegious to say that it is also worthy to be, or to contain, the Garden of Eden. There cannot be a more holy place than the Kingdom of God; although I am well aware that too many of us have made our bodies most unholy places. Paul said, " *Know ye not that ye are the Temple of God; and that the Spirit of God dwelleth in you? If any man defile the Temple of God, him will God destroy.*" Then, the human body is not only the Kingdom of God, it is the Temple of God. Suppose, I say again, it should, after all, turn out that the long-lost Garden of Eden is the human body; that these three, the Kingdom of God, the Temple of God, and the Garden of Eden, are synonymous terms and mean the same thing—are the human body? Suppose this, I say. What then? Would not the people be likely to regard it with a little more reverence than they do now? —and to treat it with a little more care? Would they not modify their pretences that, in their natural condition, any of the parts of the body can be vulgar and impure, and unfit to be discussed either in the public press or the public rostrum? Is it not fair to conclude that, with a higher conception of the body, this ought to be the result? Certainly it would be, unless the doctrine of total depravity is true in its literal sense.

I am well aware that there must be a great change in the present thoughts and ideas about the body before it can be expected that there will be any considerable difference in its general treatment. But a great change has to come, and will come. Certain parts of the body—indeed, its most important parts—are held to be so vulgar and indecent that they have been made the subject of penal laws. Nobody can speak about them without somebody imagining himself or herself to be shocked. Now, all this is very absurd, foolish, and ridiculous, since, do you not know, that this vulgarity and obscenity are not in the body, but in the associated idea in the minds of the people who make the pretence; especially in those who urge the making of, and who make these laws, and who act so foolishly as to discover their own vulgarity and obscenity to the world in this way. How long will it be before the people will begin to comprehend that Paul spoke the truth when he said, " To the pure all things are pure." He ought to be good authority to most of you, who profess him so loudly. But I must confess that I have yet to find the first professing Christian who believes a single word of that most truthful saying. I fear that the hearts of such Christians are still far away from Jesus. But give heed to the truths to which I shall call your attention, and they will help to bring you all nearer to Him both in lip and in heart.

The despised parts of the body are to become what Jesus was, the Saviour conceived at Nazareth. The despised body, and not the honoured soul, must be the stone cut out of the mountain that shall be the head of the corner, though now rejected by the builders. There can be no undefiled or unpolluted temple of God that is not built upon this corner-stone, perfectly. And until the temple shall be perfect there can be no perfect exercise by the in-dwelling spirit. " The stone which the builders disallowed, the same is made the head of the corner."—1 Peter ii. 7. Christians have been thinking of taking care of the soul by sending it to heaven, while the body has been left to take care of itself and sink to hell, dragging its tenant with it.

" That through death he might destroy him that had the power of death, that is, the devil."—Heb. ii. 14.

" And deliver them who through fear of death were all their lifetime subject to bondage."—Heb. ii. 15.

" God hath chosen the foolish things of the world, to confound the wise ; and God hath chosen the weak things of the world to confound the things which are mighty ; and base things of the world, and things which are despised, hath God chosen."—1 Cor. i. 27, 28.

" And those members of the body, which we think to be less honourable, upon them we bestow more abundant honour."—1 Cor. xii. 23.

The last two chapters of the Revelation refer to the human body saved, and as being the dwelling place of God. The first two chapters of Genesis refer to the body, cursed by the acts of primitive man (male and female), through which acts they became ashamed and covered themselves, because they had done evil to the parts that they desired to hide. Remember, that to the pure all things are pure; and do not deceive yourselves by believing that anything which can be said about the natural functions and organs of the body can be otherwise than pure. From Genesis to the Revelation the human body is the chief subject that is considered—is the temple of God, which through long ages He has been creating to become, finally, His abiding place, when men and women shall come to love Him as He has commanded that they should; and this important thing is the basis of all revelation and all prophecy.

The objection that will be raised against accepting the evident meaning of the 2nd and 3rd chapters of Genesis will be that the things of which they really treat could never have been the subject of scriptural consideration. The degradation of the human race, following the transgression of Adam and Eve, through which purity was veiled from their own lustful gaze, and virtue shut out of the human heart, can never be removed until the world can bear to have that veil lifted, and to look upon and talk in purity about the whole body alike. It was not because they ought to have been ashamed of the nakedness they desired to hide, but because their thoughts were not pure and holy, and because their eyes could not endure the sight without engendering lust within them. So it is now. Only those are ashamed of any parts of the body whose secret thoughts are impure, and whose acts represent their thoughts whenever opportunities present themselves, or can be made.

People talk of purity without the least conception of the real meaning of the term. The people who do no evil because they have no desire to do it, are infinitely more virtuous than are they who refrain because there is a legal or any other kind of penalty attached thereto. So it is with the relations of the sexes. They are the really pure who need no law to compel them to do the right. I do not say that the law has not been useful, nor that it is not useful still. It is better to be restrained by law from doing wrong, than not to be restrained at all; but it is those who need restraint who ought to be ashamed, and not those who have grown beyond the need of law and wish for freedom from its force. In one sense, as Paul said it was, "the law was our schoolmaster;" but those who have graduated from the school, no longer need a master. Shall they, however, be compelled to have one, merely because all others have not yet graduated? Shall everybody be compelled to stay at school till everybody else has left? Think of these questions with but a grain of common sense, and you will see that they who urge the repeal of law are the best entitled to be considered pure at heart, as well as pure in act.

Jesus said, that "Whosoever looketh on a woman to lust after her, hath committed adultery with her already in his heart." Judged by this standard of purity, who are not adulterers? I will tell you who, and who only. Only those are not who can stand the test of natural virtue; and this test is never to do an act for which, under any circumstances, there is cause to be ashamed. Adam and Eve were not ashamed until they had eaten the forbidden fruit—the fruit of the tree which stood in "the midst of the garden," "whose seed is within itself;" but the moment they had done what they knew to be a wrong, when they had learned of good by knowing evil as its contrast, by reason of having done the evil, then they were ashamed and made covers for themselves. They are sexually pure and virtuous who enter into the most sacred and intimate relations of life just as they would go before their God, and by being drawn to them by the Spirit of God, which is ever present in His temple.

This is to have natural virtue. This is to have natural, in place of artificial purity. People who are pure and virtuous may be brought into intimate relations, and never have a lustful thought come into their souls. Now, this is the kind of virtue, purity, and morality that I would have established; it is the kind I advocate as the highest condition to which the race can rise. Suppose that the world were in the condition in which I speak, do you not know that it would be a thousand times more pure than it is? But do you say that all this is too far in the future to be of any use now? This plea is often made—that it ought not to be given to the people till they are ready to receive it and live it. I cannot have a more complete endorsement than to have it said that the people are not yet good enough to live the doctrines that I teach. But if they really do imagine this, I can assure them that they do not give the people credit enough for goodness. Bad as they are, they are not half so bad as some would make them out to be. Place men and women on their honour. You are all familiar with this principle, but you never think of applying it to the social relations, while it is really more applicable to them than it is to almost anything else. But, if the people are not good enough to live under the law of individual honour, then it is quite time that some one should have the courage to go before the world and begin to advocate the things that are needed to make them so.

Before leaving this part of my subject, I wish again to impress it upon you that when there is purity in the heart, it cannot be obscene to consider the natural functions of any part of the body, whether male or female. I am aware that this is a terrible truth to tell to the world, but it is a truth that the world needs to be told; one which it must fully realize before the people will give that care and attention to their creative functions which must precede the building up of a perfected humanity. Who shall dare say that the noblest works—nay, this holy temple—the kingdom of God—is obscene? Perish the vulgarity that makes such thoughts possible.

Where should the Garden of Eden be found if not within the human body? Is there any other place or thing in the universe more worthy to be called an "Eden"? Then let who may, esteeming himself a better judge than myself, condemn this garden as impure. If the gravity and grandeur of this subject were once realized you would never think meanly of, or desecrate your own body, but instead, you would do what Paul commanded (1 Corinthians vi. 20): "Glorify God in your body."

Anyone who will read the second chapter of Genesis, divorced from the idea that it relates to a spot of ground anywhere on the face of the earth, must, it seems to me, come to, or near, the truth. I have shown, conclusively, that it is not a garden in the common acceptance of that term : indeed, that the Garden of Eden, according to Moses, is a physical absurdity, if it be interpreted to mean what it is held to mean by the Christian world.

The Garden of Eden is the human body ; the second chapter of Genesis was written by Moses to mean the body ; it cannot mean anything else. Furthermore, Moses chose the language used because it describes the functions and uses of the body better than any other that he could choose without using the plain terms. Could there have been a more poetic statement of what really does occur? What more complete idea could there be formed of Paradise than a perfect human body—such as there must have been before there had been corruption and degradation in the relation of the sexes ? *"Know ye not that ye are the temple of God, and that the Spirit of God dwelleth in you? If any man defile the temple of God, him shall God destroy, for the temple of God is holy, which temple ye are."*—(1 Cor. iii. ver. 16, 17.) *" What! Know you not that your body is the temple of the Holy Ghost which is in you? Therefore glorify God in your body."*—(1 Cor. vi. ver. 19, 20.)

But now let us go on with the application of our former inquiries into this garden: "And a river went out of Eden to water the garden, and from thence it was parted, and became into four heads. The name of the first river is Pison, as we have seen. It will be remembered that this term signifies changing and extension of the mouth. Now, apply this rendering to the body and see if we cannot find the river Pison in this Havilah, which we failed to find in the Arabian land. How is the body watered and fed? Is it not by a stream which is the extension of the mouth, and that changes constantly as it encircles the system? Does not the support of the body enter it by the mouth, and by the river which is the extension of the mouth run to the stomach? "And from thence it was parted, and became into four heads." Now this is precisely what is going on in the body all the time. From the stomach, or rather from the small intestines, where the separating process in the chyle, which is the digested contents of the stomach, begins, this river Pison has four principal heads; that is, it divides and becomes into four heads, giving off three branches, while the main current continues on its course to compass the whole land of Havilah. This current—this river Pison—empties itself into the heart, and then into the lungs, where it is de-carbonized and oxygenized, and returned to the heart to be distributed over the entire system by the arterial circulation. In its course toward the extremities it gives to the various parts through which it passes their necessary supplies. This constant giving-off changes the character of the current as constantly, until the circumference of the body is reached. From thence it is returned to the heart through the venous circulation, gathering up the worn-out matter to expel it from the body. This is the process by which the river Pison compasseth the whole land of Havilah, which is the land "that suffers pain and brings forth," and in which there are precious things, besides the bdellium and the onyx stone. This land that suffers pain and brings forth is the land of Havilah, which is compassed by the river Pison. Can anyone conceive a more graphic description of the process by which the body is nourished and fed? A river, to water the land of pleasure or delight, enters by the mouth, and extending by the way of the stomach, intestines, heart, lungs, arteries, and veins, waters the whole land that suffers pain and brings forth. What is there in the world to which this description of the river Pison and the land of Havilah could be applied, save to the body? It cannot be found. I challenge the world to find it. It would be absurd, simply, to say that the district south-east of Sanaa, in Arabia, which is called Havilah, suffers pain in bringing forth. Nevertheless, this is the conventionally accepted land of Havilah.

"And the name of the second river is Gihon: the same is it that compasseth the whole land of Ethiopia." The first branch that divides from the main river of the body is that which drains the body by way of the intestines. This is the river Gihon, which is the valley of grace. Could there be a more appropriate name than that of "grace" for the process by which the refuse from the river Pison is discharged from the body? or than the valley of grace for the operations that are performed within the abdomen for the elimination from the body of the refuse that is gathered there. Is not this a process of grace?—a process of natural and involuntary purification? If it were not for this purpose of grace we should be lost through the *débris* of which the system is relieved by this bursting forth of the river Gihon from this valley of grace.

And this is the river that compasseth the whole land of Ethiopia—the land of blackness (darkness), and where there is heat (see Psalm cxxxix. 12). That is to say, the intestines occupy the abdominal cavity, which is the land of darkness in Eden. All the movements that are made therein are made in darkness, and therein also is the heat which signifies the warmth that gives and maintains life; that maintains the old and that produces the new; that sustains the temperature of the body, and that gives it the power to reproduce. Physiologically this is absolutely true, just as are all the other descriptions and allegories that are given by Moses of the garden.

"And the name of the third river is Hiddekel, that is it

which goeth toward the east of Assyria." Next in importance to the maintenance of the human economy is the river that drains the system of another class of impurities, running by the way of the kidneys, uretus, bladder, and urethra. This is the river Hiddekel; or the stream that runs with a "swift current" and a "sharp sound." Search the language through and through for a more appropriate description for the elimination of the waste matter by the means of the urinary organs than this one given by Moses. And this river of Eden runs toward the east of Assyria, which is the "land of the garden," in the midst of which is the tree of life. That this may be still more evident, it is proper to remark here, that it is the female human body which is referred to by Moses, because it is her body that suffers pain in bringing forth; and it was the producing part of the garden—the reproductive female power—that was the land which was cursed in Eden by the transgressions, *by eating of the fruit of the tree of life improperly.* It was by this curse that woman's "*sorrows and conceptions were multiplied,*" as stated by Moses. So the Garden of Eden is the producing land of the human family into which the Lord God put the man whom he had formed, "to keep it and to dress it," so that it might be fruitful. Do you not see how perfect the allegorical statement is, which Moses made?

"And the fourth river is Euphrates." The last river of the Garden of Eden is that one which renders it fruitful; that makes it yield its fruit, and that flows through the reproductive system. Euphrates means fruitfulness, and this river, the last one in the order of physiological sequence, is the fruit or the result of the perfected action of all the others combined. This river was in its natural, healthful, primitive state of purity, from which physical purity primitive man and woman fell by the improper use of the functions of the garden, which were committed to their care, the same as people continue to do, and are cursed—die in Adam.

At the time when knowledge began to find root in the brain of man, it is pretty evident that the human animal, man, was pure and perfect physically; that is, that they were like the other animals, and that they are to be judged of as we judge of animals now. Considered in this light, what are the differences between man and the animals? This is a question of the most vital importance, since, if there was a fall of man from the original state of purity, it is necessary that we know of what that fall consisted before we can provide intelligently for an escape therefrom. It was not a moral fall certainly, since morality is not an attribute of animals, unless physical purity is morality. This view of ethics is not legitimate, since morals are the last development in the growth of man, are an outgrowth of, or a building upon, intellect. Nor could that fall have been intellectual, since as there had then been no knowledge of good and evil, there was no intellect; there had been no power of comparison in the human brain. We are obliged to conclude, therefore, that that sin committed by man was a physical sin.

Now what was this sin? Well, go to the animal world and compare its physical habits with our own, and it will not be difficult to discover differences sufficient to account for all that has occurred to mankind; indeed, we shall find such a disparity that we shall be left only to wonder that a second deluge has been so long deferred. What is the central point towards which all these differences gravitate? It is clearly the relations between the male and female. Undoubtedly, before the fall of man, if we accept the Biblical story, these relations between the sexes were the same then, as they are now, between the animals; that is, they were solely for propagation; and in this respect the female was and is supreme mistress.

But what has been the result of this desecration of woman? Look again to the female animals and learn; for here woman stands in lurid contrast to her sex in that domain! Where is

the animal that wastes her very life at every changing moon ?
There are no such, except among the monkeys, and the
fact exists there for the same reason that it exists among
women.

Menstruation is an hæmorrhage or exfoliation of the mucous
membrane of the uterus. Some of the higher mammals have
something similar at the period of œstus or heat, but monkeys
are the only mammals which menstruate like women. Monkeys
are the only mammals which copulate for other purposes than
reproduction.

Apes were kept in confinement thousands of years before
King Solomon's ships brought home from Tarshish " ivory,
apes and peacocks" (2 Chron. ix., 21). A monkey (kaf)
appears under the chair of a person who lived in the reign
of Cheops, 4th dynasty, proving that the word is much older
than the Sanskrit form (Wilkinson, Ancient Egyptians, vol. iii.,
p. 269: See also vol. ii., p. 190). Aristotle, who wrote upon
the resemblance of man to the monkey, takes no note of this
fact; "some animals unite in their natures the characteristics
of man and quadrupeds, as apes, monkeys, &c."

Pliny in his "Natural History" speaks of human beings and of
monkeys, but of the things *wherein they are alike* no mention
was made. Was Pliny ignorant of this fact? Monkeys and
women are the only animals which menstruate. They are the
only mammals which copulate promiscuously and at every
season. Monkeys are still monkeys in spite of this fact; they
have not evolved to something higher, so neither menstruation
nor the increased excitation of the generative organs could have
been the cause of subsequent development.

Pflüger has said "that menstruation is the result of the
growing follicle acting as an irritant to the terminations of
the nerve fibres embedded in the stromas of the ovary. This
irritation finally brings about congestion of the genital organs
by an afflux of blood to these organs. Other animals besides
monkeys and women have ovaries and yet the pressure of the

growing follicles does not cause congestion of the genital organs out of season. Moreover, if menstruation were analogous to the æstus of animals, this only appears at certain periods. The sum of the irritations of the growing Graafian follicles is not the same, evidently, as in monkeys and women. But I might ask why should the sum of these irritations become so great at periodic intervals causing the periodic congestion of the genital organs? When the ovaries become atrophied and menstruation ceases the woman is no longer capable of producing life; hence the expression, turn of life. Upon the maturity of the Graafian follicle menstruation commences, and it indicates that the female is able to produce life. Menstruation itself is not essential to life as animals who never menstruate produce life, and girls have become pregnant who have never menstruated. The essential principle of life is seated in the ovaries, and it is the excitation out of proper seasons which has brought on menstruation in the female organism. We say we cannot re-pot or transfer plants if it is not the proper season, we must not disturb the roots while the sap is running. If the ovaries are cut out of a girl before she has menstruated she never does so. Thousands of years ago the ancients must have arrived at some idea of the truth when they caused the ovaries to become atrophied by puncturing with needles which had been dipped in chemicals. Did this custom have its origin in some attempt to solve the phenomena of life?

The ovaries are not only essential for the function of menstruation, but they are also essential for the development of the female generative organs. If the ovaries are degenerate, atrophied, or arrested in their growth, the pelvis remains narrow, the uterus, the breasts, &c., are undeveloped. In diseased ovaries menstruation is intermittent or ceases; in diseased ovaries the secondary sexual characters are apt to reproduce themselves. The ovaries are responsible then for menstruation, its cessation, and the development of the generative organs. Tilt in his book on Ovarian and Uterine Inflammation, says, "when there is no ovary the uterus, should it exist, does not menstruate. It is the ovary which calls the uterus into action, imparting to it a stimulus which is either healthy or morbid, periodical or continuous. . . Menstruation is a species of parturition. *The reproductive organs are indeed the only organs of the body whose function is painful even when healthily performed.*" . . . Dr. Tyler Smith sought to prove that the bulk of diseases of women originate in the *hyper-secretion* of the mucous glands of the neck of the womb. . . . Dr. Ashwell says, Of all the organs of the human body scarcely any seem so prone either to functional or organic disuse as the ovaries; for I can with truth say that I have rarely when examining these important organs after *death found* them entirely *healthy.* . . . In Germany, Neumann did not scruple to remark that, of all the organs of the human frame, none are so often affected by disease as the ovaries. . . . If menstruation does not take place when the ovaries are absent, it follows that menstruation had its origin in something which affected or related to the ovaries. As no mammal menstruates where coition takes place for reproduction only, it was the copulation for other purposes than the perpetuation of the species which brought on menstruation—the undue excitation of the ovaries. The fact that menstruation ceases when the fertilized ovum becomes attached to the uterus would seem to prove that menstruation is the hereditary result of the *excitation of the ovaries* for other purposes than for propagation, for if there are no ovaries there is no menstruation.

It may be asked, what stimulated monkeys to copulate for other purposes than propagation? When the transition took place from the attitude of the quadruped to that of the biped, the pelvic viscera, by impact, were pressed down towards the pelvic outlet. Undue secretion of the mucous glands of the vagina corresponding to the æstus or rut of animals may have been the result. This may have incited the males to rape the females.

This truth was realized by the most ancient religious sects. They found it necessary to check the superior brute force of the male from desecrating the female by promulgating such religious laws as these. "The birth of a child is a defilement to its parents, especially to its mother who is declared impure for as many days as have elapsed months since her conception, and her purification shall be accomplished as after her natural seasons." (Manou in the Vedas.) In Leviticus we read that "her purification shall require sixty days." In the Veda—"the husband should respect his wife in her natural seasons as we respect the blossom.of the banana which announces fecundity and future harvest." If we study different religions we find it has been necessary to make religious laws to protect woman from violation. There stands the fact, ye women of the world, and there is where ye differ from the animals; and in this fact all the results of the original sin have had their source. Let any female brute lose the control of her procreative functions, as woman has been deprived of hers, and let her be subjected to the unbridled passion of the male, and she will soon begin to menstruate.

No animal menstruates which copulates for reproduction only. Some scientists have suggested to me that this may have been the cause of the subsequent intellectual development of the human race. I see no scientific truth in this theory.

Idiots have their generative organs abnormally developed. There is a great scientific truth in this which I am investigating for a future work. Except in morbid pathological conditions, the cerebral soul developes in degree as it overcomes the abdominal soul. The licentious monkeys and savages with their thick protruding lips, indicating great sensuality and small mental capacity would negative this hypothesis were there no other refutation. But if it needed any further refutation I have only to give an example from history.

History is a great teacher—it enables us to learn by the experience of others. The Spartans were taught self-control, simplicity in their way of living, that their actions must be directed by Reason, and that the vital law manifested through their beings was not to be made the instruments of beasts but the creator of gods. Here licence was not, accorded, but restraint was enforced. What was the result? The Spartans were known as the Invincibles, powerful both in body and mind. History teaches us another lesson. At Rome in the days of Juvenal when there was no such thing as self-control; Reason was a myth, civilization a mockery, and purity a jest. Energy directed too much in one direction must be at the expense of some other part. There must be an equivalence. We cut back the leaves of a plant when we want abundant bloom and pick off the bloom when we desire foliage.

An athlete who expends his energy in muscular exertion has not that energy left to expend in the artistic perception and muscular work of the eyes, or the musician of his ears. There is in either case mechanical work done and energy expended, but one is at the expense of the other. The energy of the human body is limited. If we use up our energy in diseased appetites, we have not that energy left for noble thought and artistic pursuits. The brain has developed by the *exercise* of the reasoning faculties, more exact or cumulative methods of observation. Every new scientific discovery is the means of adding to our knowledge. We have an example of what education and training can do with the youthful mind in the great disparity between men and women in this regard—the systematic collegiate education of boys and the makeshift education which has been in vogue heretofore with regard to girls.

We still further see the result of this sin in all those false ideas which are being disseminated with regard to preventive checks or means to prevent conception, as the cure for bad population. We are told that the amative impulse may be allowed full scope, so long as children be not produced, save as and when desired. Science is cited as the instrument which enables us to have many domestic comforts—that the aid of science is called where it would be injurious to the mother to have a child—why not under other circumstances? These books are criminal in their ignorance.of natural laws.

Menstruation being the hereditary result of the undue excitation of the ovaries, there could be no greater condemnation for those who advocate preventive checks.

Morbid menstruation or excessive excitation of the ovaries induced by sexual excitement is the cause of ovarian and uterine inflammation, of uterine tumours, of ovarian cysts, of ovarian dropsy, of cancer of the cervix uteri, and various other pathological conditions of the generative organs. And this pathological condition is by no means confined to the individual life. It may be handed down from generation to generation for diseased ovaries are found in mere children; cases are on record where ovariotomy has been performed on young girls, one only eight years of age, for ovarian tumour. Cysts are found in the ovaries of new-born children, showing that these pathological conditions are hereditary. And yet these ovaries influence the whole body, often rendering existence one life-long martyrdom. Poor mortals doomed to a living death! Degenerate organs of reproduction produce monsters of every description. The enormous percentage of women who die from these causes can only be realized by reading medical books on diseases of women. Constant irritation of the ovaries reacts upon the nervous centres, producing all kinds of morbid effects, headaches, lassitude, irritability, nervous chills, hysteria, hypochondria, melancholia, epilepsy, paralysis, hyperexcitability, lethargy, catalepsy, somnambulism, strange alienation, and various degrees of insanity. It is not the frequent child-bearing which is so disastrous to the mother, but the constant drain upon her available energy by too frequent sexual excitement and consequent exhaustion.

Why is it that when the testes are extirpated in the male the secondary sexual characters do not produce themselves? And when the ovaries are extirpated in the female, the secondary sexual characters do produce themselves? This would show that the test react upon the body of the male to cause increased vital activity. It is just the opposite with the female, though with savages and in some parts of the East where ovariotomy is performed for certain purposes, it is said that the women develop unusual strength. In the female the ovaries drain to themselves and store up energy for the future embryo, and when the ovaries become atrophied or are extirpated, the energy not being needed for the ova reacts upon the whole organism.

Ovarian activity therefore always means a loss to the female, a drain upon her available energy. The female organism being called upon to produce aborted life in the form of the monthly or frequent maturation of the Graafian follicle, the false corpus luteus of menstruation is a drain upon and waste to the maternal organism and no benefit to the race. Woman, as she is to-day, can be said to be undergoing perpetual child-bearing, her generative organs are never at rest, except before puberty, and after she has ceased to be fruitful. The hypothesis has been advanced, that longevity or length of life is the adaptation to the needs of the offspring, that where animals deposit a large number of eggs, there is more likelihood of some surviving, therefore the maternal organism dies young, in some instances death follows immediately. In those cases where there are a small number of offspring, or the number is limited, there is a tendency for the life of the maternal organism to be prolonged to secure the perpetuation of the species.

If this hypothesis is true, the frequent maturation of the Graafian follicle is so much loss of vitality to the human race. In those races where puberty of the female is retarded she retains her youth longer, and the average duration of the life of the race is the longest. And in those countries where the sexual sentiments have been worked by the custom of early marriages, the hereditary result has been early menstruation, shorter life, and deterioration of the race. The vital principle is developed and determined by the female and is followed by the male. Even the greater developed mental capacity of the male is largely dependent upon the mother who bore him.

In repeated pregnancies the weight of the child and the bulk of its head are increased. Schroeder, in his "Manual of Midwifery," says: "The weight of the child increases with the age and especially with the number of the previous labours of the woman. . . . The heads of male children are larger than those of female, and the most important diameter of the head—and the biparietal—increases quite out of proportion to the number of labours and the age of the mother, so that the broadest skull may be expected in a male fœtus of a pluriparæ somewhat advanced in age . . . . consequently not to expect very large heads in young primiparæ, whilst in an older woman who has often borne children, a head of a considerable size may be looked for. This proves that the function of gestating is developed in successive pregnancies, that the fœtus is better nourished, and has had the advantages of the more fully developed maternal organs. But our civilization would provide means to avoid conception when the mother has had one or two children, so that those children, who would be more developed physically and mentally, should not be born, or if born in spite of preventive checks should have the injurious effects resulting to contend against.

Sir Spencer Wells, in his book on "Ovarian and Uterine Tumours," published in 1882, gives a brief sketch of the history of Ovariotomy, and quotes the following :—

"A paper was laid before a late meeting of the Anthropological Society of Berlin for publication in their Transactions which reports that the aborigines of Australia and

New Zealand performed ovariotomy on young girls (the age is not mentioned) by incision in both inguinal regions. They do this for two purposes : first to *prevent the propagation of hereditary diseases and deformities, and other disabilities.* The writer met a woman born deaf and dumb who had been spayed to hinder her from bearing deaf and dumb children. . . . For the same reason of personal defect men are made impotent."

The preceding indicates that certain savages have at least some regard for the future members of their community. It is to be hoped, however, that when the responsibilities of parentage become more fully recognized that neither method —preventives nor spaying, will be necessary; the force of educated public opinion will deter the unfit from propagating their kind : but if human beings have not sufficiently evolved to realize that the function of their generative organs is reproduction, I would recommend the remedy of the ancient Greeks.

Scientific propagation is not a new idea which has originated with our nineteenth century civilization.

Menstruation is the result of the excitation of the ovaries, and the function of the ovaries is to develop and bring to maturity the Graafian follicle; and, as function has always preceded structure, we must seek the cause of the deviation of structure in the pathological condition of the ovaries—inflammation, cystic degeneration, dropsy, &c. The same may be said of the changes which the fertilized ovum may undergo in the uterus, or why is the purity of an animal's blood lost when it has once been crossed? It cannot be that the developing fœtus can affect a future ovum which is not yet mature. It is because the function of gestation is affected, and, if so, what effects uterine inflammation, tumours, cancer, &c., must have! What functional derangements may not be given to the developing fœtus? This negatives the hypothesis that differentiation of species is the result of the segmenting female and male pronucleus, and that only. When the generative organs are diseased they react upon the nerves governing nutrition, and this is of vital importance to the pregnant woman, for how can she impart to her child energy and rich blood when there is hyperæsthesia or anæsthesia of the nervous centres affecting these organs? And if psychical processes are to be traced back to physical processes the mother moulds the character of her child.

If we sought for the cause of nine-tenths of the insanity which is the curse of the nineteenth century, I think we should find it in sexual debauchery; that those insane had inherited weakened nervous systems through the sexual debauchery of their ancestors, or abuse in childhood of their own generative organs, or debauchery in maturity. Only the doctrine that under no circumstances ought humanity to propagate unless healthy both in body and mind, will perfect the human race. The loss of the prerogative of becoming creators when they sin against the God who gave them the right to be, would be an incentive to our sons and daughters to study such laws of life as will produce physical and psychical perfection by appealing to one of the most powerful instincts.

The maternal and paternal instincts to propagate are natural instincts; but these instincts have become diseased, and this disease is known by the term lust.

Is it not to be wondered rather that the human race enjoys anything that can be called health? Aye, still more, is it not astonishing that it even lives at all—that it has not long since been swept from the face of the earth, as it soon will be if it do not repent of this sin?

All this is feminine, since it is from the waters of the river Euphrates that the fruit of the tree of life (whose seed, as Moses said, is within itself) is developed and perfected. But this stream of life was turned to blood by the transgressions of primitive man, and has been entirely wasted to the race save that small portion which is utilized during gestation. The supposition that this river is something of which the female system ought to be relieved—that it is lifeless and corrupt—is false and wrong.

If it had no physiological value, why does menstruation cease during the period of gestation? Nature does not deem this blood corrupt and valueless then. From the Veda of ancient India is the following: " The blood is the life, it is the divine fluid that waters and fecundates the matter of which is formed the body. It is through the blood that the pure essence emanating from the Great Whole, and which is the *soul*, unites itself to the body."

But this river of life has been left to waste away the health and strength—the vigour and vitality—of the race, and no efforts have been made to remedy the destruction which it threatens, a disaster involving the fruitfulness of the garden itself, and the consequent wiping out of the race. This wasteful process is considered to be a natural function, and necessary to health and life, and so indeed it is, in the unnatural conditions in which we live, and in which the world has lived since this river was turned to waste, as described by Moses, allegorically, in the 4th and 7th chapters of Exodus. This wasting away of the life of the race is the vicarious atonement by which death is averted for the time. The fulness of time is not yet; the race, for a time, must rush madly onward toward destruction and extinction; but when the New Jerusalem (which is the purified woman) shall come in the new heaven and the new earth, as seen by St. John on Patmos, then this river of waste will return again to be "a pure river of water of life proceeding out of the throne of God"—proceeding out of His highest creative place, the Garden of Eden, through which flows the fruitful river Euphrates.

The Garden of Eden then is the human body, and its four rivers, which have their source in the extension of the mouth,

4

are the Pison, the blood; the Gihon, the bowels; the Hiddekel, the urinary organs; and the Euphrates, the reproductive functions. By these four rivers the whole garden is watered and fed or nourished and supported, drained of refuse matter, and its fruit produced. It was in this garden that mankind was planted by the Lord God after the same manner in which He performs all His other works—through the agency of law and order, as exemplified in evolution. It was the ground of this garden that was cursed, so that in sorrow man should "eat of it all the days of his life," and that it should bring forth "thorns and thistles," as Moses said it should, instead of the pleasant and agreeable fruit of perfect and beautiful children. Has not this allegorical picture been literally verified? Paul said he had only "the first fruits of the spirit;" that is to say, having the intellectual comprehension of the means for redemption of his body only.

"If any man defile the temple, him shall God destroy." Does He not do this? Does not death follow the defilement of the temple? In the temples that man has erected, and into which he enters on every seventh day to worship God, He does not dwell. These are the figures or the images only, as Paul said, of the true temple. Neither in this mountain nor at Jerusalem shall man worship; but in spirit and in truth, said Jesus. The fact that there are so many temples made with hands, into which all the professedly Christian world feels it to be necessary to enter and worship, is a certain evidence that their temples, not made with hands, are not yet the abode of God. Not having consciously the kingdom of heaven within them, where God comes and dwells with them, they still go after Him; and they are so blind that they do not see their own condemnation in the act. If a person has God dwelling in him, he need not go to church to worship Him, nor by so doing to make it evident to others that he is one of God's people, to whom He has come, and with whom He has taken up His abode.

Those who have to make a profession of faith to make it appear that they have God, only expose their own hypocrisy, for God's presence in any human being is self-evident proof of the fact.

Consider for a moment what would be the result if the people could come to recognize that their bodies are God's holy temples, and that their sexual organs, being the means by which His crowning work is created, ought never to be defiled by an unholy touch or thought, or ever made the instruments of selfish gratification merely. If the people should enter into these sacred relations only as if they were communing with God—with the same spirit in which really earnest and honest Christians enter into the temples made with hands, which they have falsely thought to be God's temples—and not with unbridled passion, what would become of the debauchery that now runs riot in the world? No; let the sexual act become the holiest act of life, and then the world will begin to be regenerated, and not before. Suppose that those who read the Scriptures, and pray regularly before eating, should go through the same ceremony before entering into the relations which should be the holiest of all relations, how long would the beastliness that now holds high carnival under cover of the law continue? If praying people believe the Bible—believe that their bodies are God's temple—why should they make such hot haste to defile them by their selfish lust and inordinate lasciviousness? Let these people become consistent at least, and in the most important act of life ask God's blessing to rest upon it.

But John saw that these fruits were to be fully realized in the new heaven and the new earth, meaning the new man and the new woman.

"Adorned as a bride prepared for her husband." Can there be any mistaking the significance of this figure? Can it mean anything save the perfected union of the sexes; and in the understanding that this perfection is coming to the world?

Why has God permitted His people to live in darkness and

death (all die in Adam) so long, the Christian will ask; and if there is any truth in the Bible as being God's truth, why did He not make it so clear that none could misunderstand it and be lost thereby, the scientist will retort. Now, here is precisely where the reconciliation between religionists and scientists will come. The very thing that the Bible declares to be a gift of God, which is to be revealed when the mystery shall be solved, is the very thing after which all science seeks—the perfect life. The ultimate fact after which both religion and science bend their energies is the self-same thing. The Spirit—God—tells what this is inspirationally in the Bible; men delve for it among the laws of nature scientifically. At the same time that it shall be discovered to the world of what this mystery of God consists: it will be demonstrated by actual life in individuals. Inspiration and evolution mean the self-same thing, spoken from the opposite extremes of the development by which it shall come—the former being the spiritual comprehension of the truth before it is "made flesh and dwells among us," and evolution being its actualization in experience.

Interpret the arbitrary commands of the Bible by the language of natural law, by which alone God works, and the reconciliation between God and nature, between religion and science, between inspiration and evolution, is completed. Inspiration is the language of men who were permeated with Divine essence, but knew nothing about the law of cause and effect. They attributed the destruction of a city by fire or by an earthquake, in short, every visitation of painful effects upon men, as a direct and arbitrary command of God as punishment for sin; while by the light of science they are only the natural effects of immutable laws, occurring because they must occur, in the evolution of the universe. All the sins and punishments of which man has been made the subject are of the same order. It was impossible that man, being an animal, should be made a son of God, save by the very process through which he has had to pass.

That the law of evolution which makes growth the method by which intellectual altitude is reached, is also the law by which physical development goes forward ; the perfected creation of man and his consequent salvation from death being physical and not moral, as has been falsely taught by almost the whole of Christendom. With a perfect physical body—man reconciled to God—all other perfections follow as its fruit, necessarily. The opposite proposition to this is the stumbling-block over which all Christians have fallen ; they have given all their attention to saving the soul hereafter, when this salvation depends entirely upon saving the body here and now.

Is it not palpable how the acceptance of this fact, and the adoption of its logic as a rule of human action, would harmonize the relations of man ? With this view, everything that occurs is a part, and a necessary part, of the evolution or the growth of man. *Suppose criminals were to be treated by this principle, what a reform might be inaugurated in this regard !* Suppose this precept were to be made a rule of life, the world could be at once transformed into a brotherhood. But this must also be a result of growth.

" And out of the ground (female-male) the Lord God formed every beast of the field, and every fowl of the air." The two sexes must have been comprised in each species, evidently a rib was not taken out of each male to make a corresponding female.

In the first dawn of the life-principle there was no such thing as sex. Life was a unit, that is, a homogeneous mass, gradually becoming heterogeneous until two sexes were evolved. The Biblical allegory of Adam and Eve, that the two sexes were evolved from one, accords with science. Had this a deeper meaning than even Moses comprehended ? Still more curious was the supposition that the male animal was the first distinct sex ; before the male animal, it was the two sexes in one of the female-male animal. And the male organs of the latter becoming gradually degenerated or suppressed the distinct female animal was evolved to correspond with the male animal.

Here we have the ideal marriage. The two unite to become as one from which the human family had its birth. Onward from the family next were formed the roving tribes which had a chosen head, who ruled the whole with arbitrary will in all respects. Next cities sprang into existence, and reaching over provinces united into nations, making their kings or queens, their rulers absolute. From this, the concentrated form of power, the sway began to re-dispose itself among the people. Through monarchs limited in rule to constitutions and republics has the power descended and now it is about to be assumed again by each and all individuals who have become a law unto themselves, into whose hearts Almighty God has put His law of love. From individuals such as these a brotherhood of man can form and live, but not from any other kind. And from a brotherhood wherein the good of each becomes the good of all, the higher and the holier family will spring into existence, whose King and Queen and Lord and Prince shall be the living God who from creation's dawn through long experience, sometimes dark but often bright, hath brought us kindly on our way to this exalted place as His abode.

THE REVELATION OF ST. JOHN THE DIVINE.
CHAPTER XXI.

And I saw a new heaven and a new earth : for the first heaven and the first earth were passed away; and there was no more sea.

2 And I John saw the holy city, new Jerusalem, coming down from God out of heaven, prepared as a bride adorned for her husband.

3 And I heard a great voice out of heaven saying, Behold, the tabernacle of God *is* with men, and he will dwell with them, and they shall be his people, and God himself shall be with them *and be* their God.

4 And God shall wipe away all tears from their eyes ; and there shall be no more death, neither sorrow, nor crying, neither shall there be any more pain : for the former things are passed away.

5 And he that sat upon the throne said, Behold, I make all things new. And he said unto me, Write; for these words are true and faithful.

6 And he said unto me, It is done. I am Alpha and Omega, the beginning and the end. I will give unto him that is athirst of the fountain of the water of life freely.

7 He that overcometh shall inherit all things; and I will be his God, and he shall be my son.

8 But the fearful and unbelieving, and the abominable, and murderers, and whoremongers, and sorcerers, and idolators, and all liars, shall have their part in the lake which burneth with fire and brimstone; which is the second death.

9 And there came unto me one of the seven angels which had the seven vials full of the seven last plagues, and talked with me, saying, Come hither, I will shew thee the bride, the Lamb's wife.

10 And he carried me away in the spirit to a great and high mountain, and shewed me that great city, the holy Jerusalem, descending out of heaven from God.

11 Having the glory of God: and her light *was* like unto a stone most precious, even like a jasper stone, clear as crystal;

12 And had a wall great and high, *and* had twelve gates, and at the gates twelve angels, and names written thereon, which are *the names* of the twelve tribes of the children of Israel:

13 On the east three gates; on the north three gates; on the south three gates; and on the west three gates.

14 And the wall of that city had twelve foundations, and in them the names of the twelve apostles of the Lamb.

15 And he that talked with me had a golden reed to measure the city, and the gates thereof, and the wall thereof.

16 And the city lieth foursquare, and the length is as large as the breadth: and he measured the city with the reed, twelve thousand furlongs. The length and the breadth and the height of it are equal.

17 And he measured the wall thereof, an hundred *and* forty *and* four cubits, *according to* the measure of a man, that is, of the angel.

18 And the building of the wall of it was *of* jasper: and the city *was* pure gold, like unto clear glass.

19 And the foundation of the wall of the city *were* garnished with all manner of precious stones. The first foundation *was*

jasper; the second, sapphire; the third, a chalcedony; the fourth, an emerald.

20 The fifth, sardonyx; the sixth, sardius; the seventh, chrysolite; the eight, beryl; the ninth, a topaz; the tenth, a chrysoprasus; the eleventh, a jacinth; the twelfth, an amethyst.

21 And the twelve gates *were* twelve pearls; every several gate was of one pearl : and the street of the city *was* pure gold, as it were transparent glass.

22 And I saw no temple therein : for the Lord God Almighty and the Lamb are the temple of it.

23 And the city had no need of the sun, neither of the moon, to shine in it : for the glory of God did lighten it, and the Lamb *is* the light thereof.

24 And the nations of them which are saved shall walk in the light of it : and the kings of the earth do bring their glory and honour into, it.

25 And the gates of it shall not be shut at all by day : for there shall be no night there.

26 And they shall bring the glory and honour of the nations into it.

27 And there shall in no wise enter into it any thing that defileth, neither *whatsoever* worketh abomination, or *maketh* a lie : but they which are written in the Lamb's book of life.

CHAPTER XXII.

And he shewed me a pure river of water of life, clear as crystal, proceeding out of the throne of God and of the Lamb.

2 In the midst of the street of it, and on either side of the river, *was there* the tree of life, which bare twelve *manner of* fruits, *and* yielded her the fruit every month : and the leaves of the tree *were* for the healing of the nations.

3 And there shall be no more curse : but the throne of God and of the Lamb shall be in it; and his servants shall serve them :

4 And they shall see his face : and his name *shall be* in their foreheads.

5 And there shall be no light there; and they need no candle neither light of the sun; for the Lord God giveth them light : and they shall reign for ever and ever.

6 And he said unto me, These sayings *are* faithful and true : and the Lord God of the holy prophets sent his angel to show unto his servants the things which must shortly be done.

7 Behold I come quickly: blessed *is* he that keepeth the sayings of the prophecy of this book.

8 And I John saw these things, and heard *them*. And when I had heard and seen, I fell down to worship before the feet of the angel which shewed me these things.

9 Then saith he unto me, See *thou do it* not: for I am thy fellowservant, and of thy brethren the prophets, and of them which keep the sayings of this book: worship God.

10 And he saith unto me, Seal not the sayings of the prophecy of this book: for the time is at hand.

11 He that is unjust, let him be unjust still: and he which is filthy let him be filthy still: and he is that is righteous, let him be righteous still: and he that is holy, let him be holy still.

12 And, behold I come quickly; and my reward *is* with me to give every man according as his work shall be.

13 I am Alpha and Omega, the beginning and the end, the first and the last.

14 Blessed *are* they that do his commandments, that they may have right to the tree of life, and may enter in through the gates in the city.

15 For without *are* dogs, and sorcerers, and whoremongers, and murderers, and idolaters, and whosoever loveth and maketh a lie.

16 I Jesus have sent mine angel to testify unto you these things in the churches. I am the root and the offspring of David, *and* the bright and morning star.

17 And the Spirit and the bride say, Come. And let him that heareth say, Come. And let him that is athirst come. And whosoever will, let him take of the water of life freely.

18 For I testify unto every man that heareth the words of the prophecy of this book, If any man shall add unto these things, God shall add unto him the plagues that are written in this book.

19 And if any man shall take away from the words of the book of this prophecy, God shall take away his part out of the book of life, and out of the holy city, and *from* the things which are written in this book.

20 He which testifieth these things saith, Surely I come quickly. Amen. Even so, come, Lord Jesus.

21 The grace of our Lord Jesus Christ be with you all. Amen.

India, according to the Vedas, entertained a respect for woman amounting almost to worship.

MAXIMS FROM THE SACRED BOOKS OF INDIA.

" He who despises woman despises his mother."

"Who is cursed by a woman is cursed by God."

" The tears of a woman call down the fire of Heaven on those who make them flow."

"Evil to him who laughs at woman's sufferings : God shall laugh at his prayers."

" It was at the prayer of a woman that the Creator pardoned Man : cursed be he who forgets it."

"Who shall forget the sufferings of his mother at his birth shall be reborn in the body of an owl during three successive transmigrations."

" There is no crime more odious than to persecute woman."

" When women are honoured the Divinities are content ; but when they are not honoured all undertakings fail."

" The households cursed by women to whom they have not rendered the homage due them find themselves weighed down with ruin, and destroyed, as if they had been struck by some secret power."

" The infinite and the boundless can alone comprehend the boundless and the infinite, God only can comprehend God."

" As the body is strengthened by muscles, the soul is fortified by virtue."

" The wrongs we inflict upon others follow us like our shadow."

" It is time to appreciate all things at their true value."

Let us repeat that story from Sufi : " There was a man, who for seven years, did every act of charity, and at the end of seven years he mounted the steps to the gate of Heaven and knocked. A voice cried, 'Who is there ?' 'Thy servant, O Lord,' and the gate was shut. Seven other years he did every other good work, and again mounted the three steps to Heaven and knocked. The voice cried, ' Who is there ?' He answered, ' Thy slave, O God,' and the gates were shut. Seven other years he did every good deed and again mounted the steps to Heaven, and the voice said, ' Who is there ?' He replied, ' Thyself, O God,' and the gates wide open flew."

And why ?

Because, as the Scripture saith,—" *The good that is done in the earth, Thou, Lord, doest it.*"

THE ARGUMENT FOR WOMAN'S ELECTORAL RIGHTS.

THE ARGUMENT FOR WOMAN'S ELECTORAL RIGHTS.

MY object in re-printing the following pages is to place on record the history of my labours, during the years 1870-1871, in the cause of Woman's claim to equality with Man, more especially as regards the right to electoral suffrage, under the existing Constitution of my country. The question of Female franchise was even then no new one, and the names of the champions of the cause are well-known : not to speak of the work of independent labourers, organized Convention meetings had been held from 1850 to 1870* in support of the movement. My own efforts were entirely outside of this organization ; its aim was throughout to obtain the desired object by amending the Constitution ; I, on the contrary, made it the head and front of my contention that no such amendment was necessary, but that equality is already granted to both sexes under the Constitution as it stands.

The effect produced by this independent action on new lines may best be shown in the words of the Appendix to the History of the Decade Meeting of October 20th, 1870 :—

At the close of the Decade meeting it was decided to hold a National Convention in Washington, January, 1871. For this convention preparations were duly made by the committee.

As the friends came together they found that the work had assumed a new phase.

The intricacy of the question seemed likely to be unravelled sooner than anticipated. When the English statesmen were all at fault and could see no way out of their embarrassments, in

---

* A History of the National Woman's Rights Movement, for twenty years, &c. New York, 1871.

relation to chattel slavery, a Woman, with a large brain and a large heart, wrote out the simple sentence, "Immediate and unconditional emancipation," and the West India question was peaceably settled in seven years. Brougham, Wilberforce, Romilly, and Clarkson sat at the feet of Elizabeth Heyrick and learned wisdom of her. They recognized the divine inspiration, and now when another woman comes with a like inspiration and offers to show the way out of a still more intricate and embarrassing question—not the giving of freedom to a small race, but to one-half the inhabitants of our country—a few of our statesmen recognize her inspiration, and gladly seize upon it to solve the problem.

The letter of Mrs. Griffing, secretary of the committee, the organizing working power at Washington, gives the history very clearly of Mrs. Woodhull's work, and of the progress since December, 1870, up to April 10, 1871. To Mrs. Woodhull's active energy and judicious conduct of her work in Washington, we, as the disfranchised class, owe a deep debt of gratitude :

My DEAR MRS. DAVIS,

Having been present at the Decade meeting, held in the City of New York in October last, 1870, and listened to your very interesting and accurate statement of the women's rights movement, since its first public inception in 1848, permit me to thank you, and to express my earnest hope that you will not fail to print it.

Such a review is already called for by those whose attention is now, for the first time, turned to the question, and to the future generations it is absolutely necessary, including as it does, the grandest lesson in the triumph of human freedom.

In this history you have not only pointed out each inductive step of progress, but have made faithful mention of the early workers, who, by indomitable energy, self-sacrifice, and devotion to truth and principle, have laid a foundation, in the moral sense of the age, for a complete recognition of woman's personality, hitherto denied, and upon which a Universal Republic shall be established that shall live, when kingdoms and thrones shall be forgotten in the civilizations of the world.

Only one thing I would add to your manuscript, which is the part taken and the name of the author of this historic statement as one of the brightest stars in the pathway that marks this glorious era of woman's struggle.

Hitherto the work has been mainly inductive,—a presentation of human rights and woman's wrongs.

For the first time it is now recognized as a political issue, and simple justice before the law, not expediency or position, is the point alone to be settled.

" The mills of God grind slowly, but they grind exceeding small."

It now appears that under the Federal Constitution and its amendments, woman is entitled to equal rights of citizenship with man; and as voting is a fundamental right of the citizen in a free government, woman not only may, but should vote.

The last Woman Suffrage Convention, held in Washington, D. C., January, 1871, called by Paulina W. Davis, J. S. Griffing, and I. B. Hooker, in behalf of the women of the country, contemplated no new issue, proposed only to discuss the moral question, the XVIth Amendment, and a more thorough system of education for the women of the country, through the issue of a monthly series of tracts.

With slight exception, this programme would have been the order of the convention, as it was the indication of the call, had not the time arrived for the bugle-note, calling all " to the front." Events of the hour at once changed the direction of thought, and inaugurated a line of movement for the practical enfranchisement of, and restoration to, woman, of her equal rights as an American citizen.

A few days previous to the time of holding this convention, Mrs. Victoria C. Woodhull, of the City of New York, memorialized Congress for the exercise of the elective franchise,

which memorial was read in the House of Representatives, by
Hon. George W. Julian, early friend of the cause, referred to
the Judiciary Committee and ordered to be printed.

This action on the part of Mrs. Woodhull was taken without
consultation with the movers for, or even knowledge of the
convention, and by unprecedented energy and great intelligence,
pressed upon the attention of both branches of Congress, upon
the plea that she was "born upon the soil and was subject to
the jurisdiction of the United States," and that as a citizen, she
desired a voice in legislation, through the only means in a free
Government, that of a vote; and on this *pivot* she based her
demand. With some difficulty she obtained permission for a
hearing before the Judiciary Committee, but at the time of the
opening of the convention, the day was not fixed.

Learning this important step taken by Mrs. Woodhull, a
stranger to the convention, a conference was held between the
parties resulting in a friendly agreement, that with consent of
the chairman of the committee, Mrs. I. B. Hooker, on the part
of the convention, should at the same time, through a constitutional lawyer, the Hon. A. G. Riddle, ex-member of Congress,
defend the memorialists (30,000 women) whose names were
already before Congress, asking also, to exercise the right of
the ballot.

Mrs. Woodhull, who personally embodied womanhood in her
defence, spoke with power and marvellous effect, as though
conscious of a right unjustly withheld, and feeling a duty, she
was forbidden to do. Under the supreme law of the land, the
Constitution and the XIVth and XVth Amendments thereto,
she asked equal protection to person, property, and full citizenship; in response to this, the key-note, Mr. Riddle followed
with an unanswerable legal argument, sweeping away all laws
of the United States, and of any State, restricting woman in
the right to vote, as directly opposed to the supreme law of the
land, as pointed out in the XIVth and XVth Amendments to

the Federal Constitution, which he showed to be consonant with both the letter and spirit of that instrument. He also suggested that the immediate action of woman, as a citizen, might be found the most speedy method of triumph.

The result of this hearing, in the printed reports of Judge Bingham and the majority, and of Judge Loughridge and Hon. B. F. Butler, the minority of the Judiciary Committee, is *already* before the country, and marks well the beginning of the end.

It was now clearly seen by the leaders of the movement that the agitation of woman's wrongs and oppressions was no longer a necessary part of the discussion. That in the statute-books, a record of this was made, and that henceforth woman's citizenship and full enfranchisement must be declared. That under the supreme law of the land her right to person, property, children and full and equal citizenship must be *pronounced* and admitted; and, finally, her *duty* to vote, and through her highest capabilities, to assume a share of the responsibility of the State, as she has already of the home, are hereafter to be the legitimate theme of discussion till woman is emancipated.

These events and this decision indicated an immediate want of a National Woman's Suffrage and Educational Committee, to carry forward measures for the speedy execution of the work, and upon consultation with the experienced and wise men and women of the convention, and with the approval of all well-wishers who were present, a committee, consisting of Mrs. I. B. Hooker (Chairwoman), Mrs. J. S. Griffing (Secretary), Mrs. M. B. Bowen (Treasurer), Susan B. Anthony, Paulina W. Davis and Ruth Carr Denison, was organized at the City of Washington, D. C., and machinery set in operation to accomplish what is now known as the work of that committee.

For the temporary use of this Committee a part of the House Education and Labour Committee-room, through the marked kindness of Hon. Mr. Arnell, Chairman of the Committee, was granted. Afterward the beautiful artistic House Agriculture Committee-room, also used for Manufacture Committee, was generously proffered by the chairmen of both, Hon. Mr. Morrell and General Smith, and is still retained.

Books are now opened for signatures to the new Declaration and Pledge, and the autograph of all women now ready to exercise the elective franchise, and thousands of tracts, constitutional arguments of Mr. Riddle and Mrs. Woodhull, reports of the minority Judiciary Committee, and an address to the women of the United States, are being sent to the whole country, carrying conviction to the weak, force to the active, and hastening the consummation of a triumph worthy of the struggle and undying faith of all who have nobly borne their part in this history.

The names of the earnest women who took part in this convention, and who participated in the inauguration of the new issue, are recorded in the books of the Committee; and now, only the funds—generous and prompt contributions—are needed to respond to the call from all the States and Territories for knowledge—either by voice or pen—to complete a reconstruction of the government "of the people, for the people, and by the people," without arms, court-martial or bloodshed. Give, *give* is the call of the Committee, and *give* is the prayer of all the true workers in the advance of the woman's rights movement; and whatsoever you mete shall be measured to you again.

Most truly,
J. S. GRIFFING.

It has been stated above as the essence of my contention, that the equality claimed is already granted by the existing Constitution: it is therefore proper to give precedence to the text of the Constitution itself:—

THE
CONSTITUTION OF THE UNITED STATES.

ARTICLE I.

SEC. I.—All legislative powers herein granted shall be vested in a Congress of the United States, which shall consist of a Senate and House of Representatives.

SEC. II.—1. The House of Representatives shall be composed of members chosen every second year, by the people of the several States; and the electors in each State shall have the qualifications requisite for electors of the most numerous branch of the State Legislature.

2. No person shall be a Representative who shall not have attained the age of twenty-five years and been seven years a citizen of the United States, and who shall not, when elected, be an inhabitant of the State in which he shall be chosen.

3. Representatives and direct taxes shall be apportioned among the several States which may be included within this Union, according to their respective numbers, which shall be determined by adding to the whole number of free persons, including those bound to service for a term of years, and, excluding Indians not taxed, three-fifths of all other persons. The actual enumeration shall be made within three years after the first meeting of the Congress of the United States, and within every subsequent term of ten years in such manner as they shall by

law direct. The number of Representatives shall not exceed one for every thirty thousand, but each State shall have at least one Representative; and until such enumeration shall be made the State of New Hampshire shall be entitled to choose three: Massachusetts, eight; Rhode Island and Providence Plantations, one; Connecticut, five; New York, six; New Jersey, four; Pennsylvania, eight; Delaware, one; Maryland, six; Virginia, ten; North Carolina, five; South Carolina, five, and Georgia, three.

4. When vacancies happen in the representation from any State, the executive authority thereof shall issue writs of election to fill such vacancies.

5. The House of Representatives shall choose their Speaker and other officers, and shall have the sole power of impeachment.

Sec. III.—1. The Senate of the United States shall be composed of two Senators from each State chosen by the Legislature thereof, for six years; and each Senator shall have one vote.

2. Immediately after they shall be assembled in consequence of the first election, they shall be divided, as equally as may be, into three classes. The seats of the Senators of the first class shall be vacated at the expiration of the second year, of the second class at the expiration of the fourth year, and of the third class at the expiration of the sixth year, that one-third may be chosen every second year; and if vacancies occur by resignation or otherwise, during the recess of the Legislature of any State, the Executive thereof may make temporary appointments until the next meeting of the Legislature, which shall then fill such vacancies.

8. No person shall be a Senator who shall not have attained the age of thirty years, and been nine years a citizen of the United States, and who shall not, when elected, be an inhabitant of that State for which he is chosen.

4. The Vice-President of the United States shall be Presi-

dent of the Senate, but shall have no vote unless they be equally divided.

5. The Senate shall choose their other officers and also a President *pro tempore*, in the absence of the Vice-President or when he shall exercise the office of the President of the United States.

6. The Senate shall have the sole power to try all impeachments. When sitting for that purpose they shall be on oath or affirmation. When the President of the United States is tried the Chief Justice shall preside; and no person shall be convicted without the concurrence of two-thirds of the members present.

7. Judgment in cases of impeachment shall not extend farther than to removal from office, and disqualification to hold and enjoy any office of honour, trust, or profit under the United States; but the party convicted shall nevertheless, be liable and subject to indictment, trial, judgment and punishment according to law.

Sec. IV.—1. The times, places, and manner of holding elections for Senators and Representatives shall be prescribed in each State, by the Legislature thereof; but the Congress may, at any time, by law, make or alter such regulations, except as to the places of choosing Senators.

2. The Congress shall assemble at least once in every year; and such meeting shall be on the first Monday in December, unless they shall by law appoint a different day.

Sec. V.—1. Each House shall be judge of the elections, returns, and qualifications of its own members; and a majority of each shall constitute a quorum to do business, but a smaller number may adjourn from day to day, and may be authorized to compel the attendance of absent members, in such manner and under such penalties as each House may provide.

2. Each House may determine the rules of its proceeding, punish its members for disorderly behaviour, and, with the concurrence of two-thirds, expel a member.

3. Each House shall keep a journal of its proceedings, and from time to time publish the same, excepting such parts, as may, in their judgment require secrecy; and the yeas and nays of the members of either House on any question, shall, at the desire of one-fifth of those present, be entered on the journal.

4. Neither House, during the session of Congress, shall, without the consent of the other, adjourn for more than three days, nor to any place than that in which the two Houses shall be sitting.

SEC. VI.—1. The Senators and Representatives shall receive a compensation for their services, to be ascertained by law, and paid out of the Treasury of the United States. They shall, in all cases, except for treason, felony and breach of the peace, be privileged from arrest during their attendance at the session of their respective Houses, and in going to or returning from the same; and for any speech or debate in either House they shall not be questioned in any other place.

2. No Senator or Representative shall, during the time for which he was elected, be appointed to any civil office under the authority of the United States, which shall have been created, or the emoluments whereof shall have been increased during such time, and no person holding any office under the United States shall be a member of either House during his continuance in office.

SEC. VII.—1. All bills for raising revenues shall originate in the House of Representatives, but the Senate may propose or concur with amendments, as on other bills.

2. Every bill which shall have passed the House of Representatives and the Senate, shall, before it become a law, be presented to the President of the United States; if he approves, he shall sign it; but if not, he shall return it, with his objections, to that House in which it shall have originated, who shall enter the objections at large on their journal, and proceed to reconsider it. If, after such reconsideration, two-thirds of that House shall agree to pass the bill, it must be sent, together

with the objections, to the other House, by which it shall like-
wise be reconsidered, and if approved by two-thirds of that
House, it shall become a law. But in all such cases the votes
of both Houses shall be determined by yeas and nays; and the
names of the persons voting for or against the bill shall be
entered on the journal of each House respectively. If any bill
shall not be returned by the President within ten days (Sundays
excepted) after it shall have been presented to him, the same
shall be a law in like manner as if he had signed it, unless the
Congress, by their adjournment, prevent its return; in which
case it shall not be a law.

3. Every order, resolution, or vote, to which the concurrence
of the Senate and House of Representatives may be necessary
(except on a question of adjournment) shall be presented to the
President of the United States; and before the same shall take
effect, shall be approved by him, or being disapproved by him,
shall be repassed by two-thirds of the Senate and House of
Representatives, according to the rules and limitations prescribed in the face of a bill.

Sec. VIII.—The Congress shall have power—

1. To lay and collect taxes, duties, imposts and excises; to
pay the debts, and provide for the common defence and general
welfare of the United States; but all duties, imposts, and
excises shall be uniform throughout the United States.

2. To borrow money on the credit of the United States:

3. To regulate commerce with foreign nations and among
the several States, and with the Indian tribes:

4. To establish a uniform rule of naturalization, and uniform
laws on the subject of bankruptcies throughout the United
States:

5. To coin money, regulate the value thereof, and of foreign
coin, and to fix the standard of weights and measures:

6. To provide for the punishment of counterfeiting the
securities and current coin of the United States:

7. To establish post-offices and post-roads:

8. To promote the progress of science and useful arts by securing, for limited times, to authors and inventors, the exclusive right to their respective writings and discoveries:

9. To constitute tribunals inferior to the Supreme Court; to define and punish piracies and felonies committed on the high seas, and offences against the law of nations:

10. To declare war, grant letters of marque and reprisal, and and make rules concerning capture on land and water:

11. To raise and support armies; but no appropriation of money to that use shall be for a longer term than two years:

12. To provide and maintain a navy:

13. To make rules for the government and regulation of the land and naval forces:

14. To provide for calling forth the militia to execute the laws of the Union, suppress insurrection and repel invasions:

15. To provide for organizing, arming and disciplining the militia, and for governing such part of them as may be employed in the service of the United States, reserving to the States respectively the appointment of the officers, and the authority of training the militia, according to the discipline prescribed by Congress.

16. To exercise exclusive legislation, in all cases whatsoever, over such district (not exceeding ten miles square) as may, by cession of particular States, and the acceptance of Congress, become the seat of Government of the United States, and to exercise like authority over all places purchased by the consent of the Legislature of the State in which the same shall be, for the erection of forts, magazines, arsenals, dock-yards, and other needful buildings:—And

17. To make all laws which shall be necessary and proper for carrying into execution the foregoing powers, and all other powers vested by this Constitution in the Government of the United States, or in any department or officer thereof.

SEC. IX.—1. The migration or importation of such persons as any of the States now existing shall think proper to admit, shall not be prohibited by the Congress prior to the year one thousand eight hundred and eight; but a tax or duty may be imposed on such importation not exceeding ten dollars for each person.

2. The privilege of the writ of *habeas corpus* shall not be suspended unless when, in cases of rebellion or invasion, the public safety may require it.

3. No bill of attainder, or *ex-post facto* law, shall be passed.

4. No capitation, or other direct tax shall be laid, unless in proportion to the census or enumeration hereinbefore directed to be taken.

5. No tax or duty shall be laid on articles exported from any State. No preference shall be given, by any regulation of commerce or revenue, to the ports of one State over those of another; nor shall vessels bound to or from one State, be obliged to enter, clear, or pay duties in another.

6. No money shall be drawn from the Treasury, but in consequence of appropriations made by law; and a regular statement or account of the receipts and expenditures of all public money shall be published from time to time.

7. No title of nobility shall be granted by the United States; and no person holding any office of profit or trust under them, shall, without the consent of the Congress, accept of any present, emolument, office, or title, of any kind whatever, from any king, prince, or foreign state.

SEC. X.—1. No State shall enter into any treaty, alliance, confederation; grant letters of marque and reprisal; coin money; emit bills of credit; make anything but gold and silver coin a tender in payment of debts; pass any bill of attainer, *ex-post facto* law, or law impairing the obligation of contracts; or grant any title of nobility.

2. No State shall, without the consent of Congress, lay any

6

imposts or duties on imports or exports, except what may be absolutely necessary for executing its inspection laws ; and the net produce of all duties and imposts laid by any State on imports or exports, shall be for the use of the Treasury of the United States; and all such laws shall be subject to the revision and control of the Congress. No State shall, without the consent of Congress, lay any duty of tonnage, keep troops or ships of war in time of peace, enter into any agreement or compact with another State, or with a foreign power, or engage in war, unless actually invaded, or in such imminent danger as will not admit of delay.

ARTICLE II.

Sec. I.—1. The executive power shall be vested in a President of the United States of America. He shall hold his office during the term of four years, and, together with the Vice-President chosen for the same term, be elected as follows:—

2. Each State shall appoint, in such manner as the Legislature thereof may direct, a number of electors, equal to the whole number of Senators and Representatives to which the State may be entitled in Congress ; but no Senator or Representative, or person holding an office of trust or profit under the United States, shall be appointed an elector.

3. [Annulled. See Amendments, Art. XII.]

4. The Congress may determine the time of choosing the elector, and the day on which they shall give their votes ; which day shall be the same throughout the United States.

5. No person except a natural born citizen, or a citizen of the United States at the time of the adoption of this Constitution, shall be eligible to the office of President; neither shall any person be eligible to that office who shall not have attained to the age of thirty-five years, and been fourteen years a resident within the United States.

6. In case of the removal of the President from office, or of

his death, resignation, or inability to discharge the powers and duties of the said office, the same shall devolve on the Vice-President; and the Congress may by law provide for the case of removal, death, resignation, or inability, both of the President and Vice-President, declaring what officer shall then act as President, and such officer shall act accordingly, until the disability be removed, or a President shall be elected.

7. The President shall at stated times receive, for his services, a compensation, which shall neither be increased nor diminished during the period for which he shall have been elected; and he shall not receive within that period any other emolument from the United States or any of them.

8. Before he enter on the execution of his office he shall take the following oath or affirmation:

" I do solemnly swear (or affirm) that I will faithfully execute the office of President of the United States, and will, to the best of my ability, preserve, protect and defend the Constitution of the United States."

Sec. II.—1. The President shall be Commander-in-Chief of the army and navy of the United States, and of the militia of the several States when called into actual service of the United States; he may require the opinion in writing of the principal officer in each of the executive departments, upon any subject relating to the duties of their respective offices; and he shall have power to grant reprieves and pardon for offences against the United States, except in cases of impeachment.

2. He shall have power, by and with the advice and consent of the Senate, to make treaties, provided two-thirds of the Senators present concur; and he shall nominate, and by and with the consent and advice of the Senate, shall appoint ambassadors, other public ministers, and consuls, judges of the Supreme Court, and all other officers of the United States, whose appointments are not herein otherwise provided for, and which shall be established by law. But the Congress may, by law, vest the appointment of

6 *

such inferior officers as they think proper, in the President alone, in the courts of law, or in the heads of departments.

3. The President shall have power to fill up all vacancies that may happen during the recess of the Senate, by granting commissions which shall expire at the end of their next session.

Sec. III.—He shall, from time to time, give to the Congress information of the State of the Union, and recommend to their consideration such measures as he shall judge necessary and expedient; he may, on extraordinary occasions, convene both Houses, or either of them, and in case of disagreement between them, with respect to the time of adjournment, he may adjourn them to such time as he shall think proper; he shall receive ambassadors and other public ministers; he shall take care that the laws be faithfully executed, and shall commission all the officers of the United States.

Sec. IV.—1. The President, Vice-President and all civil officers of the United States shall be removed from office on impeachment for, and conviction of, treason, bribery or other high crimes and misdemeanours.

ARTICLE III.

Sec. I.—1. The judicial power of the United States shall be vested in one Supreme Court, and in such inferior courts as the Congress may, from time to time, ordain and establish. The judges, both of the Supreme and inferior courts, shall hold their offices during good behaviour, and shall, at stated times, receive for their services a compensation, which shall not be diminished during their continuance in office.

Sec. II.—1. The judicial power shall extend to all cases in law and equity arising under this constitution, the laws of the United States and treaties made, or which shall be made, under their authority; to all cases affecting ambassadors, other public ministers and consuls; to all cases of admiralty and maritime jurisdiction; to controversies to which the United States shall be a party; to controversies between two or more States, between a State and citizens of another State, between citizens of different States, between citizens of the same State claiming lands under grants of different States, and between a State or the citizens thereof, and foreign States, citizens or subjects.

2. In all cases affecting ambassadors, other public ministers and consuls, and those in which a State shall be a party, the Supreme Court shall have original jurisdiction. In all the other cases before mentioned, the Supreme Court shall have appellate jurisdiction, both as to law and fact, with such exceptions and under such regulations as the Congress may make.

3. The trial of all crimes, except in cases of impeachment, shall be by jury; and such trial shall be held in the State where the said crimes shall have been committed; but when not committed within any State, the trial shall be at such place or places as the Congress may by law have directed.

SEC. II.—1. Treason against the United States shall consist only in levying war against them, or in adhering to their enemies, giving them aid and comfort. No person shall be convicted of treason unless on the testimony of two witnesses to the same overt act, or on confession in open court.

2. The Congress shall have power to declare the punishment of treason; but no attainder of treason shall work corruption of blood, or forfeiture, except during the life of the person attainted.

ARTICLE IV.

SEC. I.—1. Full faith and credit shall be given, in each State, to the public acts, records and judicial proceedings of every other State. And the Congress may, by general laws, prescribe the manner in which such acts, records and proceedings, shall be proved, and the effect thereof.

Sec. II.—1. The citizens of each State shall be entitled to all privileges and immunities of citizens in the several States.

2. A person charged in any State with treason, felony or other crime, who shall flee from justice, and be found in another State, shall, on demand of the executive authority of the State from which he fled, be delivered up to the State having jurisdiction of the crime.

3. No person held to service or labour in one State, under the laws thereof, escaping into another, shall, in consequence of any law and regulation therein, be discharged from such service or labour; but shall be delivered up, on claim of the party to whom such service or labour may be due.

Sec. III.—1. New States may be admitted by the Congress into this Union; but no new State shall be formed or erected within the jurisdiction of any other State, nor any State be formed by the junction of two or more States, or parts of States, without the consent of the Legislature of the States concerned, as well as of the Congress.

2. The Congress shall have power to dispose of and make all needful rules and regulations respecting the territory or other property belonging to the United States; and nothing in this Constitution shall be so construed as to prejudice any claims of the United States or of any particular State.

Sec. IV.—The United States shall guarantee to every State in this Union a Republican form of Government, and shall protect each of them against invasion; and, on application of the Legislature, or of the executive (when the Legislature cannot be convened), against domestic violence.

ARTICLE V.

The Congress, whenever two-thirds of both Houses shall deem it necessary, shall propose amendments to this Constitution; or, on the application of the Legislatures or two-thirds of the several States, shall call a convention for proposing amendments, which, in either case, shall be valid to all intents and purpose, as part of this Constitution, when ratified by the Legislatures of three-fourths thereof, as the one or the other mode of ratification may be proposed by Congress; provided that no amendment which may be made prior to the year one thousand eight hundred and eight, shall, in any manner, affect the first and fourth clauses in the ninth section of the first article; AND THAT NO STATE, WITHOUT ITS CONSENT, SHALL BE DEPRIVED OF ITS EQUAL SUFFRAGE IN THE SENATE.

ARTICLE VI.

1. All debts contracted, and engagements entered into, before the adoption of this Constitution, shall be as valid against the United States under this Constitution as under the Confederation.

2. This Constitution, and the laws of the United States which shall be made in pursuance thereof, and all treaties made, or which shall be made under the authority of the United States, shall be the supreme law of the land, and the judges in every State shall be bound thereby, anything in the Constitution or laws of any State to the contrary notwithstanding.

3. The Senators and Representatives before mentioned, and the members of the several State Legislatures, and executive and judicial officers both of the United States and of the several States, shall be bound by oath or affirmation to support this Constitution; but no religious test shall ever be required as a qualification to any office, or public trust, under the United States.

ARTICLE VII.

The ratification of the convention of nine States shall be sufficient for the establishment of this Constitution between the States so ratifying the same.

GEORGE WASHINGTON, *President.*

WILLIAM JACKSON, *Secretary.*

AMENDMENTS TO THE CONSTITUTION.

ARTICLE I.

Congress shall make no law respecting an establishment of religion, or prohibiting the free exercise thereof ; or abridging the freedom of speech, or of the press ; or the right of the people peaceably to assemble and to petition the Government for a redress of grievances.

ARTICLE II.

A well regulated militia being necessary to the security of a free State, the right of.the people to keep and bear arms shall not be infringed.

ARTICLE III.

No soldier shall, in time of peace, be quartered in any house without the consent of the owner ; nor in time of war, but in a manner to be prescribed by law.

ARTICLE IV.

The right of the people to be secure in their persons, houses, papers and effects, against unreasonable searches and seizures, shall not be violated : and no warrant shall issue but upon probable cause, supported by oath or affirmation, and particularly describing the place to be searched, and the persons or things to be seized.

ARTICLE V.

No person shall be held to answer for a capital or otherwise infamous crime, unless on a presentment or indictment of a grand jury, except in cases arising in the land or naval forces, or in the militia, when in actual service, in time of war or public danger; nor shall any person be subject, for the same offence, to be twice put in jeopardy of life or limb; nor shall he be compelled, in any criminal case, to be a witness against himself, nor be deprived of life, liberty or property without due process of law; nor shall private property be taken for public use without just compensation.

ARTICLE VI.

In all criminal prosecutions the accused shall enjoy the right to a speedy and public trial by an impartial jury of the State and district wherein the crime shall have been committed, which district shall have been previously ascertained by law, and to be informed of the nature and cause of the accusation; to be confronted with the witnesses against him; to have compulsory process for obtaining witnesses in his favour, and to have the assistance of counsel for the defence.

ARTICLE VII.

In suits at common law, where the value in controversy shall exceed twenty dollars, the right of trial by jury shall be preserved: and no fact tried by a jury shall be otherwise re-examined in any court of the United States than according to the rules of the common law.

ARTICLE VIII.

Excessive bail shall not be required, nor excessive fines imposed, nor cruel and unusual punishments inflicted.

ARTICLE IX.

The enumeration in the Constitution of certain rights shall not be construed to deny or disparage others retained by the people.

ARTICLE X.

The powers not delegated to the United States by the Constitution, nor prohibited by it to the States, are reserved to the States respectively, or to the people.

ARTICLE XI.

The judicial power of the United States shall not be construed to extend to any suit in law or equity commenced or prosecuted against one of the United States by citizens of another State, or by citizens or subjects of any foreign State.

ARTICLE XII.

The electors shall meet in their respective States, and vote by ballot for President and Vice-President, one of whom, at least, shall not be an inhabitant of the same State as themselves; they shall name in their ballots the person voted for as President, and in distinct ballots the person voted for as Vice-President; and they shall make distinct lists of all persons voted for as President, and of all persons voted for as Vice-President, and of the number of votes for each, which list they shall sign and certify, and transmit sealed to the seat of Government of the United States, directed to the President of the Senate; the President of the Senate shall, in the presence of the Senate and House of Representatives, open all the certificates, and the votes shall then be counted; the person having the greatest number of votes for President shall be the President, if such number be a majority of the whole number of electors appointed; and if no one has such majority, then, from the persons having the highest numbers, not exceeding three, on the list of those voted for as President, the House of Representatives shall choose immediately, by ballot, the President. But in choosing the President, the votes shall be taken by States, the representation from each State having one vote; a quorum for this purpose shall consist of a member or members from two-thirds of the States, and a majority of all the States shall be necessary to a choice. And if the House of Representatives shall not choose a President, whenever the right of choice shall devolve upon them, before the fourth day of March next following, then the Vice-President shall act as President, as in the case of the death or other constitutional disability of the President.

2. The person having the greatest number of votes as Vice-President shall be the Vice-President, if such number be a majority of the whole number of electors appointed; and if no person have a majority, then, from the two highest numbers on the list, the Senate shall choose the Vice-President; a quorum for the purpose shall consist of two-thirds of the whole number of Senators, and a majority of the whole number shall be necessary to a choice.

3. But no person constitutionally ineligible to the office of President shall be eligible to that of Vice-President of the United States.

ARTICLE XIII.

If any citizen of the United States shall accept, claim, receive or retain any title of nobility or honour, or shall, without the consent of Congress, accept and retain any present, pension, office, or emolument, of any kind whatever, from any emperor, king, prince, or foreign power, such person shall cease to be a citizen of the United States, and shall be incapable of holding any office of trust or profit under them or either of them.

ARTICLE XIV.

1. All persons born or naturalized in the United States, and subject to the jurisdiction thereof, are citizens of the United

States and of the State wherein they reside. No State shall make or enforce any law which shall abridge the privileges or immunities of citizens of the United States. Nor shall any State deprive any person of life, liberty, or property, without due process of law, nor deny to any person within its jurisdiction the equal protection of the laws.

2. Representatives shall be appointed among the several States according to their respective numbers, counting the whole number of persons in each State, excluding Indians not taxed; but whenever the right to vote at any election for electors of President and Vice-President, or for United States Representatives in Congress, executive and judicial officers, or the members of the Legislature thereof, is denied to any of the male inhabitants of such State, being twenty-one years of age and citizens of the United States, or in any way abridged, except for participation in rebellion or other crime, the basis of representation therein shall be reduced in the proportion which the number of such male citizens shall bear to the whole number of male citizens twenty-one years of age in that State.

3. No person shall be a Senator or Representative in Congress, elector of President or Vice-President, or hold any office, civil or military, under the United States, or under any State, who, having previously taken an oath as member of Congress, or as an officer of the United States, or as a member of any State Legislature, or as an executive or judicial officer of any State, to support the Constitution of the United States, shall have engaged in insurrection or rebellion against the same, or given aid or comfort to the enemies thereof; but Congress may, by a vote of two-thirds of each House, remove such disability.

4. The validity of the public debt of the United States, authorized by law, including debts incurred for the payment of pensions and bounties for service in suppressing insurrection or rebellion, shall not be questioned, but neither the United States

nor any State shall assume or pay any debt or obligation incurred in aid of insurrection or rebellion against the United States, or claim for the loss or emancipation of any slave, but all such debts, obligations, and claims, shall be held illegal and void.

ARTICLE XV.

The right of citizens of the United States to vote shall not be denied or abridged by the United States, or by any State, on account of race, colour, or previous conditions of servitude.

I NOW turn to the record of my own work. Having clearly satisfied my own mind that the existing Constitution of my country conferred this franchise on all citizens, independently of the accident of sex, and that all rights attaching to the possession of the franchise followed necessarily on with its exercise, I determined to bring matters to an issue by claiming my rights in their highest form of expression, and declared myself a candidate for the Presidency in the following terms :—

MANIFESTO.*

The disorganized condition of parties in the United States at the present time affords a favourable opportunity for a review of the political situation and for comment on the issues which are likely to come up for settlement in the Presidential election in 1872. As I happen to be the most prominent representative of the only unrepresented class in the republic, and perhaps the most practical exponent of the principles of equality, I request the favour of being permitted to address the public through the medium of the *Herald*. While others of my sex devoted themselves to a crusade against the laws that shackle the women of the country, I asserted my individual independence; while others prayed for the good time coming, I worked for it; while others argued the equality of woman with man, I proved it by successfully engaging in business; while others sought to show that there was no valid reason why women should be treated, socially and politically, as being inferior to man, I boldly entered the arena of politics and business and exercised the rights I already possessed. I therefore claim the right to speak for the unenfranchised women of the country, and believing as I do that the prejudices which still exist in

* Reprinted from the *New York Herald* of April 2nd, 1870.

the popular mind against women in public life will soon disappear, I now announce myself as candidate for the Presidency.

I am well aware that in assuming this position I shall evoke more ridicule than enthusiasm at the outset. But this is an epoch of sudden changes and startling surprises. What may appear absurd to-day will assume a serious aspect to-morrow. I am content to wait until my claim for recognition as a candidate shall receive the calm consideration of the press and the public. The blacks were cattle in 1860; a negro now sits in Jeff Davis' seat in the United States Senate. The sentiment of the country was, even in 1863, against negro suffrage; now the negro's right to vote is acknowledged by the Constitution of the United States. Let those, therefore, who ridiculed the negro's claim to exercise the right to "life, liberty and the pursuit of happiness," and who lived to see him vote and hold high public office, ridicule the aspirations of the women of the country for complete political equality as much as they please. They cannot roll back the rising tide of reform. The world moves.

That great Governmental changes were to follow the enfranchisement of the negro I have long foreseen. While the curse of slavery covered the land progress was enchained, but when it was swept away in the torrent of war, the voice of justice was heard, and it became evident that the last weak barrier against complete political and social equality must soon give way. All that has been said and written hitherto in support of equality for woman has had its proper effect on the public mind, just as the anti-slavery speeches before secession were effective; but a candidate and a policy are required to prove it. Lincoln's election showed the strength of the feeling against the peculiar institution; my candidature for the Presidency will, I confidently expect, develop the fact that the principles of equal rights for all have taken deep root. The advocates of political equality for women have, besides a respectable known strength, a great undercurrent of unexpressed power, which is only awaiting a fit opportunity to show itself. By the general and decided test I propose, we shall be able to understand the woman question aright, or at least have done much towards presenting the issue involved in proper shape. I claim to possess the strength and courage to be the subject of that test, and look forward confidently to a triumphant issue of the canvass.

The present position of political parties is anomalous. They are not inspired by any great principles of policy or economy; there is no live issue up for discussion.

A great national question is wanted, to prevent a descent into pure sectionalism. That question exists in the issue, whether woman shall remain sunk below the right granted to the negro, or be elevated to all the political rights enjoyed by man. The simple issue whether woman should not have this complete political equality with the negro is the only one to be tried, and none more important is likely to arise before the Presidential election. But besides the question of equality others of great magnitude are necessarily included. The platform that is to succeed in the coming election must enunciate the *general* principles of enlightened justice and economy.

A complete reform in our system of prison discipline having specially in view the welfare of the families of criminals, whose labour should not be lost to them; the re-arrangement of the system and control of internal improvements; the adoption of some better means for caring for the helpless and indigent; the establishment of strictly neutral and reciprocal relations with all foreign Powers who will unite to better the condition of the productive class, and the adoption of such principles as shall recognize this class as the true wealth of the country, and give it a just position beside capital, thus introducing a practical plan for universal government upon the most enlightened basis, for the actual, not the imaginary benefit of mankind.

These important changes can only be expected to follow a complete departure from the beaten tracks of political parties and their machinery; and this, I believe, my canvass of 1872 will effect.

With the view of spreading to the people ideas which hitherto have not been placed before them, and which they may, by reflection, carefully amplify for their own benefit, I have written several papers on governmental questions of importance and will submit them in due order. For the present the foregoing must suffice. I anticipate criticism; but however unfavourable the comment this letter may evoke I trust that my sincerity will not be called in question. I have deliberately and of my own accord placed myself before the people as a candidate for the Presidency of the United States, and having the means, courage, energy and strength necessary for the race, intend to contest it to the close.

VICTORIA C. WOODHULL.

THE

MEMORIAL OF VICTORIA C. WOODHULL

TO

The Honourable the Senate and House of Representatives of the United States in Congress assembled, respectfully showeth :

THAT she was born in the State of Ohio, and is above the age of twenty-one years; that she has resided in the State of New York during the past three years: that she is still a resident thereof, and that she is a citizen of the United States, as declared by Article XIV. of the Amendments to the Constitution of the United States:

That since the adoption of Article XV. of the Amendments to the Constitution neither the State of New York nor any other State, nor any Territory, has passed any law to abridge the right of any citizen of the United States to vote, as established by said article, neither on account of sex or otherwise:

That, nevertheless, the right to vote is denied to women citizens of the United States, by the operation of Election Laws in the several States and Territories, which laws were enacted prior to the adoption of the said Article XV., and which are inconsistent with the Constitution as amended, and therefore are void and of no effect; but which, being still enforced by the said States and Territories, render the Constitution inoperative as regards the right of women citizens to vote:

And whereas, Article VI., section 2, declares "That this Constitution, and the laws of the United States which shall be made in pursuance thereof, and all treaties made, or which shall be made under the authority of the United States, shall be the supreme law of the land; and all judges in every State shall be bound thereby, anything in the Constitution and laws of any State to the contrary notwithstanding:"

And whereas, no distinction between citizens is made in the Constitution of the United States on account of sex; but Article XV. of the Amendments to it provides that "No State shall make or enforce any law which shall abridge the privileges and immunities of citizens of the United States, nor deny to any person within its jurisdiction the equal protection of the laws:"

And whereas, Congress has power to make laws which shall be necessary and proper for carrying into execution all powers vested by the Constitution in the Government of the United States, and to make or alter all regulations in relation to holding elections for senators or representatives, and especially to enforce by appropriate legislation the provisions of the said Article XIV.:

And whereas, the continuance of the enforcement of said local election laws, denying and abridging the right of citizens to vote on account of sex, is a grievance to your Memorialist and to various other persons, citizens of the United States, being women—

> Therefore, your Memorialist would most respectfully petition your Honourable Bodies to make such laws as in the wisdom of Congress shall be necessary and proper for carrying into execution the right vested by the Constitution in the Citizens of the United States to vote, without regard to sex.

And your Memorialist will ever pray.

VICTORIA C. WOODHULL.

Dated NEW YORK CITY,
    December 19th, 1870.

[From *The Congressional Globe*, Dec. 22nd, 1870.]

" In the Senate :

" Mr. Harris presented the memorial of Victoria C. Woodhull, praying for the passage of such laws as may be necessary and proper for carrying into execution the right vested by the Constitution in the citizens of the United States to vote without regard to sex ; which was referred to the Committee on the Judiciary and ordered to be printed."

" In the House :

" Mr. Julian.—I ask unanimous consent to present at this time, and have printed in the *Globe*, the memorial of Victoria C. Woodhull, claiming the right of suffrage under the XIVth and XVth Articles of Amendments to the Constitution of the United States, and asking for the enactment of the necessary and appropriate legislation to guarantee the exercise of that right to the women of the United States.   I also ask that the petition be referred to the Committee on the Judiciary."

" No objection was made, and it was ordered accordingly."

FURTHER ARGUMENT IN SUPPORT OF MEMORIAL.

The foregoing Memorial having been referred to the Judiciary Committee, I then prepared and submitted the following legal deductions in support thereof:—

To the Hon. the Judiciary Committees of the Senate and the House of Representatives of the Congress of the United States.

THE undersigned, VICTORIA C. WOODHULL, having most respectfully memorialized Congress for the passage of such laws as in its wisdom shall seem necessary and proper to carry into effect the rights vested by the Constitution of the United States in the citizens to vote, without regard to sex, begs leave to submit to your honourable body the following in favour of her prayer in the said Memorial which has been referred to your Committee:—

The public law of the world is founded upon the conceded fact that sovereignty cannot be forfeited or renounced. The sovereign power of this country is perpetual in the politically-organized people of the United States, and can neither be relinquished nor abandoned by any portion of them. The people in this Republic who confer sovereignty are its citizens: in a monarchy the people are the subjects of sovereignty. All citizens of a republic by rightful act or implication confer sovereign power. All people of a monarchy are subjects who exist under its supreme shield and enjoy its immunities.

The subject of a monarch takes municipal immunities from the sovereign as a gracious favour; but the woman citizen of this country has the inalienable "sovereign" right of self-government in *her own proper person*. Those who look upon woman's status in the dim light of the common law, which unfolded itself under the feudal and military institutions that establish right upon physical power, cannot find any analogy in the status of the woman citizen of this country, *where the broad sunshine of our Constitution has enfranchised all.*

As sovereignty cannot be forfeited, relinquished, or abandoned, those from whom it flows—the citizens—are equal in conferring the power, and should be equal in the enjoyment of its benefits and in the exercise of its rights and privileges.

One portion of citizens have no power to deprive another portion of rights and privileges such as are possessed and exercised by themselves. The male citizen has no more right to deprive the female citizen of the free, public, political expression of opinion than the female citizen has to deprive the male citizen thereof.

The sovereign will of the people is expressed in our written Constitution, which is the supreme law of the land. The Constitution makes no distinction of sex. The Constitution defines a woman born or naturalized in the United States, and subject to the jurisdiction thereof, to be a citizen. It recognizes the right of citizens to vote. It declares that the right of citizens of the United States to vote shall not be denied or abridged by the United States or by any State on account of " race, colour, or previous condition of servitude."

Women, white and black, belong to races; although to different races. A race of people comprises all the people, male and female. The right to vote cannot be denied on account of race. All people included in the term race have the right to vote, unless otherwise prohibited.

Women of all races are white, black, or some intermediate colour. Colour comprises all people, of all races and both sexes. The right to vote cannot be denied on account of colour. All people included in the term colour have the right to vote unless otherwise prohibited.

With the right to vote sex has nothing to do. Race and

colour include all people of both sexes. All people of both sexes have the right to vote, unless prohibited by special limiting terms less comprehensive than race or colour. No such limiting terms exist in the Constitution.

Women, white and black, have from time immemorial groaned under what is properly termed in the Constitution "previous condition of servitude."

Women are the equals of men before the law, and are equal in all their rights as citizens.

Women are debarred from voting in some parts of the United States, although they are allowed to exercise that right elsewhere.

Women were formerly permitted to vote in places where they are now debarred therefrom.

The Naturalization Laws of the United States expressly provide for the naturalization of women.

But the right to vote has only lately been distinctly declared by the Constitution to be inalienable, under three distinct conditions—in all of which woman is distinctly embraced.

The citizen who is taxed should also have a voice in the subject matter of taxation. "No taxation without representation" is a right which was fundamentally established at the very birth of our country's independence; and by what ethics does any free government impose taxes on women without giving them a voice upon the subject or a participation in the public declaration as to how and by whom these taxes shall be applied for common public use?

Women are free to own and to control property, separate and apart from males, and they are held responsible in their own proper persons, in every particular, as well as men, in and out of court.

Women have the same inalienable right to life, liberty, and the *pursuit of* happiness that men have. Why have they not this right politically, as well as men?

Women constitute a majority of the people of this country; they hold vast portions of the nation's wealth, and pay a proportionate share of the taxes. They are intrusted with the most holy duties and the most vital responsibilities of society; they bear, rear, and educate men; they train and mould their characters; they inspire the noblest impulses in men; they often hold the accumulated fortunes of a man's life for the safety of the family, and as guardians of the infants, and yet they are debarred from uttering any opinion, by public vote, as to the management by public servants of these interests; they are the secret counsellors, the best advisers, the most devoted aids in the most trying periods of men's lives, and yet men shrink from trusting them in the common questions of ordinary politics. Men trust women in the market, in the shop, on the highway and the railroad, and in all other public places and assemblies, but when they propose to carry a slip of paper with a name upon it to the polls, they fear them. Nevertheless, as citizens women have the right to vote; they are part and parcel of that great element in which the sovereign power of the land had birth: and it is by usurpation only that men debar them from their right to vote. The American nation, in its march onward and upward, cannot paralyse the intellectual and political activity of half its citizens by narrow statutes. The will of the entire people is the true basis of republican government, and a free expression of that will by the public vote of all citizens, without distinctions of race, colour, occupation, or sex, is the only means by which that will can be ascertained. As the world has advanced in civilization and culture; as mind has risen in its dominion over matter; as the principle of justice and moral right has gained sway, and merely physically organized power has yielded thereto; as the might of right has supplanted the right of might, so have the rights of women become more fully recognized, and that recognition is the result of the development of the minds of men, which through the ages she has polished, and thereby heightened the lustre of civilization.

It was reserved for our great country to recognize by constitutional enactment that political equality of all citizens which religion, affection, and common sense should have long since accorded; it was reserved for America to sweep away the mist of prejudice and ignorance, and that chivalric condescension of a darker age, for in the language of Holy Writ, "The night is far spent, the day is at hand, let us therefore cast off the work of darkness, and let us put on the armour of light. Let us walk honestly as in the day."

It may be argued against the proposition that there still remains upon the statute books of some States the word "male" to an exclusion, but as the Constitution in its paramount character can only be read by the light of the established principle, *ita lex scripta est;* and as the subject of sex is not mentioned, and the Constitution is not limited either in terms or by necessary implication in the general rights of citizens to vote, this right cannot be limited on account of anything in the spirit of inferior or previous enactments upon a subject which is not mentioned in the supreme law. A different construction would destroy a vested right in a portion of the citizens, and this no legislature has a right to do without compensation, and nothing can compensate a citizen for the loss of his or her suffrage—its value is equal to the value of life. Neither can it be presumed that women are to be kept from the polls as a mere police regulation: it is to be hoped, at least, that police regulations in their case need not be very active. The effect of the amendments to the Constitution must be to annul the power over this subject in the States, whether past, present, or future, which is contrary to the amendments. The amendments would even arrest the action of the Supreme Court in cases pending before it prior to their adoption, and operate as an absolute prohibition to the exercise of any other jurisdiction than merely to dismiss the suit.

3 Dall., 382; 6 Wheaton, 405 ; 9 Id., 868; 3d Circ., Pa.,
1832.

And if the restrictions contained in the Constitution as to
colour, race, or servitude, were designed to limit the State
governments in reference to their own citizens, and were
intended to operate also as restrictions on the Federal power,
and to prevent interference with the rights of the State and its
citizens, how then can the State restrict citizens of the United
States in the exercise of rights not mentioned in any restrictive
clause in reference to actions on the part of those citizens having
reference solely to the necessary functions of the seneral
Government, such as the election of representatives and senators to Congress, whose election the Constitution expressly
gives Congress the power to regulate ?

S. C., 1847 ; Fox U. Ohio, 5 Howard, 410.

Your Memorialist complains of the existence of State Laws,
and prays Congress, by appropriate legislation, to declare them,
as they are, annulled, and to give vitality to the Constitution
under its power to make and alter the regulations of the States
contravening the same.

It may be urged in opposition that the Courts have power,
and should declare upon this subject.

The Supreme Court has the power, and it would be its duty
so to declare the law ; but the Court will not do so unless such
a point shall arise as shall make it necessary to determine a
controversy, and hence a case must be presented in which there
can be no rational doubt. All this would subject the aggrieved
parties to much dilatory, expensive, and needless litigation,
which your Memorialist prays your Honourable Body to dis-
pense with by appropriate legislation, as there can be no
purpose in special arguments *ad · inconvenienti*, enlarging or
contracting the import of the language of the Constitution.

Therefore, Believing firmly in the right of citizens to freely
approach those in whose hands their destiny is placed, under
the Providence of God, your Memorialist has frankly, by

humbly, appealed to you, and prays that the wisdom of Congress may be moved to action in this matter for the benefit and the increased happiness of our beloved country.

Most respectfully submitted,

VICTORIA C. WOODHULL.

Dated NEW YORK,

January 2nd, 1871.

CONSTITUTIONAL EQUALITY THE LOGICAL RESULT OF THE XIVTH AND
XVTH AMENDMENTS, WHICH NOT ONLY DECLARE WHO ARE CITIZENS,
BUT ALSO DEFINE THEIR RIGHTS, ONE OF WHICH IS THE RIGHT
TO VOTE, WITHOUT REGARD TO SEX, BOTH SEXES BEING INCLUDED
IN THE MORE COMPREHENSIVE PROHIBITORY TERMS OF RACE AND
COLOUR.

THE STATE LAWS WHICH PROSCRIBED WOMEN AS VOTERS WERE
REPEALED BY THE STATES WHEN THEY RATIFIED SAID AMENDMENTS
—THERE ARE NO EXISTING OPERATIVE LAWS WHICH PROSCRIBE
THE RIGHT OF ANY CITIZEN TO VOTE—THE PERFECTED FRUITS OF
THE LATE WAR—THE GOVERNMENT OF THE UNITED STATES IS
BOUND TO PROTECT ITS CITIZENS, MALE AND FEMALE, IN THE
EXERCISE OF THEIR RIGHT TO VOTE—THE DUTY OF CONGRESS IN
THE PREMISES.

THE time has now arrived when it becomes proper to present
the final and unanswerable proposition, which cannot by any
possibility be controverted, that the several States which, until
recently, assumed and exercised the right of defining which of
its citizens should exercise the right to vote, have by their own
voluntary act not only for ever repealed all such prohibitory
laws, but also have for ever barred their re-enactment.

Of this I have been fully aware since the proclamation by the
President that the XVth Amendment had become a part of the
Organic Law of the country.

To bring the whole matter properly before the public I published an address on the 2nd of April last, in which I announced
myself a candidate for the Presidency in 1872, and thus asserted
the right of woman to occupy the highest office in the gift of
the people.

After that address had had its legitimate effect in arousing
the press and the country to the realization that women are a
constituent part of the body politic, and to a discussion in a
much more general way than had ever been before, I published
my second address to the people, announcing that the XVIth

Amendment was a dead letter, and that the Constitution fully recognized the equality of all citizens.

In this address the general bearings of the Constitution were examined, and from the blending of its various parts the conclusion was arrived at that no State should deny the right to vote to any citizen.

I now take the final step, and show that the States themselves, by their legislative enactments, have removed the only obstacle which until then had prevented women from voting, and have for ever debarred themselves from receding to their former position. It is as follows :—

"SUFFRAGE, or the right to vote, is declared by the XVth Article of Amendments to the Constitution to be a RIGHT, not a privilege, of citizens of the United States."

A right of a citizen is inherent in the individual, of which he cannot be deprived by any law of any State.

A privilege may be conferred upon the citizen of the State, and by it may be taken away. This distinction is made to show that *to vote is not a privilege* conferred by a State upon its citizens, but a CONSTITUTIONAL RIGHT of every citizen of the United States, of which they cannot be deprived. The language of the Constitution is most singularly emphatic upon this point. It is as follows :—

"ARTICLE XV.

" 1. *The right of citizens of the United States to vote shall not be denied or abridged by the United States or by any State on account of race, colour, or previous condition of servitude.*"

It is thus for ever proclaimed, in unmistakable terms, that *to vote is a right* of citizens of the United States.

Were it an immunity, or even were it a privilege, to vote, those who possess it could not be deprived of it by any State, for the State is bound to protect every citizen within its jurisdiction in the exercise thereof. It being declared by the XVth

Amendment that citizens of the United States have the right to vote, the next step to determine is, Who are citizens? This is also definitely, though for the first time, determined by Article XIVth of Amendments to the Constitution, as follows:

"ARTICLE XIV.

"1. All persons born or naturalized in the United States, and subject to the jurisdiction thereof, are citizens of the United States and of the State wherein they reside. *No State shall make or enforce any law which shall abridge the privileges or immunities of citizens of the United States.* Nor shall any State deprive any person of life, liberty, or property without due process of law, *nor deny to any person* within its jurisdiction the equal protection of the laws."

The next point of inquiry is, How is it that the State laws, which formerly did proscribe women and exclude them from the exercise of suffrage, no longer *do so?* Simply and effectively by this fact, that, by the adoption of the XVth Article of Amendments to the Constitution, the States established, as the "SUPREME LAW of the LAND," the fact that no person born or naturalized in the United States, and subject to the jurisdiction thereof, shall be denied or abridged by the United States, or by any State, of the RIGHT TO VOTE.

Women are citizens of the United States; and the States themselves, by their own voluntary act, have established the fact of their citizenship, and confirmed their right to vote, which, by such action, has become the supreme law of the land, which supersedes, annuls and abrogates all previous State laws inconsistent therewith or contravening the same. The XVth Article of Amendments to the Constitution is as much a part of it as any originally adopted; for Art. VI., ¶ 2, says:

"This Constitution, and the laws of the United States which shall be made in pursuance thereof, and all treaties made, or which shall be made under the authority of the United States *shall be* THE SUPREME *law of* THE LAND ; and the *judges in* EVERY *State shall* BE BOUND THEREBY ; anything in *the Constitution or laws* OF ANY *State* TO THE CONTRARY NOTWITHSTANDING."

The XVth Amendment was adopted by the several States as a legislative enactment by their Legislatures, under Article V., which provides :

" The Congress, whenever two-thirds of both Houses shall deem it necessary, *shall propose amendments to this Constitution ;* or, on the application of the Legislatures of two-thirds of the several States, shall call a convention for proposing amendments, *which,* in either case, *shall be valid to all intents and purposes, as part of this Constitution,* when *ratified by the Legislatures of three-fourths thereof,* as the one or the other mode of ratification may be proposed by Congress, provided that no amendment which may be made prior to the year one thousand eight hundred and eight shall, in any manner, affect the first and fourth clauses in the ninth section of the first article ; AND THAT NO STATE, WITHOUT ITS CONSENT, SHALL BE DEPRIVED OF ITS EQUAL SUFFRAGE IN THE SENATE."

Since, therefore, all citizens have the RIGHT TO VOTE under this act, all State Laws which abridge the right are inoperative, null and void, and the exclusion of women who are citizens from the right to vote, was repealed and must stand repealed until the Legislatures of the several States shall again pass an Act positively excluding them. If we again examine Art. XV. we shall see that this right shall not be denied or abridged by the United States or any State on account of RACE, COLOUR, OF PREVIOUS CONDITION OF SERVITUDE ; it is left to be inferred that it might be on account of SEX, but this denial has not yet been attempted, nor could it be accomplished if it were, for here the XIVth Amendment again comes to our relief, saying, " That no State shall make or enforce any law which shall abridge the privileges or immunities of citizens of the United States."

Again, the Constitution is assuredly a contract between States and citizens, and Section X., Article I., provides that no State shall pass any law impairing contracts.

Article I., Section IV., ¶ 1. provides that:

" The times, places and *manner of holding elections* for senators and representatives shall be prescribed in each State by the Legislature thereof : but the *Congress may, at any time, by law, make or alter such regulations*, except as to the places of choosing senators," while the judiciary of the United States has acquired complete jurisdiction over this matter by the authority of Art. III., Sec. II., ¶ 1, which provides that :—"*The judicial power shall extend to all cases in law and equity arising under this Constitution, the laws of the United States, and treaties made, or which shall be made, under their authority*."

And for all these reasons, the State Legislatures having, by the adoption of the XVth Amendment, abrogated all previously existing conflicting laws on the subject of suffrage, are now for ever precluded by the XIVth Amendment from re-establishing any restriction to apply to women, whom the authorities of the United States, in their support of the Constitution, are in duty bound to protect in their right to vote.

Now, what was the fruit of the late war, which threw the entire nation into such convulsive throes, unless it is found in the XIVth and XVth Amendments to the Constitution, namely : that grand change in the fundamental laws which declares *who* are citizens and what are their *rights, privileges* and immunities, which cannot be abridged ? Will anyone pretend that these great enactments can be understood to mean less than the language thereof plainly conveys ? Or will anyone claim that the old, absurd State laws, which were sunk in oblivion by the adoption of these amendments to the Constitution, are still in force ? Who will *dare* to say, in the face of these plainly worded amendments, which have such an unmistakable meaning, that the women of America shall not enjoy their emancipation as well as the black slave ?

WOMEN HAVE THE RIGHT TO VOTE ! It is the duty of the

Government to see that they are not denied the right to exercise it; and, to secure the necessary action of Congress in the premises, I did, on the 21st day of December, 1870, memorialize Congress as recorded in the *Congregational Globe*, December 22, 1870 (*see* p. 34).

REPORT OF THE COMMITTEE.

HOUSE OF REPRESENTATIVES.—41*st Congress*, 3*rd Session*.

Report No. 22. *January* 30*th*, 1871.—Re-committed to the Committee on the Judiciary and ordered to be printed.

MR. BINGHAM, *from the Committee on the Judiciary, made the following Report :—The Committee on the Judiciary, to whom was referred the Memorial of Victoria C. Woodhull, having considered the same, make the following report :—*

THE Memorialist asks the enactment of a law by Congress which shall secure to citizens of the United States in the several States the right to vote " without regard to sex." Since the adoption of the XIVth Amendment of the Constitution there is no longer any reason to doubt that all persons born or naturalized in the United States, and subject to the jurisdiction thereof, are citizens of the United States and of the State wherein they reside, for that is the express declaration of the amendment.

The clause of the XIVth Amendment, " No State shall make or enforce any law which shall abridge the privileges or immunities of citizens of the United States," does not, in the opinion of the Committee, refer to privileges and immunities of citizens of the United States other than those privileges and immunities embraced in the original text of the Constitution, Article IV., Section II. The XIVth Amendment, it is believed, did not add to the privileges and immunities before mentioned, but was deemed necessary for their enforcement, as an express limitation upon the power of the States. It has been judicially determined that the first eight articles of amendment of the Constitution were not limitations on the power of the States, and it was apprehended that the same might be held of the provision of Article IV., Section II.

To remedy this defect of the Constitution, the express limitations upon the States contained in the first section of the XIVth Amendment, together with the grant of power in Congress to enforce them by legislation, were incorporated in the Constitution. The words " citizens of the United States " and " citizen of the States," as employed in the XIVth Amendment, did not change or modify the relations of citizens of the State and Nation as they existed under the original Constitution.

Attorney-General Bates gave the opinion that the Constitution uses the word " citizen " only to express the political quality of the individual in his relation to the Nation ; to declare that he is a member of the body politic and bound to it by the reciprocal obligation of allegiance on the one side and protection on the other. The phrase "a citizen of the United States," without addition or qualification, means neither more nor less than a member of the Nation.—*Opinion of Attorney - General Bates on Citizenship.*

The Supreme Court of the United States has ruled that, according to the express words and clear meaning of Article IV., Section II. of the Constitution, no privileges are secured by it except those which belong to citizenship.—*Connor* et al. v. *Elliott* et al., 18 *Howard,* 593.

In Corfield v. Correll, 4 Washington Circuit Court Reports, 380, the Court say :—

" The inquiry is, what are the privileges and immunities of citizens in the several States ? We feel no hesitation in confining these expressions to those privileges and immunities which are in their nature fundamental;

8 *

which belong of right to the citizens of all free governments; and which have at all times been enjoyed by the citizens of the several States which compose this Union, from the time of their becoming free, independent and sovereign. What these fundamental principles are would, perhaps, be more tedious than difficult to enumerate. They may, however, be all comprehended under the following general heads: Protection by the Government; the enjoyment of life and liberty, with the right to acquire and possess property of every kind, and to pursue and obtain happiness and safety, subject, nevertheless, to such restraints as the Government may justly prescribe for the general good of the whole; the right of a citizen of one State to pass through or to reside in any other State, for the purpose of trade, agriculture, professional pursuits, or otherwise; to claim the benefit of the writ of *habeas corpus;* to institute and maintain actions of any kind in the courts of the State, to take, hold, and dispose of property, either real or personal; and an exemption from higher taxes or impositions than are paid by the other citizens of the State, may be mentioned as some of the particular privileges and immunities of citizens which are clearly embraced by the general description of privileges deemed to be fundamental; to which may be added the elective franchise, as regulated and established by the laws or Constitution of the State in which it is to be exercised. . . . But we cannot accede to the proposition which was insisted on by the counsel, that under this provision of the Constitution, Article IV., section 2, the citizens of the several States are permitted to participate in all the rights which belong exclusively to the citizens of any other particular State."

The learned Justice Story declared that the intention of the clause—" the citizens of each State shall be entitled to all the privileges and immunities of citizens in the several States "— was to confer on the citizens of each State a general citizenship, and communicated all the privileges and immunities which a citizen of the same State would be entitled to under the same circumstances.—*Story on the Constitution,* Vol. II., p. 635.

In the case of the Bank of the United States *v.* Primrose, in the Supreme Court of the United States, Mr. Webster said :—

" That this Article in the Constitution (Article IV., Section 2) does not confer on the citizens of each State political rights in every other State is admitted. A citizen of Pennsylvania cannot go into Virginia and vote at any election in that State, though when he has acquired a residence in Virginia, and is otherwise qualified and is required by the Constitution (of Virginia), he becomes, without formal adoption as a citizen of Virginia, a citizen of that State politically."—*Webster's Works*, Vol. 6, p. 112.

It must be obvious that Mr. Webster was of opinion that the privileges and immunities of citizens, guaranteed to them in the several States, did not include the privilege of the elective franchise otherwise than as secured by the State Constitution. For, after making the statement above quoted that a citizen of Pennsylvania cannot go into Virginia and vote, Mr. Webster adds, " but for the purposes of trade, commerce, buying and selling, it is evidently not in the power of any State to impose any hindrance or embarrassment, &c., upon citizens of other States, or to place them, going there upon a different footing from her own citizens."—*Ib.*

The proposition is clear that no citizen of the United States can rightfully vote in any State of this Union who has not the qualifications required by the Constitution of the State in which the right is claimed to be exercised, except as to such conditions in the constitutions of such States as deny the right to vote to citizens resident therein " on account of race, colour, or previous condition of servitude."

The adoption of the XVth Amendment to the Constitution imposing these three limitations upon the power of the several States was, by necessary implication, a declaration that the States had the power to regulate by a uniform rule the conditions upon which the elective franchise should be exercised by citizens of the United States resident therein. The limitations specified in the XVth Amendment exclude the conclusion that a State of this Union, having a government republican in form, may not prescribe conditions upon which alone citizens may vote other than those prohibited. It can hardly be said that a State law which excludes from voting women citizens, minor citizens, and non-resident citizens of the United States, on account of sex, minority or domicile, is a denial of the right to vote on account of race, colour, or previous condition of servitude.

It may be further added that the second section of the XVth Amendment, by the provision that "when the right to vote at any election for the choice of electors of President and Vice-President of the United States, Representatives in Congress, or executive and judicial officers of the State, or the members of the legislature thereof, is denied to any of the male inhabitants of such State, being twenty-one years of age, and citizens of the United States, or in any way abridged, except for participation in rebellion or other crime, the basis of representation therein shall be reduced in the proportion which the number of such male citizens shall bear to the whole number of male citizens twenty-one years of age in such State," implies that the several States may restrict the elective franchise as to other than male citizens.   In disposing of this question effect must be given, if possible, to every provision of the Constitution. Article I., Section 2, of the Constitution provides :—

"That the House of Representatives shall be composed of members chosen every second year by the people of the several States, and the electors in each State shall have the qualifications requisite for electors of the most numerous branch of the State Legislature."

This provision has always been construed to vest in the several States the exclusive right to prescribe the qualifications of electors for the most numerous branch of the State legislature, and therefore for members of Congress.   And this interpretation is supported by Article I., Section 4, of the Constitution, which provides :—

"That the time, places, and manner of holding elections for Senators and Representatives shall be prescribed in each State by the legislature thereof ; but the Congress may at any time by law make or alter such regulations except as to the place of choosing Senators."

Now it is submitted, if it had been intended that Congress

should prescribe the qualifications of electors, that the grant would have read: The Congress may at any time by law make or alter such regulations, and also prescribe the qualifications of electors, &c. The power, on the contrary, is limited exclusively to the time, place and manner, and does not extend to the qualification of the electors. This power to prescribe the qualification of electors in the several States has always been exercised, and is, to-day, by the several States of the Union; and we apprehend, until the Constitution shall be changed, will continue to be so exercised, subject only to the express limitations imposed by the Constitution upon the several States before noticed. We are of opinion, therefore, that it is not competent for the Congress of the United States to establish by law the right to vote without regard to sex in the several States of this Union, without the consent of the people of such States, and against their constitutions and laws; and that such legislation would be, in our judgment, a violation of the Constitution of the United States, and of the rights reserved to the States respectively by the Constitution. It is undoubtedly the right of the people of the several States so to reform their constitutions and laws as to secure the equal exercise of the right or suffrage, at all elections held therein under the Constitution of the United States, to all citizens, without regard to sex; and as public opinion creates constitutions and governments in the several States, it is not to be doubted that whenever, in any State, the people are of opinion that such a reform is advisable it will be made.

If, however, as is claimed in the memorial referred to, the right to vote "is vested by the Constitution in the citizens of the United States without regard to sex," that right can be established in the courts without further legislation.

The suggestion is made that Congress, by a mere declaratory act, shall say that the construction claimed in the memorial is the true construction of the Constitution, or in other words, that by the Constitution of the United States the right to vote is vested in citizens of the United States "without regard to sex," anything in the constitution and laws of any State to the contrary notwithstanding. In the opinion of the Committee, such declaratory act is not authorized by the Constitution nor within the legislative power of Congress. We therefore recommend the adoption of the following resolution:—

Resolved, That the prayer of the petitioner be not granted, that the memorial be laid on the table, and that the Committee on the Judiciary be discharged from the further consideration of the subject.

MINORITY REPORT OF THE COMMITTEE.

Report No. V., Part 2.—February 1, 1871.—Ordered to be Printed.

MR. LOUGHRIDGE, *from the Committee on the Judiciary, submitted the following as the views of the minority:—In the Matter of the Memorial of Victoria C. Woodhull, referred by the House to the Committee on the Judiciary, the undersigned, members of the Committee, being unable to agree to the Report of the Committee, present the following as their views upon the subject of the Memorial:—*

THE Memorialist sets forth that she is a native born citizen of the United States, and a resident thereof; that she is of adult age, and has resided in the State of New York for three years past; that by the Constitution of the United States she is guaranteed the right of suffrage; but that she is, by the laws of the State of New York, denied the exercise of that right; and that by the laws of different States and Territories the privilege of voting is denied to all the female citizens of the United States; and petitions for relief by the enactment of some law to enforce the provisions of the Constitution by which such right is guaranteed.

The question presented is one of exceeding interest and importance, involving as it does the constitutional rights not only of the Memorialist but of more than one-half of the citizens of the United States—a question of constitutional law in which the civil and natural rights of the citizen are involved. Questions of property or of expediency have nothing to do with it. The question is not "Would it be expedient to extend the right of suffrage to women," but, "Have women citizens that right by the Constitution as it is."

A question of this kind should be met fairly and investigated in that generous and liberal spirit characteristic of the age, and decided upon principles of justice, of right, and of law.

It is claimed by many that to concede to women the right of suffrage would be an innovation upon the laws of nature, and upon the theory and practice of the world for ages in the past, and especially an innovation upon the common law of England, which was originally the law of this country, and which is the foundation of our legal fabric.

If we were to admit the truth of this, it is yet no argument against the proposition, if the right claimed exists, and is established by the Constitution of the United States. The question is to be decided by the Constitution and the fundamental principles of our Government, and not by the usage and dogmas of the past.

It is a gratifying fact that the world is advancing in political science, and gradually adopting more liberal and rational theories of government.

The establishment of this Government upon the principle of the Declaration of Independence was in itself a great innovation upon the theories and practice of the world, and opened a new chapter in the history of the human race, and its progress toward perfect civil and political liberty.

But it is not admitted that the universal usage of the past has been in opposition to the exercise of political power by women. The highest positions of civil power have from time to time been filled by women in all ages of the world, and the question of the right of woman to a voice in government is not a new one by any means, but has been agitated, and the right acknowledged and exercised, in governments far less free and liberal than ours.

In the Roman Republic, during its long and glorious career, women occupied a higher position, as to political rights and privileges, than in any other contemporaneous government. In England unmarried women have, by the laws of that country, always been competent to vote and to hold civil offices, if qualified in other respects; at least, such is the weight of authority. In "Callis upon Sewers," an old English work, will be found a discussion of the question as to the right of women to hold office in England.

The learned and distinguished author uses the following language :—

"And for temporal governments I have observed women to have from time to time been admitted to the highest places; for in ancient Roman histories I find Eudocia and Theodora admitted at several times into the sole government of the empire; and here in England our late famous Queen Elizabeth, whose government was most renowned; and Semiramis governed Syria; and the Queen of the South, which came to visit Solomon, for any-thing that appears to the contrary, was a sole queen; and to fall a degree lower, we have precedents that King Richard I. and King Henry V. appointed by commissions their mothers to be regents of this realm in their absence in France.

"But yet I will descend a step lower; and doth not our law, temporal and spiritual, admit of women to be executrixes and administratrixes? And thereby they have the rule or ordering of great estates, and many times they are guardianesses in chivalry, and have hereby also the government of many great heirs in the kingdom and of their own estates.

"So by these causes it appeareth that the common law of this kingdom submitted many things to their government; yet the statute of justices of the peace is like to Jethro's counsel to Moses, for there they speak of men to be justices, and thereby seemeth to exclude women; but our Statute of Sewers is, 'Commission of Sewers shall be granted by the King to such person and persons as the lords should appoint.' So the word persons stands indifferently for either sex. I am of the opinion, for the authorities, reasons, and causes aforesaid, that this honourable countess, being put into the Commission of the Sewers, the same is warrantable by the law; and the ordinances and decrees made by her and the other Commissions of Sewers, are not to be impeached for that cause of her sex."

As it is said by a recent writer:—

"Even at present in England the idea of women holding official station is not so strange as in the United States. The Countess of Pembroke had the office of Sheriff of Westmoreland and exercised it in person. At the assizes she sat with the judges on the bench. In a reported case it is stated by counsel and assented to by the Court that a woman is capable of serving in almost all the offices of the kingdom."

As to the right of women to vote by the common law of England, the authorities are clear. In the English *Law Magazine* for 1868-69, vol. xxvi., page 120, will be found reported the case of the application of Jane Allen, who claimed to be entered upon the list of voters of the Parish of St. Giles, under the Reform Act of 1867, which Act provides as follows: "Every man shall, in and after the year 1868, be entitled to be registered as a voter, and when registered to vote for a member or members to serve in Parliament, who is qualified as follows: 1st. Is of full age, and not subject to any legal incapacity, &c., &c.

It was decided by the Court that the claimant had the right to be registered and to vote; that by the English law, the term man, as used in that statute, included woman. In that case the common law of England upon that question was fully and ably reviewed, and we may be excused for quoting at some length :—

"And as to what has been said of there being no such adjudged cases, I must say that it is perfectly clear that not perhaps in either of three cases reported by Mr. Shaen, but in those of Catharine *v.* Surry, Coates *v.* Lyle, and Holt *v.* Lyle, three cases of somewhat greater antiquity, the right of women freeholders was allowed by the Courts. These three cases were decided by the judges in the reign of James I. (A.D. 1612). Although no printed report of them exists, I find that in the case of Olive *v.* Ingraham, they were repeatedly cited by the Lord Chief Justice of the King's Bench, in the course of four great arguments in that case, the case being reargued three times (7 Mod., 246), and the greatest respect was manifested by the whole Court for those precedents. Their importance is all the greater when we consider what the matter was upon which King James's Judges sitting in Westminster Hall had to decide. It was not simply the case of a mere occupier, inhabitant, or scot or lot voter. Therefore the question did not turn upon the purport of a special custom, or a charter, or a local act of Parliament, or even of the common right in this or that borough. But it was that very matter and question which has been mooted in the dictum of Lord Coke, the freeholder's franchise in the shire, and upon that the decision in each case expressly was that a feme sole shall vote if she hath a freehold, and that if she be not a feme sole, but a feme covert having freehold, then her husband during her coverture shall vote in her right. These then, are so many express decisions which at once displace Lord Coke's unsupported assertion and declare the law so as to constrain my judgment. It is sometimes said, when reference is made to precedents of this kind, that they have never been approved by the bar, but that cannot be said of these. Hakewell, the contemporary of Lord Coke, and one of the greatest of all Parliamentary lawyers then living—for even Selden and Granvil were not greater than Hakewell—left behind him the manuscript to which I have referred, with his comments on those cases."

Sir William Lee, Chief Justice, in his judgment in the case of Olive v. Ingraham, expressly says that he had perused them, and that they contained the expression of Hakewell's entire approval of the principles upon which they were decided, and of the results deduced; and we have the statement of Lord Chief Justice Lee, who had carefully examined those cases, that in the case of Holt v. Lyle, it was determined that a feme sole freeholder may claim a vote for Parliament men; but if married her husband must vote for her.

In the case of Olive v. Ingraham, Justice Probyn says :—

"The case of Holt v. Lyle, lately mentioned by our Lord Chief Justice, is a very strong case; '*They who pay ought to choose whom they shall pay.*' And the Lord Chief Justice seemed to have assented to that general proposition, as authority for the correlative proposition, that 'women, when sole, had a right to vote.' At all events, there is here the strongest possible evidence that in the reign of James I. the feme sole, being a freeholder of a country, or what is the same thing, of a county, of a city, or town, or borough, where, of custom, freeholders had the right to vote, not only had, but exercised the parliamentary franchise. If married, she could not vote in respect merely of her freehold, not because of the incapacities of coverture, but for this simple reason, that, by the act of marriage, which is an act of law, the title of the feme sole freeholder becomes vested for life in the husband. The qualification to vote was not personal, but real; consequently her right to vote became suspended as soon and for as long as she was married. I am bound to consider that the question as to what weight is due to the dictum of my Lord Coke is entirely disposed of by those cases from the reign of James I. and George II., and that the authority of the latter is unimpeached by any later authority, as the cases of Rex v. Stubles, and Regina v. Aberdavon abundantly show."

In Anstey's Notes on the New Reform Act of 1867, the authorities and precedents upon the right of women to vote in England are examined and summed up, and the author concludes:—

"It is submitted that the weight of authority is very greatly in favour of the female right of suffrage. Indeed, the authority against it is contained in the short and hasty dictum of Lord Coke, referred to above. It was set down by him in his last and least authoritative institute, and it is certain that he has been followed neither by the great lawyers of his time nor by the judicature. The principles of the law in relation to the suffrage of females will be found in Coates v. Lyle, Holt v. Ingraham, and The King v. Stubles, cases decided under the strict rules for the construction of statutes."

It cannot be questioned that from time whereof the memory of man runneth not to the contrary, unmarried women have been by the laws of England competent voters, subject to the freehold qualification which applied alike to men and women. Married women could not vote because they were not freeholders; by the common law their property upon marriage became vested in the husband.

So that it appears that the admission of women to participation in the affairs of government would not be so much of an innovation upon the theories and usage of the past as is by some supposed.

In England the theory was that in property representation, all property should be represented. Here the theory is that of personal representation, which of course, if carried out fully, includes the representation of all property. In England, as we have seen, the owner of the property, whether male or female, was entitled to representation, no distinction being made on account of sex. If the doctrine contended for by the majority of the Committee be correct then the Government is less liberal upon this question than the government of England has been for hundreds of years, for there is in this country a large class of citizens of adult age, and owners in their own right of large amounts of property, and who pay a large proportion of the

taxes to support the Government, who are denied any representation whatever, either for themselves or their property—
unmarried women of whom it cannot be said that their interests
are represented by their husbands. In their case, neither the
English nor the American theory of representation is justified
upon the ground alone that this class of citizens are women.

Surely we cannot be so much less liberal than our English
ancestors! Surely the Constitution of this Rupublic does not
sanction an injustice so indefensible as that!

By the XIVth Amendment of the Constitution of the United
States, what constitutes citizenship of the United States is for
the first time declared, and who are included by the term
citizen. Upon this question, before that time, there had been
much discussion judicial, political and general, and no distinct
and definite definition of qualification had been settled.

The people of the United States determined this question by
the XIVth Amendment to the Constitution, which declares
that—

" All persons born or naturalized in the United States and subject to the
jurisdiction thereof are citizens of the United States, and of the State
wherein they reside. No State shall make or enforce any law which shall
abridge the privileges or immunities of citizens of the United States; nor
shall any State deprive any person of life, liberty, or property, without due
process of law; nor deny to any person within its jurisdiction the equal
protection of the law."

This amendment, after declaring who are citizens of the
United States, and thus fixing but one grade of citizenship,
which insures to all rights which accrue to that condition, goes
on in the same section and prohibits these privileges and
immunities from abridgment by the States.

Whatever these "privileges and immunities" are, they
attach to the female citizen equally with the male. It is
implied by this amendment that they are inherent, that they
belong to citizenship as such, for they are not therein specified
or enumerated.

The majority of the Committee hold that the privileges guaranteed by the XIVth Amendment do not refer to any other than the privileges embraced in Article IV., Section 2, of the original text.

The Committee certainly did not duly consider this unjustified statement.

Article IV., Section 2, provides for the privileges of "citizens of the *States*," while the first section of the XIVth Amendment protects the privileges of "*citizens of the United States*." The terms citizens of the *States* and citizens of the *United States* are by no means convertible.

A Circuit Court of the United States seems to hold a different view of this question from that stated by the, Committee.

In the case of The Live Stock Association *v.* Crescent City (1st Abbott, 396), Justice Bradley, of the Supreme Court of the United States, delivering the opinion, uses the following language in relation to the 1st clause of the XIVth Amendment :—

"The new prohibition that 'no State shall make or enforce any law which shall abridge the privileges or immunities of citizens of the United States' is not identical with the clause in the Constitution which declared that 'the citizens of each State shall be entitled to all the privileges and immunities of citizens in the several States.' It embraces much more.

"It is possible that those who framed the article were not themselves aware of the far-reaching character of its terms; yet, if the amendment does in fact bear a broader meaning, and does extend its protecting shield over those who were never thought of when it was conceived and put in form, and does reach social evils which were never before prohibited by constitutional enactment, it is to be presumed that the American people, in giving it their *imprimatur*, understood what they were doing and meant to decree what in fact they have decreed.

"The 'privileges and immunities' secured by the original Constitution were only such as each State gave to its own citizens, ... but the fourteenth amendment prohibits any State from abridging the privileges or immunities of citizens of the United States, whether its own citizens or any others. It not merely requires equality of privileges, but it demands that the privileges and immunities of all citizens shall be absolutely unabridged and unimpaired."

In the same opinion, after enumerating some of the "privileges" of the citizens, such as were pertinent to the case on trial, but declining to enumerate all, the Court further says :—

"These privileges cannot be invaded without sapping the very foundation of republican government. A republican government is not merely a government of the people, but it is a free government. . . . . It was very ably contended on the part of the defendants that the fourteenth amendment was intended only to secure to all citizens equal capacities before the law. That was at first our view of it. But it does not so read. The language is, ' No State shall abridge the privileges or immunities of citizens of the United States.' What are the privileges and immunities of the citizens of the United States ? Are they capacities merely ? Are they not also rights ? "

The Court in this seems to intimate very strongly that the amendment was intended to secure the natural rights of citizens, as well as their equal capacities before the law.

In a case in the Supreme Court of Georgia, in 1869, the question was before the Court whether a negro was competent to hold office in the State of Georgia. The case was ably argued on both sides, Mr. Akerman, the present Attorney-General of the United States, being counsel for the petitioner. Although the point was made and argued fully, that the right to vote and hold office were both included in the privileges and immunities of citizens, and were thus guaranteed by the XIVth Amendment, yet that point was not directly passed upon by the Court; the Court holding that under the laws and constitution of Georgia the negro citizen had the right claimed. In delivering the opinion, Chief Justice Brown said :—

"It is necessary to the decision of this case to inquire what are the ' privileges and immunities' of a citizen, which are guaranteed by the fourteenth amendment to the Constitution of the United States. Whatever they may be, they are protected against all abridgment by legislation. . . . Whether the ' privileges and immunities' of the citizen embrace political

9

rights, including the right to hold office, I need not now inquire. If they do, that right is guaranteed alike by the Constitution of the United States and of Georgia, and is beyond the control of the legislature."

In the opinion of Justice McKay, among other propositions, he lays down the following:—

"2nd. The rights of the people of this State, white and black, are not granted to them by the Constitution thereof; the object and effect of that instrument is not to *give*, but to restrain, deny, regulate, and guarantee rights; and all persons recognized by that Constitution as citizens of the State have *equal, legal and political rights*, except as *otherwise expressly declared*.

"3rd. It is the settled and uniform sense of the word ' citizen,' when used in reference to the citizens of the separate States of the United States, and to their rights as such citizens, that it describes a person entitled to every right, *legal and political*, enjoyed by any person in that State, unless there be some express exceptions made by positive law covering the particular persons whose rights are in question."

In the course of the argument of this case, Mr. Akerman used the following language upon the point, as to whether citizenship carried with it the right to hold office :—

"It may be profitable to inquire how the word (citizen) has been understood in Georgia. . . . . It will be seen that men whom Georgians have been accustomed to revere believed that citizenship in Georgia carried with it the right to hold office in the absence of positive restrictions."

The majority of the Committee having started out with the erroneous hypothesis that the term "privileges of citizens of the United States," as used in the XIVth Amendment, means no more than the term "privileges of citizens," as used in Article IV., Section 2, discuss the question thus :—

"The right of suffrage was not included in the privileges of citizens as used in Article IV., Section 2; therefore that right is not included in the privileges of citizens of the United States, as used in the fourteenth amendment."

Their premise being erroneous, their whole argument fails. But if they were correct in their premise, we yet claim that their second position is not sustained by the authorities, and is shown to be fallacious by a consideration of the principles of free government.

We claim that, from the very nature of our government, the right of suffrage is a fundamental right of citizenship, not only included in the term "privileges of citizens of the United States," as used in the XIVth Amendment, but also included in the term as used in Article IV., Section 2, and in this we claim we are sustained both by the authorities and by reason.

In Abbott *v.* Bayley (6 *Pick.*, 92), the Supreme Court of Massachusetts says :—

" ' The privileges and immunities ' secured to the people of each State, in every other State, can be applied only to the case of a removal from one State to another. By such removal they become citizens of the adopted State without naturalization, and have a right to sue and be sued as citizens; and yet this privilege is qualified and not absolute, for they cannot enjoy the right of suffrage or eligibility to office without such *term of residence* as shall be prescribed by the constitution and laws of the State into which they shall remove."

This case fully recognizes the right of suffrage as one of the "privileges of the citizen," subject to the right of the State to *regulate* as to the *term of residence*. The same principle was laid down in Corfield *v.* Correll.

In the case of Corfield *v.* Correll in the Supreme Cour of the United States, Justice Washington, in delivering the opinion of the Court, used the following language :—

" ' The privileges and immunities conceded by the Constitution of the United States to citizens in the several States,' are to be confined to those which are in their nature fundamental, and belong of right to the citizens of all free governments. Such are the rights of protection of life and liberty, and to acquire and enjoy property, and to pay no higher impositions than other citizens, and to pass through or reside in the State at pleasure, and to enjoy the elective franchise as regulated and established by the laws or constitution of the State in which it is to be exercised."

And this is cited approvingly by Chancellor Kent.—2 *Kent*, Section 72.

9 *

This case is cited by the majority of the Committee, as sustaining their view of the law, but we are unable so to understand it. It is for them an exceedingly unfortunate citation.

In that case the Court enumerated some of the "privileges of citizens," such as are "*in their nature fundamental and belong of right to the citizens of all free governments*" (mark the language), and among those rights place the "right of the elective franchise" in the same category with those great rights of life, *liberty* and *property*. And yet the Committee cite this case to show that this right is *not* a fundamental right of the citizen!

But it is added by the Court that the right of the elective franchise "is to be enjoyed as regulated and established by the State in which it is to be exercised."

These words are supposed to qualify the right, or rather take it out of the list of fundamental rights, where the Court had just placed it. The Court is made to say by this attempt in the same sentence, "the elective franchise *is* a fundamental right of the citizen, and it is *not* a fundamental right." It is a "fundamental right," provided the State sees fit to grant the right. It is a "fundamental right of the citizen," but it does not exist, unless the laws of the State give it. A singular species of "fundamental rights!" Is there not a clear distinction between the regulation of a right and its destruction? The State may regulate the right, but it may not destroy it.

What is the meaning of "regulate" and "establish?" Webster says—"Regulate: to put in good order. Establish: to make stable or firm."

This decision then is, that "the elective franchise is a fundamental right of the citizen of all free governments, to be enjoyed by the citizen, under such laws as the State may enact to regulate the right and make it stable or firm." Chancellor Kent, in the section referred to, in giving the *substance* of this opinion, leaves out the word establish, regarding the word regulate as sufficiently giving the meaning of the Court.

This case is, in our opinion, a very strong one against the theory of the majority of the Committee.

The Committee cite the language of Mr. Webster, as counsel in United States v. Primrose.

We indorse every word in that extract. We do not claim that a citizen of Pennsylvania can go into Virginia and vote in Virginia, being a citizen of Pennsylvania. No person has ever contended for such an absurdity. We claim that when the citizen of the United States becomes a citizen of Virginia, that the State of Virginia has neither right nor power to abridge the privileges of such citizen by denying him entirely the right of suffrage, and thus all political rights. The authorities cited by the majority of the Committee do not seem to meet the case—certainly do not sustain their theory.

The case of Cooper v. the Mayor of Savannah (4 Geo. 72) involved the question whether a free negro was a citizen of the United States ? The Court, in the opinion, say :—

"Free persons of colour have never been recognized as citizens of Georgia; they are not entitled to bear arms, vote for members of the Legislature, or hold any civil office; they have no political rights, but have personal rights, one of which is personal liberty."

That they could not vote, hold office, &c., was held evidence that they were not regarded as citizens.

In the Supreme Court of the United States, in the case of Scott v. Sandford (19 Howard, p. 476), Mr. Justice Daniel, in delivering his opinion, used the following language as to the rights and qualities of citizenship :—

"For who, it may be asked, is a citizen? What do the character and status of a citizen import? Without fear of contradiction, it does not import the condition of being private property, the subject of individual power and ownership. Upon a principle of etymology alone, the term citizen, as derived from *civitas*, conveys the idea of connection or identification with the State or Government, and a participation in its functions. But beyond this there is not, it is believed, to be found, in the theories of writers on government, or in any actual experiment heretofore tried, an exposition of the term citizen which has not been understood as conferring the actual possession and enjoyment, or the perfect right of acquisition and enjoyment, of an entire equality of privileges, civil and political."

And in the same case Chief Justice Taney said—"The words 'people of the United States' and 'citizens' are synonymous terms, and mean the same thing; they both describe the political body, who, according to our republican institutions, form the sovereignty, and who hold the power, and conduct the Government through their representatives. They are what we familiarly call the sovereign people, and every citizen is one of this people, and a constituent member of this sovereignty."— 19 *Howard*, 404.

In an important case in the Supreme Court of the United States, Chief Justice Jay, in delivering the opinion of the Court, said—"At the Revolution the sovereignty devolved on the people, and they are truly the sovereigns of the country, but they are sovereigns without subjects (unless the African slaves may be so called), and have none to govern but themselves. The citizens of America are equal as fellow-citizens, and joint tenants of the sovereignty."—*Chisholm* v. *Georgia*, 2 *Dallas*, 470.

In Connor v. Elliott (18 Howard), Justice Curtis, in declining to give an enumeration of all the "privileges" of the citizen, said—"According to the express words and clear meaning of the clause, no privileges are secured except those that belong to citizenship."

The Supreme Court said, in Corfield v. Correll, that the elective franchise is such privilege; therefore, according to Justice Curtis, it belongs to citizenship. In a case in the Supreme Court of Kentucky (1 *Littell's Ky. Reports*, p. 333) the the Court say :—

"No one can, therefore, in the correct sense of the term be a citizen of a State who is not entitled upon the terms prescribed by the institutions of the State to all the rights and privileges conferred by these institutions upon the highest class of society."

Mr. Wirt, when Attorney-General of the United States, in an official opinion to be found on p. 508, 1st volume Opinions of Attorney-Generals, came to the conclusion that the negroes were not citizens of the United States, for the reason that they had very few of the "privileges" of citizens, and among the "privileges of citizens" of which they were deprived, that they could not vote at any election.

Webster defines a citizen to be a person, native or naturalized, who has the privilege of voting for public officers, and who is qualified to fill offices in the gift of the people.

Worcester defines the word thus—"An inhabitant of a republic who enjoys the rights of a citizen or freeman, and who has a right to vote for public officers as a citizen of the United States."

Bouvier, in his Law Dictionary, defines the term citizen thus—"One who, under the Constitution and laws of the United States, has a right to vote for Representatives in Congress and other public officers, and who is qualified to fill offices in the gift of the people."

Aristotle defines a "citizen" to be one who is a "*partner in the legislative and judicial* power, and who shares in the honours of the State."—*Aristotle de Repub.*, Lib. III., cap. 5, D.

The essential properties of Athenian citizenship consisted in the share possessed by every citizen in the legislature, in the election of magistrates and in the courts of justice.—See *Smith's Dictionary of Greek Antiquities*, p. 289.

The possession of the *jus suffragii*, at least, if not also of the *jus honorum*, is the principle which governs at this day in defining citizenship in the countries deriving their jurisprudence from the civil law.—*Wheaton's International Law*, p. 892.

The Dutch publicist, Thorbecke (*Rev. and Fr. Etr.*, Tom. V., p. 333), says:—

" What constitutes the distinctive character of our epoch is the development of the right of citizenship. In its most extended, as well as its most restricted sense, it includes a great many properties.

" The right of citizenship is the right of voting in the government of the local, provincial or national community of which one is a member. In this last sense the right of citizenship signifies a participation in the right of voting, in the general government, as member of the State."

In a recent work of some research, written in opposition to female suffrage, the author takes the ground that women are not citizens, and urges that as a reason why they can properly be denied the elective franchise, his theory being that if full citizens they would be entitled to the ballot. He uses the following language :—

" It is a question about which there may be some diversity of opinion what constitutes citizenship or who are citizens. In a loose and improper sense the word citizen is sometimes used to denote any inhabitant of the country, but this is not a correct use of the word. Those, and no others, are properly citizens who were parties to the original compact by which the government was formed, or their successors who are qualified to take part in the affairs of government by their votes in the election of public officers.

" Women and children are represented by their domestic directors or heads in whose wills theirs is supposed to be included. They, as well as others not entitled to vote, are not properly citizens, but are members of the State, fully entitled to the protection of its laws. A citizen, then, is a person entitled to vote in the elections. He is one of those in whom the sovereign power of the State resides."—*Jones on Suffrage*, p. 48.

But all such fallacious theories as this are swept away by the XIVth Amendment, which abolishes the theory of different grades of citizenship, or different grades of rights and privileges, and declares all persons born in the country or nautralized in it to be citizens, in the broadest and fullest sense of the term, leaving no room for cavil, and guaranteeing to all citizens the rights and privileges of citizens of the republic.

We think we are justified in saying that the weight of authority sustains us in the view we take of this question. But considering the nature of it, it is a question depending much for its solution upon a consideration of the government under which citizenship is claimed. Citizenship in Turkey or Russia is essentially different in its rights and privileges from citizenship in the United States. In the former, citizenship means no more than the right to the protection of his absolute rights, and the "citizen" is a subject; nothing more. Here, in the language of Chief Justice Jay, there are no subjects. All native-born and naturalized, are citizens of the highest class; here *all citizens are sovereigns*, each citizen bearing a portion of the supreme sovereignty, and therefore it must necessarily be that the right to a voice in the Government is the right and privilege of a citizen as such, and that which is undefined in the Constitution is undefined because it is self-evident.

Could a State disfranchise and deprive of the right to a vote all citizens who have red hair; or all citizens under six feet in height? All will consent that the States could not make such arbitrary distinctions the ground for denial of political privileges; that it would be a violation of the first article of the XIVth Amendment; that it would be abridging the privileges of citizens. And yet the denial of the elective franchise to citizens on account of sex is equally as arbitrary as the distinction on account of stature, or colour of hair, or any other physical distinction.

These privileges of the citizen exist independent of the Constitution. They are not derived from the Constitution or the laws, but are the means of asserting and protecting rights that existed before any civil governments were formed—the right of life, liberty and property. Says Paine, in his Dissertation upon the Principles of Government :—

"The right of voting for representatives is the primary right, by which other rights are protected. To take away this right is to reduce man to a state of slavery, for slavery consists in being subject to the will of another; and he that has not a vote in the election of representatives is, in this case. The proposal, therefore, to disfranchise any class of men is as criminal as the proposal to take away property."

In a state of nature, before governments were formed, each

person possessed the natural right to defend his liberty, his life, and his property from the aggressions of his fellow men. When he enters into the free government he does not surrender that right, but agrees to exercise it, not by brute force, but by the ballot, by his individual voice in making the laws that dispose of, control and regulate those rights.

The right to a voice in the government is but the natural right of protection of one's life, liberty and property, by personal strength and brute force, so modified as to be exercised in the form of a vote, through the machinery of a free government.

The right of self-protection, it will not be denied, exists in all equally in a state of nature, and the substitute for it exists equally in all the citizens after a free government is formed, for the free government is by all and for all.

The people "ordained and established" the Constitution. Such is the language of the preamble. "We the people." Can it be said that the people acquire their privileges from the instrument that they themselves establish? Does the creature extend rights, privileges, and immunities to the creator? No; the people retain all the rights which they have not surrendered; and if the people have not given to the Government the power to deprive them of their elective franchise, they possess it by virtue of citizenship.

The true theory of this Government, and of all free governments, was laid down by our fathers in the Declaration of Independence, and declared to be "self-evident." "All men are endowed by their Creator with certain inalienable rights; among these are life, liberty, and the pursuit of happiness. That to secure these rights governments are instituted among men, deriving all their just powers from the consent of the governed."

Here is the great truth, the vital principle, upon which our Government is founded, and which demonstrates that the right of a voice in the conduct of the government, and the selection of the rulers, is a right and privilege of all citizens.

Another of the self-evident truths laid down in that instrument is :—

"That whenever any form of government becomes destructive of these ends, it is the right of the people to alter or abolish it, and to institute a new government, laying its foundations on such principles, and organizing its powers in such form, as to them shall seem most likely to effect their safety and happiness."

How can the people carry out this right without the exercise of the ballot; and is not the ballot then a fundamental right and a privilege of the citizen, not given to him by the Constitution, but inherit, as a necessity, from the very nature of government ?

Benjamin Franklin wrote :—

"That every man of the commonalty, except infants, insane persons, and criminals, is, of common right, and by the laws of God, a freeman, and entitled to the free enjoyment of liberty. *That liberty or freedom consists in having an actual share in the appointment of those who frame the laws,* and who are to be the guardians of every man, life, property, and peace for the all of one man is as dear to him as the all of another ; and the poor man has an *equal* right but *more* need to have representatives in the legislature than the rich one, *That they who have no voice nor vote in the electing of representatives do not enjoy liberty, but are absolutely enslaved to those who have votes and to their representatives;* for to be enslaved is to have governors whom other men have set over us, and be subject to laws made by the representatives of others, without having had representatives of our own to give consent in our behalf."—*Franklin's Works*, Vol. II., p. 372.

James Madison said :—

"Under every view of the subject it seems indispensable that the mass of the citizens should not be without a voice in making the laws which they are to obey, and in choosing the magistrates who are to administer them."—*Madison Papers*, Vol. III., p. 14.

Taxation without representation is abhorrent to every principle of natural or civil liberty. It was this injustice that drove our fathers into revolution against the mother country.

"The very act of taxing exercised over those who are not represented appears to me to be depriving them of one of their most essential rights as freemen, and if continued, seems to be, in effect, an entire disfranchisement of every civil right. For what one civil right is worth a rush, after a man's property is subject to be taken from him at pleasure without his consent? If a man is not his *own assessor*, in person or by deputy, his liberty is gone, or he is entirely at the mercy of others."—*Otis's Rights of the Colonies*, p. 58.

Nor are these principles original with the people of this country. Long before they were ever uttered on this continent they were declared by Englishmen. Said Lord Somers, a truly great lawyer of England :—

"Amongst all the rights and privileges appertaining unto us, that of having a share in the legislation, and being governed by such laws as we ourselves shall cause, is the most fundamental and essential, as well as the most advantageous and beneficial."

Said the learned and profound Hooker :—

" By the natural law whereunto Almighty God hath made all subject, the lawful power of making laws to command whole politic societies of men belongeth so properly unto the same entire societies that for any prince or potentate of what kind soever upon earth to exercise the same of himself (or themselves), and not either by express commission immediately received from God, or else by authority derived at the first from their consent upon whose persons they impose laws, it is no better than mere tyranny! Agreeable to the same just privileges of *natural equity*, is that maxim for the English constitution, that 'Law to bind all must be assented to by all;' and there can be no legal appearance of assent without some degree of representation."

The great champion of liberty, Granville Sharpe, declared that—

" All British subjects, whether in Great Britain, Ireland, or the colonies, are equally *free* by the laws of nature; they certainly are equally entitled to the same natural rights that are essential for their own preservation, because this privilege of 'having a share in the legislation' is not merely a *British right*, peculiar to this island, but it is also a natural right, which cannot, without the most flagrant and stimulating injustice, be withdrawn from any part of the British Empire by any *worldly authority* whatsoever.

" No tax can be levied without manifest robbery and injustice where this legal and constitutional representation is wanting, because the English law abhors the idea of taking the least property from freemen without their free consent.

"It is iniquitous (*iniquum est*, says the maxim) that freemen should not have the *free* disposal of their own effects, and whatever is iniquitous can never be made lawful by any authority on earth, not even by the united authority of king, lords, and commons, for that would be contrary to the eternal laws of God, which are supreme."

In an essay upon the "First Principles of Government," by Priestly, an English writer of great ability, written over a century since, is the following definition of political liberty :—

"Political liberty, I would say, consists in power, which the members of the State reserve to themselves, of arriving at the public offices, or at least of having votes in the nomination of those who fill them.

"In countries where every member of the society enjoys an equal power of arriving at the supreme offices, and consequently of directing the strength and sentiments of the whole community, there is a state of the most perfect political liberty.

"On the other hand, in countries where a man is excluded from these offices, or from the power of voting for proper persons to fill them, *that man*, whatever be the form of the government, has no share in the government, and therefore has no political liberty at all. And since every man retains and can never be deprived of his natural right of relieving himself from all oppression, that is, from everything that has been imposed upon him without his own consent, this must be the only true and proper foundation of all the governments subsisting in the world, and that to which the people who compose them have an inalienable right to bring them back."

It was from these great champions of liberty in England that our forefathers received their inspiration and the principles which they adopted, incorporated into the Declaration of Independence, and made the foundation and framework of our government. And yet it is claimed that we have a Government which tramples upon these elementary principles of political liberty, in denying to one-half its adult citizens all political liberty, and subjecting them to the tyranny of taxation without representation. It cannot be.

When we desire to construe the Constitution, or to ascertain the powers of the Government and the rights of the citizens, it is legitimate and necessary to recur to those principles and make them the guide in such investigation.

It is an oft-repeated maxim set forth in the bills of rights of many of the State constitutions that " the frequent recurrence to fundamental principles is necessary for the preservation of liberty and good government."

Recurring to those principles, so plain, so natural, so like political axioms, it would seem that to say that one-half of the citizens of this republican Government, simply and only on account of their sex, can legally be denied the right to a voice in the government, the laws of which they are held to obey, and which takes from them their property by taxation, is so flagrantly in opposition to the principles of free government, and the theory of political liberty, that no man could seriously advocate it.

But it is said in opposition to the " citizen's right " of suffrage that at the time of the establishment of the Constitution, women were in all the States denied the right' of voting, and that no one claimed at the time that the Constitution of the United States would change their status ; that if such a change was intended it would have been explicitly declared in the Constitution, or at least carried into practice by those who framed the Constitution, and, therefore, such a construction of it is against what must have been the intention of the framers.

This is a very unsafe rule of construction. As has been said, the Constitution necessarily deals in general principles ; these principles are to be carried out to their legitimate conclusion and result by legislation, and we are to judge of the intention of those who established the Constitution by what they say, guided by what they declare on the face of the instrument to be their object.

It is said by Judge Story, in " Story on Constitution," " Contemporary construction is properly resorted to to illustrate and confirm the text. . . *It can never abrogate the text ; it can never fritter away its obvious sense;* it can never narrow down its true limitations."

It is a well-settled rule that in the construction of the Constitution, the objects for which it was established, being expressed in the instrument, should have great influence; and when words and phrases are used which are capable of different constructions, that construction should be given which is the most consonant with the declared objects of the instrument.

We go to the preamble to ascertain the objects and purpose of the instrument. Webster defines preamble thus: " The introductory part of a statute, which states the reason and intent of the law."

In the preamble, then, more certainly than in any other way, aside from the language of the instrument we find the intent.

Judge Story says :—

" The importance of examining the preamble for the purpose of expounding the language of a statute has been long felt and universally conceded in all juridical discussions. It is an admitted maxim . . that the preamble is a key to open the mind of the matters as to the mischiefs to be remedied and the objects to be accomplished by the statute. . . It is properly resorted to where doubts or ambiguities arise upon the words of the enacting part, for if they are clear and unambiguous there seems little room for interpretation, except in cases leading to an obvious absurdity or to a direct overthrow of the intention expressed in the preamble."—*Story on the Constitution,* Sec. 457.

Try this question by a consideration of the objects for which the Constitution was established, as set forth in the preamble, " to establish justice." Does it establish justice to deprive of all representation or voice in the Government one-half of its adult citizens and compel them to pay taxes to and support a Government in which they have no representation ? Is " taxation without representation" justice established ?

" To insure domestic tranquillity." Does it insure domestic tranquillity to give all the political power to one class of citizens, and deprive another class of any participation in the government ? No. The sure means of tranquillity is to give " equal political rights to all," that all may stand " equal before the law."

" To provide for the common defence." We have seen that the only defence the citizen has against oppression and wrong is by his voice and vote in the selection of the rulers and law-makers. Does it, then, " provide for the common defence," to deny to one-half the adult citizens of the republic that voice and vote ?

" To secure the *blessings of liberty* to ourselves and our posterity." As has been already said, *there can be no political liberty to any citizen deprived of a voice in the government.* This is self-evident; it needs no demonstration. Does it, then, " secure the blessings of liberty to ourselves and our posterity" to deprive one-half the citizens of adult age of this right and privilege ?

Tried by the expressed objects for which the Constitution was established, as declared by the people themselves, this denial to the women citizens of the country of the right and privilege of voting is directly in contravention of these objects, and must, therefore, be contrary to the spirit and letter of the entire instrument.

And according to rule of construction referred to, no " contemporaneous construction, however universal it may be, can be allowed to set aside the expressed objects of the makers, as declared in the instrument." The construction which we claim for the first section of the fourteenth amendment is in perfect accord with those expressed objects ; and even if there were anything in the original text of the Constitution at variance with the true construction of that section, the amendment must control. Yet we believe that there is nothing in the original text at variance with what we claim to be the true construction of the amendment.

It is claimed by the majority of the Committee that the

adoption of the fifteenth amendment was by necessary implication a declaration that the States had the power to deny the right of suffrage to citizens for any other reasons than those of race, colour, or previous condition of servitude.

We deny that the fundamental rights of the American citizen can be taken away by "implication."

There is no such law for the construction of the Constitution of our country. The law is the reverse—that the fundamental rights of citizens are not to be taken away by implication, and a constitutional provision for the protection of one class can certainly not be used to destroy or impair the same rights in another class.

It is too violent a construction of an amendment which prohibits States from, or the United States from, abridging the right of a citizen to vote, by reason of race, colour, or previous condition of servitude, to say that by implication it conceded to the States the power to deny that right for any other reason. On that theory the States could confine the right of suffrage to a small minority, and make the State government aristocratic, overthrowing their republican form.

The XIVth Article of Amendment to the Constitution clearly recognizes the right to vote, as one of the rights of a citizen of the United States. This is the language:—

" The right of citizens of the United States to vote shall not be denied or abridged by the United States, or by any State, on account of race, colour, or previous condition of servitude."

Here is stated, first, the existence of a *right*. Second, its nature. Whose right is it? The right of citizens of the United States. What is the right? The right to vote. And this right of citizens of the United States, States are forbidden to abridge. Can there be a more direct recognition of a right? Can that be *abridged* which does not *exist* ? The denial of the power to abridge the right, recognizes the existence of the right. It is said that this right exists by virtue of State citizen-

10

ship, and State laws and Constitutions? Mark the language: "The right of citizens of the *United States* to vote;" not citizens of *States*. The right is recognized as existing independent of State citizenship.

But it may be said, if the States had no power to abridge the right of suffrage, why the necessity of prohibiting them?

There may not have been a necessity; it may have been done through caution, and because the peculiar condition of the coloured citizens at that time rendered it necessary to place their rights beyond doubt or cavil.

It is laid down as a rule of construction by Judge Story that the natural import of a single clause is not to be narrowed so as to exclude implied powers resulting from its character simply because there is another clause which enumerates certain powers which might otherwise be deemed implied powers within its scope, for in such cases we are not to assume that the affirmative specification excludes all other implications. —*Story on Constitution*, II., Sec. 449.

There are numerous instances in the Constitution where a general power is given to Congress, and afterwards a particular power given, which was included in the former; yet the general power is not to be narrowed, because the particular power is given. On this same principle the fact that by the fifteenth amendment the States are specifically forbidden to deny the right of suffrage on account of race, colour, or previous condition of servitude, does not narrow the general provision in the fourteenth amendment which guarantees the privileges of all the citizens against abridgment by the States on any account.

The rule of interpretation relied upon by the Committee in their construction of the fifteenth amendment is, "that the expression of one thing is the exclusion of another," or the specification of particulars is the exclusion of generals.

Of these maxims Judge Story says :—

" They are susceptible of being applied, and often are ingeniously applied, to the subversion of the text and the objects of the instrument. The truth is, in order to ascertain how far an affirmative or negative provision excludes or implies others, we must look to the nature of the provision, the subject, matter, the objects, and the scope of the instrument; these, and these only, can properly determine the rule of construction."—*Story*, II., Sec. 448.

It is claimed by the Committee that the second section of the fourteenth amendment implies that the several States may restrict the right of suffrage as to other than male citizens. We may say of this as we have said of the theory of the Committee upon the effect of the fifteenth amendment. It is a proposal to take away from the citizens guarantees of fundamental rights, by implication, which have been previously given in absolute terms.

The first section includes all citizens in its guarantees, and includes all the "privileges and immunities" of citizenship, and guards them against abridgment, and under no recognized or reasonable rule of construction can it be claimed that by implication from the provisions of the second section the States may not only abridge but entirely destroy one of the highest privileges of the citizen to one-half the citizens of the country. What we have said in relation to the Committee's construction of the effect of the fifteenth amendment applies equally to this.

The object of the first section of this amendment was to secure all the rights, privileges, and immunities of all the citizens against invasion by the States. The object of the second section was to fix a rule or system of apportionment for representation and taxation ; and the provision referred to, in relation to the exclusion of males from the right of suffrage, might be regarded as in the nature of a penalty in case of denial of that right to that class. While it, to a certain extent, protected that class of citizens, it left the others where the previous provisions of the Constitution placed them. To protect the coloured man more fully than was done by that penalty was the object of the XIVth Amendment.

In no event can it be said to be more than the recognition of an existing fact, that only the male citizens were, by the State laws, allowed to vote, and that the existing order of things was recognized in the rule of representation, just as the institution of slavery was recognized in the original Constitution, in the article fixing the basis of representation, by the provision that only three-fifths of all the slaves ("other persons") could be counted. There slavery was recognized as an existing fact, and yet the Constitution never sanctioned slavery, but, on the contrary, had it been carried out according to its true construction, slavery could not have existed under it; so that the recognition of facts in the Constitution must not be held to be a sanction of what is so recognized.

The majority of the Committee say that this section implies that the States may deny suffrage to others than male citizens. If it implies anything, it implies that the States may deny the franchise to all the citizens. It does not provide that they shall not deny the right to male citizens, but only provides that if they do so deny they shall not have representation for them.

· So, according to that argument, by the second section of the fourteenth amendment, the power of the States is conceded to entirely take away the right of suffrage, even from that privileged class—the male citizens. And thus this rule of "implication" goes too far, and fritters away all the guarantees of the Constitution of the right of suffrage, the highest of the privileges of the citizens; and herein is demonstrated the reason and safety of the rule that fundamental rights are not to be taken away by implication, but only by express provision.

When the advocates of a privileged class of citizens under the Constitution are driven to implication to sustain the theory of taxation without representation, and American citizenship without political liberty, the cause must be weak indeed.

It is claimed by the majority that by Article I., Section 2, the Constitution recognizes the power in States to declare who shall and who shall not exercise the elective franchise. That section reads as follows:—

"The House of Representatives shall be composed of Members chosen every second year by the people of the several States, and the electors in each State shall have the qualifications requisite for electors of the most numerous branch of the State legislature."

The first clause of this section declares *who* shall choose the Representatives. Mark the language—"Representatives *shall be chosen by the people* of the States," not by the male people, not by certain classes of the people, but by the people; so that the construction sought to be given this section, by which it would recognize the power of the State to disfranchise one-half the citizens, is in direct contravention of the first clause of the section, and of its whole spirit, as well as of the objects of the instrument. The States clearly have no power to nullify the express provision that the election shall be by the people, by any laws limiting the election to a moiety of the people.

It is true the section recognizes the power in the State to regulate the qualifications of the electors; but as we have already said, the power to regulate is a very different thing from the power to destroy.

The two clauses must be taken together, and both considered in connection with the declared purpose and objects of the Constitution.

The Constitution is necessarily confined to the statement of general principles. There are regulations necessary to be made as to the qualifications of voters: as to their proper age, their domicile, the length of residence necessary to entitle the citizen to vote in a given State or place. These particulars could not be provided in the Constitution but are necessarily left to the States, and this section is thus construed as to be in harmony with itself, and with the expressed objects of the framers of the Constitution and the principles of free government.

When the majority of the Committee can demonstrate that "the people of the States," and one-half the people of the States, are equivalent terms, or that when the Constitution provides that the Representatives shall be elected by the people, its requirements are met by an election in which less than one-half the adult people are allowed to vote, then it will be admitted that this section, to some extent, sustains them.

The Committee say, that if it had been intended that Congress should prescribe the qualifications of electors, the grant would have given Congress that power specifically. We do not claim that Congress has that power; on the contrary, admit that the States have it; but the section of the Constitution *does* prescribe who the electors shall be. That is what we claim—nothing more. They shall be "the people;" their qualifications may be regulated by the States; but to the claim of the majority of the Commiteee, that they may be "qualified" out of existence, we cannot assent.

We are told that the acquiescence by the people, since the adoption of the Constitution, in the denial of political rights to women citizens, and the general understanding that such denial was in conformity with the Constitution, should be taken to settle the construction of that instrument.

Any force this argument may have it can only apply to the original text, and not to the fourteenth amendment, which is of but recent date.

But, as a general principle, this theory is fallacious. It would stop all political progress; it would put an end to all original thought, and put the people under that tyranny with which the friends of liberty have always had to contend—the tyranny of precedent.

From the beginning, our Government has been right in theory, but wrong in practice. The Constitution, had it been carried out in its true spirit, and its principles enforced, would have stricken the chains from every slave in the republic long since. Yet, for all this, it was but a few years since declared, by the highest judicial tribunal of the republic, that, according to the "general understanding," the black man in this country had no rights the white man was bound to respect. General understanding and acquiescence is a very unsafe rule by which to try questions of constitutional law, and precedents are not infallible guides toward liberty and the rights of man.

Without any law to authorize it, slavery existed in England, and was sustained and perpetuated by popular opinion, universal custom, and the acquiescence of all departments of the government as well as by the subjects of its oppression. A few fearless champions of liberty struggled against the universal settlement, and contended that, by the laws of England slavery could not exist in the kingdom; and though for years unable to obtain a hearing in any British court, the Sommersett case was finally tried in the Court of King's Bench in 1771, Lord Mansfield presiding, wherein that great and good man, after a long and patient hearing, declared that no law of England allowed or approved of slavery, and discharged the negro. And it was then judicially declared that no slave could breathe upon the soil of England, although slavery had up to that time existed for centuries, under the then existing laws. The laws were right, but the practice and public opinion were wrong.

It is said by the majority of the Committee that "if the right of female citizens to suffrage is vested by the Constitution, that right can be established in the courts."

We respectfully submit that, with regard to the competency and qualification of electors for members of this House, the courts have no jurisdiction.

This house is the sole judge of the election return and qualification of its own members (Article I., Section 5, of Constitution); and it is for the House alone to decide upon a contest who are, and who are not, competent and qualified to vote. The judicial department cannot thus invade the prerogatives of the political department.

And it is therefore perfectly proper, in our opinion, for the House to pass a declaratory resolution, which would be an index to the action of the House, should the question be brought before it by a contest for a seat.

We therefore recommend to the House the adoption of the following resolution :—

Resolved, by the House of Representatives, That the right of suffrage is one of the inalienable rights of citizens of the United States, subject to regulation by the States, through equal and just laws.

That this right is included in the " privileges of citizens of the United States," which are guaranteed by Art. XIV., Section 1, of the amendments to the Constitution of the United States ; and that women citizens, who are otherwise qualified by the laws of the State where they reside, are competent voters for Representatives in Congress.

WM. LOUGHRIDGE.
BENJ. F. BUTLER.

CONSTITUTIONAL EQUALITY.

A LECTURE BY VICTORIA C. WOODHULL,

AT

Lincoln Hall, Washington, D.C., Thursday, February 16th, 1871.

It was an honest zeal which first influenced me to appear before the public as a champion of a cause which receives alike the jeers of the common multitude and the railery of the select few. It is an honest zeal in the same that inspires me with confidence to continue before it as its advocate, when but too conscious that I am of that portion of the people who are denied the privileges of freedom; who are not permitted the rights of citizens; and who are without voice, in the pursuit of justice, as one of that sovereignty to whom this Government owes its existence, and to whom it will be held accountable, as it holds all accountable who set themselves against Human Rights.

I have no doubt it seems strange to many of you that a woman should appear before the people in this public manner for political purposes, and it is due both to you and myself that I should give my reasons for so doing.

On the 19th of December, 1870, I memorialized Congress, setting forth what I believed to be the truth and right regarding Equal Suffrage for all citizens. This memorial was referred to the Judiciary Committee of Congress. On the 12th of January

I appeared before the House Judiciary Committee and submitted to them the Constitutional and Legal points upon which I predicated such equality. January 20th, Mr. Bingham, on behalf of the majority of said Committee, submitted his report to the House, in which, while he admitted all my basic propositions, Congress was recommended to take no action. February 1st, Messrs. Loughridge and Butler of said Committee submitted a report in their own behalf, which fully sustained the positions I assumed, and recommended that Congress *should* pass a Declaratory Act, for ever settling the mooted question of suffrage.

Thus it is seen that equally able men differ upon a simple point of Constitutional Law, and it is fair to presume that Congress will also differ *when* these Reports come up for action. That a proposition involving such momentous results as this should receive a one-third vote upon first coming before Congress has raised it to an importance which spreads alarm on all sides among the opposition. So long as it was not made to appear that women were denied Constitutional rights, no opposition was aroused; but now that new light is shed, by which it is seen that such is the case, all the Conservative weapons of bitterness, hatred and malice are marshalled in the hope to extinguish it, before it can enlighten the masses of the people, who are always true to freedom and justice.

Public opinion is against Equality, but it is simply from prejudice, which but requires to be informed to pass away. No greater prejudice exists against equality than there did against the proposition that the world was a globe. This passed away under the influence of better information, so also will present prejudice pass, when better informed upon the question of equality.

I trust you will pardon me the expression when I say that I do not comprehend how there can exist an honest and perfect appreciation of the fundamental propositions upon which the

superstructure of our Government is based, and, at the same
time, an honest hostility to the legitimate deductions of them,
therefore I appear before you to expound, as best I may, the
law involved by these propositions, and to point out the
inconsistences of those who evince hostility to such deductions.

I come before you to declare that my sex are entitled to the
inalienable right to life, liberty, and the pursuit of happiness.
The first two I cannot be deprived of, except for cause, and by
due process of law ; but upon the last, a right is usurped to
place restrictions so general as to include the whole of my sex,
and for which no reasons of public good can be assigned. I ask
the right to pursue happiness by having a voice in that Government to which I am accountable. I have not forfeited that
right, still I am denied. Was assumed arbitrary authority ever
more arbitrarily exercised ? In practice, then, our laws are false
to the principles which we profess. I have the right to life, to
liberty, unless I forfeit it by an infringement upon others'
rights, in which case the State becomes the arbiter and deprives
me of them for the public good. I also have the right to pursue
happiness, unless I forfeit it in the same way, and am denied it
accordingly. It cannot be said, with any justice, that my pursuit
of happiness in voting for any man for office would be an infringement of one of his rights as a citizen or as an individual. I hold,
then, that in denying me this right without my having forfeited
it, that departure is made from the principles of the Constitution,
and also from the true principles of government, for I am denied
a right born with me, and which is inalienable. Nor can it be
objected that women had no part in organizing this government.
They were not denied. To-day we seek a voice in government
and *are* denied. There are *thousands* of male citizens in the
country who seldom or never vote. They are not denied :
they pursue happiness by not voting. Could it be assumed, because
this body of citizens do not choose to exercise the right to vote,
that they could be *permanently* denied the exercise thereof ?

If not, *neither* should it be assumed to deny women who wish to vote, the right to do so.

And were it true that a majority of women do not wish to vote, it would be *no* reason why those who do should be denied. If a right exist, and only *one in a million* desires to exercise it, *no* Government should deny its enjoyment to that one. If the thousands of men who do not choose to vote should send their petitions to Congress asking them to prevent others who do vote from so doing, would they listen to them? I went before Congress to ask for myself and others of my sex who wish to pursue our happiness by participating in Government protection in such pursuit, and I was told that Congress had not the necessary power.

If there are women who do not desire to have a voice in the laws to which they are accountable, and which they must contribute to support, let them speak for themselves; but they should not assume to speak for me, or for those whom I represent.

So much for the fundamental propositions upon which government is organized. Women did not join in the act of constructing the Constitution. So far as I know, none expressed a desire so to do, and consequently were not denied. But *what* is government, and *what* a Republican form of government? Government is national existence organized. Government of some form exists everywhere, but none would assume to say that the government of *China* is similar to that of *England*, or that of *Germany* to that of the *United States*. When government is fashioned *for* the people it is not a republican form, but when fashioned *by* the people it is a republican government. *Our* form of government is supposed to emanate from the people, and whatever control it possesses *over* the people is supposed to be exercised by and with their consent; and even more than this, *by their direct will and wish.* If, at any time, there are powers exercised by a Government which emanates from, and is dependent upon, the will of the people, which the majority of the people do not desire to be continued, they have it in their power, and it is their duty, to compel their suspension. If, at any time, the majority of the people from whom has emanated, and who support, a republican form of government, desire that it should assume *new* functions, exercise more extended control, or provide for *new* circumstances, *not* existant at its primary organization, they have the power and it is their duty to *compel* their Government to take such action as is necessary to secure the form that shall be acceptable.

The people are virtually the government, and *it* is simply the concentration and expression of their will and wisdom through which they assume form as a body politic or as a nation. The government is an embodiment of the people, and as *they* change so also must *it* change. In this significant fact lie all the true beauty and wisdom of our form of polity. It can be changed without actual revolution, and consequently possesses the inherent qualities of permanency. It is capable of adaptation to all contingencies and circumstances, and provides how changes shall be made. It nowhere positively declares that its citizens, or the people, if you please, shall *not* have the right to vote under its provisions; and, *mark you*, it nowhere provides that any portion of the people *shall* vote.

Before government was organized there were no citizens, but there were *people,* and these people had the *human right* to organize a government under which they could become citizens. In the absence of organized government, individual government alone exists, every individual having the human right to control himself and herself.

Now, if a people—an aggregate of individuals—not having a government, undertake to construct one, wherein but *one-half* should engage, the *other* half taking no part therein, and its functions should be exercised over the *whole*, it is *plain* that, so far as the non-engaged part would be concerned, it would be an *usurped* authority that dispossessed them of the inherent right which all people have in organized government. But so long as the unconsulted part quietly acquiesce in such a government, there can be none to question its right to control. At the moment, however, when the unconsulted portion should demur from such government, they would begin to assert the right to self-government possessed equally by all. The fact that such right had not been made known by expression could in no wise invalidate it. It would remain an inherent possession, and whenever expressed it could be maintained and enjoyed.

The condition of the people of this country to-day is this :—

I and others of my sex find ourselves controlled by a form of government in the inauguration of which we had no voice, and in whose administration we are denied the right to participate, though we are a large part of the people of this country. Was George III.'s rule, which he endeavoured to exercise over our fathers, less clearly an assumed rule than is this to which we are subjected? He exercised it over them without their consent and against their wish and will, and naturally they rebelled. Do men of the United States assume and exercise any less arbitrary rule over us than *that* was? No, not one whit the less. To be sure, his cabinet were *few*, while they are *many;* but the principle is the same; in both cases the inherent elemental right to self-government is equally over-ridden by the assumption of power. But the authority King George's Parliament exercised was even more consistent than *this* is which they assume and exercise: his Government made no pretension to emanation from the people.

When our fathers launched "Taxation without representation is tyranny " against King George, were they consistent? Certainly. Were they justified? Yes; for out of it came our national independence. Revolutionary war, which gave our country independence, grew from this tyranny. Was that war justifiable? Most assuredly it was. We find that the same declarations of tyranny were raised by Congress in the lengthy discussions upon enfranchising the negro. Such sentiments as the following were often repeated, and with great effect: "A considerable part of the people of the United States embraced under the preamble to the Constitution, 'We, the people,' are left without representation in the Government; but, nevertheless, held within the grasp of taxation of all kinds, direct and indirect, tariff and excise, State and national. This is tyranny, or else our fathers were wrong when they protested against a kindred injustice. This principle is fundamental. It cannot be violated without again dishonouring the fathers," whose rights were so ably and eloquently asserted and defended by James Otis, who, in his "Rights of the Colonies," says—"The very act of taxing exercised over those who are not represented appears to me to be depriving them of their most essential rights as freemen, and if continued, seems to be, in effect, an entire disfranchisement of civil right. For what one civil right is worth a rush, after a man's property is subject to be taken from him at pleasure without his consent? If a man is not his own assessor, in person or by deputy, his liberty is gone, or he is entirely at the mercy of others." Could *stronger words* than these be found or used in favour of universal suffrage? They applied with sufficient force *then* to rouse a few men, whose souls were fired with its injustice, to resist a powerful oppressor. It was one of the most forcible arguments by which the cause of the negro was advocated. *Is it* any less forcible in its application to women? Is the tyranny now exercised over women, under, as some say, the authority of the Government—but we say, without any authority—any less tyrannous than that over our fathers? or than that of the negro, for whom many plead so earnestly? Or is *nothing* tyranny for women? If a civil right is "not worth a rush" to a *man* when he is taxed and not represented, how much is it worth to a woman? If a "*man's* liberty is gone," and he is "at the mercy of others" when thus taxed, what becomes of *woman's* under the same tyranny? If "every man of sound mind should vote," by what principle can every *woman* of sound mind be deprived from voting? Or are all women of *unsound* mind? Not exactly; they are found to be very proper persons as the assigns of men in many instances.

In the records of the early days of the Republic there are found *numerous* authorities bearing directly upon this point, such as, "That by the law of nature no man has a right to impose laws more than to levy taxes upon another; that the freeman pays no taxes, as the freeman submits to no law but such as emanate from the body in which he is represented." If the freeman pays no taxes without representation, how is it that the free woman is compelled to do so? Not long since I was notified by a United States officer that if I did not pay a certain tax the Government had imposed upon me, my property would be levied upon and sold for that purpose. Is *this* tyranny, or can men find some *other* word to take the place of that used by our fathers so freely, and by Congress, not so long ago as to be forgotten, with such powerful effect? Has oppression become less odious, that in these days twenty of the forty millions of people who compose the sovereign people of this country must *quietly* submit to what has been, in all ages of representative government, denounced as *tyranny?*

But let us hear more of the principles which actuated our fathers: "All men having sufficient evidence of permanent common interest with, and attachment to, the community, have he right of suffrage, and cannot be taxed or deprived of their property for public uses without their own consent or that of their representatives so elected, nor bound by any law to which they have not in like manner assented for the public good."— *Virginia Bill of Rights,* January 12th, 1776.

So it appears that our fathers declared that *no one* should be bound by *any* law in the making of which he had no voice. *How* would this principle operate to-day should I refuse to pay the taxes levied against me without my consent and in direct opposition to my wishes? Would I be justified in declaring that I would not pay? I might be *justified*, but I do not think I should escape the tyranny.

Franklin said, "That every man of the community, except infants, insane people and criminals, is of common right, and by the laws of God, a freeman, and entitled to the free enjoyment of liberty. *That freedom or liberty consists in having an actual share in the appointment of those who frame* the laws, and who are to be the guardians of every man, for the all of one man is as dear to him as the all of another man; and the poor man has an equal right, but more need, to have representatives than the rich one." "That they who have no voice nor vote in the election of representatives do not enjoy liberty, but are *absolutely enslaved;* for to be enslaved is to have governors whom others have set over us."

If freedom consists in having an *actual share* in appointing those who frame the laws, are not the women of this country in absolute *bondage*, and can government, in the face of the XVth Amendment, assume to deny them the right to vote, being in this "condition of servitude?" According to Franklin we are absolutely enslaved, for there *are* "governors set over us by other men," and we are "subject to the laws" they make. Is *not* Franklin good authority in matters of freedom? Again, rehearsing the arguments that have emanated from Congress and applying them to the present case, we learn that "It is idle to show that, in certain instances, the fathers failed to apply the sublime principles which they declared. Their failure can be *no* apology for those on whom the duty is now cast." Shall it be an apology *now?* Shall the omission of others to do justice keep the government from measuring it to those who now cry out for it? I went before Congress like Richelieu to

11

his king asking for justice. Will they deny it as he did until the exigencies of the case compel them?

I *am* subject to tyranny! I am taxed in every conceivable way. For publishing a paper I must pay; for engaging in the banking and brokerage business I must pay; of what it is my fortune to acquire each year I must turn over a certain per cent.; I must pay high prices for tea, coffee, and sugar. To *all* these must I submit, that *men's* government may be maintained, a government in the administration of which I am denied a voice, and from its edicts there is no appeal. I must submit to a heavy advance upon the first cost of *nearly everything I wear* in order that industries in which I have no interest may exist at my expense. I am compelled to pay extravagant rates of fare wherever I travel, because the franchises, extended to gigantic corporations, enable them to *sap* the vitality of the country, to make their *managers money kings*, by means of which they boast of being able to control not only legislators but even a State judiciary.

To be compelled to submit to *these* extortions that *such* ends may be gained, upon *any* pretext or under *any* circumstances, is bad enough; but to be compelled to submit to them, and also denied the right to cast my vote *against* them, is a tyranny *more* odious than that which, being rebelled against, gave this country independence.

But usurpations do not stop here. The Constitution, as it stood on the day of its original adoption, under the interpretation of *that* day, guided by the principle of *self*-government, admits *perfect* equality among the people. There are *no* limitations contained in it by which any part of the people from whom it emanated could be placed *unequally* with any other part. Permit me to quote from a speech delivered by Mr. Sumner, in the Senate of the United States, March 7th, 1866, upon the following proposition:—

"Representatives shall be appointed among the several

States which may be included in this Union, according to their respective number of persons included in each State, excluding Indians not taxed: Provided, That whenever the elective franchise shall be denied or abridged by any State on account of race or colour, all persons therein of such race or colour shall be excluded from the basis of representation." "Adopt this," said Mr. Sumner, "and you will stimulate anew the war of race upon race. Slavery itself was a war of race upon race and this is only a new form of this terrible war. Adopt it, and you will put millions of fellow-citizens under the ban of excommunication. You will declare that they have no political right which 'white men' are bound to respect. Adopt it, and you will cover the country with dishonour. Adopt it, and you will fix the stigma upon the very name of Republic." In express terms there is an *admission of the idea* of inequality of rights founded on race and colour. That this unrepublican idea should be allowed to find a place in the text of the Constitution will excite especial wonder, when it is considered how conscientiously our fathers excluded from that text the kindred idea of property in man. Mr. Madison "thought it wrong to admit in the Constitution the idea of property in man." "But," says Mr. Sumner, "is it less wrong to admit in the Constitution the idea of inequality of rights founded on race and colour?" Is it not, *I* ask, a *graver* wrong to insist that *one-half of the people of all races* and colours have not equal right, because they are *women;* and *this,* too, when there are *no* provisions contained in the Constitution which can by *any* possibility be construed to give the other half disfranchising power? Fathers, husbands, brothers, sons, does not your blood tingle with shame in your veins at this ignoble distinction? How can you look in your sisters' faces and declare they shall not enjoy the citizen's rights, granted to the lowest orders and classes in the human race?

11 *

Therefore it is, that instead of growing in republican liberty, we are departing from it. From an unassuming, acquiescent part of society, woman has gradually passed to an individualized human being, and as she has advanced one after another evident right of the common people has been accorded to her. She has now become so *much* individualized as to demand the full and unrestrained exercise of *all* the rights which can be predicated of a people constructing a government based on individual sovereignty. She asks it, and shall Congress deny her?

The formal abolition of slavery created several millions of male negro citizens, who, a portion of the acknowledged citizens assumed to say were *not* entitled to equal rights with themselves. To get over this difficulty, Congress in its wisdom saw fit to propose a XIVth Amendment to the Constitution, which passed into a law by ratification by the States. Section I. of the Amendment declares: "All persons, born or naturalized in the United States, and subject to the jurisdiction thereof, are citizens of the United States and of the State wherein they reside. No State shall make or enforce any law which shall abridge the privileges and immunities of citizens of the United States. Nor shall any State deprive any person of life, liberty, and property without due process of law, nor deny any person within its jurisdiction the equal protection of the law."

But there is an objection raised to our broad interpretation of this amendment, and that is obtained from the wording of the second section thereof :—"But whenever the right to vote," &c., "is denied to any of the male inhabitants of such State, being twenty-one years of age, and citizens of the United States," &c., &c., "the basis of representation then shall be reduced in the proportion which the number of such male citizens shall bear to the whole number of male citizens twenty-one years of age." *Consistency* is said to be a bright jewel when possessed, but I doubt its possession by those who have the boldness to

advance *this* as an argument in opposition to this point. We
surely have a right to use the logic of objectors in interpreting
their own propositions, and we therefore reply, *ita lex scripta est.*
If the Constitution means *nothing* but what is expressed, how
can it be presumed to infer anything from the use of the word
male in this second section, except what it expresses? The
right of women to vote, or the *denial* of that right to them,
is not involved by this section under the furthest-fetched
application.

I am perfectly well aware of the attempt which was made in
the Congress of 1866 to add a special, but indirectly, restrictory
clause to the Constitution, providing that the basis of representation should be the then recognized legal voters. It was
perceived that the arguments advanced for political equality
for the negro were equally potent for women. The inconsistency
of women forming a part of the basis of representation, and
being denied participation in it, was *too* apparent to escape
sagacious minds. The attempt, however, did not succeed. Its
promoters *did not dare* openly to avow their intentions, but it
is known that they *felt* the time would come when women
would claim equal political rights, which could not consistently
be denied them, unless, when it should be *necessary so to do,*
that proper restrictory legislation should be contained in the
Constitution.

The only point which I can see the report of the majority of
the Judiciary Committee attempts to make against my demand
I propose to meet by quoting authority, which I am positive no
one will think of questioning.

Chief Justice Taney, in Howard, Rep. 404, thus defines the
words people and citizen. The words *"people of the United
States"* and *citizens* are *synonymous* terms, and mean the *same
thing.* They *both* describe the *political* body, *who,* according to
our republican institutions, *form* the *sovereignty,* and who *hold*
the power and *conduct* the Government through their repre-

sentatives. They are what we *familiarly* call the *sovereign* people, and *every* citizen is *one* of this people and a *constituent* member of this sovereignty.

Ibid., p. 476: "There is not, it is believed, to be found in the theories of writers on government, or in any actual experiment heretofore tried, *any* exposition of the term *citizen*, which has not been considered as conferring the *actual possession* and *enjoyment* of the *perfect right* of acquisition and enjoyment of an *entire* equality of privileges, *civil* and *political*." *Such* authority as this, couched in such strong words, leaves no doubt about the Constitutional meaning of these terms.

I do not think it possible that the Congress or the people of the United States, when they give this matter due consideration, will refuse to accept *such* authority upon the rights of citizens, the decisions of the report referred to, to the contrary notwithstanding. The XIVth Amendment has compelled said Committee to admit *just enough too much* to make their *entire* position untenable. Being citizens, women are of the " sovereign people," and entitled to the enjoyment of an " *entire equality of privileges, civil and political*."

After the adoption of the XIVth Amendment it was found that still more legislation was required to secure the exercise of the right to vote to all who by it were declared to be citizens, and the following comprehensive amendment was passed by Congress, and ratified by the States : " The right of citizens of the United States to vote shall not be denied or abridged by the United States or by any State on account of race, colour, or previous condition of servitude." Nothing could be more explicit than this language, and nothing more comprehensive. " But," says the objector, ever on the alert, " it may be denied on account of sex." It must be remembered " that is law which is written," and all *inferences* drawn must be in accord with the *general intent* of the instrument involved by the inference. *If* the right to vote cannot be denied on account of race, *how* can it be denied on account of a constituent part of race, unless the power of denial is specially *expressed*. The larger *always* includes the smaller, which, if reserved, the reservation must be expressed. No *inference* can be allowed to determine that *any* part of the citizens covered by the term *race* can be denied the right to vote, unless the denial is expressed. It seems to me that no logic can be plainer than this. Had this amendment recited that the right to vote should not be denied on account of race, except to *females*, it would have left the right of denial to the States, but *even then*, under the XIVth Amendment, the denial would have to be made, with woman participating therein, and although there are those who assert that the majority of women do not desire to vote, I think none of you can imagine that, *possessing* the right, they would remain at home and permit it to be taken away.

This amendment is *just as much* a part of the Constitution as though it had been one of its original provisions. The effect of the Constitution, as it *now* stands, upon the *present* citizens must be the same that it would have been upon the citizens at the time of its original adoption, had it contained *all* its present provisions. Previous to its adoption there were no citizens of the United States. Immediately it was adopted persons became citizens, but had not voted as citizens of the United States under it. Under *these* circumstances, with *these* provisions *in* the Constitution, which declare that Representatives shall be elected *by the people*, that *all people* are *citizens*, and that the right to vote shall not be denied on account of race, colour, or previous condition of servitude, I ask Congress, and I ask them upon their solemn oaths, to give vitality to the provisions of the Constitution, and to guarantee a republican form of Government to every State, *who* among the people, persons, citizens, who resided in the States, could have been denied the right to vote for Representatives. We must regard this amendment as though there had been no negroes requiring enfranchisement.

We must divorce our minds from the negro and look at the Constitution *as it is.* We must not be biased by surrounding circumstances. It must apply to these conditions and interpret them. It is the basis of equality constructed *by all* and *for all,* and from which all partake of *equal* rights, privileges, and immunities.

Because this amendment was framed to apply to the African race, and to *black* people, and to those who had been slaves, it must not be concluded that it has no *broader* application. Whoever it may include, under logical construction, to them the right to vote shall not be denied. Take the African race and the black colour and the previous slaves out of the way, and what application would this amendment *then* have ? This is the way to test these things, the way to arrive at what they mean. *Who* will pretend to say this amendment would mean nothing were there no negroes, and there had been no Southern slaves ? Who will pretend to say that the amendment would mean nothing in the coming election, provided that there never before had been an election under the Constitution ? If you provide a Constitutional amendment, having *one* race specially in view, it must not be forgotten that there are *other* races besides. Thirty-seven States constitute the United States. If you speak of the United States you speak of all the States, for they are all included. If you speak of a *part* of the United States, you must designate *what* part, in order that it may be known what you mean. A race is composed of two sexes. If you speak of a race you include both sexes. If you speak of a *part* of a race, you must designate *which* part in order to make yourselves intelligible.

The same line of reasoning applies to the word colour, although some assume to say that colour in this amendment means black, as white is no colour. But how should any know what specific colour is referred to in this amendment ? One might say it was intended to mean a copper colour ; another a mulatto colour, and still another that of a Spaniard or an Italian. How can any one determine absolutely that the word race or colour in this amendment referred to the African race and to black colour? Hence you must see the complete absurdity of interpreting this to mean *any* special race or colour, or *any* number of races and colours less than the whole number.

I have learned that high judicial authority has been invoked upon this question of law, and that this authority has declared that neither the XIVth nor XVth Amendment gave anybody the right to vote. I think I give the exact words. I have not claimed that the XVth Amendment gave *any one* the right to vote. There is no language in either the XIVth or XVth Amendment which confers rights not possessed; but 1 will state what these amendments *do* say, and if it is not equal to the declaration of the right of all to vote I confess that my perceptions are at fault, for I cannot perceive the difference. They declare positively—not negatively—that "All persons born or naturalized in the United States are citizens of the United States," and, mark you, of the State wherein they reside. I am a person, one of the sovereign people, a citizen of the United States and of the State of New York. Does the State of New York enforce any law which abridges my privileges or immunities as a citizen? Is it nothing to be denied the right to vote? What privileges and immunities have I differing from those of the subjects of the most *absolute* monarch? They are subject to such laws as he sees fit to impose. Am I subject to any laws other than are imposed upon me? It does not appear possible to me that men are conscious of the tyranny they exercise over women. It may be mildly exercised, but it is, nevertheless, absolute tyranny. I can have what they will give. Could the veriest slave have less? Therefore, Government permits the State of New York, in the face of the XIVth Amendment, to enforce laws which abridge my privilege and immunities, as well as those of every other woman who resides therein, who is responsible, taxed, and who contributes to the maintenance of an organized Government.

"But," says the authority, "neither does the XVth Amendment give anybody the right to vote." What does it do? or was it an utter abortion of Congressional wisdom? "The right to vote shall not be denied on account of race, colour, or previous condition of servitude." The right to vote, then, is possessed. It may be, as some say, a negative admission of the existence of the right; nevertheless, it is an admission, and one under which I claim to be a voter.

I now come to the previous condition of servitude, and there is much *more* in this than is at first apparent. We had become so accustomed to regard African slavery as servitude that we forgot there were other conditions of servitude besides. Slavery, or a condition of servitude, is, plainly speaking, subjection to the will of others. The negroes were subject to the will of their masters, were in a condition of servitude, and had no power or authority as citizens over themselves.

I make the plain and broad assertion, that the women of this country are as *much* subject to men as the slaves were to their masters. The extent of the subjection may be less and its severity milder, but it is a complete subjection nevertheless. What can women do that men deny them? What could not the slave have done if not denied?

It is not the women who are happily situated, whose husbands hold positions of honour and trust, who are blessed by the bestowal of wealth, comforts and ease that I plead for. These do not feel their condition of servitude any more than the happy, well-treated slave felt her condition. Had slavery been of this kind it is at least questionable if it would not still have been in existence; but it was not all of this kind. Its barbarities, horrors, and inhumanities roused the blood of some who were free, and by their efforts the male portion of a race were elevated by Congress to the exercise of the rights of citizenship. Thus would I have Congress regard woman, and shape their action, *not* from the condition of those who are so well cared for as not to wish a change to enlarge their sphere of action, but for the *toiling female millions*, who have human rights which should be respected.

It may be affirmed that the exercise of suffrage will not ameliorate their conditions. I affirm that it will, and for authority will refer to the improved condition of our fathers, and also to the improved condition of the negroes since they acquired the rights of citizenship ; since they were enfranchised : *and how enfranchised ?* The XVth Amendment does not grant them the right to vote. Neither does it to me ; *but it forbids* that a right already possessed shall be denied. If the male negroes, as citizens, possessed the right to vote, shall it be assumed that women citizens do not possess the same right ?

It is said the amendment does not give any one the right to vote. Suppose we admit that for a moment. I think men will desire to disown it. If the XIVth and XVth Amendments give none the right to vote, let me ask them where they obtain their right to vote ? Do they get it from the Constitution ? Nowhere does it say " the right to vote," except in this XVth Amendment. Do they vote by right, or is this another usurpation which they exercise ? Where do they get their right to vote ? I will tell them where they get their right to vote. They inherit it from their God, and every one of the sovereign people inherits it from the same infinite source, Who knows no such ignoble limitation as that of sex. The right to vote is *higher* than State laws, *higher* than countries' Constitutions. It can neither be given nor taken by laws or by Constitutions. These are but means for its exercise, and when our laws and Constitutions shall have been reduced to *this* standard we shall have a republican form of Government, and not till then.

One more point and I shall dismiss this amendment. It has been insisted, again and again, that the denial may be made on account of sex, and that it was not intended by those who framed this amendment to make such a broad application and such a sweeping enfranchisement as my interpretation embraces. This is not the first time, even in legislation, that people, having a single point in view which they were determined to gain, have overreached themselves ; happily, however, this time it was in the cause of liberty, humanity, and equal rights.

All law may not be the deductions of logic, but where law does not apply fact and logic must. Here, however, law and fact do apply, while the deductions are very clear.

This amendment declares that the right to vote shall not be denied on account of race. The class of opposers who still wish to deny women the right to vote, declare this means the *African* race. Let us see how this would read. The right to vote shall not be denied on account of the African race. To WHOM shall it not be denied on account of the African race ? *This* certainly does not inform us, for it simply declares that it shall not be denied on account of the *African* race. Therefore, if this amendment were even modified by saying the African race, it would still fail to leave any room for denial. But it does *not say African* race, and cannot, therefore, be interpreted to *mean* the African race, when there are so many other races represented in this country. Who would pretend that though the right to vote could not be denied to the African race, it *might* be denied to the Teuton, the Celt, or the Scandinavian ? Under any other interpretation of this amendment than the broad one I make, the right to vote *may* be denied to *any* race or *all* other races except the African.

Does Congress desire that an interpretation shall stand upon the Constitution, that, should the time come when the Anglo-Saxons would not be predominant, would permit other races to unite and deny the right to vote to the Anglo-Saxon race? *See* the dilemma in which this matter is placed by persisting in denying women the right to vote?

There is but one construction the language of this amendment is susceptible of, and this becomes apparent if the section is properly rendered. It simply means that the right to vote shall not be denied on account of race to ANYBODY. By the interpolation of this word the sense of this amendment is complete and unmistakable. From the simple negative it changes it to an all-powerful command, by which the sovereign people declare that the right to vote shall not be denied by the United States nor by any State to any person of any race.

We are now prepared to dispose of the sex argument. If the right to vote shall not be denied to any person of any race, how shall it be denied to the female part of all races? Even if it could be denied on account of sex, I ask, what warrant men have to presume that it is the *female* sex to whom such denial can be made instead of the *male* sex? Men, you are wrong, and you stand convicted before the world of denying me, a woman, the right to vote, not by any right of law, but simply because you have usurped the power so to do, just as all other tyrants in all ages have, to rule their subjects. The extent of the tyranny in either case being limited only by the power to enforce it.

And this brings us to the "qualification" argument; which before entering upon I must premise by saying, I consider it the most *stupid* of them all. If there is little of sound logic in the other objections, in this there is none at all. It is the purest attempt at *quackery* that was ever palmed off upon a nation.

The only reason that can be offered for which women can be denied the right to vote is that they do not "possess the requisite qualifications for electors of the most numerous branch of the State Legislature." Article I., Section 2, of the Federal Constitution.

Again: " The times, places, and manner of holding elections for Senators and Representatives shall be prescribed in each State by the Legislature thereof; but the Congress may at any time, by law, make or alter such regulations." Federal Constitution, Article I., Section 4, paragraph 1.

Upon *these* two words, "qualifications" and "regulations," must be based the whole authority for denying to women the right to vote. It has been said that the right to vote exists, but has been denied. A person being denied the right to vote is disfranchised. Are the terms qualification, regulation, and disfranchisement synonymous? Qualifications are what citizens can acquire, and after having acquired can use them or not. Disfranchisement cannot be overcome. Anything that is made a qualification, which cannot be attained, which is an impossibility, is not a qualification, either within the meaning of the Constitution or of dictionaries. Sex cannot be made a disqualification. To be denied the right to vote on account of sex is the pure essence of disfranchisement; for how can a person, a citizen, being a woman, obtain the qualification of being a man? I regret that I am compelled to impugn your good sense by the argument, but I have had "sex" sounded in my ears until I can scarcely *think* of it with patience or *speak* of it with courtesy. Sex is a quality obtained by nature, and with what degree of regard for common honesty shall men continue to call this a *disqualification* which women must overcome? Was ever a more intolerable thing; It is like saying to the starving, "You may eat; here is a stone." The kingdom of human rights cannot be invaded to furnish qualifications for voters; these qualifications must be of a character equally attainable by all citizens. No more can be required of woman than of man. If men become qualified by residence, property, education, character, age, &c., so, too, must women be able to qualify by the same means.

I do not care what qualifications the States require for electors. What I ask is, that they shall apply equally to all

citizens of the United States, whether they are men or women.
For men to say to women, "You shall not vote because you are
women" is *intolerable;* is *unbearable,* and it will not do for
Congress to quietly allow this disfranchisement to continue.
Congress *has* the power to make and alter the regulations of a
State, and I respectfully ask Congress to make and alter the
regulations of the State of New York, so that I shall not be
disfranchised under the misnomer of the qualification of sex.

Nor is authority wanting upon this point, and that, too, from
our fathers who framed the State Constitutions, of which we
hear so much, and who thought so differently from what is now
predicated of them.

Mr. Madison, as a member of the Virginia Convention, said :
" *Some* States might regulate the elections on the principle of
equality, and *others* might regulate them otherwise. Should the
people of any State, by any means, be deprived of the right of
suffrage IT WAS DEEMED PROPER THAT IT SHOULD BE REMEDIED BY
THE GENERAL GOVERNMENT." One-half of *all* citizens of the
United States are disfranchised because they are not men a
something to which they can never attain. Nature has made a
distinction which it is impossible to get over. How do the
arguments which were used in Congress not many months ago
pale before the awful magnitude of this National dishonour ?
They were then entreated to not continue the disfranchisement
of a *few* millions of negroes, but they *unblushingly* continue the
disfranchisement of *many* millions of women.

If there are good and consistent reasons why some should not
be electors let them be applied without regard to sex or any
other general condition. Let men as well as women be subject
to them. If they include me I will not complain ; I will but
ask that every man shall be prevented for the same reasons that
I am, and for none other. If men were unreasonably prevented
from suffrage I would as earnestly plead their cause. No person
felt more for the emancipated negro race than myself ; but with
their enfranchisement I could not forget that the whole female

sex was labouring under the same disabilities from which they were raised. Negroes could not qualify to become voters, Congress assisted them and they are voters; hence I come to Congress to plead for women. The negro found many advocates—men whose souls were large enough to take in all God's family. But with this great effort they closed. Woman must be her own advocate. Few of the male sex—few of those who battled so manfully for the negro—now come forward and lift their voices against this *thrice* greater, this *terrible* wrong.

Slavery will ever be regarded by all our descendants as a foul blotch upon the escutcheon of this country's honour, which ages alone can wash away. Congress know this, but they do not yet know how much *more* foul will this greater wrong be regarded by future ages. It should be the task of the next Congress to remove this damning thing. That Congress which recognized negroes as citizens is already reverenced for its mighty work. So, too, will that Congress which shall recognize women as citizens of equal rights with the negro be regarded with reverence in proportion to the magnitude of the result of its labours.

I assume then—

1st. That the rights, privileges, and immunities of all citizens are equal.

2nd. That no citizens, as a class, can be denied the right to vote, except they first forfeit it as a class.

3rd. That the qualifications which a State may require of electors must be such as can be acquired by all persons by the same means.

4th. That the State may make regulations but cannot enforce prohibitions.

5th. That anything that may be required which is impossible of one-half of the people or any considerable class, possessing all the other qualifications required for electors, is not a qualification, but disfranchisement.

6th. That a State which disfranchises any part of its citizens on account of any natural quality is not possessed of a Republican form of government.

7th. That if a State has not a Republican form of government it is the solemn duty of Congress, under its Constitutional obligations, to guarantee it to its citizens resident therein.

Thus have I endeavoured, as briefly as possible, to place before you my reasons for claiming the right to vote for myself and others of my sex who desire it. Neither upon general principles nor by special provision of the Constitution can I perceive that men have any right to deny it to us. So long as we did not *claim* it, it was not denied, but I do now claim that I am, *equally* with men, possessed of the right to vote, and if *no others* of my sex claim it, I will stand alone, and reiterate my claim, and if the right is possessed, men have *no power* other than an usurped one to deny me.

The first official duty of every Congressman is to take a solemn oath to support and give vitality to the Constitution of the United States, not as they would, or might wish it to be, but as it is. That Constitution declares that women are citizens, and that citizens shall not be denied the right to vote. In the face of these facts, how can they, with that oath recorded, deliberately set at naught these plain declarations?

I went before Congress to demand a right, and memorialized them, setting forth my grievances, and frankly and fully to the extent of my ability I endeavoured to make my claim clear. This is a vital matter, fraught with more momentous events than have ever yet dawned upon the world. Through it civilization will make a giant stride from barbarism toward perfection—a stride which will land the human race near the haven where every person living will become a law unto himself, where there shall be no need of Constitutions, Houses of Congress and Executives, such as are necessary now.

Regarding it as I do, it becomes to me the most sacred duty of my life to attain to my rights under the Constitution.

12

I think I have examined this subject quite thoroughly; to me it appears very plain, but to others it may not. I have no doubt about the common rights of citizens under the original text of the Constitution. There is *no room* for doubt since the addition of the XIVth and XVth Amendments. Whatever doubts there may yet be in the minds of opponents, I now propose to show you that whether equality is Constitutional or not, Congress has *already* given its verdict in favour of my position, whether *intentionally* or *unwittingly* I *know* nor *care* not; it is *sufficient* that it is given, and *that*, too, in the form of *positive* law.

Permit me to return for a moment to Mr. Bingham, who has played so prominent a part, who has wrought so much better than he knew. In his report adverse to my memorial, which asked for an Act to place the right of all citizens to vote above question, he says in the outset: "Since the adoption of the XIVth Amendment of the Constitution there is no longer any reason to doubt that *all persons* born or naturalized in the United States, and subject to the jurisdiction thereof *are* citizens of the United States and of the State wherein they reside." And in closing: "We are of opinion, therefore, that it is not competent for Congress to establish by law the right to vote, without regard to sex, in the several States of this Union, without the *consent* of the *people* of such States, and against their constitutions and laws; and that such legislation would be, in our judgment, a violation of the Constitution of the United States, and of the rights reserved to the States. We therefore recommend that the prayer of the petitioner be not granted."

This report was made to the House of Representatives, January 30, 1871. It is almost impossible to conceive that the author of this report was the same person who drew the XIVth Amendment, and AN ACT to enforce the rights of citizens of the United States to vote in the several States of the Union, and for other purposes, approved May 31, 1870. If Mr. Bingham, can harmonize these three instruments and maintain himself before the people of the United States as the great legal authority of the Congress of the United States, he will accomplish something no other person living would be able to *do*. But let us refer to this Act of less than a year ago, which I have taken the precaution to produce, Section 2 of which is as follows :—

"*And be it further enacted*, That if, by or under the authority of the constitution or laws of any State, or the laws of any Territory, any act is or shall be required to be done as a prerequisite or qualification for voting, and by such constitution or laws persons or officers are or shall be charged with the performance of duties in furnishing to citizens an opportunity to perform such prerequisite, or to become qualified to vote, it shall be the duty of every such person or officer to give to all citizens of the United States the same and equal opportunity to perform such prerequisite, and to become qualified to vote without distinction of race, colour, or previous condition of servitude ; and if any such person or officer shall refuse or knowingly omit to give full effect to this section, he shall, for every such offence, forfeit and pay the sum of five hundred dollars to the person aggrieved thereby, to be recovered by an action on the case, with full costs and such allowance for counsel fees as the Court shall deem just, and shall also, for every such offence, be deemed guilty of a misdemeanour, and shall, on conviction thereof, be fined not less than five hundred dollars, or be imprisoned not less than one month and not more than one year, or both, at the discretion of the Court.

"Sec. 3. *And be it further enacted*, That whenever, by or under the authority of the constitution or laws of any State, or the laws of any Territory, any act is or shall be required to [be] done by any citizen as a prerequisite to qualify or entitle him to vote, the offer of any such citizen to perform the act required to be done as aforesaid shall, if it fail to be carried into execution by reason of the wrongful act or omission aforesaid of the person or officer charged with the duty of receiving or permitting such performance or offer to perform or acting thereon, be deemed and held as a performance in law of such act; and the person so offering and failing as aforesaid, and being otherwise qualified, shall be entitled to vote in the same manner and to the same extent as if he had in fact performed such act; and any judge, inspector or other officer of election whose duty it is or shall be to receive, count, certify, register, report or give effect to the vote of such citizen upon the presentation by him of his affidavit stating such offer and the time and place thereof, and the name of the officer or person whose duty it was to act thereon, and that he was wrongfully prevented by such person or officer from performing such act, shall for every such offence forfeit and pay the sum of five hundred dollars to the person aggrieved thereby, to be recovered by an action on the case, with full costs and such allowance for counsel fees as the Court shall deem just, and shall also for every such offence be guilty of a misdemeanour, and shall, on conviction thereof, be fined not less than five hundred dollars, or be imprisoned not less than one month and not more than one year, or both, at the discretion of the Court.

"SEC. 16. *And be it further enacted,* That all persons within the jurisdiction of the United States shall have the same right in every State and Territory in the United States to make and enforce contracts, to sue, be parties, give evidence, and to the full and equal benefit of all laws and proceedings for the security of person and property as is enjoyed by white citizens, and shall be subject to like punishment, pains, penalties, taxes, licenses and exactions of every kind, and none other, any law, statute, ordinance, regulation or custom to the contrary notwithstanding. No tax or charge shall be imposed or enforced by any State upon any person immigrating thereto from a foreign country which is not equally imposed and enforced upon every person immigrating to such State from any other foreign country ; and any law of any State in conflict with this provision is hereby declared null and void."

Thus we find Mr. Bingham, in the XIVth Amendment, declaring that *all persons are citizens;* in an Act approved May 31, 1870, making it a penal offence for any officer of election in any State to refuse to permit *all citizens* the *same* and *equal* opportunities to perform the prerequisites to become qualified to vote ; less than a year afterward informing us that women are *not citizens,* and on January 30, 1871—less than two months thereafter—very decidedly expressing a contrary opinion, and adding that Congress has no power to enforce their rights as citizens in the States, which is a complete stultification of the Act of last May. At present Mr. Bingham does not think women are entitled to vote. What he may think to-morrow or next month it would be quite impossible to predict. Whether we are to account for his inconsistencies by presuming that he has not attained to the knowledge that the States, through their respective legislatures, by the act of adopting and ratifying the XIVth and XVth Amendments, did remove all obstructions to the right of women citizens to vote or by some other disability of mind it is impossible to determine.

What did Congress ask the States to do ? To ratify the Amendments. They did ratify them, and thereby enfranchised women as citizens. Mr. Bingham does not yet seem to conprehend what the States were asked to do, nor that they did what was requested of them.

It is clear from the report of the majority of the Judiciary Committee that they take the view that there is " something " in the Constitutions or Laws of the State which is contrary to the language, spirit, intent and purpose of these Amendments, and that this inconsistent something must be removed by the States. I contend that by the adoption of these Amendments the States did legislate upon the subject, and remove all inconsistencies and all obstructions to the right to vote, leaving them as parts and parcels of the " Supreme Law," before which *all existing legislation contrary* to and *inconsistent* therewith *did* fall, and was rendered null and void.

The Constitution can be amended as follows:—" Congress, whenever two-thirds of both Houses shall deem it necessary, shall propose Amendments to the Constitution, which shall be valid to all intents and purposes as part of this Constitution, when ratified by the legislatures of three-fourths of the several States." (Article V.) Again it says:—"This Constitution and the Laws of the United States which shall be made under authority of the United States, shall be the supreme law of the land." (Article VI.)

These amendments *were* thus proposed by two-thirds of both Houses, *were* thus *ratified* by the Legislatures of three-fourths of the several States, and were thus formally legislated upon by all the several State Legislatures and *adopted* by them in the due and solemn manner in which they pass all laws. From the moment the official declaration was made that they *were* so adopted by State legislation they became a part of the " supreme law of the land," which they *never* could have become without such legislation.

Are not these amendments in question, as a part of the supreme law, the *very creatures* of the State Legislatures, and as *such* do they not supersede all legislative Acts in *all the* States not in harmony therewith? Nor can the States *recede* from these Acts without similar formal legislation in which three-fourths of all the States must concur. *And what do they establish? The status of every native born or naturalized person in the country as a citizen of the United States and of the State, and the right to vote as vested in every such person.* And to go further: The State of New York has declared—Article I. of the Constitution of New York—and every other State holds that: " No *member of this State shall be disfranchised* or deprived of *any* of the rights or privileges secured to *any* citizen thereof,

unless by the law of the land or the judgment of his peers."
As the State cannot pass any law which deprives *any* citizen of
his or her citizenship and the declared right to vote, it follows
that the Legislatures *have* acted directly upon this question by
the adoption of these amendments, and *for ever* precluded themselves from receding, except by a similar proceeding, viz.: by
another amendment to the Constitution which would annul and
repeal the XIVth and XVth Amendments.

These amendments are therefore not only the law of the
United States, but the Constitutional law of New York and
every other State in the Union.

Therefore, I would have Congress, in the pursuit of its duty,
to enforce the Constitution by appropriate legislation, *pass* a
Declaratory Act plainly setting forth the right of *all* citizens to
vote, and thus render unnecessary the thousands of suits for
damages which will otherwise arise. What legislation could be
more appropriate than defining the rights of *one-half* the
citizens of the country, when they are in question? This
matter has passed *beyond* the States. They have delegated this
power to *Congress* by these amendments. Could the legislatures of the States think of legislating upon the question of
who are citizens? *How* can they then upon the *rights* of these
same citizens, which are no less clearly a part of the Constitution that the fact of citizenship.

If Congress refuse to legislate appropriately in this matter,
every woman who desires to vote should take all the steps
required as prerequisite to become qualified, and, if prevented
from voting, should prosecute those who prevent them, under
the plainly worded Act of May 30, 1870, and so *continue* to do
until the Government of the United States and of the several
States shall be made to *enforce* the supreme law of the land,
and thus secure to every citizen *equal* right and *exact* justice
under a Republican form of Government.

THE XIVTH AND XVTH AMENDMENTS TO THE CONSTITUTION OF THE UNITED STATES.

A Speech before the National Woman's Suffrage Convention,

At Apollo Hall, May 11th, 1871.

SINCE this is not a convention for the consideration of general political questions, I am not certain that I have anything to say which will prove of interest or profit to you. But with your permission I will endeavour to state the position which the movement for political equality now occupies, and attempt to show therefrom the duties which devolve upon those who advocate it.

Whatever there may have been spoken, written, or thought in reference to the constitutional rights of women citizens of the United States, as defined by the XIVth and XVth Articles of Amendments to the Supreme Law of the Land, the first practical movement under it to secure their exercise was made in the Congress of the United States during the past winter. A memorial, setting forth the grievances of a woman citizen, who was denied the right of citizenship, was introduced into both Houses of Congress, and by them referred to their Judiciary Committees. Upon this memorial the House Judiciary Committee made two reports ; that of the majority, while admitting the validity of the foundation upon which the memorial was based, was averse to congressional action thereon, naively attempts to ignore the force of the argument by thrusting the responsibility back upon the States, which have acted upon the point in question by the adoption of said Amendments. That of the minority, than whom there is no more conclusive judiciary authority in the United States, took issue with the entire pleading of the majority, and fortified their position by such an array of authority, judicial decisions, and logic, as to fully establish the fact of the right of women to the elective franchise in every unprejudiced mind.

So forcible was the conviction which this report carried wherever analyzed that even Democrats who, everybody well knows, are constitutionally predisposed against the extension of suffrage, acknowledged it as unanswerable. Besides this, there has been so much high judicial authority also expressing itself in the same terms of approbation that there can be no question whatever about the fact that women, equally with men, are entitled to vote. This conclusion, though at first received with great scepticism by very many who wished it were really so, is gradually spreading among the people, and settling into a well-defined conviction in their hearts. Many of your own journals even ridiculed the matter more I presume from dislike to the movers in it than from convictions of its incapacity to meet the required demand.

I am glad, however, to now announce that most of these journals have reconsidered the subject, since there has been such enthusiasm and action raised all over the country by it, resulting in bringing women forward to demand their rights, which have been accorded to them in a sufficient number of cases to finally decide the true value of the movement. If I mistake not some of those who were instrumental in preventing the exercise of these claimed rights will have the pleasure of paying for their presumption in money, if not by imprisonment, both of which may be meted to them under the Act which it seems was almost providentially passed by Congress in May, 1870, to meet just such cases as are now required to be met.

There are two ways by which the success already gained may be pushed on to ultimate and complete victory, both of which I count as legitimate and justifiable. One is to continue the appeals to the courts, until by a final decision of the Supreme Court it shall be fully determined. The other is for Congress to pass an Act declaring the equal rights of all citizens to the elective franchise. To this method some object that it stultifies the position that the Constitution already grants everything we ask. But these objectors forget that by Article I., Section 8, par. 17, of this same Constitution it is made one of the duties of Congress to make all laws which shall be necessary and proper for carrying into execution all powers vested by the Constitution in the Government of the United States, and that one of the special powers vested in Congress is the right to make *all* laws necessary for enforcing the provisions of the XIVth and XVth Amendments. It seems to me that petitioning Congress to enforce the provisions of these Amendments is eminently proper, and that any who object thereto either do not understand the powers and duties of Congress or do not wish so easy a solution of the franchise question, which solution cannot be expected from the courts, as a decision therein may be deferred for years.

A Washington correspondent of the *Tribune*, of May 2nd, speaking of this matter, says :—

" There is no probability that the women of this district will vote by the next Presidential election, if they depend on a decision of the courts in their favour for the privilege. The action is brought in the Circuit Court of the District, which will adjourn before reaching the case. It cannot, then, be decided until the October term ; but, no matter what the decision may be, the case will be appealed to the United States Supreme Court, which, judging from the present condition of its docket, will not be able to render an opinion in less than two or three years."

The matter of time is an important element in this issue. I

am aware that women do not yet fully appreciate the terrible
power of the ballot, and that they have made no calculations
what they will do should the right to vote be accorded them the
next session of Congress. I hold that when women are fully
decided in their minds that they are entitled by law to the
elective franchise, it is their solemn duty to determine how they
shall use this new power.

The enfranchisement of ten millions of women is a revolution
such as the world has never seen, and effects will follow it
commensurate with its magnitude and importance. Whatever
the women of the country shall determine to do that will be
done. It seems to me that nothing could be more wise and
judicious than for them even now to begin to consider what
they will do.

I have had ample occasion to learn the true worth of present
political parties, and I unhesitatingly pronounce it as my firm
conviction if they rule this country twenty years to come as
badly as they have for twenty years past, that our liberties will
be lost, or that the parties will be washed out by such rivers of
blood as the late war never produced. I do not speak this
unadvisedly. I know there are men in Congress—great men—
who know that unless change for the better come this will.

What do the Republican leaders care for the interests of the
people if they do not contribute to their strength? They have
prostituted and are prostituting the whole power of the Government to their own selfish purposes. They have wrung the very
last possible dollar from the industries of the country and are
now hoarding it in the vaults of the Treasury. One hundred
and thirty millions of dollars in actual cash is a great power, a
dangerous power it might be made by unscrupulous men, and I
do not think but that there are those near the head of the
Government who are ambitious and unscrupulous enough to
take advantage of any favourable opportunity in which to make
use of this power.

True, the Republican party did a mighty work to which all future ages will look back with reverence. True, that they opened the door, unwittingly though it was done, to our enfranchisement. True, that they have made the name of slavery odious, and added new lustre to that of freedom.

But having delivered us from one curse shall they be permitted to sell us to another, compared to which the first is but a cipher? They have told us that the Southern slave oligarchy had virtual control of the Government for many years, and that the terrible war which we waged was the only means by which this power could be humbled.

But do they tell us of a still more formidable oligarchy which is now fastening upon the vitals of the country? Do they tell us that they have given four hundred millions of acres of the public domain, millions of dollars and tens of millions of credit to build up this new tyrant? Do they tell us that this tyrant is even now sufficiently powerful to buy up the whole legislation of the country, to secure the confirmation of any nomination which it desires made, and to bribe officials everywhere to the non-performance of their duty? Do they tell us matters have been so arranged that all the revenue they can extract from the people is turned over to this power, by which process the vitality of the country is being gradually absorbed? No, not a bit of it. This they will leave us to learn through bitter experience, as we were left to learn what were the fruits of forty years' plotting by the slave oligarchy. This new oligarchy has plotted less than ten years and it has already attained the most threatening and alarming proportions.

Shall we turn to the Democratic party with the hope that they may prove the necessary salvation from the wrath to come? To do this would indeed be to show the dire extremity to which we are driven. I hold that the Democratic party is directly responsible for the late war. The Democratic party South would not have rebelled had not the Democratic party North promised them their support. Can we expect anything better from them than from the Republican party? They are not now making themselves so antagonistic to the true interests of the country as are the Republicans, simply because they have not got the power so to do. But where they have the power, their leaders do not hesitate to make the most use of it to their own aggrandisement.

Therefore, it is my conviction, arrived at after the most serious and careful consideration, that it will be equally suicidal for the Woman Suffragists to attach themselves to either of these parties. They must not—cannot afford to—be a mere negative element in the political strife which is sure to ensue in the next Presidential election. They must assume a positive attitude upon a basis compatible with the principles of freedom, equality and justice which their enfranchisement would so gloriously demonstrate as the true principles of a republican form of government. I do not assume to speak for any one. I know I speak in direct opposition to the wishes of many by whom I am surrounded. Nevertheless, I should fail to do my duty did I conceal what I feel to be the true interests of my sex, and through them, those of humanity; for the interests of humanity will never be understood or appreciated until women are permitted to demonstrate what they are, and how they shall be subserved. I have thus as briefly as possible given what I conceive to be the position which the Woman's Rights Party occupies at this time, their prospective power, importance and duties, and the dangers by which this country is threatened, from which they may save it.

If Congress refuse to listen to and grant what women ask, there is but one course left them to pursue. Women have no Government. Men have organized a Government, and they maintain it to the utter exclusion of women. Women are as much members of the nation as men are, and they have the same human right to govern themselves which men have. Men have none but an usurped right to the arbitrary control of women. Shall free, intelligent, reasoning, thinking women longer submit to being robbed of their common rights? Men fashioned a Government based on their own *enunciation* of principles: that taxation without representation was tyranny; and that all just government exists by the consent of the governed. Proceeding upon *these* axioms, they formed a Constitution declaring all persons to be citizens, that one of the rights of a citizen is the right to vote, and that no power within the nation shall either make or enforce laws interfering with the citizen's rights. And yet men deny women the first and greatest of all the rights of citizenship—the right to vote.

Under such glaring inconsistencies, such unwarrantable tyranny, such unscrupulous despotism, what is there left women to do but to become the mothers of the future government.

Because I have taken this bold and positive position; because I have advocated radical political action; because I have announced a new party and myself as a candidate for the next Presidency, I am charged with being influenced by an unwarrantable ambition. Though this is scarcely the place for the introduction of a privileged question, I will, however, take this occasion to, once and for all time, state that I have no personal ambition whatever. All that I have done I did because I believed the interests of humanity would be advanced thereby.

Had I been ambitious to become the next President I should have proceeded very differently to accomplish it. I did announce myself as a candidate, and this simple fact has done a great work in compelling people to ask: and why not? This service I have rendered women at the expense of any ambition I might have had, which is apparent if the matter be but candidly considered.

In conclusion, permit me again to recur to the importance of following up the advantages we have already gained, by rapid and decisive blows for complete victory. Let us do this through the courts wherever possible, and by direct appeals to Congress during the next session. And I again declare it as my candid belief, that if women will do one-half their duty until Congress meets, that they will be compelled to pass such laws as are necessary to enforce the provisions of the XIVth and XVth Articles of Amendments to the Constitution, one of which is equal political rights for all citizens.

A NEW POLITICAL PARTY

AND

A NEW PARTY PLATFORM.

*At the Suffrage Convention held in Apollo Hall, May 11th and
12th, 1871, by request of Mrs. LUCRETIA MOTT, the following
Platform of Principles of a Just Government was read by
VICTORIA C. WOODHULL, and is embodied in this history
that it may have a wide circulation and be deeply considered
in all its bearings on the future of this country.*

SUFFRAGE is a common right of citizenship. Women have the
right of suffrage. *Logically* it cannot be escaped. Syllogis-
tically it is self-evident, thus :—

First—All persons—men and women—are citizens.
Second—Citizens have the right to vote.
Third—Women have the right to vote.

Though the right to vote be now denied, it must eventually
be accorded. Women can be neither Democrats nor Republicans. They must be something more than Democratic or
Republican. They must be humanitarian. They must become
a positive element in governmental affairs. They have thought
little; they must be brought to think more. To suggest food
for thought, a new party and a new platform is proposed for
the consideration of women and men: the party, the Cosmo-
political—the platform, a series of reforms, to wit:

A reform in representation, by which all Legislative Bodies and the Presidential Electoral College shall be so elected that minorities as well as majorities shall have direct representation.

A complete reform in Executive and Departmental conduct, by which the President and the Secretaries of the United States, and the Governors and State Officers, shall be forced to recognize that they are the servants of the people, appointed to attend to the business of the people, and not for the purpose of perpetuating their official positions, or of securing the plunder of public trusts for the enrichment of their political adherents and supporters.

A reform in the tenure of office, by which the Presidency shall be limited to one term, with a retiring life pension, and a permanent seat in the Federal Senate, where his Presidential experience may become serviceable to the nation, and on the dignity and life emolument of Presidential Senator he shall be placed above all other political position, and be excluded from all professional pursuits.

A radical reform in our Civil Service, by which the Government, in its executive capacity, shall at all times secure faithful and efficient officers, and the people trustworthy servants, whose appointment shall be entirely removed from, and be made independent of, the influence and control of the legislative branch of the Government, and who shall be removed for "cause" only, and who shall be held strictly to frequent•public accounting to superiors for all their official transactions, which shall for ever dispose of the corrupt practices induced by the allurements of the motto of present political parties, that "to the victor belong the spoils," which is a remnant of arbitrarily assumed authority, unworthy of a Government emanating from the whole people.

A complete reform in our system of Internal improvements, which connect and bind together the several States in commercial unity, to the end that they shall be conducted so as to administer to the best interests of the whole people, for whose benefit they were first permitted, and are now protected; by which the General Government, in the use of its postal powers and in the exercise of its duties in regulating commerce between the States, shall secure the transportation of passengers, merchandize and the mails, from one extremity of the country to the opposite, and throughout its whole area, at the actual cost of maintaining such improvements, plus legitimate interest upon their original cost of construction, thus converting them into public benefits, instead of their remaining, as now, hereditary taxes upon the industries of the country.

A complete reform in commercial and navigation laws, by which American-built or purchased ships and American seamen shall be practically protected by the admission of all that is required for construction of the first, or the use and maintenance of either, free in bond or on board.

A reform in the relations of the employer and employed, by which shall be secured the practice of the great natural law, of one-third of time to labour, one-third to recreation, and one-third to rest, that by this, intellectual improvement and physical development may go on to that perfection which the Almighty Creator designed.

A reform in the principles of protection and revenue, by which the largest home and foreign demand shall be created and sustained for products of American industry of every kind; by which this industry shall be freed from the ruinous effects consequent upon frequent changes in these systems; by which shall be secured that constant employment to working-men and working-women throughout the country which will maintain them upon an equality in all kinds and classes of industry; by which a continuous prosperity—which, if not so marked by rapid accumulation, shall possess the merit of permanency—will be secured to all, which in due time will reduce the cost of all products to a minimum value; by which the labouring poor shall be relieved of the onerous tax, now indirectly imposed upon them by Government; by which the burden of governmental support shall be placed where it properly belongs, and by which an unlimited national wealth will gradually accumulate, the ratio of taxation upon which will become so insignificant in amount as to be no burden to the people.

A reform by which the power of legislative bodies to levy taxes shall be limited to the actual necessities of the legitimate functions of Government in its protection of the rights of persons, property and nationality; and by which they shall be deprived of the power to exempt any property from taxation; or to make any distinctions directly or indirectly among citizens in taxation for the support of Government; or to give or loan the public property or credit to individuals or corporations to promote any enterprise whatever.

A reform in the system of criminal jurisprudence, by which the death penalty shall no longer be inflicted; and by which, during that term, a portion of the prison employment shall be for, and the product thereof be faithfully paid over to, the support of the criminal's family; and by which our so-called prisons shall be virtually transformed into vast reformatory workshops, from which the unfortunate may emerge to be useful members of society, instead of the alienated citizens they now are.

The institution of such supervisatory control and surveillance over the now low orders of society as shall compel them to industry, and provide for the helpless, and thus banish those institutions of pauperism and beggary which are fastening upon the vitals of society, and are so prolific of crime and suffering in certain communities.

The organization of a general system of national education which shall positively secure to every child of the country such an education in the arts, sciences and general knowledge as will render them profitable and useful members of society, and the entire proceeds of the public domain should be religiously devoted to this end.

13 *

Such change in our general foreign policy as shall plainly indicate that we realize and appreciate the important position which has been assigned us as a nation by the common order of civilization ; which shall indicate our supreme faith in that form of government which emanates from, and is supported by the whole people, and that such government must eventually be uniform throughout the world; which shall also have in view the establishment of a Grand International Tribunal, to which all disputes of peoples and nations shall be referred for final arbitration and settlement, without appeal to arms ; said Tribunal maintaining only such an International army and navy as would be necessary to enforce its decrees, and thus secure the return of the fifteen millions of men who now compose the standing armies of the world, to industrial and productive pursuits.

A reform by which the functions of Government shall be limited to the enactment of general laws ; and be absolutely prohibited from enacting any special law upon any pretext whatever ; by which all laws shall be repealed which are made use of by Government to interfere with the rights of adult individuals to pursue happiness as they may choose; or with the legitimate consequences of such pursuit; or with contracts between individuals, of whatever kind, or their consequences, which will place the intercourse of persons with each other upon their individual honour, with no appeal, and the intercourse of the general people upon the principles of common honesty ; which will be a nearer approach to self-government and a wider departure from arbitrary control than has ever been exemplified. And finally that all legislative action shall be approved by the people before becoming law.

Thus in the best sense do I claim to be the friend and exponent of the most complete equality to which humanity can attain ; of the broadest individual freedom compatible with the public good, and that supreme justice which shall know no distinction among citizens, upon any ground whatever, in the administration and the execution of the laws ; and also, to be a faithful worker in the cause of human advancement; and especially to be the co-labourer with those who strive to better the condition of the poor and friendless ; to secure to the great mass of working people the just reward of their toil. I claim from these, and from all others in the social scale, that support in the bold political course I have taken which shall give me the strength and the position to carry out these needed reforms, which shall secure for them, in return, the blessings which the Creator designed the human race should enjoy.

If I obtain this support, woman's strength and woman's will, with God's support, if he vouchsafe it, shall open to them, and to this country, a new career of greatness in the race of nations, which can only be secured by that fearless course of truth from which the nations of the earth, under despotic male governments, have so far departed.

VICTORIA C. WOODHULL.

New York,
  January 10th, 1871.

A REVIEW OF THE NEW DOCTRINE OF STATE RIGHTS.

A Speech before the National Suffrage Association,

BY

VICTORIA C. WOODHULL,

AT

Lincoln Hall, Washington, D. C., January 10th, 1872.

"WE hold these truths to be self-evident: that all men are created equal; that they are endowed by the Creator with certain inalienable rights; that among these are life, liberty, and the pursuit of happiness; that to secure these rights governments are instituted among men, deriving their just powers from the consent of the governed."

Such, my friends, are the propositions which resulted from that famous Philadelphia Conference, in which Washington, Franklin, Rush, and Adams, when hesitating and undecided, called on Tom Paine to solve their difficulty. Rising from his seat when he had attentively listened to their doubts and queries, and towering high above them, Mr. Paine answered them, "We want independence, and I mean revolution."

And our wants to-day are what their wants were at that time. We want independence; and if we can't get it without it, we mean revolution. Do you doubt that we are in slavery? Franklin himself said, to be enslaved is to have governors appointed over us by other men. Women have governors appointed over them by other men, and, according to Franklin, are absolutely enslaved. Freedom has been the watchword which has echoed through the centuries; and to-day it rises higher, and touches the souls of mankind with a profounder meaning than ever before. With each succeeding year it has gathered in volume, and expanded its boundaries, until every human soul leaps with a new pulsation when touched by its magnetic power.

Something more than a year ago I went before Congress with a simple petition, setting forth that I was a citizen of the United States and of the State of New York, under the provisions of the XIVth Amendment to the Constitution of the United States, and that the State of New York unlawfully deprived me of one of the dearest rights of a citizen, in direct contravention of that amendment, and asking for the necessary legislation to prevent the continuation of such tyranny.

I adopted that course because I believed myself aggrieved as set forth, and because I believed I had just as good a right to participate in government as most men had, and because I was not willing to await the willingness of men to graciously say, " We will now consent that you shall vote." I did not ask any other woman whether she believed as I believed, or if she felt as I felt. I acted of my own accord, scarcely realizing that my demand would grow into the great National Question it since has.

But why did I go to Congress with my demand? I will tell you. I had carefully watched the legislation of Congress following the war, which was fought and won upon the very idea upon which all that legislation was founded—and that was the sovereignty of the United States over that of the States. It was held by all Republicans, up to the time of my demand upon Congress, that that was the result of the war and the effect of the amendments.

I saw that all the qualifications for electors, of which use had been made by the States, were wiped out by the Amendments and the Force Act; I saw that the provisions of race, colour, and previous condition of servitude, removed all restrictions upon the right of negroes to vote, although, as in the State of New York, they were not prevented from voting because they were negroes, but because they did not have the property qualification; I saw all these restrictions and obstacles melt away before the potent concentration of power, by which the sovereign people of the whole country forbade the sovereign people of any one State to discriminate against citizens who owed their first allegiance to the United States.

I saw that I was first a citizen of the United States, and, by virtue of so being, also a citizen of the State of New York, and that the State had no right to even require me to conform to any of its regulations in order to be entitled to be recognized as a citizen.

But the State of New York did assume to interfere with my rights as a citizen of the United States, by depriving me of the right to participate in the government of the United States. Therefore, as a citizen of the United States, I appealed to the Government of the United States for redress. Was I right or was I wrong? But how was I met? By the flat contradiction of my whole demand. It was denied that I was a citizen. I was simply a woman—not even a person, since to be a person was to be a citizen.

That was a year ago. How does the question stand to-day? Then, the Republican Party claimed to have demolished—aye, destroyed—the doctrine of States' rights. Now they are compelled either to acknowledge that my demand was a legal and just one, or themselves become the champions of those very doctrines to purge the country from which they murdered hundreds of thousands of their brothers. Thus, what required rivers of blood and years of severest struggle to gain, my simple demand has caused them to abandon. Verily, there must be a mighty power behind that demand, to cause the Republican Party to even hesitate to grant it. While not to grant it is to enter up a verdict of condemnation against themselves, which time even will never be able to efface.

I hold, then, that I was right in going to Congress to demand redress ; and I further hold that everything that has since occurred, connected with this question as relating to women, proves that I was right—proves that we have no hope whatever for redress by any other means. In a State where men specially desire to invite the immigration of women, they were denied an amendment to the State Constitution by a vote of six to one. If that is to be taken as a sample of what men will do where they should be specially favourable to women on account of their scarcity, what may we expect in States where women predominate ? Do you, my friends, see any hope that way ? I confess I do not.

Turn you to Wyoming, and what do we see there as a result of the theory that citizens may be enfranchised and disfranchised at will simply because they don't choose to vote as it is desired that they should vote ? Is that the kind of Republicanism under which you want to live ? Do you want your State to grant you suffrage one day and take it away the next ? Have men ever undertaken to play that game with their own sex ? Not a bit of it. And, were it ever attempted, I think I can name a hundred Congressmen who would launch their oratorical thunder till the whole country should ring with its echoes. And it would be right. It would be ignoble in them not to do so. But in our case—why, it is quite a different matter. They don't deem it quite expedient. They don't know exactly what use we shall make of the ballot if they permit us to get it. We are only women, you know—between whom and men, it is said, there is an impassable political gulf fixed. But let me simply say to those expedient Congressmen, who think more of their positions and prospects than they do of justice, that they cannot afford to maintain that position.

But let us enter into a close analysis of the situation, and the law which applies. We, as women citizens, are either entitled to vote under the law, or we are not. Let us take it up, and see for ourselves just how the matter stands. We do not need to ask anything. I think we are capable of reading and getting at the real sense of it for ourselves. And if we read, and find that we are entitled to the ballot, under the very laws men have made, we are surely justified in demanding the benefit of such laws.

One of the following positions must be correct. Either the States have the right to deny the right to vote to all citizens, or they have no right to deny it to any citizen. Now, we claim that they have no right to deny any citizen the right to vote. But if we admit that they have no right to deny any citizen the right to vote, we must claim that that is not a Republican form of Government which makes such denial. And if the Government which makes such denial is not a Republican Government, is that form of government which will admit of such denial a Republican form? I say, most emphatically, no! But what say the Republican party?

During last summer, Mr. Tilton addressed an exhaustive argument to Senator Sumner upon this question, ending by asking him to become the champion of this movement in Congress, as he was the champion of the Slavery movement. Though several months have elapsed, Mr. Sumner has made no reply. Whether he thinks it unworthy his attention, or whether, like many Republicans, he thinks it inexpedient to broach this question upon the eve of a Presidential election—since they are not capable of seeing how it will affect that election—or whether he is indifferent to it, we are not able to determine. But I must confess to not a little astonishment that a Senator who played so honourable a part in the destruction of African slavery, and advocating human rights, and whose speeches only need to be amended by substituting the word "sex" for "negro" to furnish us all the argument we require, should, for any reason whatever, hesitate to become a champion against this greater slavery. I may be in error in supposing he will not. I trust I may be.

But as yet he has made no reply, though another honourable Senator has. And I think we are justified in assuming, and I do assume, that the address of Mr. Tilton to Mr. Sumner was not considered as simply a personal address, but as addressed, through Mr. Sumner, to the Republican Party, and that since Mr. Sumner could not consistently take adverse grounds, and since the party could not permit itself to be committed to Woman Suffrage by an indorsement of it, that Mr. Carpenter was selected as the person to break the force of Mr. Tilton's onset, and to bridge the question over another Presidential election, when, as I have been informed by several prominent men, they will be willing that we get our rights. And to such things, my friends, has our Republic descended. Justice, when placed in the scales with party expediency, is found wanting, and goes by the board. What business have these men to deny us our rights because a Presidential election is impending? Had they a particle of the sense of honour and true patriotism ; had they a single feeling of love for their country, as above their love for self and position, they would the more gladly welcome us just at this time. Hence I say—and I declare it boldly—that these men whom other men send to Congress to legislate for themselves and against us, are traitors to their country, and unfit to occupy seats in so honourable a place as the Capitol of this country, representative of freedom to the world, if they for a single moment deny us justice. We ask no favour. We want no alms. We beg for no charity. We demand what is ours of right. And woe betide them if they shut their ears to our demands, since—

"Ever the right comes uppermost,
And ever is justice done."

But, as I have said, the question is now narrowed down to a very small point—a single point—but around it are grouped several important questions which, it appears to me, must have been either totally ignored, or, at best, but casually observed by those who established it, as the position from which to resist the attack of Woman Suffrage under the Constitution as it is. It has seemed to me ever since I thought upon this subject that we had a queer sort of a Republican form of Government whose Constitution had to be amended in order to meet each new contingency. It appeared to me that "We, the people," included all the people. But our wise governors seated in the Capitol inform us quite to the contrary. They tell us that we, the people, are only those persons whom from time to time their graciousness permits the privilege of interest in government.

That is to say, though our Constitution is based upon individual equality, exact justice and perpetual freedom, yet those whom men choose to legislate have the right to decide who are to be the recipients of these blessings which the Constitution was ordained to guard, protect, and defend. Some of you may be able to comprehend such a position, and see its benign results ; but, for my part, I freely confess I am too obtuse. I can understand the simple propositions of the theory of our Government ; but, for the life of me, I lose sight of the theory altogether if I attempt to grasp the application which is made of it in practice—since the paradox is too obscure for me to discover its truth. And this Republican Paradox, enunciated by Senator Carpenter, became to me still more enveloped in clouds and fogs after it passed the searching ordeal of Justice Cartter's logic. The paradox, as stated by Mr. Carpenter (as far as can be discovered from his language), is this : We have a Republican form of Government, because we are compelled by the Constitution to have it, and it consists of the right of States to deny the right to vote to any citizen, except male negroes, which after passing through the judicial furnace of Justice Cartter's brain, becomes still further attenuated—since he says that to admit the theory that the right to self-government is an inherent right is to destroy our civilization—hence the right does not exist.

Now, before going further, I submit to you whether Justice Cartter's logic, added to Senator Carpenter's wisdom, should not compel us, out of respect to ourselves, if not from deference to them, to adjourn and go home, convinced that we form no part of "We, the people," nor of the persons whom this amendment made citizens; or, if we are citizens, that we must wait with due patience for our gracious masters to extend us the ballot, since they instruct us that we have no rights that men are bound to respect.

Let us examine the questions that are grouped about the new Republican doctrine of States' Rights, as remodelled and announced by the modern Lycurgus, and made law by the later Daniel. And first let us examine as to what a Republican form of Government is. Mr. Carpenter says :—" It is a strong point in favour of your position, that under the old Constitution it is made the duty of the United States to guarantee a Republican form of Government to every State." But he sweeps that point away by the assertion that, since when women did not desire to vote, the States were held to have a Republican form of Government; that, though women do now desire the right to vote, and are denied, the States, nevertheless, are Republican. Is that strictly logical ? I say, emphatically, NO ! It is neither logic nor common sense, as I will shortly show.

A hundred years ago women made no demand for the exercise of the elective franchise. They simply did not want it. They were not denied it, however ; and they freely exercised such other citizen's rights as that of pre-empting lands, obtaining passports, and clearing vessels. Nobody thought of denying them these rights. But it is quite different now since women do demand the elective franchise, thousands strong, and are denied. The argument hurled at us, that the majority of women do not want the ballot, instead of being against our position, is directly and forcibly in its favour—since a Government might be held to be Republican which had non-voting citizens from choice, but could not be so held having non-voting citizens from compulsion.

Would Mr. Carpenter assume that to be a Republican form of government which deprived every man of the ballot? We hardly think he would go to that extreme. How, then, can he assume the same of one that denies the ballot to every woman? And do you not see, to admit that if all women wanted the ballot they should have it, is to admit that if any one desires it, it is clearly her right to have it, since rights are individual, not collective? If it is the right of all women, then it follows necessarily that it is the right of each one constituting the all. Is not that a clear statement?

But Mr. Carpenter facetiously says:—"The Constitution, deriving its powers from the will of the people, must be construed as it was understood by the people." Admit all that, and it proves nothing; since, if the people a hundred years ago construed indefinite language to mean one thing, the people of to-day may very properly give the same language a very different construction. Or are we always to accept the theories of past ages? The Constitution exists to-day under the authority and by the will of the people who exist to-day; and it is for *them* to determine for themselves what a Republican form of government is to-day, not what it may have been held to be a hundred years ago.

But how are we to know whether the States ever had a Republican form of government? Mr. Carpenter says:—"The Courts would undoubtedly have held that the States under the old Constitution were Republican;" but, unfortunately, that question was never raised, and of course it was never decided. It seems to me, however, that Mr. Madison did not so understand the matter, since he said :—" Some States might regulate the elections on the principle of equality, and others might regulate them otherwise. Should the people of any State by any means be deprived of suffrage, it was deemed proper that it should be remedied by the General Government."

Now, what did Mr. Madison mean by the principle of equality in elections ? Mr. Carpenter will hardly contend that he meant admitting one-half the citizens to suffrage and excluding the other half, since that would be *inequality*. If Mr. Madison were now here, and should make that assertion, he would at once be set down by our opponents as in favour of Woman Suffrage.

If a Republican form of government means the equality to which Mr. Madison referred, then neither the United States nor any of the States ever had it ; and they have not got it now. Mr. Carpenter saw the force of this, and said, " Well, it is a strong point."

A Republican form of government means a government guaranteeing equality of rights among its citizens exercising the right of self-government, in opposition to a monarchical form, in which citizens submit to be ruled by a monarch, as women submit to be ruled in this country by men. There is no mistaking the meaning of these terms. There is no chance left for equivocation, reservation, or interpretation. Ours is either a monarchical or a Republican government, and there is no half-way house at which to stop. Leaving a monarchy, we must go to the other extreme to find a Republic. To do otherwise is to set up a false pretence—is to practice a cheat either upon rights or upon credulity. And I do not mean that men shall think any longer it is upon my credulity that they are practising. I am for exposing this monstrous fraud, and for compelling the enforcement of that provision of the Constitution which demands a Republican form of government in every State of the Union.

But now let us see about the muddle into which Senator Carpenter, in his zeal to establish his new-fledged doctrines, would precipitate the XIVth Amendment. The language of its first section is : " All persons born or naturalized in the United States are citizens of the United States and of the State wherein they reside. No State shall make or enforce any law that shall abridge the privileges and immunities of citizens of the United States, nor deny to any person the equal protection of the laws."

Of this language Mr. Carpenter says : " *Had the XIVth Amendment stopped with the first section, I think the right of all citizens, black and white, male and female, to vote and hold office, would have been secured.*" He *thinks* only !

But is such the actual fact ? Had there been no second section, would the right to vote have been secured alike to men and women ? That is the question, and it is the only one. The language is positive. It does not leave any room for doubt, or place for construction to step in and quibble over words. The States shall not (that is the language) make or enforce any law that shall abridge the privileges and immunities of citizens of the United States. Now, everybody who knows anything about the definition given to the term citizen knows it describes a person entitled to participate in government, and that was distinctively and expressly settled as the law of the United States in one of the most important cases that ever came before the Supreme Court of the United States—the Dred Scott case. In delivering the opinion of the Court, Mr. Justice Daniels said : " Who, it may be asked, is a citizen ? What do the character and status of citizens import ? Upon a principle of etymology alone the term citizen, as derived from *civitas*, conveys the idea of connection or identification with the State or Government, and a participation in its functions. But beyond this there is not, it is believed, to be found in the theories of writers on government, or in actual experiment heretofore tried, an exposition of the term citizen which has not been understood as conferring the actual possession and enjoyment or the perfect right of acquisition and enjoyment, of an entire equality of privileges, civil and political."

Now, what are political privileges ? Are voting, being elected and appointed to office, political privileges ? If they are not, then there are no political privileges. Take them away from politics and there would be nothing remaining. Then the right to vote is a political privilege which every citizen has the perfect right to possess or acquire and enjoy; and since every woman born or naturalized in the United States is a citizen, every such woman, by the supreme tribunal of the nation, has the right to vote : and that decision of that tribunal stands the supreme law, unreversed by any later decision.

It inevitably and unavoidably follows, then, that the first section of the XIVth Amendment *does* give to "black and white, male and female," the right to vote; and no proposition can be more clearly and forcibly established.

Now, then, let us see about that second section, upon which Senator Carpenter makes so magnificent a retreat, saying, "Although *all* citizens have been made voters by the first section, the second section clearly recognizes the right of the States to exclude a *portion* of the same from voting." If a portion only, why not the whole—but if only a portion, what portion ? "Oh! but—but—but it doesn't tell us who may be excluded. That, you know, we left for the States to decide." And who, pray, are the States ? Do they consist of men only, and is it for them, having usurped the power to do so, to say that all women are the portion who may be excluded ? Is that the magnificent result obtained by all the wisdom expended since the war in legislation, to which Congress has been almost exclusively devoted ? It seems to me that such an abortion is better described by that little game "first you see it, and then you don't," than anything else that ever emanated from Congressional brains for the sake of ushering negroes into the mysteries of citizenship, Congress set themselves to work and made everybody citizens; but, being frightened at the grandeur and extent of the result, straightway they turned about and gave the States the right to exclude a *portion* of the newly-made voters from voting, and magnanimously left it to the States to say that that portion should be women. Such patriots; such lovers of their country; such devoted adherents to the right of the States, to do whatever they please with citizens of the United States so that they let men alone, is truly astonishing. And Mr. Carpenter, the Raphael of the Nineteenth century, presents them to us in such life-like colours and in such grandeur, that we fain must bow down and worship at their shrine.

But let us analyze these beautiful pictures of the gods of Wisdom and Justice, to see if indeed they are the only true gods. We have been so often deceived that we must be pardoned for having become just a little bit sceptical. This amendment declares that when the right to vote shall be denied by a State to a portion of the male citizens of the United States, the basis of such State's representation shall be reduced, &c.; and this, Mr. Carpenter says, is clearly an acknowledgment of the right of the States to deny the right to vote to women. General Butler a year ago said of a certain argument, that it was "the slimmest he ever heard." That may be the slimmest he had ever heard, but Mr. Carpenter had not then advanced this one, of which we are speaking. I think General Butler will be obliged to revise his assertion in favour of Mr. Carpenter's last effort. When the States shall deny the right to vote to a single man, then they shall have the right because of such denial to deny the same right to all women. Wonderful wisdom; wonderful indeed!

But again: this provision is in the form of a penalty; it provides if any State shall do a certain thing to certain citizens of the United States that it shall suffer a certain penalty. Now that is all that can be made of the language. And it may be well to remember that that only is law which is written; *ita lex scripta est* is the rule everywhere. It is the only safeguard to law, since if we are at liberty to infer anything we please, then we might as well have no law at all.

But Senator Carpenter tells us that because the sovereign people have declared, if the States shall assume to commit a certain crime against citizens, they shall suffer a certain penalty, that gives them the right to commit all other crime against all other citizens with perfect impunity. Undoubtedly Senator Carpenter and Justice Cartter will give to the world a new system of logic; but I hope I shall not be called upon to formulate its rules.

Let us try by the same rule a similar kind of a case outside of voting, and see how it would work. The people say that if a person commit the crime of murder he should be hanged; therefore, any person has the right to commit all other crimes and suffer no penalty at all.

But there is still another face to this remarkable thing, which we are called upon to admire. If men are denied the right to vote, then the representation must be reduced. But all women may be excluded from voting and still be retained in the basis of representation. This pretence, however, is too shallow to dwell upon. Any school-girl of twelve years who could not detect it ought to be accounted a dullard. But these logicians must stick to this line of argument, since it is their last line of defence. Give this up and woman suffrage is inevitable.

But we will bid adieu to this part of the subject by calling attention to the fact everywhere recognized in law, that anything granted by positive law cannot be taken away by imputation.

Justice Story, in speaking of Constitutional law, said:—

"Contemporaneous construction is properly resorted to, to illustrate and confirm the text; it can never abrogate the text; it can never fritter away its obvious sense; it can never narrow

14 *

down its true limitations. There seems little room for interpretation, except in cases leading to an obvious absurdity, or to a direct overthrow of the intention expressed in the preamble."

Now the text to the XIVth Amendment is clear and positive, making, as Senator Carpenter even is compelled to admit, all persons voters. Then, if the common rule is applied, how can the inference drawn by Senator Carpenter, from the indefinite and negative language of the second section, be held to "abrogate that text;" and "fritter away its obvious meaning;" and "narrow down its true limitations," and finally to directly overthrow not only the intent but the positively expressed meaning of the text? In other words, how can what is granted to women in express terms by the first section be taken away from them by the inference it is found convenient to draw from the second section?

"But," says Senator Carpenter, "the XVth Amendment is equally damaging to the right of female suffrage, since if by the XIVth Amendment the elective franchise had been secured to every citizen, the XVth Amendment would have been unnecessary." Now mark the consistency of the three points of his argument which we have reached: First, he informs us that the first section of the XIVth Amendment secured the right to vote to all citizens, black and white, male and female; second, that all persons having been enfranchised, the second section of the same amendment confers the power upon the States to disfranchise any citizens, for any reason whatever; and that since the States continued to disfranchise male negroes, the XVth Amendment was necessary to take that power away from the States. Now, if it was the intention of Congress from the first to arrive at this end, why did they proceed by such a roundabout way? Why did they not at once specifically state that all this legislation was for the purpose of securing the votes of male negroes, since that, according to Senator Carpenter, is the final result. The States may deny the right to vote to any citizens except to male negroes. Suffrage in all other cases stands just as it did before the amendments, the fact of all persons having been made citizens counting for nothing.

All men, save negroes, voted then. All men, including negroes, vote now. So that the result of all the work and talk about human rights has ended in securing the exercise of the elective franchise to, say, a million negroes; and all this was conducted with specific care that the same right should not be secured to 15,000,000 women. In other words, the men of the United States have declared by these amendments that all men may vote if they choose, but that no woman shall vote under any circumstances whatever. I submit to you if, according to their own showing, this is not what has been accomplished.

But we object to this conclusion, and propose to show that men have proceeded upon an opposite theory quite too long to permit them to shift its application, now that women demand what belongs to them. The Courts have held that all limitations of rights must be made in express terms: we must demand that the same rule shall operate in our case, especially since it has been held to apply in cases arising under this amendment.

Justice McKay laid down the following proposition:—"The rights of the people of a State, white and black, are not granted them by the Constitution thereof; the object and effect of that instrument is not to give but to restrain, duly regulate, and guarantee rights; and all persons recognized by the Constitution as citizens of the State have *equal legal and political rights* except as *otherwise expressly declared.*"

Again:—"It is the settled and uniform sense of the word citizen, when used in reference to the citizens of the separate States of the United States, and to have rights as such citizens, that it describes a person entitled to every right, legal and political, enjoyed by any person in that State, unless there be some express exceptions made by positive law covering the particular persons whose rights are in question."

Let me ask, is there any language in these amendments by which women are excluded from suffrage "by positive law covering the particular persons " whose rights are involved? On the contrary, there is no direct reference made to women whatever, and no particular persons excluded. Therefore, by still another argument we are compelled to conclude that since women in common with all other persons are made citizens and consequently voters, all women are voters,· with the exception of those who have been excluded by express constitutional provisions.

Again: Senator Carpenter tells us that before the adoption of the XVth Amendment any citizen could be excluded for any reason whatever, but since that adoption any citizen may be excluded for any reason other than race, colour, or previous condition of servitude.

Now I claim, if language have any definite meaning, and if there are any rules of logic by which such meaning is to be arrived at, and if the construction of general law as announced by the Courts has any weight, that the XVth Amendment forbids the denial or abridgment of the right to vote to any citizen whatever. The language is plain and explicit :—

"The right of citizens of the United States to vote shall not be denied or abridged by the United States or by any State on account of race, colour, or previous condition of servitude."

Now, the question is not what that language was framed to cover, nor what it has been construed to mean ; but what does it say, and what would it be considered as meaning if it were to be interpreted by people having no interest in the matter as citizens of the United States, and no knowledge of the circumstances under which it became the law of the land?

It asserts, first, that the right to vote is a citizen's right; and, secondly, that that right shall not be denied or abridged by any Government on account of race, colour, or previous condition. Now, what do these terms cover? We know that the African race were denied the right to vote, and that by this amendment the male portion were raised to the exercise of that right. But we also know that if the Celtic race had also been denied the same right they would have been affected in the same way. Hence it must be held to mean that not only are the States prohibited from denying the right to vote to the African race, but also to all other races—that is, that no person of any race shall be denied the right to vote because he belongs to that specific race.

If none can be denied the right to vote on account of race, can any be denied that right on account of anything that goes to make up race? That is, since the African race cannot be denied the right to vote, can any part of that race be denied? We say, emphatically, NO! The larger always includes the parts of which it is composed, and if the whole is granted a privilege, or the exercise of a right, no part of the whole can be excluded, unless the exclusion of that specific part is expressly provided for; as I have shown, it must be by the decisions quoted, which have never been reversed. If we say the citizens of the United States may vote, it could not be held that the citizens of any of the States could be prevented, unless such States were excluded in definite terms. If the United States could not deny the right to vote to citizens of the United States, they surely could not to the citizens of the State of New York, unless there was a specific provision granting the right to exclude New York. And what applies to citizens in general must apply to all classes of citizens, no part of whom can legally be excluded, except such exclusion is made in express terms, so as to specially declare who are excluded.

But let us look at this provision from another standpoint, that we may judge of it upon some other issue than of voting. Suppose that negroes, instead of having been denied the right to vote, had been denied the right to register vessels or to pre-empt land, which, equally with his right to vote, are citizen's rights; and that the XVth Amendment had read: "The right of citizens of the United States to register vessels and to pre-empt lands shall not be denied by the United States, or by any State, on account of race, colour, &c.," would that have been construed to leave the privilege of denying those rights to citizens on account of sex? Why are not those rights denied on account of sex? That they are not, under the interpretation of the language of the amendment, is clear and unmistakable; since what would apply in one class of cases must also apply in all classes of cases. Nobody would think of denying a negro woman the right to register a ship, or to pre-empt land, or to obtain a passport. She is a citizen, and entitled to these citizen's rights; but the moment another citizen's right is involved—that one by which men hold their usurped power—then they are denied the exercise of that right, and are quietly informed that that right may be denied to citizens being women.

The right to vote shall not be denied on account of race. Now, if it may be denied to anybody covered and included by that term, then everybody included by the term race may be excluded for various other reasons, which would render the provision utterly nugatory. To assume such a position would be to make all legislation negative and void. And arguing upon the plea of intent, of which opponents make such constant though thoughtless use, it was the intent of the framers of the XVth Amendment to prevent negroes from being denied the right to vote for any reason whatever.

Now, what does the term race include in comparison with the sex? A race is composed of two sexes. Thus sex is a component part of race. But who ever heard that a sex was composed of two or more races? Therefore, if the right to vote cannot be denied on account of race, it cannot be denied on account of sex, which is a constituent part of race, unless it is specially provided, in express terms, that exclusion may be made on account of sex, and stating which sex may be excluded.

Our State constitutions provide that male citizens are electors. Why may we not just as reasonably assume that some male citizens may be excluded for other reasons than simply because they are males? Men say that the women are excluded for other reasons than because they belong to a race. We say that men may also be excluded by the same rule for other reasons than because they are males. Is not that statement clear? The several races include all people, and the right to vote cannot be denied on account of race. But a part of the race are denied because they are women. Now, by the other proposition, all men are included in the phrase "all male citizens," and they cannot be denied the right to vote, but a part of all male citizens, even the negro part, may be excluded for any other reason it may be convenient to invent. That would not be excluding them because they are males, but because they had a certain coloured hair, or because they were not a certain number of feet in height, or for any other reason of which use might be made to compel arbitrary distinctions. This would be the same rule which men now apply to the term race. Women are not excluded because they belong to the African or any other race, but because they are women, who are a part of a race; as different colour-haired men are a part of the sum total of men; and as different sized men are a part of the sum total of men. But while exclusions are made on account of sex, they are not made upon the other accounts, simply because men don't choose to make them; which resolves the whole question into its real position: that men exclude women from voting because they have got the power to do so, and that is the sum and substance and all there is of it since it completes the argument, and the conclusion is impossible of escape.

Do you not see it as I asserted in the beginning, that this doctrine of Mr. Carpenter's, to which he has committed the Republican party, and which they have made no effort to reverse, is the most complete possible statement of the old and exploded doctrines of States' Rights in a new form, to meet a specific contingency ? It seems to me that it was an unfortunate oversight in the Southern States that they did not take this view of the question ; since, when they were forbidden to deny negroes the right to vote because they belonged to the African race, they might have invented any other reason and have excluded them in spite of Congress. If this doctrine prevail, I do not see why the States may not go on and find reasons to exclude every negro in them from the ballot. Senator Carpenter says they have the right. I am quite certain some of the people of some of the States would like to have it done. Then I say do it, and have the sincerity of these self-constituted advocates of freedom and equality put to the test, as to whether their affections run to the negro rather than to women.

We are all aware of the desperate strait in which the Democratic party find themselves. They are seeking in every direction for an escape from the toils the Republicans have woven about them ; they supposed themselves "foundered " on the rock of a Centralized Government, from which there was no chance of escape except to accept the situation and make a " New Departure." Even the astute and learned, and legal and excessively constitutional *New York World* lately acknowledged that it was not only the intent but the effect of the amendments to vest the control of citizenship in the General Government, and to put it entirely beyond the control of the States. Now, I do not state this of my own knowledge, but I have been privately informed that Senator Carpenter is ambitious to be the next President, and since he saw that in the Republican party there was no chance for him, he put forth this new doctrine reviving the theory of States' Rights as a bid for the Democratic nomination. As I said, I cannot state that this is so, but this I can say : He ought to have it, since he has had the temerity to assert in a new form a doctrine which the most earnest old-line Democrat had abandoned not only as impracticable but obsolete.

The further we pursue this argument the clearer it becomes

that women are excluded from a right common to all citizens by the despot's right of might, which in all ages has been the argument of tyrants. Each succeeding proposition which we examine results in demonstrating this by a new method. Each analysis proves the logic of the right of men to be the flimsiest assumption, the merest pretence.

But, for all that, we will go through the list. Senator Carpenter says the States have the right to exclude women. This would have been a little more satisfactory had he explained what the States are. Suppose we admit his proposition. There must be some definite method of procedure by which to accomplish it. How must they do it? First, it must be determined what the States are to which this power is entrusted. Next, have the States excluded any citizens from suffrage? Lastly, was that exclusion made in proper form?

States are not certain territorial areas, having definite limits abstracted from their inhabitants. But they are the people and their effects living in such defined limits. It is impossible to conceive of a State without people. A State is a people under the jurisdiction of a certain organized government. I think no person can object to that definition. Now, the State of New York consists of all the people who are included within specified limits, and over whom its Constitution and Laws hold jurisdiction. Now, have those people ever denied to the women of New York the right to vote? There has never been any such procedure, or any attempt at such procedure. The Courts say that all persons who are citizens are entitled to every right, civil and political, enjoyed by any person in the State, unless excluded by express terms covering the persons excluded. I have examined the Constitution and Laws of New York, and I find no express terms excluding women from equal political rights. There is no such provision existent. By what authority, then, are women denied the right to vote? I answer, by the authority of the right of might.

In the State of Nebraska this question came before the people, but the men absolutely prevented a part of the people from expressing their opinion. And yet they say that the people of Nebraska rejected Woman Suffrage. Were there ever such insults heaped upon a class of citizens as this? Will Senator Carpenter assume that the people of Nebraska have denied women the right to vote? If he cannot, neither can he escape the inevitable conclusion that they are wrongfully and illegally deprived of a right exercised by other citizens of Nebraska, and consequently he must admit that it is the duty of the General Government to interpose its power to prevent the continuation of the wrong.

More recently, in Wyoming, an attempt was even made to take from women the right to vote, exercised by them for two years, and, as Governor Campbell testifies, in a manner worthy of the best citizens. Now, what is the lesson to be learned from this attempt at despotic power in Wyoming? That to allow the right of the States to deny suffrage to any of its citizens is a dangerous precedent, and that it will be a fatal error for women to rely upon this tenure for their rights, since every governor may not be like Governor Campbell, and some Legislatures may not have even six men out of twenty who will admit that women have any rights that men are bound to respect. Governor Campbell wisely remarks, "If this Legislature deprive women of the right to vote, the next may deprive men."

There is but one position for women to assume, and that they should advocate first, last, and all the time. They must take the Amendments, as they have the legal and established right to take them, to mean just what they say, utterly regardless of whatever might or might not have been the intent of their framers. These Amendments have completely reversed the order of government. Formerly citizens were originally citizens of the State. Now they are first citizens of the United States, and by virtue of being so are citizens of the States wherein they reside.

The first duty of every citizen is allegiance to the United States sovereignty; secondly, when it does not interfere with his first allegiance, allegiance to the sovereignty of the State. And if the State interfere with any of his privileges as a citizen of the greater sovereignty, then he must appeal for relief to that greater sovereignty. State sovereignty then is merged in the sovereignty of the United States. And the people of this larger sovereignty have decreed that neither that sovereignty nor that of any State shall interfere in any way whatever with the rights of citizens of the United States. This is as we read the Constitution, and all the authority there is supports this reading. Those who read it differently invite all the dangers of a return to despotism. It must be all the people governing themselves; or it *may* be one of them governing all the rest; since to begin discrimination is to open the way to discriminate against all, and to permit a government to deny one class of citizens a right that is exercised by another class, is to admit its right to deny all kinds of rights to all classes of citizens; and there is no escaping that conclusion, unless it be by the remarkable logic of Justice Cartter, which we will presently admire.

There are several other points in Senator Carpenter's "New Departure," which, with these examined, are equally felicitous. But I have not time to notice them here. I wait, however, to hear him advocate them from his seat in the Senate, and to hear his brethren of the Republican party say, Amen!

But we hear of opposition from another quarter, and must take some time to look after it. Since this constitutional question has been raised this matter has found its way into the Courts, notwithstanding the oft-repeated wail from Boston that the raising of this question by those "ungodly people" has done irreparable harm to the cause. It has ruined the prospects for women, since it has sunk the question from a mere matter of glittering generalities into the depths of Constitutional law. Now, I am willing to accept suffrage, even if we have to drag it through such low and filthy slums as this to get it. I want it, and want it at once. I am even willing to get it by a "Short Cut," across lots, and through a gate left open by those who loved the negroes so well that they forgot there were any women. Even by a "trick" am I willing to get back our rights. When we deal with thieves, who have stolen our birthrights, it is not only our right but our solemn duty to take advantage of all their oversights to make safely off with their booty. I am for stealing every possible march upon them, and for confronting them in the places to which they have fled for safety and security. They have built up a something which we have shown to be a mere pretence, but which they now desire the Courts to confirm, and to thus fortify their position against us for ever.

This *entrée* into the Courts caused a considerable flutter among politicians and political journals. Farmer Horace, in the *Tribune*, recently said that we might as well keep away from the Courts, since if we went there with our troublesome petitions we would be requested to go home and mind our own business. But we did go to the Courts; and the Courts, having forgotten the injunctions of the Philosopher, listened.

Justice Howes, of Wyoming, even rendered a decision, in which he declared that all women citizens in the United States acquired the right to vote by the XIVth Amendment. And Justice Underwood, of Virginia, announced, semi-officially, the same doctrine. This frightened the press, and straightway they roused to the fact that there really was such a question before the people. Even the *Nation*, in its critical clumsiness, felt called upon to enter its protest; and so it went the round, until Justice Cartter, of the Supreme Court of the District of Columbia, solved the whole question to the complete satisfaction of both parties. He is so remarkably clear in his elucidation of the subject that I am satisfied; and our opponents assert that they are also satisfied. This decision is almost as remarkable in its possibilities as the amendments themselves appear to be, which it pretends to interpret.

Since that portion of this decision which satisfies me is the latter part, I will begin with that. He says, in giving expression to my own judgment of this clause (the first clause of the XIVth Amendment), it does advance them (women) to free citizenship, and clothes them with the right to become voters. Now, I hold that is the law. Women are full-fledged citizens, with the right to become voters in the same manner that men become voters, by qualifying under the existing regulations. But we found the Constitution of the States standing in the way of our becoming voters. Hence, I asked Congress to compel the removal of the obstructions by passing an act forbidding the States to make distinctions of sex a bar to voting. Such action will also meet the legal objection raised by Justice Cartter, since he says: "It is a constitutional provision that does not execute itself. It is the creation of a constitutional condition that requires the supervention of legislative power to give it effect. The capacity to become a voter created by this amendment lies dormant until made effective by legislature action." Now, while I deny the possibility of such a thing as dormant rights existing in one class of citizens which is active in another class, being equal in other respects and which require legislation to make them legal, still legislation is the readiest way to compel the removal of the distinctions, and hence we seek it.

But Justice Cartter strikes a blow at the very existence of our theory of government, when he argues that the right to vote is not a natural right, existing regardless of constitutions and laws. He says: "The legal vindication of the natural right of citizens to vote would involve the destruction of civil government, hence the right does not exist." Civil government does exist, even with all the accumulation of male depravity. Justice Cartter in substance tells us if women participate they would destroy it, hence women do not have the right to participate. Complimentary, truly; isn't it?

Men are bad enough : but women—oh, no, that will never do; they would ruin us. Since some men make bad use of the ballot, therefore women have no right to it. Since some people abuse their stomachs, through their appetites, therefore the right to eat and drink does not exist. Since some people steal, therefore the right to possess anything does not exist. Since some people commit suicide, therefore the right to life does not exist. A wise man! A wondrous wise man! I stand abashed before the awful majesty of such wisdom!

But this is not all the discoveries in constitutional law made by this latter-day Columbus. It has been his fortune to find out that women have been rescued from one unpleasant condition by this amendment. " It has done so much as to distinguish them from aliens," says this Solomon. " To be an alien," says Webster, " is not to belong to the same country or government;" "belonging to one who is not a citizen;" "estranged;" "foreign;" "not allied;" "adverse to;" "one not entitled to the privileges of a citizen." Now we are informed that we are rescued from these conditions; that we now "belong to the same country and government;" that we are "citizens;" that we are not "estranged," or "foreign;" that we are "allied," and not "adverse to;" and that we are "entitled to the privileges of a citizen." All this may be consistency, but I am free to confess that my obtuseness will not permit me to appreciate the application of it made by Justice Cartter.

But, besides this statement of Justice Cartter, he proposes a principle which is fatal to all his elaboration. By his own argument he proves that our Government never had, and has not now got, a legal existence, since civil government can have no legitimate existence anywhere unless it have a lawful begin-

ning somewhere. How can a legal legislative body be organized
if there is no one qualified to vote until that right is conferred
by legislation? How were the first legislators elected, and who
elected them? and if they were elected by the people who had
no right to vote, how shall we go about to establish the validity
of our laws? I assume that, if the right to vote or the right to
self-government do not exist in the people, independent of constitutions and laws, that there never can be a lawful constitution in existence, since all constitutions and all laws must then
emanate from an arbitrary assumption of power on the part of
somebody.

It is scarcely necessary to pursue this absurd fallacy, since
the matter has been so thoroughly passed upon by a higher
authority than Justice Cartter, who must have been oblivious of
Chief Justice Taney's decision in the Dred Scott case. Justice
Cartter assumes that the Government confers the right to vote.
Hear him rebuked by Taney, who said : " The words 'people of
the United States' and 'citizens' are synonymous terms, and
mean the same thing. They both describe the political body,
who, according to our republican institutions, form the sovereignty, and who hold the power and conduct the Government
through their representatives. They are what we familiarly
call the sovereign people, and every citizen is one of this people,
and a constituent member of this sovereignty."

Can anything be clearer than this exposition, or more pointed
as to our claim? Every woman is a member of the sovereignty,
who hold the power and conduct the government through their
representatives. Against the pandering to despotism of this
late decision I oppose the broad republican sentiment of the
former one; nor do I fear the judgment of the American people
when they shall come to see this matter properly—Senator
Carpenter and all whom he represents, and Justice Cartter and
his confederates to the contrary notwithstanding.

But I must call your attention to another fact that this

15

decision brings into the argument, because when it is stripped
of subterfuges and inconsistencies, it has a few substantial
points left. He says that women are made full citizens by a
constitutional provision which does not execute itself. He
scarcely need have told us that, though I thank him for having
done so. If anybody ever saw a constitutional provision
executing itself, he has witnessed something that if he can
reproduce and take it to Barnum's Menagerie, I am sure he can
realize a fortune from it. We go to a deal of trouble and
expense, and pay seventy thousand men four years' salary, who
do scarcely anything else than work for the election of a
President, to execute the constitutional provisions; from all of
which we should have been exempt had the Constitution been
self-executing. And, moreover, one of these constitutional
provisions is specially framed in this view, and since it is made
one of the positive duties of the President "to take care that
the laws be faithfully executed," the provisions of the Constitution itself being the supreme law. Now I ask, in all candour
and seriousness, if the President has taken care that this part
of the supreme law relating to women was faithfully executed ?
If Congress want to impeach him they had better take some
clear case of neglect of duty, and here, according to Justice
Cartter, is a very plain one.

But let us take another view of this question of dormant right
raised by Justice Cartter. He says legislation must supervene
before it can become a right to be exercised. Is that the view
Congress took of the amendment in its application to negroes ?
If the negroes acquired any benefits by this amendment, women
also acquired the same benefits. If it made negroes citizens and
voters, so also did it make women citizens and voters. Is there
any escape from that logic ? How did negroes become voters ?
Did the State make them so ? No. This amendment is all
the legislation there has been upon the subject. And if it only
made them citizens having the dormant right to become voters,

how is it they are voters? As Judge Underwood has naively remarked: "If by a constitutional enactment a word of five letters was stricken out of the State Constitutions and Laws, why cannot a word of four letters be also stricken out?" Justice Cartter seems to have ignored history in this matter. Or does he hold that the "Force Act" was the legislation that raised negro suffrage from its dormant stage? If so, should not Congress also, and for the same reason, make the same sort of legislation, or rather, enforce the same act, for the benefit of women?

That act has never been understood, and I here desire to call the attention of Senator Carpenter to it, since it stabs his whole plea to the heart, and sweeps away the dust with which he endeavoured to blind the eyes of thoughtless people. Section 2 of this act reads as follows:—

"*And be it further enacted,* That if, by or under the authority of the Constitution or Laws of any State, or the Laws of any Territory, any act is or shall be required to be done as a prerequisite or qualification for voting, and by such Constitution or Laws, persons or officers are or shall be charged with the performance of duties in furnishing to citizens an opportunity to perform such prerequisite, or to become qualified to vote, it shall be the duty of every such person or officer to give to all citizens of the United States the same and equal opportunity to perform such prerequisite and become qualified to vote."

We know this Act was framed for the negro, but we must again demand the attention of our lords and masters. They must not object to being held to laws they have themselves made, and we beg them to remember that having made it the duty of officers of election to give all citizens the same and equal opportunity to become qualified and to vote, that if they intended to make any exception, they should have done so in the act and in specific terms covering the particular citizens

15 *

intended to be excluded from its benefits. In the name of justice and common sense as well as in that of law, I ask you, my friends, if that is not a reasonable demand. And if they failed to make the requisite exception to exclude women, shall we not claim under the Act? And I will *now* state that Judge Woodward, of Pennsylvania, while I was at Washington last winter, brought this act to me and said, "There is no question about women being able to vote under it." Many other eminent men have said the same thing to me. But such plain language as is used scarcely needs authoritative exposition to make its meaning clear.

And this brings us face to face with the last argument, to which everybody alike resorts when driven from all other possible positions. Invariably they come at last back to the baby objection, which is considered as a sort of general antidote to Woman Suffrage. "Well," they say, "if all you say is just as you assume it to be, why, babies have got the same right to vote that women have." That is exactly what we claim, only we claim a little more—that men have got no right to vote that the women and babies do not possess. All we ask is that men, women and babies shall exercise the right equally and under the same regulations, as James Madison said they ought, otherwise it was the duty of the Government to remedy it.

It is a strange fact that people can never see that this baby objection applies equally and as forcibly to man suffrage as it does to woman suffrage. If it is an objection in the last-mentioned, it is equally so in the first instance. Though this objection is, as General Butler has termed it, "the slimmest he ever heard," I will take the pains to sweep it out of our path.

Infants consist of male and female persons. But men would have it inferred that there are no male infants since they ask, "Are women born in the United States?" and reply, "so are babies." Male and female babies are both born in the United States, and consequently both are citizens, and both possess the right to vote; but the regulations prevent its being exercised until they have resided twenty-one years in the United States. On arriving at that age they have the requisite qualification of age, and both arrive at that qualification by the same process—by living twenty-one years. But just at that point the discrimination between the male and the female, as against the latter, begins. The male is permitted to begin the exercise of the right to vote, while the female is quietly informed that no age to which she can attain will ever qualify her to vote. This is an unequal exercise of power against which I rebel. It is neither a regulation nor the establishment of the citizen's right to vote, but a flat and unqualified denial of it.

Again, criminals, paupers and lunatics are citizens, but, by the common law, by which all legal construction of law is governed, are held to be incompetent to exercise the suffrage. Still there is no inequality here. All criminals, all paupers, all lunatics, be they men or women, are alike excluded. To make men's logic sound they should say that these classes of citizens, being women, should, while those being men should not, be excluded from suffrage. This would make their reasoning consistent. Now, will men say that adult women are to be placed in the same category with these classes of citizens and excluded from the suffrage for the same reasons that they and infants are excluded? But if they are not excluded for the same reason that these classes of citizens are, pray tell us what the reason is for which they are excluded. I have never heard one given.

On arriving at the age of twenty-one, men become entitled to the exercise of the suffrage. Why women should not also become entitled by the same reason, men may be sufficiently wise to determine. I hope they may. I am sure none will be more ready to give them credit than I. But if they cannot give a good, lawful and constitutional reason why women twenty-one years of age cannot vote, then I shall hold their assumptions as valueless.

Now, what did Mr. Madison mean by "the principle of equality?" Evidently he meant equality among citizens in regard to the right of suffrage. Suppose Mr. Madison were now living and should make that declaration, would he not be justly set down as an advocate of the right of women citizens to vote under the provisions of the Constitutions; and further, that he would deem it proper that the General Government should remedy any inequality in such States as should regulate elections upon the principles of inequality? The Constitution itself now declares that women are citizens, and that the right to vote is a citizen's right. The States deny the right to vote to women citizens. Is not that an inequality, according to Mr. Madison, to be remedied by the General Government?

But we suppose Senator Carpenter would at this stage of the argument again remind us of that "fatal," second section of the XIVth Amendment. None of our opponents now attempt to say that women are not citizens. This is admitted by them all. Now if to be a citizen is to have the right of suffrage, or, if the elective franchise is included among the privileges of citizens, then women have the right to vote. I will prove both propositions, and thus doubly establish our claim by two other methods.

A citizen possesses all his rights of citizenship from birth, else he can never possess them legally as I have shown; but some of these rights, like the right to bear arms, he does not exercise till the military age; others, like the right to vote, and to possess inherited property, till the legal age; and others, still, like the holding of the higher offices of State, till a yet wiser age: and till different ages for different offices. No one will pretend to say that there is a single citizen possessing the qualifications, who has not got the right to become President, though he or she cannot do so until thirty-five years of age.

I make the broad assertion that a citizen (whether man or woman) by virtue of simple citizenship (and with nothing else as his or her credentials) possesses constitutionally the right of suffrage. What is a citizen?

Noah Webster says that "a citizen is a person, native or naturalized, who has the privilege of voting for public officers, and who is qualified to fill offices in the gift of the people."

Worcester says that "a citizen is an inhabitant of a republic who enjoys the rights of a citizen, or freeman, and who has a right to vote for public officers, as a citizen of the United States."

"Bouvier's Law Dictionary," which gives the legal meaning of the word, says that "a citizen is one who, under the Constitution and Laws of the United States, has a right to vote for Representatives to Congress and other public officers, and who is qualified to fill offices in the gift of the people."

Thorbecke says that "the right of citizenship is the right of voting in the government of the local, provincial, or national community of which one is a member."

Turning to the Courts, I quote the Supreme Court of Kentucky, which declares that "no one can be in the correct sense of the term a citizen of a State who is not entitled, upon the terms prescribed by the institutions of the State, to all the rights and privileges conferred by these institutions upon the highest classes of society."

And, finally, in the Supreme Court of the United States, in, perhaps, the most important case that was ever decided—the Dred Scott case—Justice Daniels said, as I have already quoted, "that to be a citizen is to have the actual possession and enjoyment, or the perfect right of acquisition and enjoyment, of an entire equality of privileges, civil and political."

Mark the force of the words of Justice Daniels : "*The actual possession and enjoyment, or the perfect right of acquisition and enjoyment, of an entire equality of privileges, civil and political.*"

How lame and how impotent beside such authority as this is the decision of Justice Cartter, that though the amendments had conferred upon women the right to vote, it was a *dormant* right not to be enjoyed *until men should graciously see fit to make it active.*

But let us see more of this business.

In the opinion of Justice McKay, among other propositions, he lays down the following: and here we must again repeat

"Third. It is the settled and uniform sense of the word 'citizen,' when used in reference to the citizens of the separate States of the United States, and to their rights as such citizens, that it describes a person entitled to every right, *legal and political*, enjoyed by any person in that State, unless there be some express exceptions made by positive law covering the particular persons whose rights are in question."

Now, you all know that the phrase "all male citizens" in our State Constitutions is what men make use of to prevent women from voting. I ask, in all seriousness, is that an *express exclusion made by positive law* covering the *particular persons* whose rights are in question? It does not even refer to women, and therefore there is no law that covers the particular women whom the men seek to exclude from the exercise of a citizen's right. But even if this were not so—if there *were* express laws in the States, of what force would they be as against the Constitution of the United States, which declares itself to be the *supreme law* of the land, the constitution and laws of any State to the contrary notwithstanding? Now, if the Constitution of the United States give women the right to vote, how can the States take it away or deny its exercise? Some of these wise governors of ours may tell us, but I confess I cannot see how it can be lawfully done.

But let us look still a little further, since the further we look the clearer our case becomes:

The Supreme Court of Massachusetts says:

"'The privileges and immunities' secured to the people of each State, in every other State, can be applied only to the case of a removal from one State into another. By such removal they become citizens of the adopted State without naturalization, and have a right to sue and be sued as citizens;

and yet this privilege is qualified and not absolute, for they cannot enjoy the right of suffrage or eligibility to office without such *term of residence* as shall be prescribed by the constitution and laws of the State into which they shall remove."

This case fully recognizes the right of suffrage as one of the "privileges of the citizens," subject to the right of the State to *regulate* as to the *term of residence*—the same principle was laid down in Corfield v. Correll. Justice Washington, in delivering the opinion, used the following language :—

" ' The privileges and immunities conceded by the Constitution of the United States citizens in the several States,' are to be confined to those which are in their nature fundamental, and belong of right to the citizens of all free governments. Such are the rights of protection of life and liberty, and to acquire and enjoy property, and to pay no higher impositions than other citizens, and to pass through or reside in the State at pleasure, and to enjoy the elective franchise as regulated and established by the laws or constitution of the State in which it is to be exercised."

The elective franchise, then, is *one* of the privileges referred to in the XIVth Amendment which shall not be abridged. To complete our case it only remains to ask what is meant by regulating and establishing the Elective Franchise, since the Court says " as regulated and established by the States."

I have never heard any objection made to the regulations established for the protection of the ballot. Nobody objects that a person is forced to reside a year in a State to which he may remove before he can vote. This changing, however, does not impair the right. But we make this objection. We object that when a man and a woman remove from one State to another, that the woman is not permitted to vote after a year's residence. We want these things to fall equally upon all classes of citizens : and they must be made to do so ; we no longer say they ought.

To regulate, Webster says, is "to put in order," not to put out of existence. To establish is "to make stable and firm," not to nullify and destroy. Now, that is all we ask. We demand that our elective franchise shall be so "put in order" that we may have the enjoyment of a perfect equality of political privilege with men, and that it shall be made "stable and firm." We want nothing but what the law gives us, and that, too, in terms *so plain* that "the wayfaring man, though a fool, can understand."

But men say there was "no intent" to enfranchise women. There ought not to have been any need of intent, and I do not know how they can say there was any; but since they do, I presume both men and women will be compelled to leave that matter as the Supreme Court of the United States has decided it. Justice Bradley, in delivering the opinion of the Court in the case of The Live Stock Association v. The Crescent City, said:—

"It is possible that those who framed the article were not themselves aware of the far-reaching character of its terms, yet if the amendment *does* in fact bear a broader meaning and *does* extend its protecting shield over those who were never thought of when it was conceived and put in form, and *does* reach social evils which were never before prohibited by constitutional enactment, *it is to be presumed* that the American people, in giving it their *imprimatur*, *understood* what they were doing and *meant* to decree what in fact they *have* decreed."

Again I say, if words have any definite meaning, or Court decisions any weight, I submit that I have established: first that by the mere fact of being citizens women are possessed of the elective franchise; and secondly, that the elective franchise is one of the privileges of the XIVth Amendment which the States shall not abridge: that the States cannot regulate the suffrage out of existence, as they attempt to do, and have done, in the case of women; and finally, that whether it was, or was not, the intent of the framers of the XIVth Amendment to give women the elective franchise, *they have done so*, past all hop of retreat except by getting the woman's consent to another amendment to the Constitution repealing the XIVth.

But let us look at this matter in the light of a common business transaction, and see it in a still more ridiculous position. There are joint-stock companies in which women are stockholders. What would even men say if the male stockholders of such companies should get secretly together and pass a resolution reciting that all male stockholders may vote? Do you think the female stockholders would submit to such a usurpation of powers? But women submit to a still more despotic and tyrannical usurpation. Our government is a joint-stock company, in which *every* citizen has an interest, and yet men, without even so much as consulting women, have denied them all right to participate in the administration of that interest. Is that despotism, or can a better term be found by which to designate it?

The majority of men oppose us, and as men only have power, they may, under the present form of government, continue to exclude us. Suppose there are fourteen million of adult citizens who would vote—seven million of men and seven million of women. At least two million of the men are in favour of Woman Suffrage. Add them to the seven million of women, and our majority would be nine million to five million. Shall that majority remain bound hand and foot by such a minority? But men say that women won't vote. That is too late in the day. Wyoming has shown this statement to be untrue.

Thus have I carefully gone through the arguments, *pro* and *con*, and, as I think, both legally and logically, fully established the fact that women have, not only just as clear a natural right to participate in government as men have, but also that they have a constitutional and legal right conferred by the Supreme Court, and therefore that they are illegally, unconstitutionally, and tyrannically excluded.

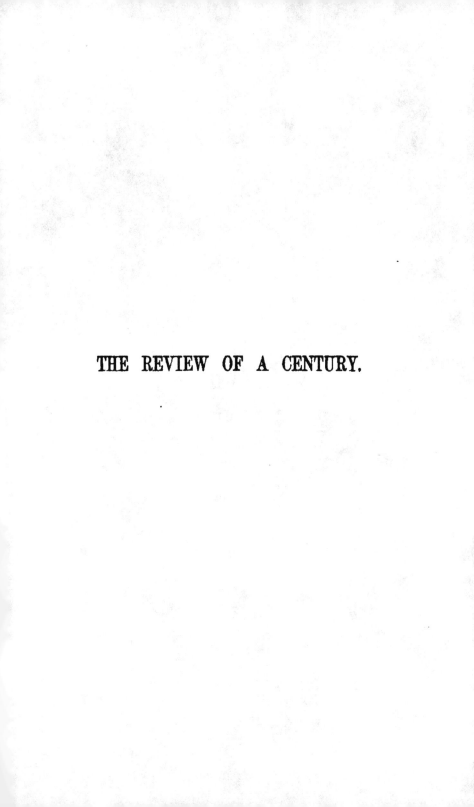

THE REVIEW OF A CENTURY.

THE

REVIEW OF A CENTURY;

OR,

THE FRUIT OF FIVE THOUSAND YEARS.

A LECTURE BY VICTORIA C. WOODHULL,

IN THE

Boston Theatre, Boston, October 22nd, 1876.

A HUNDRED years ago, in an upper room in Philadelphia, five men were gathered—men of noble bearing, of brilliant intellects, of undoubted character. Their faces wore a look of stern determination, as if the theme of their consideration were matters of grave import; were matters destined to be the beginning of the most important era that had ever dawned upon the earth. A century and eighty years before, a single shipload of men, women, and children had landed on this virgin soil at Jamestown in Virginia; and a few years later, another one at Plymouth Rock in Massachusetts. To these, additions had been made until the thirteen States then numbered full three million souls, over whom "the king" had placed obnoxious rulers, and upon whom he had imposed onerous taxation. The tea had been destroyed in Boston harbour, and the people were wrought up to the intensest pitch by their oppressions. They had come from their native lands to escape from tyranny, and were not disposed to brook it here. In this wild, free land, they had become pregnant of liberty, and were even then struggling in the throes of travail. These five men had met to find a way in which the delivery might be safely made, so that both the mother and the child should live to bless the world.

THE EARLY FATHERS.—Washington, Adams, Franklin, Rush, Paine—every one of them immortal names—struggled with the task with which God had entrusted them. They felt the great responsibility, and their faces, as they looked into each other's eyes, spoke their anxiety. Each knew that every other as well as self had something in his heart that he dared not utter. They looked inquiringly again and again for some yielding in some face. But they hesitated all. And well they might; for it was not the fate of three million people merely that was in their hands, but the future destinies of the world. One of these men had said but little; but the set features of his face showed a stern resolve; showed that he was waiting for the proper time in which to speak. He knew it would fall to him to break the way to say the words that each one felt but dared not speak; and speak at last he did; and they were the words of mighty import that came forth from him; words that were to deliver the people who had come to their full time—a birth that should herald a new race of people to the world; and they came forth from him as if all his powers were concentrated in the effort; as if that effort were the last struggle of the mother to bring forth her child; and the "four" caught up the child and became godfather to it, and they bore it to the people. The people recognized it as their own; took it to their hearts, and at once adopted it. Its name was—revolution—independence; and the words rang up and down the wave-washed shores, and fired the people with their inspiration—revolution as the means—independence as the end.

One hundred years have come and gone since that eventful

day, great with the future's destinies. Its hundredth anniversary has passed, and forty million people have commemorated the work of those five men; of those three million people commemorated it by re-affirming the truths that then were uttered for the first time in the world; commemorated it by brilliant flights of oratory, by firing cannon, and by profuse displays of "stars and stripes" harmoniously blended with the flags of almost every other nation of the globe, whose sons and daughters were participating in the glory of the day; with feasting, fireworks, with general rejoicing everywhere. As if, with a universal assent, these swarming millions re-echoed with a will the words that that stern man had uttered on that never-to-be-forgotten day a hundred years ago.

OUR COMMERCIAL GREATNESS.—But those three million people have expanded into forty; and the thirteen States to thirty-eight, besides ten territories and one district. The country now, excepting the stretch from the west shore of Lake Superior, and from the south-west point of Texas westward to the ocean, has a continuous water-front of not less than fifteen thousand miles, equal to that of the whole of Europe, available for commercial purposes. It is five thousand miles from east to west, and four thousand from north to south. It contains vast ranges of mountains, the longest river in the world, and the most fertile plains. Its climate is so varied and extensive that it produces almost everything that is grown anywhere in the world—the fruits of the tropics as well as of the latitudes north and south; and it will be the granary from which the world must ultimately draw its bread. It has all the different forms of mineral wealth—gold, silver, copper, iron, lead, besides coal, oil, and salt. No other country on the globe can begin to compare with it in the variety of its products; it combines the utilities of them all. It is as if all others had contributed their choicest seeds, as they have their peoples, to fill up the variety with which this should be blessed. In what-

16

ever sense in which it may be regarded, it is the great country of the world. No other can for a moment enter into comparison with it save in some single sense—while this combines the greatnesses of them all. Blessed with such a country—with a land such as God promised to His chosen people—"a land flowing with milk and honey"—how ought the people to have returned their gratitude to Him who gave it? Or rather, how have they done so?

Having already entered upon a second century, there could be a no more appropriate time in which to see what use there has been made of the "ten talents" with which the Great Husbandman has entrusted us; how we have shown our love for Him by that which we have given to our brethren; to see whether from His bounteous gifts to all, a part has stolen the inheritance from others, and when His servants have been sent whether they have been beaten away empty; whether some, having an abundance, have "shut up their bowels of compassion," though seeing their brothers in need; whether they have "fought the good fight," whether "kept the faith," whether "entitled to the crown" that St. Paul bespoke for them that love Him?

WHAT ARE OUR CENTENNIAL FRUITS?—In other words, what is the condition politically, industrially, socially, religiously? Is it such as will make us rejoice in its review? Are our centennial fruits such as He would pronounce good, so that we may rest upon the "seventh day from all our labours"?

In the first place, what have we done politically? It is to government that people largely owe their prosperity or adversity —a good government meaning continuous prosperity; a bad one, continuous adversity, or else alternate seasons of each, in which the latter consume the fruits of the former; in which the people see-saw, up and down, each decade; in which, like the Israelites, the people journey in the wilderness "forty years" in search of the promised land, to which God would bring them suddenly, if they would keep all His commandments, and neither worship nor sacrifice to the "Golden Calf."

The last estimates are, that there are forty-four million people now in the United States. It is by no means, however, to be inferred that these are all citizens who constitute the "sovereignty;" from whom the Government has its source, and upon whom it sheds its benignant rays. For, although the Constitution declares that "all persons born or naturalized in the United States, and subject to the jurisdiction thereof, are citizens:" and although there are unreversed decisions of the Supreme Court, that declares that every person in the country "constitutes a part of the political sovereignty," and that every such person is entitled to every right, civil and political, enjoyed by anyone in the State,—notwithstanding all this authority and law upon the subject, only a minority of the forty-four millions are really citizens. For, in the Dred Scott decision, the law of citizenship was declared to be this: "To be a citizen is to have the actual possession and enjoyment, or the perfect right to the acquisition and enjoyment, of an entire equality of privileges, civil and political." Dred Scott did not possess or enjoy these rights; therefore the court held that he was not a citizen. As this is the law of citizenship now, we must conclude that only those are citizens who have "the actual possession and enjoyment, or the perfect right of acquisition and enjoyment, of an entire equality of privileges, civil and political," the constitution to the contrary notwithstanding. The constitution in the hands of "the few," is a mere toy, with the plain language of which they play, making it to mean anything or nothing as it suits them now and then. Later we shall see that this was what it was intended to be; that it was a fraud, a cheat, from the beginning, into which neither the letter or spirit of the Declaration of Independence ever entered.

WHO ARE CITIZENS?—But who are citizens? Why, those who possess and enjoy, or have the right to acquire and enjoy,

16 *

an equality of political and civil privileges. Only certain classes of men possess these rights. These certain classes having possessed themselves of the machinery of the Government, tread upon the constitution and the decisions of the Supreme Court. They have stolen the birthrights of the "many," and say, "help yourselves if you can." The despoiled people are not able to help themselves now, but let these usurpers be warned that the judgments of God are upon this nation, and that He will come to help those who cannot help themselves against such tyranny ; come to deliver His people out of the hands of the Egyptians, who have imposed tasks upon them grievous to be borne; come to send them some "Moses," who shall cause "Pharaoh " to let the people go, and who shall bring them down from "Sinai's Mount " a new and better code of laws.

But who are not citizens, who neither possess or enjoy, nor have the right to acquire or enjoy, an equality of privileges, civil and political ? There are three classes of these people : Indians, Chinese, and women, and these constitute by a million more than one-half of all the people. The political lords have selected nice company for the women to keep politically, and yet they put on such monstrous airs if they are told that they have no respect for their mothers, wives, and daughters in this respect. Here is a subject for some Raphael, who should have reduced it to canvas and exhibited it at the Centennial, in honour of the mothers and daughters of the land. Upon the one hand there should have been grouped the women of the country, flanked upon the right and left by Indians and Chinese, and the subject named—political slaves; while upon the other the citizens should have been grouped, and labelled political sovereigns.

THE PRINCIPLES OF OUR GOVERNMENT.—The principles under the inspiration of which this government had its birth, are set forth in the Declaration of Independence. They were when realized by the people, when incorporated into the organic law,

to give them independence; and they were thought to be of so
much importance that the people fought a long and bloody war
to acquire a right to their possession and enjoyment. Who can
think of Bunker Hill, of Brandywine, of Princeton, of Valley
Forge, of Yorktown, think of those long eight years of alternate
hope and despair, and not feel that the price paid for independence was too great to have it limited to a mere minority of the
people, when it was purchased for the whole; was too great a
price to pay for principles that were to be restricted to less than
one-half of the descendants of those who paid it? Our fathers
would have never fought for the liberty to have a king or an
aristocratic ruler of their own. They endured the hardships and
privations of that war for independence for themselves and
their posterity. Nothing less than this was the inspiration of
those years of suffering, nothing less than this could have given
them inspiration to gain their independence.

But this was scarcely more than won before those from
whom this inspiration came were doomed to see their work
robbed of one-half its value. At the convention that met to
frame a government, there were men whose minds were too
narrow to grasp the significance of the truths that had been the
inspiration of the people; that had sustained them through the
war. They were men bred and born in English customs. They
were not willing to make a complete departure from the established legal forms of the mother-country, and make the declaration the inspiration of the Constitution, as it had been of the
revolution. That inspiration came from these truths, and they
were declared to be self-evident "that all men are created equal;
that they are endowed by their Creator with certain inalienable
rights; that among these are life, liberty, and the pursuit of
happiness; that to secure these rights governments are instituted among men, deriving their just powers from the consent
of the governed." No trace of any single one of these truths is
to be found in the Constitution as then adopted; nor in any of

the amendments that have since been added, save in Sec. I.
Art XIV., which the self-constituted citizens have rendered
nugatory.

OUR COPYING OF ENGLAND.—Our Constitution and laws have
nothing specifically American about them. They are copies
from the English modified in some particulars, which have been
the inducement "to gather the spoils while we may." The
President is an English king under another name, selected by the
"caucus," the worst element in politics, and elected by the people
because, under the vicious methods that are in vogue, they have
no way to vote save for one of the two at whom ten thousand
papers vie with each other in throwing mud during the campaign. Many who have come to know how Presidents are made
have abandoned the polls in disgust. The Senate is a badly
abridged edition of the House of Lords, while the House of
Representatives is the same as the House of Commons. In the
law of primogeniture only do our laws differ materially from
those of England, this good feature having been borrowed from
another source. Nor have we any political literature save the
Declaration of Independence which has a distinct national
character about it that is purely American, and it is this that
we celebrate year after year; it is this, and this only, that calls
out the patriotism of the people.

So far as the Constitution is concerned, it is Dead Sea fruit.
It is an old and musty English sermon to which we have
prefixed a new and vital text, the text and sermon having no
common ground or meaning. The condition of the people and
the country could scarcely have been worse had we had a king
and Parliament, instead of President and Congress. A tree,
let it be called by whatever name, is known by the fruit
it bears. If we are to judge the political tree in this country in
this way, shall we not be forced to say that we have gathered
thorns from grapes and thistles from figs? In purity in the
administration of justice our Government can stand no com-

parison with that of England. Money here is king, and judge and jury also. Then must there not be something radically wrong somewhere, and what can this be, except the engrafting of a new political idea into an old political system ? This is what is the matter, and, cringe as we may, there can never be a change greatly for the better until the institutions of the country are remodelled by the inspiration of that which led to their establishment.

OUR LACK OF GREAT STATESMEN.—Had there been any really great men among our statesmen they would have discovered the cause of the alternate "ups and downs " in the prosperity of the country, and, at least, attempted some remedy. But we may look in vain through the whole list of those who have, one after another, prominently occupied the public attention, for a great mind in the sense of instituting reforms in government; in replacing vicious by beneficent legislation. Washington, who will always be revered, was in no sense a great man save in goodness. As a general or statesman he has been excelled by dozens since his time, not one of whom has left anything behind him that will make his name immortal. Immortality in history requires to rest on some living basis of reform effected in the Government, or in the industrial habits, or in the religious faiths or rites, of the people. Buddha in India, Confucius in China, Zoroaster in Persia, Mahomet among Mahommedans, and Jesus among Christians, have immortality. But the religious element, *per se,* never would have civilized the world. Indeed, the nations most under the influence of religious sentiments have done the least to spread civilization into unknown countries. It is the warlike and intellectual, in contradistinction to the religious and æsthetic, nations to whom we owe the almost world-wide enlightenment of the present, while the latter have remained shut up within themselves, and are nothing but what their religion makes them. The contrast between Egypt and India or China is, in this respect, most striking. Egypt, becoming great at home, pushed out into the surrounding world. With its immense armies under Sesostris and its no less potent power emanating from the wise men who made the Alexandrian library a possibility, it left its impress so fixed upon the world that, even to this day, there are many things in the habits and customs of the people, especially in their literature and philosophies, that are Egyptian. It was an Egyptian colony which laid the foundation in Greece, at Athens, for the splendid civilization that was there developed; for the glory, the military renown, and the arts and sciences that afterwards made Greece at once the admiration and wonder of the world.

GREAT MINDS THE FOUNTAIN OF ALL GOOD.—The Egyptians were also a maritime people who made voyages for discovery. It was under the instructions of one of its kings—Nechos—that some skilful Phœnician sailors first sailed round the coast of Africa. Six hundred years B.C. an attempt was also made to do what the French engineer, Lesseps, has since done—to cut a canal across the Isthmus of Suez. I mention these facts to show how all the really great things that have done the world most good had their origin in some one great mind who still lives in the immortality of his creations, having impressed himself inexpugnably upon the descent of the race and on civilization; and by this showing to call attention to the further fact that the number of the great who live in the present is extremely small, and to finally show that this country has not produced even one such mind outside the purely intellectual plane. The names of Fulton and Field will live until steam, as a motor power, shall be superseded by some more potent agent, and until the telegraphic wires shall be no longer required to transmit the thoughts of one to another at the antipodes of the earth; but in government the list is blank.

Our basis must, however, be made still broader. Greece was founded upon principles brought from Egypt; but in that small country a new era was born. Egyptian achievements were the culmination of an era of civilization of which Greece was the fruit, and became the seed for the next. Not only did Greece dim the splendour of Egyptian warfare, but she also surpassed her in intellectual attainment. The names of Plato, Socrates, Aristotle, Archimedes, Xenophon, will live in philosophy as long as there is a literature; while Marathon, Thermopylæ, Salamis, Platæa, and Mycale will stand for ever unapproachable in military and naval glory, conclusive evidence of the power of order and organization over mere numbers and brute force.

THE POWER OF ELOQUENCE.—There was, however, another power behind this one of order which made it invulnerable, irresistible. Philip of Macedon, the father of Alexander the Great, testified of this power in these words: "The eloquence of Demosthenes did me more harm than all the armies and fleets of the Athenians. His harangues are like machines of war and batteries raised at a long distance, by which all my projects and enterprises are ruined. Had I been present and heard that vehement orator declaim, I should have been the first to conclude that it was necessary to declare war against me. Nor could I reach him with gold, for in this respect, by which I had gained so many cities, I found him invulnerable." Antipater also said of the same power: "I value not the galleys nor armies of the Athenians. Demosthenes alone I fear. Without him the Athenians are no better than the meanest Greeks. It is he who rouses them from their lethargy and puts arms into their hands almost against their wills. Incessantly representing the battles of Marathon and Salamis, he transforms them into new men. Nothing escapes his penetrating eye, nor his consummate prudence. He foresees all our designs, he countermines all our projects, and disconcerts us in everything. Did the Athenians confide in him and follow his advice we should be irredeemably undone."

'Tis true that this was in the days of the declining Grecian glory; but it is none the less true that it was the same power in others previously that lifted a whole people to sublime achievements and into grand and noble character. It was here, also, that patriotism had birth ; here that men devoted their lives to their country for the country's sake rather than for private gain or glory. In this respect the character of Grecian generals and statesmen has never been approached in any other nation. It was this character that gave the Greeks as a nation, and to the world as an example, the first code of laws ; gave a constitution as a conservatory of the people's rights, and made a Lycurgus possible, the principles of whose Spartan code are only now beginning to be appreciated. It is to this code that we must look as the prime source of political economy, and it has been the inspiration of all the modifications of laws ever made in the interests of the people. In this respect, Lycurgus will be known in future ages as the Spartan law-giver of the world.

LESSONS FROM ROMAN HISTORY.—Roman history is a second edition of Grecian, enlarged in its sphere of operations and in influence over the world. Rome, however, would have never been possible, had Greece not been at first a fact. But Rome was vitiated in the character of her public men, as compared with those of Greece, in about the same ratio that she was greater in other respects. Greece was the admiration of the world, but Rome was its astonishment. All that she was, sunk with her as she went down into the dark ages. The best of what made Greece still lives in the people of the world. Greece was the garden of modern civilization and will remain its inspiration until three elements of character—the religious, the intellectual, and the social—shall join their powers to construct the future government of the world.

Charlemagne was the basis of the first great national character that evolved after the dark ages, and Otho the Great laid the foundation for the present dominance of Bismarck and Von Moltke in Central Europe. Cromwell, more than any other, is the inspiration of English character, modified by its respect for the political rights of women through the influence of Queen Elizabeth, under whom England reached the acme of its power and glory. But in French history is to be found the most distinct evidence of a communication to a whole people of the character of a single individual that there is to be found anywhere. The French character, both as a nation and as an individual, may be summed up in one word—Bonaparte. With the advent of this giant mind came a crisis over all modern Europe. Under his influence not only did the national character of the French people change, but the individual character also underwent many modifications. Nor was this confined to France, for this man's genius was felt in every capital in the world. He conquered the nations and compelled them to change their laws, while to France he gave an entire new Code, to which, more than to anything else, France owes her position among nations. It was the result of these laws that gave to France the capacity to rise from the disaster inflicted upon her by Prussia. Her immense loans came in small sums from the peasantry, and when paid will remain in France, which will not suffer the double impoverishment that most nations suffer from a public debt. The possibility of this was due to the far-reaching statesmanship of Napoleon Bonaparte, when he changed the laws regarding the inheritance of property, taking the estate from the deceased and dividing it equally among all the children —the greatest innovation that had ever been made upon the old feudal system, and together with other reforms fixing France in a position to become more prosperous internally than any other European nation. Bonaparte also broke down the barriers that divided the nations and races of Europe, and opened up the way for closer commercial and literary relations, and performed, during the twenty years that he was in France, a greater service for the advancement of civilization than was ever performed by any other person who ever lived. In a sense, and in a good sense too, it may be said that he dictated to the world, because the changes that he instituted and compelled have produced a modifying influence over the whole world.

LYCURGUS AND BONAPARTE.—It is, therefore, to Lycurgus and to Bonaparte, more than to any others, to whom we must look as the master-minds in government; as those who instituted sweeping changes in the political institutions of the world. Many slight reforms have been effected; but they alone conceived and reduced to a system the changes that revolutionized and replaced the old beneficently to the people.

Bonaparte himself recognized that his greatness consisted in this, for, when he asked his friends to which of his achievements he would owe his place in history, and they replied naming some campaign or battle, he corrected them and said : "I shall go down in history with my *Code Napoleon* in my hands." So it was not Marengo, not Wagram, not Austerlitz, not Dresden, not any nor all his great victories to which he looked as his best achievement; but it was the code of laws by which he made France the happiest country in Europe. It is not to be wondered at that his name lives in the hearts of the French and moves them as no other name ever moved a people.

Great as Bismarck may be, he is not great in the true sense of greatness, for he is building up a power that the next fifty years will have to overthrow. True greatness works in the direction of and not against progress, and its works live. Compared with him, Disraeli may after all, should his intentions towards India have a humanitarian tendency, turn out to be the greater man.

In this view of greatness, to whom shall we look among our statesmen for any of its evidences ? Beyond the legislation that the abolition of slavery forced upon us, the homestead act and one recently introduced by General Banks, enlarging its scope in the interests of the settler, and some concessions to the people, like the eight-hour law, we may search the legislation of the country through in vain for any evidence of humanitarian tendencies in our legislators. On the contrary, the inspiration of the privileged classes, the power and use of wealth will be found everywhere; 'tis true that we have a Republican Government in name and form, but it is also true that money rules, that it elects the officers and controls the legislation. The people who are outside the privileged classes, outside the offices and the press, are powerless to help themselves. The machinery of the government is in the hands of those who want things to continue as they are, while the few in power who are devoted to the public welfare, beat the air in vain attempts to strike either the causes of or the remedy for existing evils.

NEED OF A NEW CODE OF LAWS.—But they may be summed up in a few words. The causes lie in the fruitless attempt to run a Republican Government upon an aristocratic code of laws, and the remedy is to remodel the code by the principles of the declaration which should be made the inspiration of every provision, as well as the key to its construction. I might enumerate the special evils that have grown out of the error made in the Constitution—the vicious legislation for which this error laid the foundation—that the rule of the majority is not a republican idea; that "the majority" is another name for the despot; that minorities are entitled to, and can be represented; I might show that the United States is, after all, nothing but a confederation of equal and antagonistic powers, and not a Federal Union; that Washington is more a place in which representatives from the several States assemble to quarrel over the spoils of office, and to lay the ropes for the succession, than it is the capital of a free and mighty people; that there is such a contrariety of laws in the several States upon any given subject, that it puzzles a Philadelphia lawyer to tell whether a given act is a crime, a misdemeanour, or whether actionable at all in the different States; if people be married in one State, whether they are so legally in any other; or if divorced, the same. I might show that taxation is unequal and oppressive, and the revenue unjust; and if there were need of it, which there is not, that official patronage is a polite name for public plunder, and that the public service is a vast system of organized corruption. Had the original error not been made, had the fountain been kept pure, none of these baneful things could have been engrafted into the system. But they have now obtained a root so deep that they can never be exterminated save by uprooting the system. They are the Canada thistles in the fertile meadow that spread themselves until they absorb the whole vitality of the soil and thrust out the useful harvest. These thistles have spread and seeded in the government until they have thrust out every honest servant of the people, and until one who has any care for his reputation cannot afford to meddle with the government.

MUST WE HAVE A REVOLUTION ?—How can such a state of things be remedied save by revolution ? The people may listen to the "outs" who pretend to tell them that it may; but should they come to the "ins" they would follow in the footsteps of their predecessors. The machine is running down-hill too fast to be now stopped ; the tide of power is set too strongly toward corruption to be reversed ; the political body is too thoroughly impregnated with the poison to make its purging possible by any change of medicine. The disease is incurable because it is in the system more than in the individual men who run it. It has had its youth, its manhood, and is now in its old and decaying age. No power can save it ; and those who think they can, who think that they can patch it up with tonics for a time, are only preparing for a worse ruin when the crash shall come.

But the people would not care so much about the government ; they would be willing to let the politicians run it as they please and enjoy its spoils as they have for a century;

they would even endure, as they have, uncomplainingly, any extortion that their earnings would permit without reducing them to the starvation point; but when in addition to the absorption of all their earnings to pay the debts of official extravagance and vicious legislation it is threatened to foreclose the mortgages on the industries and sell them out, and thus take away their means of livelihood, they have a right, indeed it is their duty, to object, and they are beginning to do it in real earnest.

Like all other people engaged in a bad cause, when given rope enough, the politicians are preparing to hang themselves and those whom they have served so well, who perhaps are not aware of what fate is in store for them; that there is already a noose tightening around their throats, that the long and silently suffering people, when they shall see the game that has been played upon them, will not hesitate to draw the cords until some reparation shall be made for the ills that have been brought upon the country.

THE ROOT OF THE TROUBLE.—We come now in logical order to the grand and fundamental error that has been made and which lies at the back of all political fallacies, and to which are to be primarily attributed all industrial and financial ills from which we suffer, both as a nation and as individuals: since, let the Government be as good as they may, with this error lying between it and the industries, it were impossible that evil should not come upon the people. Hence, let the Government and the public service be as bad as they may; let the people suffer from bad legislation as much as they have; the fault is, after all, more to be charged against the system than against the individuals who, for the time, are its administrators. No matter how skilful the engineer may be, nor how watchful the fireman, if the engine itself be faulty in construction, it will explode; or if the engine be perfect in itself, but connected with other machinery that is not fitted to run at the same speed as the engine, then the machinery will fly in pieces. The same is true of the relations between the Government—the political organization of the people—the wealth producers—the industrial organization of the people, as we shall see, for the Government is a machine constructed after the highest known principles of political mechanism, while intimately connected with it, is the industrial organization, running upon the very lowest—the rudimental—industrial mechanism. Consequently when the political machinery runs at a high rate of speed, requiring an extra amount of fuel and water, the industrial machinery, in its efforts to supply this demand, and urged on by its connection to keep pace with the rapid motion, flies in pieces; becomes prostrated and useless as we see it everywhere in the country now, when to keep the political machinery running at the present high rate of speed, it has to draw upon its accumulated stock of fuel, as it is doing now to the amount of $700,000,000 annually.

If we go back, and examine the evolution of government and industry, all this will be made clear; so clear that all may understand it. Certainly, fixed laws direct and regulate the growth of everything, and they are the same for all departments in the universe. The statement of the laws by which the sidereal and solar systems have been evolved, will also describe those which the earth has obeyed, and are the laws of all material, governmental, industrial, intellectual, social, moral, and religious change. This law as applied to government and industry may be stated in philosophic terms, thus: The progress of government and industry is a continuous establishment of physical relations within the community, in conformity to physical relations arising within the environment, during which the government, industry, and the environment pass from a state of incoherent homogeneity to a state of coherent heterogeneity; and, during which, the constitutional units of the government and industry become ever more distinctly individualized.

If we examine the growth of industry and government, and the relations that exist between them now, in this country, we shall discover how far they have advanced from incoherent homogeneity toward coherent heterogeneity. Looking through the dim vistas of the past into the pre-historic time, we find a time when there were no aggregations of individuals larger than the family; that the family was the only government and the only organization for industry; that its head ruled with arbitrary sway, having no one to whom he was accountable, each family having to depend wholly upon itself for subsistence. The people then were in the same state politically and industrially, and this was the homogeneous or original state. Afterwards we find that, for protection or for conquest, two or more families combined in a political sense and formed tribes, having an absolute head, but remaining in the rudimentary state industrially; next, tribes came together and built cities, and cities then coalesced and constituted nations (whereof the rulers still used arbitrary power), until single rulers aspired to the dominion of the world; and in a sense succeeded. But all this time, industrially, the people remained in the original state. There had been no coalescings for the purpose of subsistence as there had been for government. While politically the people had evolved through several stages of progression, industrially they were still in the rudimentary state.

Having arrived at the culmination of growth in the line of absolute power, one man having controlled the destinies of the world (thus typifying the future yet to be when the world shall be united under a humanitarian, in place of a despotic government; under the rule of all, instead of that of one), a new departure was set up in the direction of this future condition, and the power to which one man aspired began to redistribute itself in limited and constitutional monarchies, down through kings and queens, nobility and republics, to the people generally,

17

in this country advancing so far as to be divided practically among nearly one-half of the people, and theoretically among the whole. Evolution on this line will go on till every person in the world shall form a part of the government. Then the great human family will be a possibility.

SOCIAL EXPERIMENTS.—But up to the present time, what have the people done industrially? Almost nothing, save to subsist themselves on the rudimental plan! Nothing, save to make a few experiments at coalescing. There are a few illustrations of the first step in progress in this respect, which correspond to the coming together of families politically. But there are no industrial cities, to say nothing about nations. There were Brook Farm, New Harmony, and several other attempts at industrial tribes, and there are Oneida and a dozen lesser attempts still in existence, besides numerous co-operative movements. There are the railroad, the telegraph, insurance companies, banks and other corporations, all evidences that a real departure is about to be made in industrial organization; that is, that the people are preparing to depart from the homogeneous state industrially. The Granger movement in which, to protect themselves against the rapacity of merchants and railroads, they combine to purchase from first hands and realize a saving of from twenty to fifty per cent., is the most positive evidence of the moving of the people generally in this direction. This is an illustration of coalescing for protection. Most of the other illustrations, such as railroads, banks, &c., are in many cases for aggressive purposes. Nevertheless, they are all evidences of progress in the industrial sense; those for aggression in the end compelling others for protection. That there are so many forms of coalescing for aggressive purposes, is conclusive evidence that the time is near when the people will be driven into organizing themselves into industrial communities, cities, and nations, and eventually into one nation for the whole world. The first departure having been made, nothing can prevent industry from passing through the same stages of progress through which government has passed, and eventually becoming "at one" with government.

Has the evolution of government proved a blessing to the people? Are we, as a people, in a better condition politically? Are we nearer the ultimate condition than were they of ancient time, when the family was the highest form of government? If we are, then we should be equally improved, industrially, if we were upon the same plane in this respect. There are no contradictions in natural growth. Like degrees of evolution bring equal good in all; the same to government, to industry, to intellect, to morals, to religion. But this development does not mean for the rich what it is inferred by them to mean, unless, indeed, they attempt to resist its progress, which, if they do, the same fate will overtake them that came upon those who attempted to stay the tide of political growth. It means for them just what the development of government meant for those who held and exercised its power. The political relations of the monarch and nobility are repeated in the industrial relations of the capitalists and working-men. The "levelling," politically, has not been down but up. Instead of the rulers having been degraded into serfdom, the serfs have been elevated to the plane of rulers in this country. In the place of one man ruling over others, all men rule themselves, at least in theory. In this transformation no one has been deprived of anything that of right belonged to him; but the masses have received their natural rights from those who held them from them by the right of might. When the industries shall rise to the stage of growth which the Government occupies, a like "levelling up" will take place; a like relinquishment of industrial power will be made in favour of the toiling masses. None who are independent now will be made dependent then; but the dependent will rise to independence. Hence the alarm of the rich is wholly without foundation. Such a move does not mean the slightest harm for them; it

17 *

means equal good for all. It does not mean the taking away of any comfort or luxury from anybody; but the extension of every comfort and luxury that any have to all—to those who suffer or hunger, from nakedness, for shelter.

OUR NATIONAL DEBT.—If this analysis be applied to the present situation we shall see what is the matter with the industries. When the South rebelled, the North was compelled to resist or else permit the national unity to be destroyed. Let it be borne in mind what stress was put upon the necessity of preserving the oneness of the people politically. To do this an army was required. When volunteers ceased to offer in sufficient numbers to keep the army to its necessary strength, the Government, acting upon the right of a representative of a politically united people, resorted to drafting to determine which of the members of this unity should go into the army and jeopardize their lives for its preservation. This was in perfect harmony with the principles of government upon which this order rests, and was fully endorsed by the people. But what did the Government do to subsist these men, and to provide the munitions of war? Did it proceed the same way that it did to secure the men? Not at all! It borrowed the money from the bankers of New York, Hamburg, and London, and agreed to pay them a rate of interest double that demanded of any other first-class nation, parting with its bonds to them at "60." In other words, it borrowed $1,800,000,000 at 10 per cent., and gave $1,200,000,000 in bonds as bonus for making the loan.

Now this was the error that was committed; for, although the people were industrially upon a lower order of development than they were politically, nevertheless, since necessity knows no law save that of its own conditions, the Government should have proceeded as though we were upon the same plane in both respects. When it called for volunteers to raise an army, and the ranks of industry responded liberally, it should at the same time have also called for volunteer assistance from the ranks of wealth to subsist that army; and, as it resorted to drafting to maintain the necessary number of fighting men when volunteering failed to do it, so should it have resorted to drafting the means with which to pay their expenses when volunteer assistance should have failed to do it. Had the people been one industrially as they were one politically; had the industrial organization of the people been upon the same plane with their political organization, this would have been done naturally, and there would have been no bonded debt incurred.

What does this show? This, clearly—that, while the Government can command the lives of the working-men, and put them in jeopardy—even sacrifice them without stint to maintain itself —it has no power over the property of the rich to compel them to assist in that maintenance. Had it been so that the Government could not have borrowed any money, it would have fallen from this disparity between the political and industrial development. Is not this clear? And if it be, does not it show a very great and grave defect in the wisdom of our institutions?

But what has been the effect of this error in this instance? The present prostration of industry, necessarily; and it has come about in this way: The armies were made up from the ranks of industry; the "rank and file" were so many men taken away from producing, and therefore from adding to the accumulated wealth; but the maintenance of the army was borrowed at an exorbitant rate of interest from the accumulated wealth, which was wholly in the hands of those who never fired a shot in defence of the country, nor added a dollar to its aggregate wealth by labour. While the war continued, the men who were left in the ranks of industry were called upon to pay this interest; and when it was over, those who had survived the war and returned to productive toil were included with them. And it is expected that the industrial classes will continue to pay this interest until the bonds mature, and then the bonds themselves, as I shall show you that they do hereafter; or, what is more to the point, for the $1,800,000,000 that the Government borrowed from the money-lenders it would compel the people to return them as bonus, interest, and principal, the enormous sum of $5,000,000,000.

INDUSTRY OVERBURDENED.—Hence, by this error, made possible by the false relations of government and industry, the Government has not only compelled industry to furnish the men to fight its battles, win its victories, and maintain its integrity, but it also compels it to pay all the expenses of the war, besides to continue adding to the wealth of the rich. The gentlemen in whose interests it was principally fought, who have sat quietly at home in luxury and drawn the life-blood from the poor, now go out of all the effects of the war with their fortunes trebled by having merely loaned the Government the money it needed to maintain itself in the struggle.

This is a true picture, moderately drawn, of the real facts. While I do not desire to stir up the wrongs that industry has suffered in this matter, and drive the weary toilers to seek redress, it is nevertheless time, when thousands of families are suffering the pangs of hunger as a consequence of this wrong, to lay it open before the people who have been its cause and who have profited by it; it is time that the Government should be shown the errors that it has committed, and be told that the people are coming to an understanding of them; time that the bondholders should know that the people are aware of the tenure by which they hold these mortgages on the industries. Let the one protest as it may, and the other plead innocence under the revelations as they will, I intend to do everything in my power to rouse them to a sense of the danger in which they stand from the still sleeping masses, who, when they shall come to a full realization of the impositions that have been practised upon them, will not hesitate at any means of redress; especially will they not hesitate when the modern Shylocks shall relentlessly demand the last "pound of flesh" from them, in utter disregard of the blood that it may cost to yield it. The people already begin to learn that the Government has no sympathy for their sufferings, and that it declares that it has no power to alleviate them, which they will think is strange enough, since it had the power to inflict them.

WHAT LABOUR WILL SAY.—Under these conditions they will soon come to argue like this : Was it not enough to demand of industry that it could fight the battles for the Government ? Was it not enough that the working classes should lay down their lives by thousands upon a hundred fields of battle ? Was it not enough that mothers and wives should give their sons and husbands to fill the soldier's grave that the wealth of the country might remain inviolate ? Was it not enough that we did all this, without now being forced to give our toil year after year to return these rich, who did nothing, these loans ? Is it too much to ask of wealth that it pay the expenses of the war ? Should we not rather demand that it shall pay them, in tones of thunder if lower ones are insufficient to rouse its holders to a sense of their duty, that it shall bear its part of the burden ? We have looked on quietly and seen the sufferings to which this people are reduced by the rapacity of the usurers, until we can no longer hold our peace ; and, if it be in our power, we intend that wealth, and not industry, shall yet be made to pay what it should have been made to pay at first ; that it shall return to the Government the bonds which the toiling masses have redeemed by the rivers of blood that they have shed, and that it shall also return the $2,000,000,000 of interest that it has already filched from industry for interest on this most unjust debt. In other words, since we gave from our ranks the lives that it was necessary to sacrifice in order to conquer the rebellion, we intend that the rich shall give from what they had when the rebellion broke out, to pay all the expenses of the war, and we will never rest until this be done.

These, I say, are the arguments to which the suffering

labourers will resort if you permit them to be driven to desperation by hunger from want of employment. If the rich were wise, they would forestall all opportunity for such arguments to be used, by coming forward voluntarily to do them justice. If what I have suggested as their arguments be true, as you know that it is, then wealth should pay the expenses of the war without any further delay, because it is a gross injustice, not to say an unwarrantable imposition on good nature, to make the men who did the fighting also pay this debt, while those for whom it was mostly fought have done nothing but to speculate out of it. Perhaps you have never looked at it in this light; but if you have not, then I pray you look at it so now, before your attention shall be called to it in an unpleasant way; for, unless relief comes soon to those who are suffering the pangs of hunger, by reason of your blindness, there will be an imperious demand made of you.

THE SILVER QUESTION.—As if they were not yet satisfied with the oppressions already in operation, some of those whom you have sent to Washington to conduct your business, and who have got you into all this difficulty, think that silver is not good enough money in which to pay interest, because it is not now worth quite so much as gold. Where has the wisdom and prudence of this people fled? Have they no care for what *may* come upon their families, that they sit by and see indignity after indignity piled mountain-high upon the people? The lives, the labour, the all of the poor may be taken for the public good; but your bonds, your money, your usury must not be touched. They are of more consequence than life and toil and everything else that the poor have got to be taken!—your revenue must be sacred, and the Shylocks must take their "pound of flesh" from the daily labourer, let it cost whatever blood it may in the cutting of it; and no wise Portia comes to stay the hand already dripping with the life of the toilers—for is not the interest wrenched from their toil, their life? Look at the poor of the country; millions of them without work and their families either starving or else on the verge of it. Let me read you extracts from two articles from the New York *Sun*, July 20th, so that you may see that I am not overdrawing the picture: "Starvation in New York. The sufferings among the poor are fearful. The sufferers are chiefly widows and young children, who, for lack of nourishment, are unable to withstand the intense heat. Instances of actual starvation are mentioned. A widow and her young daughter and son, who are unable to find work, have been for some time living on two dollars a week. In a garret, without any other furniture than an old dry goods box for a table and a broken chair, live a widow and her five young children. In a closet are a mattress and a blanket, which at night make a bed for the whole family. An aged woman, who was once in affluent circumstances, was some time ago found nearly dead from hunger; it was only by careful nursing that she was saved. A young man, whose family were gradually starving, was driven to despair and intended suicide. The child of another died, and not only was the father unable to bury it but he was unable to provide food for the living." These are only a few of the cases that come under the observation of a single church relief society. What shall we say of the great city? The other was entitled "'Widespread Destitution in Brooklyn.' At the meeting of the King's County Charity Commissioners yesterday Mr. Bogab said that there was almost as much destitution in the city now as at midwinter. The families of unemployed men, who up to this time have never asked for a cent of charity, were daily besieging his office. The system of outdoor relief had been abandoned, and there was no way to provide for the needy except out of his private purse. The heads of families were forced into idleness by the hard times, and, having exhausted all their means, were face to face with starvation." Is not this a fearful picture of those who have helped to make the wealth with which the store-houses of the country are loaded? African slavery was a blessing compared with the condition of thousands of the poor. Let its evils have been as great as we know that they were, the negroes never suffered for food; the women and children never died of starvation; never suffered from cold or went naked. Oh, that some master mind, some master spirit, might be sent of God to show you the way out of this desolation and the necessity of deliverance. But I fear you will not be wise enough to avoid the penalty for neglecting to keep your industrial institutions on the same plane with your political organization, which is the only possible remedy for the present evils. The people must be made as much one industrially as they are politically. Then there would be harmony and consequent peace and prosperity.

Is CASTE A NECESSITY?—But to this the common objection is raised, that it is impossible to make industrial interests common, on account of the necessary differences in labour: that there must be caste in industry. This was the reply that the king made to the people, who wanted a political republic; of course it will be the reply that the privileged classes will make to those who want an industrial republic. You know how fallacious the objection has been politically. The king deprived of his crown has not been compelled to sleep with the scavenger. It will prove equally as fallacious industrially. The money and railroad kings will not have to live with the men who do the rough work of the industrial public, unless they choose to do so, any more than they do now. The foundation-stones of a house always remain at the bottom, covered up in the dirt; nevertheless, they are even more important to the safety of the house than any upper part. So it will be in the industrial structure when it shall be erected. There will always be Vanderbilts, Stewarts, Fields and Fultons—the agents of the people industrially, as there are now presidents, governors, and mayors, agents of the people politically. And do you not see how perfectly this corresponds to the teachings of Jesus when He said : " Let him who would be greatest among you be the servant of all," and with this falls the objection of the aristocrat to the industrial republic, as utterly untenable.

The real inspiration of this objection, however, springs from quite another source. Those who make it know that, with the coming of industrial organization, the power which money has to increase will fall, and make it impossible for anybody to live without labour. Money has no rightful power to increase. Its origin and sphere distinctly forbid this power as can be clearly shown. The theory that money is wealth is false. It came to be accepted from the fact that valuable things have been used as money.

Wealth is the product of labour; is anything that labour produces or gathers. But the functions of money are representative wholly. Money takes the place of wealth for the time—stands for it. Here is the fallacy of a specie basis for money : Specie is wealth and can be made a basis for the issue of money, but the error consists in making a distinction against other kinds of wealth, which would be equally as good. Anything that has value may properly be made a basis for the issue of a currency.

If we trace the origin of money, all this will be made plain. At the basis of all questions relating to wealth and money lie the elements—the land, the water, the air, and these are the free gifts of God to man. None have the right to dispossess others of their natural inheritance in these elements. The right to life carries along with it the right to the use of so much of each of these elements as is necessary to support it. No one has a natural right to more than this. Hence, men have no more right to seize upon the land and deprive others of its use, or part with it to others for a consideration, than they have to bottle the air for the same purpose. There can be no ownership of the elements; no more of the land than in the air or water. Pretended ownership is another name for an usurpation. But the elements, unused, are valueless. Labour applied to them yields results, and these are valuable, consequently wealth ; the net results after assisting the people are the accumulated wealth of the world, and there is no other wealth.

MONEY THE ROOT OF ALL EVIL.—If every person were to produce all the different things he needs or wants, there would be no use for money, and the people would escape the curses that follow in its trail, but experience taught labourers that it was an economy for each to labour in some special way, and to exchange his surplus products for those of others labouring in different ways. Besides, the different climates produce different commodities, of each of which all other climates require a share. Out of these facts came agencies for effecting exchanges—money, the merchant, and commerce. In their origin and normal functions they are the agents, the servants of labour: but when from exchanging the products of labour they grew into speculating in these products, then they assumed abnormal functions and became the masters of labour. It must be seen, therefore, that the only legitimate method by which wealth can increase is by adding to itself the net results of labour; indeed that is the only way in which it can increase. It must also be clear that these results belong *in toto* to their producers, since, if nothing were exchanged save equivalents, these results could never pass from the hands of their producers. But by permitting the representatives of wealth—money—to have the power to increase, the makers of money have been able to filch all the net earnings from labour, and as a result of this, most of the accumulated wealth of the world is in the hands of the makers of money instead of in those of the makers of wealth. This may be legal, but can never be made just. Had the labourers been let alone they would have continued to produce and exchange their commodities among themselves without any trouble, and they could have always maintained themselves comfortably. But the "middle men"—their agents—conceived, constructed, and thrust upon them a vicious system of money, by which they are to pay tribute on everything that passes from, or is received by, them, which tribute amounts to the total net products of all the industries.

THE FEAR OF COMMUNISM.—But it may be objected that all this tends towards communism. Only bigots and the unthinking are frightened by a name or a shadow from an examination into anything. Perhaps at first it will create surprise when I tell you that the only really good institutions that we have are purely communistic. The public highways are a perfect illustration of communism. They are constructed and maintained at the public expense for the public benefit. All grades of people meet upon them on an equality, and yet no one either loses his identity in the mass or is deprived of any of his private rights, or of any of his personalities. By the principles upon which the industries are conducted and that governs their relations to wealth, the poor man who owns no property would have no right to use the highways. The same is true of the public schools. The children of the rich, who, it is falsely pretended, pay the taxes to support the schools, and the children of the poor there, meet upon an equality. The schools are not a public necessity, they are only a public good. Who will pretend to say that they are not an improvement on the old system, of every family conducting its own education, or of a few families combining to do so? Everybody recognizes the public advantage of a communal basis for the education of all the children; recognizes that the public good demands that the community shall not only provide school privileges, but shall insist on every child having the benefit of them, not for the good of the child so much as for the common good. Now this is communism. Why are you not frightened at the communistic tendencies of the public schools? Because, without thinking them to be communistic, you have adopted them and found them to be good.

Next is the post-office—a still better illustration in an industrial sense. Here the Government conducts the business of the people. If the system were maintained wholly instead of partially from the public treasury, it would be purely communistic. Is there anyone who is prepared to say that the postal system is not an improvement on the transmission of letters by private enterprise? And yet nobody is affrighted at the communistic character of the modern post-office. Suppose that this system were extended to the transportation of every-thing that is interchanged among the people, have we not a right to assume that the same beneficent results that have followed the development of the public mails would also follow there? We have not only the right to assume, but we have the reason to know, that it would, and that the railroad question and railroad wars would be for ever settled by such an advance towards communism, and an immense stride be made towards the organization of the industries as a whole; and this is what we have done industrially.

THE ELEMENTS OF OUR POPULATION.—It is an instructive lesson to analyze the population of the country, to resolve them into the several classes. First, from the 44,000,000 there are to be taken the classes that count for nothing—the Indians, the Chinese, and the women, for though they are permitted to live in the country, they form no part of the sovereignty. "They are," as Justice Cartter asserted when endeavouring to prove that women are not entitled to the ballot, "citizens in whom citizenship is dormant." In round numbers these classes are 23,000,000. Of the remaining 21,000,000, 11,000,000 are adults, who are the sovereignty and who conduct the govern-ment. Of these 3,000,000 are farmers; 2,000,000 are manu-facturers, miners, and lumbermen; 1,000,000 are unskilled labourers; 1,000,000 are merchants of all kinds, including dispensers of leaf and liquid damnation; 1,000,000 are gentle-men of ease who live by their wits—their sharpness and shrewdness—bond-holders, money-lenders, landlords, gamblers, confidence men, &c., &c.; 500,000 are clerks; 250,000 are permanent invalids; 200,000, criminals; 100,000, paupers; 100,000, insane; 100,000, weak-minded; 100,000, professional teachers; 100,000, employés of the national Government; 100,000 of the State, county and municipal governments; 90,000, physicians; 60,000, ministers; 50,000, lawyers; and 50,000, editors and professional writers and actors. A large part of the property of the farmers is mortgaged to the money-lenders, and the same is true of the manufacturers, while the liabilities of the merchants exceed their assets. So, really, the fifth class—the gentlemen of ease—either own or else hold mortgages on the whole property of the country. Can such a state of injustice as this continue? And if it cannot, what shall take its place? It is time that those who hold the wealth should, for their own sake, be asking this question seriously, unless they would incur the risk of having it answered for them as the same was answered in France in '93. Public injustice, unless remedied peaceably, always has terminated in revolution; and it will continue so to terminate as long as it is not remedied in a wiser way by those who have the power to do it.

A LAW-GIVER NEEDED.—Having fallen into the errors to which I have referred; into the hands of mediocre and incompetent legislators, without even a single statesman among them all; into the times of small minds and smaller measures that do not look beyond the day in which they are proposed; into industrial, financial, and commercial ruin, with one-half the wealth-producing power starving in idleness, and no one seeming to even think what the end of this must be; having fallen into all these ills, the country needs that a giant mind shall spring into its councils, or else into its legislation, which shall be able to grasp the helm of the ship of State now floundering hopelessly in the trough of the industrial sea, and put her before the wind again; a mind that shall have tho wisdom and the courage to show their puerility to those who occupy the posts of honour, and, by the mere force of will, lift them into the right path; show them that beneath the surface of that which they seem to think is peaceable enough, there is a raging, seething earthquake ready at the slightest occasion to burst forth and swallow everything in its path, and compel them by active measures to guide its powers rather than by inaction to provoke an eruption. This country needs that God shall let loose a law-giver upon it: one who shall understand what has led to the present situation; what the exigencies of the people demand, and who shall have the ability to propose and the power to enforce the needed remedies—a Lycurgus to give a new code of laws that shall be the incarnation of the principles of the Declaration of Independence, which alone of all principles have any influence to mould the people and from which they draw the characteristics that distinguish them from the other nations of the earth; and a Bonaparte to sweep out of the way the accumulating débris of years of vicious legislation and in its place inaugurate that code: a Lycurgus with his code of laws ; a Bonaparte with his genius to command, and, combined with these, the vehement power of a Demosthenes to rouse the people to a sense of the danger in which they stand and whether they will or no lead them through a peaceable, rather than permit them to plunge into a bloody revolution. Let this be done, no matter in what form this power may come, and a change of greater magnitude for good to this people than that proposed by Lycurgus for the Spartans, or that instituted in France by Bonaparte, will be inaugurated here.

But what has been done socially? Much of which I have not the time to speak, but this, as to what I would have for the social condition:

WORDS TO WOMEN.—If the evils of industry were removed a great many social ills would cease. For instance, if women were independent, industrial members of the community, they would never be forced into distasteful, ill-assorted, or convenient marriages, which are the most fruitful of all the sources of vice and crime in children, and consequently in the community. But beyond the industrial and dependent relations of the sexes there are many purely social ills that as much as those of industry require a remedy. Marriage is regarded as a too frivolous matter; is rushed into and out of in a haste that shows an utter ignorance or else a total disregard for its responsibilities and as if it were an institution specially designed for the benefit of the selfish wishes and passions of the sexes. But to look at marriage in this light is to not see it at all in that of the public good, or, ultimately, in that of individual happiness. Marriages that are based upon selfishness or passion can never result in anything save misery to all concerned. Men and women who cannot look above these interests, who do not recognize that these interests should be secondary, who, after finding that their personal feelings would lead them to marry, cannot coolly ask themselves, Are we prepared to become God's architects to create His images? and be governed by the truthful reply, are not fit to marry. Many have the idea that I am opposed to marriage; but nothing could be further from the truth. I am opposed to improper marriages only: to marriages that bring unhappiness to the married, and misery to their fruits; and such as do this, had I the power, I would prohibit. I would guard the door by which this state is entered with all the vigilance with which the young mother watches her first-born darling babe; I would have no one enter its precincts save on bended knee and with prayerful heart, as if appproaching the throne of God; as if to enter there were more than in any other way to give one's self to the service of God. So strictly would I regard it that none who should once enter could ever wish to retrace their steps. I would make divorces an unknown thing by abolishing imprudent and ill-assorted marriages. I would make the stigma so great that woman should find it impossible to confront the

18

world in a marriage for a home, for position, or for any reason save love alone ; and I would have her who should sell her person to be degraded in marriage, as culpable, as guilty, as impure at heart, as she is held to be who sells it otherwise. I would put every influence of the community against impure relations and selfish purposes, in whatever form they might exist, and encourage honour, purity, virtue, and chastity. I would take away from marriage the idea that it legally conveys the control of the person of the wife to the husband, and I would make her as much its guardian against improper use as she is supposed to be in maidenhood. It should be her own, sacredly, never to be desecrated by an unwelcome touch. I would make enforced commerce as much a crime in marriage as it is now out of it, and unwilling child-bearing a double crime. As the architects of humanity, I would hold mothers responsible for the character and perfection of their works ; make them realize that they can make their children what they ought to be, every one of them God's image in equality. I would have them come to know that their bodies are the temples of God, and that within their inner sanctuaries, within "the holy of holies " God performs his most marvellous creations ; that it is there that God himself dwells, there that He will make Himself manifest to man, and that every act that He does not inspire is sacrilege, is worship of the Evil One ; while every other is an offering of sweet incense to the Heavenly Father. I would have man so honour woman that an impure or improper thought or a self-desire, other than a wish to bless her, could never enter in his heart ; would have him hold her to be the holy temple to which God has appointed him to be High Priest as elaborately set forth by St. Paul in Hebrews ; as the Garden of Eden into which the Lord God put him, "to dress it and to keep it," forbidding him to eat of the fruit of the tree that stands in the midst of the garden ; would have him awake to the consciousness that, by not so regarding her, he is repeating the sin of Adam, and by not compelling him to so regard her, she is repeating the sin of Eve; and that by these sins they are thrust out of the garden and prevented from eating of the fruit of the tree of life and living for ever; more than this, I would enlarge the sphere of parental responsibility so that they should be held accountable for the instruction of their children in all of the mysteries of sex, so that none could go into marriage in ignorance of the laws and uses of the reproductive functions. I would rob the subject of the mawkish sentimentality in which it is submerged and make it a common and proper matter for earnest consideration and complete understanding. Indeed, I would make it a crime to enter marriage in ignorance of any of its possible duties and responsibilities; and twice a crime to bear improper children; for they who, to satisfy their own propensities, bring children into the world marked with the brand of Cain or Judas, are the worst kind of criminals. I would frown upon prostitution in every form; and make promiscuousness an abomination in the sight of man as it is in that of God; and I would drive out of the race the morbid passions that are consuming it. I would stop marrying until it should be no longer done in ignorance; and child-bearing until it could be done intelligently, so that every child might be a son or else a daughter of the living God. And I would have every woman remember the injunction of St. Paul, "Wives, submit yourselves unto your own husband, as it is fit in the Lord," but in no other way; and men, "Husbands, love your wives, and be not bitter against them." And if there be any other things, let St. Paul also speak for me of them. "Whatsoever things are true, whatsoever things are honest, whatsoever things are just, whatsoever things are lovely, whatsoever things are of good report; if there be any virtue, and if there be any praise, think on these things" (Phil. iv. 8).

PRESS NOTICES.

PRESS NOTICES

Lectures delivered in America and England from 1869-1882.

1869.

The World, January 28th, 1869. New York City.

THE COMING WOMAN.

"In the *Star* newspaper of the 21st instant, published in Washington, I read an article commendatory in a high degree of Mrs. Woodhull, of this city; uttering the opinion that she was destined to act no inferior part in coming conflicts and reforms in the country. I felt pleased to see this notice in a journal published at the capital of the nation, and while it was able and truthful so far as it went, it did not seem sufficiently full in detail, and I have thought the public would be interested in knowing more of this interesting woman; and having been honoured with several interviews with her, I may be able to give some account which may not prove wholly uninteresting.

"Personally, Mrs. Woodhull has a more than ordinarily fine and commanding figure, above the medium height. Her face, when at rest, does not impress the beholder at the first sight as being exquisitely beautiful, so far as the chiselling of the features is concerned, but when some great thought stirs the soul within (the radiant cause and source of all real external beauty), then her spiritual eyes 'flashing, like sunlit gems,' emit rhetoric, whose pure and, I may well say, sacred beams are enough to convert a soul to her heavenly mission; and then it is that both her face and form present a spectacle of bewildering loveliness such as Praxiteles might worship.

"The subject of the sketch is now thirty years old, but her experiences have been more than those generally of twice that age. Suffice it to say she has the experience of both wife and mother, as well as that of a most devoted worker as regards both body and soul.

"From her childhood, her parents tell me, the little Victoria gave evidence of genius as well as beauty of person, and as she grew older her mind rapidly developed into fine proportions, combining a singular masculine grasp with the most gentle and womanly attraction. This rare juxtaposition of opposite qualities is, to my own mind, the charm and marvel of this noble woman's life. Now she is conversing with engineers and others, and with the most perfect understanding, as to the methods of removing the obstructions to navigation at 'Hell Gate,' or the practicability of 'elevated railways and pneumatic dispatches.' Anon, with the most womanly tenderness, she listens to the sad story of some sick unfortunate sufferer whose life is nearly quenched in night, and gently as a careful and skilful nurse she administers the healing antidote.

"Mrs. Woodhull takes the most lively interest in all the genuine reforms of the day, and entertains her own distinctive views. Upon the woman question I deem her particularly sound. She believes in woman most completely, but she also believes in man just as thoroughly. She has just been attending the National Female Suffrage Convention, but only partially agrees with the doings of that body."

THE WALL STREET HIPPODROME.

HOW TO MANAGE A BALKY TEAM.

1870.

New York Herald, January 20th, 1870.

FINANCIAL AND COMMERCIAL.

" The general routine of business in Wall Street was somewhat varied to-day by the mingling in its scenes of two fashionably dressed ladies as speculators. Who they were few seemed to know, except that they were from the Hoffman House. Where they obtained their knowledge of stocks was a matter of puzzling conjecture with those whom they met. After investing to the extent of several thousand shares in some of our principal stocks and selling others, and announcing their intention to become regular *habitués* of Wall Street, they departed, the observed of all observers."

New York Herald, January 22nd, 1870.

THE QUEENS OF FINANCE.

"A NEW PHASE OF THE WOMAN'S RIGHTS QUESTION.

"THE LADY STOCK OPERATORS OF WALL STREET—THE FIRM OF WOODHULL, CLAFLIN & CO.—VANDERBILT PROTÉGÉS—INTERVIEW OF A 'HERALD' REPORTER WITH THE FUTURE PRINCESSES OF ERIE.

"With the progress of the woman's rights agitation we have noted from time to time various isolated instances in which women have stepped aside from their hitherto recognized sphere and engaged in pursuits and reaped profits which from time immemorial have been considered as the sole vested rights of the other sex. In the *Herald* of January 20th there appeared a very brief notice of a firm of female stockbrokers, who have been

doing a lively business on the ' street ' for some time past.   The
notice drew forth the following communication from the firm :—

"NEW YORK, Jan. 20, 1870.
" TO THE EDITOR OF THE HERALD:—
" We were not a little surprised at seeing our appearance in Wall Street
noticed in your columns of to-day.   As we intend operating as mentioned, we
should be glad to make your acquaintance.
"WOODHULL, CLAFLIN & CO."

" Enclosed within the letter were two delicately engraved
cards upon boards of the finest texture.   They read as follows :—

MRS. VICTORIA C. WOODHULL,

Hoffman House.

Parlors 25 and 26.

MISS TENNIE C. CLAFLIN,

Hoffman House.

Parlors 25 and 26.

"A *Herald* reporter called on the ladies yesterday at their apartments in the Hoffman House, and was ushered into their parlour No. 25. The parlour is a small, comfortable room fronting on the avenue and profusely decorated with oil paintings and statuary, and is furnished with a sofa, chairs, a piano, and the various other articles, useful and ornamental, which go to the make-up of a ladies' drawing-room. This is the present headquarters of Woodhull, Claflin & Co. Casting our eye around we observed a small frame, gracefully finished and glazed, containing the motto, ' Simply to Thy Cross I cling.' It was not ascertained whether the uncertainties and vicissitudes of the profession which the ladies have chosen suggested the idea; but it seemed at the moment that females, about to engage in fierce combat with cautious and calculating speculators, amid the terrific yells of ' bulls ' and ' bears,' should have something to cling to, something to keep the nerves easy and the eye clear, when the storm of financial agitation breaks in merciless billows over the devoted head of the operator.

"A desire to see and converse with one of the members of the firm was quickly granted. Miss Tennie C. Claflin entered the room. She introduced herself, and in a business-like manner bade the reporter be seated. Miss Claflin is a young lady. Her features are full, and a continuous smile plays upon her countenance. She is, to all appearance, the photograph of a business woman—keen, shrewd, wholesouled, and apparently a firm foe of the ' girl of the period ' creation, whom she describes as a sickly, squeaming nondescript, unworthy to breathe the free air of heaven. She was very plainly dressed, and spoke business in every gesture. In response to inquiries made our reporter received the following information :—

"REPORTER—You are a member of the firm of Woodhull, Claflin & Co., and you are doing business as stockbrokers and bankers ?

"Miss C.—Yes. Myself and my sister, Mrs. Woodhull, are

the active members of the firm. We have been interested in stocks in this city some two or three years. We have lately used these apartments as our offices; but within a few weeks we shall have suitable offices for the transaction of our business in Wall Street, or in that vicinity.

"REPORTER—It is a novel sight to see a woman go on the street as a stock operator, and I presume you find it rather awkward?

"Miss C.—Were I to notice what is said by what they call 'society,' I could never leave my apartments except in fantastic walking-dress or in ball-room costume. I think a woman is just as capable of making a living as a man; and I have seen men so vain of their personal appearance and so effeminate that I should be sorry to compare my intellect with theirs. I don't care what society think; I have not time to care. I don't go to balls or theatres. My mind is in my business, and I attend to that solely.

"REPORTER—But stock speculations are dangerous, and many persons of great experience, and with large capital at their backs, have been swamped, as you are aware, and I presume your experience is rather limited.

"Miss C.—I studied law in my father's office six years, and I know as much of the world as men who are older. Besides, we have a strong back. We have the counsel of those who have more experience than we have, and we are endorsed by the best backers in the city.

"REPORTER—I have been told that Commodore Vanderbilt is working in the interest of your firm. It is stated that you frequently call at his office in Fourth Street about business. Is this true?

"Miss C.—I know the Commodore, and frequently call to see him on business, but I am not prepared to state anything as to whether he is working with us. I will say that we have the advice and assistance of the shrewdest and most respectable financiers in the city.

Mrs. Victoria C. Woodhull.

"At this point in the conversation Mrs. Woodhull entered. She was very plainly dressed, having no ornament but a single rose tastefully inserted in her hair and the ring that decorated the third finger of her left hand. She is evidently of a sanguine, nervous temperament, and it might be apprehended that a serious financial shock would not tell well on her constitution. She immediately entered into the spirit of the conversation, and told a story of the work she performed, and the difficulties she had to contend with in her efforts to establish the Arcade Railway. She stated that the firm have on hand a project for the incorporation and working of a silver ledge company in Nevada, which they believe will yield them large profits. She stated that since she has been in the business in New York —some two or three years—although their operations were conducted solely through agents in the street, they have made about seven hundred thousand dollars, and she expects that when they establish an office in Wall Street and go in earnest into gold and stocks, that they will do much better.

Women in Wall Street—A New Phase of the Woman Question.

"A few days since our financial writer, whose observation is only equalled by his gallantry, recorded the fact that a couple of fashionably dressed ladies made their appearance upon the busy *trottoirs* of Wall Street and were conspicuous for extensive purchases and sales of stocks, the transactions in which they conducted with a *savoir faire* of the routine of the Stock Exchange that could have been derived only from an intimate familiarity with the intricacies of operations in that moneyed region. We have been at the pains since to learn further of these speculative daughters of Eve, and have fallen upon the astounding discovery that woman in extending her career of usefulness under the teachings of the modern school of female progressionists has entered upon the novel profession of stock brokerage. If *finesse* is woman's gift, why not finance also? We all know the skill with which she administers the domestic exchequer. Why may not her abilities take a wider range? Woman has made no mean mark in poetry and sculpture. Why should she not distinguish herself in all branches of the arts and sciences? If woman can regulate the expenditures of a household and audit a grocer's bill, why may she not manage a bank account? If she can keep a shop, why may she not sell bills of exchange? Why should she be compelled to restrict her talents to certain departments of business and be denied their exercise in all? And as to Wall Street, she would be quite in her element. The nursing of a 'corner' would enjoy her maternal skill. 'Calls' would be her delight.

"The capacity of woman for this new sphere of business being conceded, some little difficulty arises as to the specific nomenclature it would be her duty to assume. It is the experience of Wall Street that all who go there, no matter how unbiassed at first, gradually take sides with either of the respective opposing elements of the Stock Exchange. Now our politeness prevents us from conjecturing that she would become a 'bear.' We are aware, of course, that there are such things as female ursines, but they are confined to the kingdom of the lower animals. On the other hand, we are loath to think that she could be so Hibernian as to become a 'bull.' But this difficulty is one that may be easily obviated. The question of her status will settle itself in some way when woman regularly takes her place in the stock board. Meantime we congratulate the brokers that their labours are to be shared by the fair sex. How refreshing the time when the bass and baritone of 'seller sixty' shall harmonize with the tenor and soprano of 'buyer thirty,' and the halls of the Stock Exchange shall exhibit a variety of costume as diverse as the floors of a ballroom."

IN THEIR OFFICE ON BROAD STREET, NEW YORK.

19

New York Sunday News, January 80th, 1870. New York City.

WOMAN'S PROGRESS—THE FEMALE OPERATORS OF WALL ST.

"The firm of Woodhull, Claflin & Co. has for its leading business members Mrs. Victoria C. Woodhull and Miss Tennie C. Claflin. Accomplished, clever, business women, full of the necessary pluck and determination, with a good schooling in the business part of life, ready to see a good thing and grasp it, with the necessary nerve to hold their own against all opposition, we will find that their success will open up to female minds a great outlet for their present pent-up energy.

"At the present time this firm has its headquarters at the Hoffman House, Parlours Nos. 25 and 26, where they conduct their business among all the comforts of the drawing-room, but in a few days their office will be in Broad Street, when they expect to have a great increase in their business. Already they have on their books some of the oldest names in the street, who are willing to testify to their ability; and when we find such men as Commodore Vanderbilt lending them his counsel and countenance, we cannot but think it is sure of success.

"Among the many operations they are interested in, not the least is the proposed Arcade Railway, which they, in combination with some of their friends, are successfully pushing through, and also are incorporating a Silver Mining Company in Nevada, from which they anticipate large profits.

"Taking a well-balanced view of the whole subject, and putting aside prejudices which will gradually die out in time, we must come to the conclusion that the firm will, in time, reach the summit of its ambition, and have a standing equal to some of the oldest firms in the 'street;' and the firm of Woodhull, Claflin & Co. will come out in flying colours, and when the battle has been fought, and the victory gained, the future 'Princesses of Erie' can rest on their laurels, well satisfied with the work which they have accomplished, and the results achieved in the cause of *progress*."

19 *

New York Herald, February 5th, 1870.

THE QUEENS OF FINANCE.

THE PALACE OF THE FEMALE SOVEREIGNS OF WALL STREET—
COMMODORE VANDERBILT AS PRIME MINISTER—ESTABLISHING
THE CONNECTIONS—TELEGRAPHY AND WOMAN'S FINESSE.

" In every potent and picturesque event in the world's history woman has played a leading part. In the camp, in the court, in intrigue, in diplomacy, in partitioning kingdoms, and in fact in settling the destiny of the world, women have frequently had the trump card in their hands, and they have played it with all the enthusiasm and ingenuity which are theirs by nature. Joan of Arc, as was suggested by the lady members of the firm of Woodhull, Claflin & Co. to the *Herald* reporter, was only a woman who felt she had a mission and set about developing the rich resources of her intellect and her heart.

" In one field alone have the triumphs of women been miserably meagre. For some cause best known to society it has allocated commerce almost exclusively to man, and not commerce only, but all its kindred professions. Like many hidden forces, however, such as steam and electricity, which this century has developed, it is now found that woman can ably deal with large monetary interests as well as do mere shopping —can, as a matter of fact, exhibit the pluck, persistency, and fortitude which have built up the commercial fame of a Vanderbilt and a Stewart.

" In connection with the announcement made some weeks back in the *Herald*, our reporter called on the leading members of the firm of Woodhull, Claflin & Co. yesterday at their new offices, No. 44, Broad Street, and ascertained that they had made arrangements to enter immediately upon banking business upon a solid and wide basis. He inquired for Miss Claflin, and that lady, with her usual prepossession of manner, made her appearance. The *Herald* reporter inquired who inspired the new undertaking, as novel as it was plucky.

"She answered, ' Commodore Vanderbilt.'

"REPORTER—You have more confidence in the Commodore than many of the Wall Street people.

"Miss CLAFLIN—Yes, I have; for all my monetary transactions with him have been strictly honourable and perfectly satisfactory.

"Miss Claflin then said that their operations, which had turned 750,000 dollars, were up to the present incidental and belonging too much to the mere study of the market; that her firm determined rather to live with and in the money market, to risk all its ' ups and downs' and to take all the dangers and advantages of money transactions in the usual course of business. She said they were not only prepared to face the bustling, yelling, stormy crowd of men, whose pulses beat with the ' rise and fall of the monetary barometer;' but that she knew she would receive active support and sympathy from even the ' bulls and bears,' though she yet intended to do business according to the ' broad principles of justice and the keen and paying principles of common arithmetic.' Justified by former success, they had taken a large banking house and would enter upon business.

"This new, original, and very probably, successful idea—probably the occasion of millions of dollars' gain—will be worked out at No. 44, Broad Street, where every accommodation is provided, not alone for the transaction of business, but also for the comfort of those who, coming from a distance, desire to find the best advice and suitable monetary accommodation.

"The offices are magnificently fitted up. The best ' Marvin safes' are conspicuous. Walnut desks, finely finished and covered with green baize, give an air of comfort to the concern quite of a piece with the whole idea connected with this original and unique firm. In looking around the office one is struck by the ease and magnificence of the lounges and sofas and the general comfort it affords.

"Arrangements have been made so that the telegraph wires will work the whole day through with London, Paris, Vienna and Constantinople, as well as with the grand centres of trade in the South and West at home, and chiefly with St. Louis, Baltimore, Philadelphia, Chicago and Boston. This world-wide accommodation is afforded and given in the ordinary course of trade, not involving the annoyances hitherto incidental to those doing money business in the city. In a word, the requirements of the age have been all considered by these enterprising ladies. Monetary genius, which has proved its value by its success in a thousand fearful moneyed frays, has been duly consulted, and may be regarded as the chief source of inspiration in this matter. Hence, as far as an intelligent eye can take in the situation, nothing seems wanting to supplement the boldness, spirit, grandeur and enterprise of the new idea. There is nothing squeamish about it. It is founded upon pure matter of fact—arithmetic and hard calculation being the component towering elements—and so, those setting this novel establishment afloat believing, as they state, in the simple but comprehensible maxim that God helps those who help themselves, intend to work not by a mere leaden rule, but by the grander natural principles of broad justice and sheer calculation, two things which can, they believe, result in nothing but unerring success, and which they regard as the soul and source of fortune in the undertaking of George Peabody and similar representatives of ideas of old pagan notions of common honesty and of modern ideas of genuine progress, as they naively expressed it.

"Such are the suggestions which have fallen under the observation of the *Herald* reporter in his visit to the banking house of the first ' female stockbrokers ' in the world."

Evening Express, February 5th, 1870.   New York City.

"At an early hour there was a steady stream of people down Broad Street. Following the crowd, we brought up at 44,

Broad Street, and were introduced to Mrs. Victoria C. Woodhull and Miss Tennie C. Claflin, the active partners of the new female stock brokerage firm of Woodhull, Claflin & Co.

"These ladies are in the prime of life, and were very affable and agreeable in their manner. They entered into an explanation of their intended operations in Wall Street, and spoke with the same confidence as an old *habitué* of the 'street.' They intend to transact a legitimate business, and will probably in time apply to the Stock Exchange for an 'amendment' to its constitutions, in order that they may become active participants in the daily operations of the Board. The office of this new firm was crowded with people attracted by the novelty of the whole affair."

Evening Post, February 5th, 1870. New York City.

"Now for the first time, we believe, in the history of the street, a firm has been formed both of whose active members belong to what is styled the fair sex. This firm is that of Woodhull, Claflin & Co. The active members of this firm are Mrs. Victoria C. Woodhull and Miss Tennie C. Claflin. The new firm propose doing a general banking and stock brokerage business, and will be represented in the Board by different brokers. They have taken offices at No. 44, Broad Street."

The Sun, February 7th, 1870. New York City.

WOODHULL, CLAFLIN & CO.

WOMEN ESTABLISHING A BANKING HOUSE IN WALL STREET.—AN
EVENTFUL SATURDAY.

"Mrs. Victoria C. Woodhull and Miss Claflin, on Saturday, opened a general banking and brokerage business at 44, Broad Street.

" The announcement that these ladies had gone into business produced great excitement in Wall Street. The fact was

announced in both the Gold and Stock Exchanges. Woodhull,
Claflin & Co. opened their office at 10 A.M. Mr. Edward
Van Schaick was the first gentleman who called upon them.
The ladies received him very cordially. They told him that as
soon as they were firmly established they should be happy to
receive his orders for the purchase of stock. While Mr. Van
Schaick was conversing with the members of the firm, Mr.
George B. Alley and Mr. Abram B. Baylis entered, and wished
the new firm much joy. A few minutes afterwards Messrs. W.
B. Beckman, George H. Bend, and John Bloodgood paid the
ladies a visit, and left apparently satisfied that the firm was well
established, and meant to have their fair share of business in
Wall Street. Mr. S. J. Blood and Mr. George T. Bonner were
the next callers, followed by Mr. H. A. Bostwick, Mr. James
Bayed, Mr. Edward Brandon, and Mr. Hugh Hastings. The
latter regarded the ladies with evident astonishment. After
some further conversation the party left. Mr. Daniel Drew
and Mr. O. D. Ashley meanwhile paid their respects to the
partners. Mr. Drew was evidently deeply impressed with
the importance of the movement. As he went out he met
Mr. Jay Cooke and Mr. John Bonner. At this moment a
group of well-dressed men approached No. 44. Among them
were Mr. James Austin, Mr. Frank Baker, Mr. Andrew
Barstow, Mr. G. S. Bowdain, Mr. N. G. Bradford, jun., and
the dignified Mr. C. L. Cammann. The ladies received the
distinguished party with business-like consideration, and they
departed much pleased with their interview.

" Colonel John H. Almy and his brother Albert accompanied
him. During their visit numerous capitalists entered the room.
Among them were noted : Messrs. J. L. Brownell, A. B. Baylis,
jun., J. W. Blatchford, H. G. Chapman, Luther G. Clarke,
Alfred Colvill, Thomas Denny, jun., Harrison Durkee, A.
Morton Ferriss, O. Gelpke, W. H. Neilson, Reuben Howes,
T. L. Hoyt, and Edward King. These gentlemen listened to the

MISS CLAFLIN RECEIVING ORDERS FOR STOCK SPECULATIONS.

business plans of the new firm with sceptical faces, but heartily
wished the ladies success in their undertaking. After this party
had gone out, the amiable Mr. W. B. Clerke, accompanied by
Mr. Theodore Cox and Mr. E. D. Dibble, entered the room.
They asked for the latest figures on Mariposa. Mrs. Woodhull
stepped to the telegraphic instrument, and after a glance at the
snaky strip of white paper, replied : ' Mariposa's on the rise.
The latest quotation preferred is $19\frac{3}{8}$.'

"At this moment Mr. George A. Fanshaw, Mr. Mortimer,
Mr. L. Fowler, Mr. Lombardi, and General David Groesbeck
entered the office. The next visitors were Mr. S. W.
Harned and Mr. Rufus Hatch. These gentlemen looked at the
principal of the house in grim silence, and departed without
vouchsafing a word. On the threshold they were met by the
Hon. Oliver Charlick, Mr. John H. Jacquelin, and Charles A.
Lamont. The ladies listened to Mr. Charlick's advice with
much interest. He gave them some points on Long Island
stock, which they dotted down upon an ivory memorandum-book,
after thanking him for his information.

"Messrs. R. L. Cutting, jun., Edward Dodge, H. S. Fearing,
and the Hon. E. B. Hart paid their respects to the new bankers.

"Mr. Hart said he thought that there was something back
of this movement, to which Miss Claflin replied, 'Yes, there is
something back of it; Commodore Vanderbilt is back of
it.' The party left in good humour. The next comers were
Messrs. J. W. Hartshorn, D. C. Hays, Richard Schell (Mr.
Schell was in excellent spirits, but he thought the ladies
foolish. He said they would lose more money than they
could make), O. W. Joslyn, George Henriques, W. R. Travers,
and H. R. Le Roy. Mr. Travers told the ladies that they
would lose their money in Wall Street. Mrs. Woodhull replied
that they did not come to Wall Street to lose money, but to
make money. She thought it more probable that Mr. Travers
would lose his money if the firm was given a fair showing.

Mr. James A. Patteson, Mr. O. W. Schaick, Mr. John D.
Slayback, and Mr. John Ten Brock entered during the conversation. Then came Mr. Robert Waller, Mr. John R. Warren,
and Mr. M. A. Wheelock. The party departed after looking at
the closing prices. For some time there was a lull in the
visitors; about 4 o'clock, however, Mr. S. V. White, Mr. H. T.
Morgan, Mr. R. Manley, and Mr. J. Marie entered the door.

"Just as the doors were being closed some gentlemen called
upon the fair brokers. They were told that it was after
business hours, and if they had any orders to give, they would
be received after 9 o'clock on Monday morning.

"It is understood that the new firm have refused to join
either the Stock Exchange or the Gold Board."

The World, February 8th, 1870. New York City.

"THE BROAD STREET NOVELTY IN BROKERAGE — PROGRESS OF
THE BUSINESS OF THE FEMININE FIRM—GREAT EXCITEMENT
AMONG THE BULLS AND BEARS.

"The offices of the lady bankers and brokers, Mesdames
Woodhull, Claflin & Co., at 44, Broad Street, were again
besieged yesterday by the members of the Board, and the
heavy operators in the street, who called to tender their congratulations and express their recognition of these new labours
in the broad field of finance. All were disposed to give to
the ladies all the advice and assistance in their power, and
offers of loans and pecuniary facilities were without number.
Mrs. Woodhull and Miss Claflin received their visitors in a
quiet, business-like manner, discussed their new enterprise,
talked financial matters intelligently, seemed thoroughly posted
on all points, and altogether made a very favourable impression.

"STREET SCENES.

"Outside on the walk there was gathered throughout the day
an assemblage of men, who looked anxiously in at the windows,
peered anxiously through the doors, and uttered expressions of

surprise and pleasure if they could but catch a glimpse of one of the members of the firm. A clarence remained in front of the door the greater part of the day, and as the ladies frequently had occasion to drive here and there in pursuance of their business, these hangers-on and morbid curiosity-seekers had ample opportunity to gratify their sight-seeing propensities. Inside the office door a doorkeeper had been placed, who excluded all those who had no real business with the firm. On the door of the private office was a card, on which was written,—

All Gentlemen
will state their business
and then
retire at once.

"The offices engaged by them at 44, Broad Street are very spacious and convenient, extending the entire width and depth of the building on the ground-floor. The outer office is sufficiently large and roomy for the transaction of a very large business, while the inner room contains the private desks of the firm, and comfortable accommodations for their customers. The desks are of walnut and gold, the sofas and chairs of oak and green leather, while the carpets are the finest velvet, and handsome engravings hang about the walls.

"The ladies will not apply for admission themselves at any of the Boards, and when once settled will rarely leave their offices. They have engaged a manager, a gentleman who is a member of both the Stock and Gold Board, who will do all their buying and selling, and attend to most of the out-door business. Other gentlemen of great experience and knowledge of the ways and customs of the street have been engaged to attend to the office duties, the ladies themselves exercising the general supervision over everything.

"They expect to do a legitimate, straightforward banking and brokerage business, and see no reason why, if their capital is sufficient, their purchases and sales made promptly at the best figures, and all their business operations conducted with shrewdness and ability, they may not succeed in amassing a fortune as readily as hundreds who have gone before. At all events, they express themselves as ready and willing to take the chances. They will keep accounts at the Fourth National Bank, and also at the Bank of New York, and state that, if necessary, they can control $700,000 for business purposes.

"The ladies say that Commodore Vanderbilt is backing them with his influence and his advice. Gentlemen well known in Wall Street, and relatives of the Commodore Vanderbilt, fully indorse all their statements, and say these *protégés* of the great financier are certain to succeed, his patronage and friendship being all-powerful.

"THEY ARE INTERESTED IN THE ARCADE RAILWAY.

"Through their influence the Arcade Railway has received the support of Commodore Vanderbilt and his friends; and Mr. M. C. Smith, the projector, states that through their efforts alone he gained the aid of the great capitalist—most important and all-powerful in projects of the kind.

" SENTIMENTS OF THE BROKERS.

" In the Stock and Gold Boards the new firm was the general subject of conversation, some arguing success of the project, while by far a greater number were very sceptical. A prominent member of the Gold Board said, that if Woodhull, Claflin & Co. had brought $700,000 into the street, it would be a fine thing for the brokers, as they (the brokers) would have it in less than inside of six months. Others remarked that with Commodore Vanderbilt's influence, added to their own business capacity, they might prove really dangerous rivals. One and all, however, were disposed to give them a fair chance, and extend to them a helping hand, and it is not likely they will be at all annoyed by any actions on the part of members of the Board.

"The ladies say, from the first, they have received the most courteous treatment from every one."

New York Herald, February 10th, 1870.

THE BEWITCHING BROKERS.

WOODHULL, CLAFLIN AND CO. IN HIGH FEATHER—VISITORS OFFER-
ING BUSINESS AND SUPPORT—THE FIRM FULLY ESTABLISHED.

"A large number of prominent bankers and brokers visited
the office of the lady brokers, Mrs. Woodhull, Claflin & Co.,
yesterday, and offered their encouragement and support in the
conduct of the contemplated business. These were received by
the firm in due form and much conversation of a profitable
nature was indulged in. The gentlemen offering their advice
and services were hearty in their congratulation, and the ladies
were polite, dignified, and business-like. A number of letters
were also received by the firm from different bankers and brokers
offering to extend a helping hand in the enterprise of the
bewitching brokers. In the morning the street was surprised
to observe a number of carriages with ladies roll up to the door
of Mrs. Woodhull's office and enter the private room in the
rear, where the divinities of finance presided. It was not an
organized raid of strong-minded women on the safes of the firm,
or a party of charitable ladies looking for subscriptions for the
shivering savages of Feejee, but a regular stream of customers
the highest and wealthiest in the city. They wanted to make
deposits of money and to give orders for the buying and selling
of stocks. One lady wished to purchase one thousand shares
of a stock that seemed to be going up, and others were anxious
to transact business in gold and bonds to equally heavy amounts.
The firm, however, as was stated in the *Herald* of yesterday, are
not yet prepared for business, but will be in a very short time.
They were, therefore, obliged to decline the offers of their eager
customers, but booked their names for future transactions.

"Mrs. Woodhull attended in the office the entire day; but
Miss Claflin went up town early, having to attend to some real
estate business which demanded her attention. Considering the
numbers and persistency of annoying visitors, Mrs. Woodhull

maintained her good temper throughout the day, and received everybody who called, either through curiosity or on business, with equal urbanity and tact, thereby showing herself to be possessed of the first essential requisite to successful business. She told the *Herald* reporter that while the affairs of the firm were in their present embryo state she had nothing to communicate beyond the ordinary news of monetary movements, which could be obtained just as well in any other broker's office in the street. Her firm, however, were negotiating at present and operating heavily, and in a few days she would have some interesting information to communicate."

New York Herald, February 13th, 1870. New York City.

THE BEWITCHING BROKERS.

THE BUSINESS OF WOODHULL, CLAFLIN & CO. INCREASING.

" The notices published in the *Herald* of the newly established firm of Woodhull & Claflin, the female brokers, have had the effect of causing considerable commotion in down town monetary circles, and inspiring flashy young men to visit their establishment. Many of the latter called during the week to see the ladies, intent on administering lectures and showing off their exquisite figures. With the courtesy, urbanity, and tact characteristic of the firm, they were received, spoken to, and dismissed, just as if they had called at any other broker's office in the city. Surprised, if not delighted, these exquisites of the street realize for the first time that young ladies can be wise and discreet, and young men rash and foolish. The business of the firm is already commenced. Their extraordinary coolness and self-possession, and evident knowledge of the intricacies of the difficult *rôle* they have undertaken, is far more remarkable than their personal beauty and graces of manner, and these are considerable. They are evidently women of remarkable coolness and tact, and are capable of extraordinary endurance."

New York Courier, February 14th, 1870. New York City.

THE WOMEN BROKERS OF BROAD STREET.

"We found both ladies present at their magnificent office, 44, Broad Street, surrounded by all the bustle of business and evidences of preparation for the work they have undertaken. Mistresses Woodhull and Claflin received us with the manners of duchesses, or better—of straightforward, well-bred American women, and chatted as freely and decidedly as if they had been on the 'street' a dozen years. We know our hundred thousand female readers are dying to hear what they are like. As for the men, we don't care a pin for them. They do not in fact amount to a row of pins in this regard. Besides, they can see for themselves. All they have to do is to buy a thousand shares of stock daily, get Mistresses Woodhull and Claflin to do the buying and selling and have an ecstatic five minutes' interview over a highly polished rosewood counter. . . .

"They strike you at once as women of good taste, who have with great care and judgment adapted their dress to their occupation. They resemble each other closely, in both looks and manner; both have clear, decided, and excessively wide-awake blue eyes, delicately chiselled features and transparent complexions. In short, with their well-developed, yet lithe figures, flashing blue eyes, fine-cut features, and inflexible self-possession, they present absolutely perfect types of the thoroughbred American woman. There, now female readers have before them truthful portraits of Mistresses Woodhull and Claflin in words as well as woodcuts. As for our male readers amongst the Wall and Broad Street brokers, we invite them to take a good look into those ladies' eyes the first time they have to transact business with them, and see if they don't agree with us that they are perfectly capable of taking care of themselves.

"Having satisfied our anxious readers with a description of the *personel* of the ladies, we will let them tell their own story

20

as they told it to us, condensing it only into a quasi narrative, since space forbids us to give the dramatic form assumed in our conversation. 'Yes,' said they, 'we like newspapers and newspaper men, they are the salt of the earth just now—keep everything from spoiling. We hope they will not spoil us by flattery. We do not want flattery, we do not want detraction, we want fair play—nothing more. Ask to be taken for exactly what we are good for, as men are. We are business women. Give us a fair show as you give business men. That is all we ask. We like all the newspapers, they have been very kind to us. When we were turning this thing over in our minds, and debating whether we should start into it, our friends, of course, started all manner of objections. No women had ever been stock or gold brokers; Wall Street was tabooed to petticoats. We said we did not intend to let our petticoats interfere with anybody, or take up any more room in the street than the other brokers' trousers. Women stood behind counters, wrote books, acted upon the stage, kept stores, dealt in gentlemen's furnishing goods—came in business contact with men in a thousand different ways, and it was right. Nobody thought any harm of it, or said they had no right to do it for an honest living. Custom had sanctioned it. Why shouldn't they just as well be stock-brokers as keep stores and measure men for shirts? We couldn't see why. So, you see, here we are—brokers; and we mean to be so. We do not propose to go out and buy and sell on the street or at the Board as a general thing, but if we should be entrusted with the business of a client, and our broker were too busy to attend to it, our petticoats should not interfere with our loyalty to a customer's interests. We would go out and attend to his business—men or no men. All the talk about women's rights is moonshine. Women have every right. All they need do is exercise them. That's what we are doing. We are doing daily more for women's rights, by prac-tically exercising the right to carry on our own business, than all the diatribes of papers and platform speeches will do in ten years. We have had a great deal of business experience already. We did not commence building until we had counted the cost. Besides, since we opened our offices capitalists and banks have offered to carry stocks for us to any amount we please. Very plucky in us to undertake this, they say. Oh dear no, not at all; it does not seem so to us. That is a bit of your newspaper flattery.'

"Here the business pressure on the fair brokers became urgent, and we bowed ourselves out of the inner office.

"We do not know that much can be added. We believe Strong, Nichois, Strong have been their brokers, before they set up for themselves. Mistresses Woodhull and Claflin have been bold and successful operators on the street for some time, and have not much to learn about either gold or stocks. For their courtesy and frank business-like way of treating it, the *Courier* wishes them 'success' in all their doings and plentiful increase. The foolish jests and flutter in the street caused by their advent have died completely out, and they are already accepted as one of its regular features."

Chronicle, February 14th, 1870. Cincinnati (Ohio).

"J. P. Kilbreath, Esq., has just returned from New York City. He states that, up to Saturday last, it was estimated that seven thousand persons had called upon Woodhull, Claflin & Co. They recognized all their old Cincinnati friends, and informed them that the firm was ready to receive orders."

Cincinnati Chronicle, March 3rd, 1870.

"A gentleman, who left New York on Monday, informs us that Miss Claflin claims to be doing a large business with the West, and that she feels confident that the firm of Woodhull, Claflin & Co. is a success beyond their brightest anticipations."

The World, March 20th, 1870.   New York City.

THE CHEQUE FRAUDS.

ATTEMPT TO VICTIMIZE THE FEMALE BROKERS—THEY PROVE TOO
SMART FOR THE FORGERS—THE GREENWICH BANK TAKEN IN.

" The forgers who have acquired much proficiency of late in
altering cheques from small amounts to large sums, and have
already victimized several banks and brokers' firms, were
yesterday discovered in a new attempt in their peculiar line of
business, but too late to prevent their realizing a handsome sum
by their shrewd operations.

" On Thursday afternoon a person of gentlemanly and business-
like appearance called at the office of the lady bankers, Mesdames
Woodhull, Claflin & Co., and stepping up to the cashier's window
presented a cheque of Park & Tilford's, the well-known
Broadway grocers, for $4,366.52, remarking at the same time
that he was an agent for that firm, and desired to buy some gold
for them.   He came in entirely alone, and there was nothing
either in his manner, appearance, or address that would excite
suspicion, while the cheque bore Park & Tilford's signature,
was neatly drawn, bore the proper stamp, and called for the
amount from the Greenwich Bank.

" Miss Claflin says that the clerk handed the cheque to her
for inspection and she took it to her sister, Mrs. Woodhull.
Observing that the cheque was not certified, the members of the
firm took the wise precaution of sending it by a clerk to the
Greenwich Bank for certification, the agent of the grocers waiting
in the meantime in the outer office.   The boy soon returned with
the cheque properly indorsed by the paying-teller, the gold was
bought, the commission deducted, and Messrs. Park & Tilford's
agent left the office with the specie.

" On Friday afternoon another stranger made his appearance
presented a cheque of Park & Tilford's for $6600 and said that
he wanted $5500 invested in gold and would take a cheque for

the balance. The members of the firm said that this cheque, like the first one, was uncertified and that they would send it to the New York County Bank on which it was drawn to have that delicate operation performed. The gentleman stranger said that he had a little business down the street and would step out for a few minutes and return by the time the cheque was certified. On passing out of the door he was joined by the party who brought the first cheque, who was overheard to ask ' Is it all right?'—to which the reply was made ' Not yet.'

" In the meantime the clerk with the cheque reached the New York County Bank and presented it to the paying-teller. The latter glanced at it, and hastily wrote his signature across the face of it, then seemed to think there was something wrong, and after scrutinizing it carefully and consulting with the cashier, deliberately and carefully scratched out his certification, and sent it to Park & Tilford's place of business to ascertain its genuineness. The latter gentlemen on being shown the cheque were decidedly puzzled, and although they acknowledged the signature, said that they had given no cheque for that amount, and investigation proved that the figures and writing had been skilfully altered from an order for a small sum.

" A first-class forgery and attempt to defraud was at once developed, and the cashier of the New York County Bank accompanied by Woodhull & Claflin's clerk, returned to the office in Broad Street, where they awaited the return of the person who pretended to be Park & Tilford's agent, but that gentlemanly individual failed to again put in an appearance, no doubt having been on the watch from some convenient nook, and discovered the failure of the second attempt from the clerk being accompanied by the cashier.

" It appears that Messrs. Park & Tilford when they draw cheques fill in the body of the documents as well as add their signatures, and it was the fact that the writing and figures representing the amount was not in the same handwriting as the signature that first aroused the suspicion of the paying-teller at the New York County Bank. The first cheque was deposited by Mesdames Woodhull & Claflin in the Fourth National Bank and went through the exchange, where it was discovered that that also was a forgery, having been originally drawn for $40. When the fact was ascertained there was, of course, much excitement, both at the office of the ladies and at the bank; and the Greenwich Bank having certified the cheque in good faith, will be held for the amount.

"Mr. Thomas Sampson, the chief detective of the Custom House and Stock Exchange, has been engaged to ferret out the offender, and assisted by Captain Garland of the First Precinct, was on hand yesterday. They are of the opinion that the cheques were altered by the same parties who so successfully victimized Vermilye & Co. and Fisk & Hatch a few days since.

"The ladies of the firm have come out of the affair with flying colours. Their shrewd management and business tact were equal to the emergency, and the precautions they took in regard to certification guarded them from all loss."

New York Herald, April 2nd, 1870 (Editorial). New York City.

THE COMING WOMAN.

"The passage of fifteenth amendment to Constitution of the United States has had at least one beneficial effect, so far as our political status is concerned in this country—to wit, the clearing of the track for the sixteenth and as many other amendments as may be deemed necessary and becoming toward the attainment of a liberal and benignly comprehensive system of representation, and participation both in the making and the administration of laws. The woman is inevitable, and she is 'coming' on the chariot-wheels of woman's sweet wilfulness, and her irresistibly captivating appeal for a chance to experiment among the rulers.

"Now, however, there is fitting opportunity for the women throughout the land to show their might, independent of any of these petty organizations, by voting for a candidate for the Presidential succession of 1872, and by inducing men to vote, ' just for once,' in favour of a woman-President.

"Mrs. Woodhull, the lady broker of Broad Street, independent of all suffrage tea-parties and Grundy associations, proclaims herself as a candidate for the occupancy-in-chief of the White House, and asks it on the score solely that she has the means, courage, energy, and ability necessary to contest the issue to its close. Now there can certainly be no objection to such a competition as this : it possesses the merits of novelty enterprise, courage, and determination. Women always take the part of each other, and if the women can be allowed to vote, Mrs. Woodhull may rely on rolling up the heaviest majority ever polled in this or any other nation. Her platform, which will be found in another column, is short, sharp, decisive, and has the true ring in it. Now for victory for Victoria in 1872 !"

New York Dispatch, April 3rd, 1870. New York City.

THE LADY BROKERS.

" Mesdames Woodhull and Claflin and Co., the lady brokers, of 44, Broad Street, received many calls yesterday from their friends on 'Change, all desirous to offer congratulations on the advent of the ladies in the political arena ; Mrs. Woodhull having announced herself, in yesterday's *Herald*, as a candidate for the Presidency in 1872. A majority of their visitors were, undoubtedly, actuated by curiosity ; but the ladies have many sincere friends of our wealthiest citizens. Their interviews with Commodore Vanderbilt are of daily occurrence, and ex-Mayor Kingsland is said to uphold them in their new move, while ex-Mayor Opdyke and H. B. Claflin, Esq., have been in consultation with them at their office in Broad Street.

" Mrs. Woodhull announces her intention to spend a fortune in advocating her views on ' *Equality* ' and governmental policy, and will soon begin the publication of a campaign-sheet, in which she promises to make some rare disclosures that will both interest and astound the political world."

New York Herald, April 3rd, 1870 (Editorial).   New York City.

" We published yesterday the *pronunciamiento* (a powerful document on behalf of woman's rights) of Mrs. Victoria C. Woodhull as a candidate for the next Presidency. Mrs. Woodhull, then, may be considered in the field ; and, being of the female firm in Wall Street of Woodhull, Claflin & Co., who can tell the extent of her financial resources among the brokers, bulls, and bears ? A woman, and a smart and handsome woman, she is the proper person to stand forth against the field as the woman's rights candidate for the White House."

The Press, April 7th, 1870.   Philadelphia (Pa.).

" Coming from the South, the land of conservatism and fixed ideas, the first thing that startled me on my arrival in Philadelphia was the proclamation of Mrs. Victoria Woodhull, the Wall Street broker, for the next Presidential campaign. This was a total change of life. In the South we didn't know anything, save by hearsay, of woman's rights, woman's suffrage, labour and capital, and the other issues that are in men's mouths all over the North. Mrs. Woodhull and her sister, Miss Claflin, had sprung into the world as new stars on the astronomer's gaze since my departure from New York. Making inquiry about them of a lady friend, I was asked would I like an introduction. I said I should indeed, for that I thought their course indicated fearless independence at least. This day I had the honour of paying my respects to the ladies.

" My own preconceptions or expectations are of no importance. Anticipation very, very rarely justifies realization. Both ladies have been subjects of description and criticism, friendly and severe. A great deal has been predicated in utter ignorance, sheer envy, or reckless malevolence. For myself, I found two ladies who are quick, active, energetic, yet womanly, moving rapidly, giving their orders decidedly but calmly, and receiving their many guests, both business and private, with perfect ease, and without either confusion or hurry. Both are young, something more than good looking. Mrs. Woodhull has a sweet voice, is eloquent, and has a wide range of subjects at her conversational command, which she handles with force and without reticence, speaking earnestly, and as though under conviction. It is impossible to be indifferent in their presence. Both have perceptive powers of the highest order, and if I may judge from what I heard and saw, their quickness and accuracy of perception will be justified by an unusual share of logical acumen and reasoning capacity.

" The sense of incongruity of two young, pretty women being engaged in Wall Street brokerage passed away the moment I saw them. They were serene and unperturbed, and twenty times as pleasant as Belmont or Jay Cooke.

" I may conclude by saying that Mrs. Woodhull, in the right of her age, would appear to have more sagacity and depth; though, as they are inseparable, and always work in concert, the distinction may be more apparent than real."

The Sun, April 11th, 1870. New York City.

" If there does not soon ensue a general immigration of the fair sex from Europe to the United States it will not be the fault of the *Indépendance Belge*. Speaking of the influence exerted by women in America, that journal says : ' In Washington women are employed as clerks, heads of departments, &c. In New York a banking-house has been established, in which all departments are filled by the *beau sexe*. On the opening day they received 4000 clients, to which number the grace and beauty of these ladies has since added an enormous increase."

Democrat, April 18th, 1870. St. Louis (Mo.

"The Wall Street female brokers, Woodhull, Claflin & Co., are about starting a weekly to support Mrs. Woodhull for the Presidency, advocate woman's rights and suffrage."

Central Illinoian, May 12th, 1870. Beardstown (Ill.).

"'*Upward and Onward.*'—This is a title of rather a novel publication that is to make its appearance about the 14th of the present month. It is to be devoted to the vital interests of the people. It will be termed *Woodhull & Claflin's Weekly*, and support Mrs. Victoria C. Woodhull for President. They propose to take the widest range on the subject of labour and capital, liberal education, and heartily support the honesty and efficiency of all public servants, and view the Democratic party in the light of a party that has long been the shade of a name, and the Republican party as the effete, and that Conservatism is impracticable. We are rather anxious to see this anomaly in the newspaper arena. Progress is their motto."

New York Herald, May 15th, 1870. New York City.

"The latest literary sensation is *Woodhull & Claflin's Weekly*, edited and owned by the famous firm of Wall Street brokers, and the first number of which is before us. In the language of the editors the paper 'will be primarily devoted to the vital interests of the people and will treat of all matters freely and without reservation.' Of course it is a strong advocate of woman's suffrage, and discusses finances learnedly and acutely. In contents and appearance, *Woodhull & Claflin's Weekly* is interesting and agreeable. Among its literary papers is the opening part of 'In Spite of All,' translated expressly from the French of Madame George Sand, for the paper, and which reads well. Altogether the *Weekly* promises to be well managed, and we wish it all success."

New York Herald, May 18th, 1870. New York City.
THE LADY BROKERS OF WALL STREET.

" While the two hostile divisions of woman's righters are passing all their time in refusing to coalesce with each other and in flooding the country with resolutions and chatter, there are, at least, two advocates of the women movement that endeavour to show by example and precept that their sex, with ordinary fair play and industry, can take care of itself. We refer to the lady brokers who recently created a stir among the bulls and bears of Wall Street, and who have more recently opened the eyes of the slow old fogies who think women not fit for much, by starting an excellent weekly newspaper, under the business-like title of *Woodhull & Claflin's Weekly*, right in the midst of the periodicals of Park Row. The paper itself, of which the first number only has been issued, already gives evidence of talent and aptness in that most difficult of all the art of journalism. It is a neat sixteen-page paper, about the size and shape of the usual literary hebdomadal; but in addition to the stories, essays, and poetry, inseparable from these papers, it launches boldly into politics, finance, outdoor sports and fashions, and even thus early rejoices in a cheering amount of advertisements. The *Weekly*, bearing the motto 'Upward and Onward,' strongly advocates woman's rights, and even nominates and supports a woman for the next Presidency. There can, therefore, be no reasonable doubt of its devotion to the woman cause, and we suggest to the female agitators who waste their breath and their hearers' patience at conventions and mass meetings, that while the press is not so noisy an organ as the tongue, it is heard much further. The example of Woodhull & Claflin is a highly commendable one, as they do more and talk less than any two divisions of female agitators put together."

New York Standard, May 18th, 1870. New York City.

" We acknowledge the receipt of *Woodhull & Claflin's Weekly*, a handsome and readable newspaper, to advocate suffrage without distinction of sex, and support Mrs. Victoria C. Woodhull for President. It regards the Democratic party as 'effete,' and the Republican party as little better, and always lively, readable, and intelligent, largely devoted to Progress and Liberty."

The Day, June 7th, 1870. Philadelphia (Pa.).

A WOMAN'S PAPER.

"Some months ago financial circles had a novel sensation in the advent of two ladies in Wall Street as brokers. It was regarded as a very good joke, and furnished theme of various comments to the press of the county. But the firm turned out to be anything but a joke, and succeeded in establishing the financial equality of the sex in spite of ridicule, in the very heart of the American stockbroking world. The firm of Woodhull & Claflin has taken a step forward, and now comes before the public with a handsome sixteen-page journal, entitled *Woodhull & Claflin's Weekly*, and devoted to the true equality of woman. The editorials are remarkable for the practical wisdom they inculcate; are generally sound in their views, and liberal in range of both thought and subject. It is undoubtedly the ablest journal of its class, and can hardly fail of success. Its editors are sisters, and appear to be working earnestly to advance woman to her proper position in the social and business world. Fifty thousand copies of the *Weekly* are circulated every week. It is but fair to say that its financial page loses nothing by comparison with the best of the New York journals." .

Inquirer, June 8th, 1870. Philadelphia (Pa.).

WOMAN'S RIGHTS.

"In these days of political progression the ladies claim that their voices should be heard. Without venturing our opinion on this delicate subject, we must confess that the new weekly of Mesdames Woodhull & Claflin is one possessing more than ordinary merits. It contains many articles which are at once entertaining and instructive."

New York Commercial Advertiser, November 11th, 1870. New York City.

A STARTLING ANNUNCIATION.

" We believe it is Locke who, in substance, says that our ideas often die before us, and our minds represent those tombs to which we are all approaching, where, though the brass and the marble remain, yet the inscriptions are effaced by time, and the imagery moulders away. How happy, then, should he or she be who can claim exemption from this common law of decay, and like Mrs. Victoria C. Woodhull find better uses for her ' brass ' than the posthumous mummery of shaft or tablets. Almost we envy her the ecstasy which a consciousness of imperishable intellectual vigour excites, and shall never cease wondering that a mind so majestic should have ever been imprisoned in a mere temple of flesh. To such reflections are we spurred by the perusal of a ' Startling Annunciation,' which proclaims the establishment of female suffrage by ' positive law and recent events,' and declares the Sixteenth Amendment to be a dead letter ! In this document the victory of Victoria is manifestly complete. Disdaining the vulgar method of controversy, she assails all logic with the invincible weapon of assertion, and through the breach thus made, comes trooping a rabble of deductions with which the most skilful fencer would scarcely have the temerity to cope."

Republican, December 28th, 1870. St. Louis (Mo.).

" Mr. Wendell Phillips says, in his *National Standard* of this week, that the President favours woman's suffrage. General Grant says women are right in pushing their franchise, but he believes with Mrs. Woodhull that the Fifteenth Amendment as it now stands confers the right of suffrage upon women as well as men, their legal status as citizens not being denied before any court of record."

1871.

New York Herald, January 12th, 1871.
ENFRANCHISEMENT OF WOMEN.

" A delegation of ladies met by appointment with the House Judiciary Committee for the purpose of stating their side of the question, and sustaining their several memorials by argument.

" Shortly after ten o'clock, Mrs. Victoria C. Woodhull, of New York, opened the ball at the suggestion of Judge Bingham, the chairman. Mrs. Woodhull will be a candidate for the Presidency in 1872, should Congress legalize female suffrage, and intends to run as an independent candidate on the platform of free suffrage and equality before the law. Her theory is that, by the Fifteenth Amendment to the Constitution, women have already the right to vote, though she is anxious to have it more specifically enacted into the Statutes. Judging from the expressions of the committee after the meeting adjourned, there is no doubt that she made a favourable impression. Some members said that she had presented the case in as good style as any Congressman could have done. She contended that the Constitution of the United States made woman a citizen with the right to vote, and desired to know by what ethics any free government imposed taxes on women without giving them a voice upon the subject, or a participation in the public declarations as to how and by whom these taxes shall be applied for the common public use. Women constituted a majority of the people of this country, and were entrusted with the most vital responsibilities of society. They bear, rear, and educate the men ; train and mould their characters, inspire the noblest impulses in men, and often hold the accumulated fortunes of a man's life for the safety of the family and as guardians of the infants, and yet they are debarred from uttering any opinion by public vote. Women had the right to vote, and it was by usurpation only that they are debarred. In her address she quoted from many legal authorities in support of her argument.

" Other speeches were made, but Mrs. Woodhull had captured the committee, and the others were not needed."

WASHINGTON, D.C.—THE JUDICIARY COMMITTEE OF THE REPRESENTATIVES RECEIVING A DEPUTATION OF *FEMALE SUFFRAGISTS*, JANUARY 11TH, 1871. VICTORIA C. WOODHULL READING HER ARGUMENT IN FAVOUR OF WOMAN'S VOTING ON THE BASIS OF THE 14TH AND 15TH CONSTITUTIONAL AMENDMENTS.

The World, January 12th, 1871. New York City.
"THE SUFFRAGE."
"ARGUMENT BEFORE THE HOUSE JUDICIARY COMMITTEE. MRS.
WOODHULL ON THE FIFTEENTH AMENDMENT.

"The House Judiciary Committee having set apart this forenoon to hear the argument of Mrs. Victoria C. Woodhull, on her paper claiming the elective franchise for women to the Federal Constitution, the room of the committee was crowded. Messrs. Bingham, Butler, Cook, Peters, Loughridge, Kerr, Eldridge, and Kellogg, of the committee, were present, and listened attentively to the arguments presented.

"Mrs. Woodhull's argument.—She contended the constitution of the United States made woman a citizen, with the right to vote, and desired to know by what ethics any free government imposes taxes on woman without giving her a voice upon the subject or participation in the public declaration as to how and by whom these taxes shall be applied for the common public use. Women constituted a majority of the people of this country and were intrusted with the most vital responsibilities of society. They bear, rear, and educate men, train and mould their characters, inspire the noblest impulses in men, and often hold the accumulated fortunes of a man's life for the safety of the family and as guardians of the infants, and yet they are debarred from uttering any opinion by public vote. Women had the right to vote, and it was by usurpation only that they were debarred. In her address she quoted from many legal authorities in support of her argument.

"Mr. A. G. Riddle, an ex-member of Congress from Ohio, spoke next. He thought no man was born to lord it over woman, or no woman born to queen it over man. Every one was born with the rights of citizenship, and should exercise those rights upon arriving at the age of maturity. The constitution of the United States or any other amendments never CONFERRED the elective franchise upon any human being. In that instrument the right was recognized, and the manner of its use provided.

21 *

Minors could not use the elective franchise until arriving at the age of maturity, but EVERY ONE WAS BORN WITH THOSE RIGHTS.

"The Woman's National Suffrage Convention met this afternoon in the presence of a large audience, almost crowding Lincoln's Hall. Mrs. Beecher Hooker introduced Mrs. Woodhull, of New York, as a business woman to whom all Wall Street rendered respect. This was announced to be the lady's maiden effort at speech-making, she has made her *début* at reading in public this morning in the committee-room at the Capitol. Mrs. Woodhull evinced timidity. She read her resolutions as presented to Congress."

Commercial Advertiser, January 12th, 1871. New York City.

"The female suffragists appeared before the Judiciary Committee of the House to advocate their claims. The orator and special pleader of the occasion was Mrs. Victoria C. Woodhull, who, as Miss Anthony said, that Wall Street came to open the eyes of the committee. Mrs. Woodhull's plea was a strong one. Briefly stated, it is that the Constitution recognizes no sex ; a woman is a citizen ; it is her right as a citizen to vote ; women, no more than men can be proscribed on account of race, colour, or previous condition of servitude. The Committee was captured by the persuasive eloquence of the Wall Street Banker and Editor. But Mrs. Butler, to thwart the force of the blow, suggested that matrimony was a 'condition of servitude.'

"It is announced that the Woodhull Memorial will be reported on Friday, and that a resolution will be introduced, declaring that the Constitution nowhere denies women the right to vote.

"This is the bravest and best movement that women have yet made, and no one can tell what momentous results may depend upon it. The new era dawns where there shall be no distinction of sex."

Republican, January 13th, 1871. Chester (Del.).

"Mrs. Victoria C. Woodhull of New York, on Wednesday last, appeared before the Judiciary Committee of the House of Representatives at Washington, and presented a powerfully written memorial, setting forth the rights vested by the Constitution of the United States in the citizens to vote, without regard to sex. It is a bold step for a woman to assert the rights of sex in person before Congress, but it has been made, and earnestly made. In our next paper we shall publish the document, which deserves a wide circulation."

The Star, January 13th, 1871. New York City.

"Mrs. Woodhull is taking a short, direct, business-like, and constitutional way to obtain for women the full rights of citizenship.

"For twenty years the strong-minded sisters have talked, harangued, and circumlocuted. They have called conventions, declaimed concerning the wrongs and oppressions inflicted on them by the tyrant man, and passed volumes of resolutions, which have served no better use than to benefit the paper trade and encourage the art of printing. They have prayed and petitioned Legislatures and Congress to have the right granted to them.

"The National Woman's Suffrage Convention, sitting this time at Washington, has had the wind completely taken out of its sails by that lively little yacht Mrs. Woodhull, who has sailed in between it and the august body whose port it intended to bring its guns to bear upon. She has in a logical and consistent manner set forth her claim to the right of franchise, basing it on the wording of the Constitution, and on the Fourteenth and Fifteenth Amendment. Under the broad shadow of her Memorial, the Biblical argument, logical argument, and aerial asseverations of the pioneers, dwindle into insignificance . . .

"Nevertheless, if the women want it they may be sure Mrs. Woodhull has taken the only proper or feasible · method of obtaining it, viz. through the Constitution of the United States itself. If they have a constitutional right to it, and only one woman demands it on that ground, it should not be longer withheld. Those who do not desire to avail themselves of it need not, and those who do will certainly make no more confusion in our legislation than some of the elements that work in it now."

Tribune, January 16th, 1871. New York City.

THE WOODHULL AND CLAFLIN CAMPAIGN IN WASHINGTON.

"After long grief and pain the Anthony-Stanton faction at last found it was possible to hit upon leaders whose beguiling ways and numerous ducats foreshadowed success to the cause. In the fair persons of Mrs. Victoria C. Woodhull and Miss Tennie C. Claflin, bankers and brokers, woman suffrage discovered the Paladins best fitted to rescue it from dusty oblivion. Its revival must be dated from the hour when in the pure and noble atmosphere of the Capitol Mrs. Woodhull, attended by Miss Anthony, Mrs. Beecher Hooker, Mrs. Paulina Wright Davis, *et al.* bore the memorial that was to lift them from the station of down-trodden suffering they now occupy. In the assertion that the Fourteenth and Fifteenth Amendments give them the rights they want they find all delights and comforts—especially as they, at last, have something new to talk about. To be sure, the committee to whom the memorial was read refused, in the most hard-hearted and *unreasonable* manner, to be convinced, and refused also the motion for a presentment to the House—*but that is of little consequence.* The banking and brokerage business still lives; and General B. T. Butler promises Mrs. Woodhull something shall be done.

" All the past efforts of Miss Anthony and Mrs. H. B. Stanton sink to insignificance beside the ingenious lobbying of the new leader and her daring declaration of political powers under the present provisions of the Constitution. What joy could be greater than that of the organizers of the Convention when lumbering up heavily to Washington upon their venerable hobby the Sixteenth Amendment, they found waiting in the shape of the Fifteenth Amendment a mettlesome spirit, that is to bear them straight to the White House? What slave was there with soul so dead that could resist the temptation of listing under a captain capable of originating so grand an idea, and more than that, capable of subscribing $10,000 to the cause if she wanted to?

Mrs. Victoria C. Woodhull and her sister were the chief ornaments of the Convention."

Tribune, February 17th, 1871.   New York City.

"WASHINGTON, FEBRUARY 16TH.—Lincoln Hall was filled to overflowing, this evening, by a curious audience who assembled to hear the argument which Mrs. Woodhull and Mrs. Beecher Hooker were refused permission to deliver in the House of Representatives. On the platform were seated, among others, Gen. Butler, Mrs. Julian, Mrs. Paulina Wright Davis, Senator and Mrs. Ames, Judge Lawrence, Col. and Mrs. Tappon, while in the audience were many Senators and Representatives.

" Mrs. Woodhull appeared quite nervous, and evidently laboured under considerable excitement; her voice, a little tremulous at first, soon made itself distinctly heard throughout the hall. She read from printed slips an argument intended to be of a logical and legal character, occupying about an hour and a quarter in delivery, to which, after the first few minutes, the audience paid marked attention, with occasional applause. The argument was a careful elaboration of the memorial already printed by the *Tribune*, claiming that Republican government can only exist with the consent of the people, included men and women ; under the Constitution women were citizens ; that citizenship included all rights belonging to citizens of the United States ; shall not be abridged by the States. She argued that the right to representation is herent to all in a government by all ; that, according to Otis and Franklin, a government denying this, and taxing without consent, is a tyranny. One of the points made was on the use of the word qualification, as applied to the franchise. A qualification, she said, must be such as can be obtained by all citizens, otherwise it amounts to disfranchisement. Sex cannot be pleaded as a qualification, because it cannot be changed at the will of any person."

New York Herald, February 17th, 1871.   New York City.

" Mrs. Woodhull has opened her Presidential campaign with

a very effective speech, which she delivered to a full audience in Lincoln Hall at Washington last evening."

" Mrs. Woodhull delivered a lecture in Washington at Lincoln last night on Constitutional equality. The audience was the largest that has appeared in the hall, and although an admission fee was charged hundreds of persons were forced to go away, unable to get inside. General Butler was to have introduced Mrs. Woodhull, but he did not arrive in time, so that duty fell upon Mrs. Paulina Wright Davis. General Butler, accompanied by Senator Ames, his son-in-law, appeared upon the platform soon after Mrs. Woodhull began to speak and took a seat in front. He looked extremely happy, and seemed to be thinking of the excellent chance he would have of being elected President of the United States when the women shall be allowed to vote— that is, provided Mrs. Woodhull is not a candidate. She seems to be the head and front of the movement now, having pushed the others aside, who never could manage to stir up public enthusiasm and enlist prominent politicians in the cause as Mrs. Woodhull has done.

" In addition to General Butler and Senator Ames, Representatives Lawrence, Judge Loughbridge, and Ela were on the platform. These are all converts made by Mrs. Woodhull to the woman suffrage movement. The lecture was listened to with great attention, those parts of it hitting hard at Bingham, the majority of the Judiciary Committee, and the members of the Congress who refused to allow Mrs. Woodhull to have the Hall of the House for her speech, were loudly applauded. Altogether it was a great success."

The Chronicle, February 17th, 1871. Washington (D. C.).

" A vast concourse of intelligent men and women sat in Lincoln Hall last evening, and listened with rapt attention to the masterly argument delivered by Mrs. Woodhull upon the legal aspects of female suffrage. Long before the commencement of the lecture the ushers were busy in procuring chairs for those who could not find other seats, and with all that men and

STORMING THE CAPITOL FOR VOTES.

women stood by scores all around the sides of the room. At eight o'clock Mrs. Paulina Davis advanced to the footlights and stated the object of the lecture in a few clear, earnest words, and then introduced Mrs. Woodhull. This was her first attempt at public speaking. During the remarks of Mrs. Davis she had sat with perfect composure, but those who knew her face saw at a glance that nothing but a tremendous effort of will enabled her to maintain that demeanour. When she commenced to speak, her voice was clear, distinct, and without the least tremor, but her face was perfectly colourless, and she was obliged to stop an instant between each sentence to gain strength to utter the next. It was a grand exhibition of will. But as she progressed and became warmed in her argument, much of the fire of her ordinary conversation returned, her face flushed, and she was herself. The lecture was a triumph, and she demonstrated that, with a little experience, Mrs. Woodhull will be as strong upon the rostrum as she is with the pen."

The Sunday Gazette, February 19th, 1871. Washington (D. C.).

"The audience was the largest that ever congregated in Lincoln Hall, and her speech was applauded throughout."

Daily Republican, February 20th, 1871. Washington (D. C.).

"In Lincoln Hall, on Thursday last, Mrs. Victoria Woodhull delivered an argument upon the legal aspects of the claims of woman to the right of suffrage under the Fourteenth and Fifteenth Amendments of the Constitution.

"Mrs. Woodhull discussed the principles of the republican government as expounded by our revolutionary fathers, and applied them to the great questions of the present day. Of course she found no difficulty in proving woman's natural right to the exercise of the elective franchise. Coming to our own time, the reconstruction measures, both in constitutional amendment and in legislation, were fully discussed by the orator, and by them she fully proved the impregnable position she has assumed. That woman are citizens, and that no State has a right to abridge the rights, privileges, or immunities of citizens and of citizenship, no man of common sense can deny, for these facts are plainly stated in the Constitution. Congress has passed more than one bill to enforce the right of citizens to vote, and hence Bingham's claim that Congress cannot enforce this right on behalf of women is absurd.

" The thanks of all the women in the United States, and of the men, too, are due to Mrs. Woodhull for her brave, eloquent, unanswerable argument."

The New York Herald, March 2nd, 1871. New York City.

" Last evening the Cooper Institute was crowded to overflowing with a fashionable audience of ladies and gentlemen, who had come for the first time to hear Victoria C. Woodhull.

" If the Woman's Movement has a Joan of Arc, it is the gentle and yet fiery spirit, Victoria Woodhull. She is one of the most remarkable women of her time. Little understood by the public, she has been denounced by people who cannot appreciate her moral worth. She is a purest gem of the first water. Her sincerity, truthfulness, nobility, and uprightness of character rank her as a pious Catholic would rank Theresa. She is a devotee, a religious enthusiast, a seer of visions. I was astonished at the singular revelation of her character to me, as one of the most upright, truthful, religious, unsullied souls I have ever met with."

The Times, March 2nd, 1871. New York City.

" The house was crowded, and, inasmuch as when the doors were opened a surging multitude was doing its best to get inside, there is little doubt that the hall could have been filled twice over. She was loudly cheered as she left the stage, and received a shower of floral offerings."

The World, March 2nd, 1871. New York City.

" Victoria C. Woodhull delivered her lecture last evening to one of the largest audiences ever seen in Cooper Institute. The door-keeper could scarcely take and separate the tickets. She closed her lecture and walked off amid immense thunders of applause. She was literally covered with bouquets as she made her exit."

The Daily News, March 2nd, 1871. New York City.

"Mrs. Woodhull has a clear, musical voice, a commanding intellect, and remarkable executive ability, and will undoubtedly play a conspicuous part in the future."

The World, March 2nd, 1871. New York City.

"The large hall of Cooper Institute was literally crowded last evening." .

The Tribune, March 2nd, 1871. New York City.

"There was a full attendance of ladies and gentlemen, and the lecture was an undoubted success."

The Democrat, March 2nd, 1871. New York City.

"Before the doors opened, a large crowd gathered on the street, and the result was suggestive of the Piccolomini Opera Matinées, where the women thought nothing of crushed bonnets and torn dresses, provided they obtained front seats."

The Evening Telegram, March 2nd, 1871. New York City.

"There was an audience of magnificent proportions assembled at Cooper Institute last evening, to hear Victoria C. Woodhull. At an early hour the hall began to fill, and by eight o'clock every seat was filled, and as the price of admission was one dollar, the result, financially, must have been very gratifying."

The Evening Post, March 2nd, 1871. New York City.

"Victoria C. Woodhull lectured last evening before a large audience."

The Globe, March 2nd, 1871. New York City.

"Cooper Institute was thronged with men and women, and Mrs. Woodhull delivered her celebrated Constitutional Washington Lecture."

The Post, March 22nd, 1871. Philadelphia (Pa.).

"The Academy of Music was filled last evening, and the continuous applause of the audience, if it did not endorse her sentiments, at least demonstrated how doubly potent is genius

'when wielded by lovely woman.' Her style was trenchant,
and the scathing manner in which she handled Congress in
general, and Mr. Bingham in particular, gave evidence of the
logical force in her composition.

" '. . . I am of that portion of the people who are denied
the rights of citizens, and who, without voice in the pursuit of
justice, am one of that sovereignty to whom this Government
owes it existence and to whom it will be held accountable, as
it holds all accountable who set themselves against human
rights.'

" 'On December 19th, 1870, I memorialized Congress, setting
forth what I believe to be the truth and right regarding equal
suffrage for all citizens. This memorial was referred to the
Judiciary Committee of Congress ; on January 12th I appeared
before the House Judiciary Committee and submitted to them
the constitution and legal point upon which I predicated such
equality. On January 20th Mr. Bingham on behalf of the
majority of said Committee submitted his report to the House,
in which, while he admitted all my basic propositions, Congress
was recommended to take no action. February 1st, Messrs.
Loughbridge and Butler of said Committee submitted a report
in their own behalf and recommended that Congress should
pass a Declaratory Act, for ever settling the mooted question of
suffrage.

" 'Thus it is seen that equally able men differ upon a simple
point of constitutional law, and it is fair to presume that Congress will also differ when these points come up for action.
That a proposition involving such momentous results as this
should receive a one-third vote upon first coming before
Congress, has raised it to an importance which spreads alarm
on all sides among the opposition. So long as it was not made to
appear that women were denied constitutional rights, no opposition was aroused, but now that new light is shed, by which it is
seen that such is the case, all the conservative weapons of
bitterness, hatred, and malice are marshalled in the hope to

extinguish it before it can enlighten the masses of the people, who are always true to freedom and justice. . . . .

" ' Public opinion is against equality, but it is simply from prejudice, which requires but to be informed to pass away. No greater prejudice exists against equality than there did against the proposition that the world was a globe. This passed away under the influence of better information ; so also will present prejudice pass when better informed upon questions of equality.

" ' It cannot be said with justice that my pursuit of happiness in voting for any man for office would be an infringement of one of his rights as a citizen or as an individual. I hold, then, that in denying me this right without my having forfeited it, departure is made from the principles of Constitution, and also from the true principles of Government, for I am denied a right born with me, and which is inalienable. Nor can it be objected that women had no part in organizing this Government. They were not denied. To-day we seek a voice in Government and are denied. There are thousands of male citizens in the country who seldom or never vote. They are not denied ; they pursue happiness by not voting. Could it be assumed because this body of citizens do not choose to exercise the right to vote, that they could be permanently denied the exercise thereof ? If not, neither should it be assumed to deny women, who wish to vote, the right to do so.

" ' If there are women who do not desire to have a voice in the laws to which they are accountable and which they must contribute to support, let them speak for themselves, but they should not assume to speak for me or for those whom I represent.

" ' The condition of the people of this country to-day is this. I and others of my sex find ourselves controlled by a form of Government in the inauguration of which we had no voice, and in whose administration we are denied the right to participate, though we are a large portion of the people of this country. Not long since I was notified by a United States officer than if I did not pay a certain tax the Government had imposed upon

me, my property would be levied upon and sold for that purpose.
Is this tyranny, or can men find some other word to take the
place of that used by our fathers so freely, and by Congress, not
so long ago as to be forgotten, with such powerful effect?

" 'I am subject to tyranny, I am taxed in every conceivable
way. For publishing a paper, I must pay—for engaging in the
banking and brokerage business, I must pay—of what it is my
fortune to acquire each year, I must turn over a certain per
cent. I must pay high prices for tea, coffee, and sugar. To all
these I must pay. I submit to men's government, in the
administration of which I am denied a voice, and from whose
edicts there is no appeal.'

" Mrs. Woodhull at this point went into an exhaustive logical
attack upon the injustice with which our statesmen expounded the
Fifteenth Amendment. She said, when I was before Congress, I
said to Mr. Bingham, ' I want to vote because I am a citizen ;'
he replied, ' You are not a citizen.' ' What am I ?' I asked.
' You are a woman,' he said. I told him I knew that before I
came to Washington. And it is just such frivolous and illogical
arguments that are brought to bear against the woman's suffrage
question. By the very working of that amendment every
woman is allowed to vote as well as every man. The question
of sex is urged as an objection, but nowhere is the sex specified.
Perhaps no men were intended to vote. The qualification argument is the most stupid of all, and needs no comment.

" 'Therefore, I would have Congress, in the pursuit of its
duty, to enforce the constitution by appropriate legislation, pass
a declaratory act plainly setting forth the right of all citizens
to vote, and thus render unnecessary the thousands of suits for
damages which will otherwise arise. What legislation could be
more appropriate than defining the right of one-half the citizens
in the country, when they are in question ? This matter
has passed beyond the States. They have delegated this power
to Congress by these amendments. Could the Legislatures of
the States think of legislating upon the question of who are

citizens? How can they then deny the rights of these same citizens.
which are no less clearly a part of the Constitution than the fact
of citizenship? If Congress refuse to legislate appropriately in
this matter, every woman who desires to vote should take all
the steps required as prerequisites to become qualified, and if
prevented, then under the plainly worded act of May 30th,
1870, so continue to do until the Government of the United
States and of the several States, shall be made to enforce the
supreme laws of the land, and thus secure to every citizen equal
right and exact justice under a Republican form of Government.

" ' The new woman Government will do away with the thousand abuses that now palsy the arm of legislation. Under its
operation we propose to reform the conduct of public officials;
the tenure of office, making it one term, and civil service.

" 'The Finances . . . . the system of internal improvements,
commerce and navigation, the relation of the employée and the
employer; protection and revenue. . . . . To organize a general
system of education, &c. And in the furtherance of this noble
object, I ask the concurrence of every woman in this house and
in the land. If they do not wish to vote, I alone, however, will
stand and reiterate my claim. My paper, *Woodhull & Claflin's
Weekly*, is devoted to this and every glorious and ennobling
cause. But I do not believe I stand alone, and could we but get
forwarded to Congress the names of those women who wish to
vote the question would be speedily settled, as I believe Congress
willing to do.' "

Press, March 22nd, 1871.   Philadelphia (Pa.).

RIGHTS OF WOMEN UNDER THE CONSTITUTION.

" Last evening, at the Academy of Music, Mrs. Victoria C.
Woodhull delivered her lecture upon ' Constitutional Equality.'
The lecturess was accompanied by Mrs. Lucretia Mott, Mrs.
Paulina W. Davis, Mrs. Wright, and Mrs. M. E. Davis, they

22

making their appearance upon the platform about eight o'clock. The lecturess was introduced by Mrs. Paulina W. Davis, who said in substance as follows:

" ' The only vital living question of to-day is the enfranchisement of women. It has become so important that it can no longer be ignored or ridiculed. The question has taken a new form as well as a new interest during the last year. Men now acknowledge the right of women to franchise and are in favour of giving it to the mothers of the race. There has been a good champion of this cause, a Joan of Arc, in defence of the rights of women, and that one she now has the honour to introduce in the person of Mrs. Victoria C. Woodhull.' (Applause.)

" The lecturess, who has a very intellectual face, clear cut features, was very plainly dressed in dark blue broadcloth, wearing no ornaments."

Daily Times, May 9th, 1871. New York City.

" At the evening session at Apollo Hall, Mrs. Victoria Woodhull read a lengthy manuscript. Her theme was ' The Relation of Capital to Labour.' The production abounded with copious extracts from Government reports, library quotations, and statistical tables. She said: There are three questions of vital importance to the human family. These are equal political rights, social order, and moral responsibility. If the first is guaranteed the others follow."

Daily Tribune, May 10th, 1871. New York City.

" The Woman's Suffrage Bureau met at Washington, during the progress of the great campaign which Mrs. Woodhull and Mrs. Beecher Hooker conducted against Congress. We quote from the official report in the *Chronicle.*

" Mrs. Senator Stearns, of Minnesota, then rose and said that she desired to offer a resolution that deeply affected every woman interested in the cause of Woman's Suffrage. She hoped it would be concurred in by the meeting. It was as follows :—

"'BE IT RESOLVED, That we honour Victoria C. Woodhull for her fine intellectual ability, her courage and independence of character, her liberality and high moral worth, and, since every word, look, and act impresses us with the conviction that she is profoundly in earnest, we feel that for this earnestness and fearlessness we, as women, owe her a debt of gratitude which we can only repay by working with and for her with our whole hearts.'"

Tribune, May 12th, 1871. New York City.

"The lady whose intellectual ability and high moral worth we lately indorsed. For ourselves, we toss our hats in the air for Woodhull. She has the courage of her own opinion. She means business. This is a spirit to respect. Would that the rest of those who burden themselves with the enfranchisement of one-half our whole population now lying in chains and slavery but had her sagacious courage."

Standard, August 12th, 1871. New York City.

CANDIDATE FOR CONGRESS.

"Miss Tennie C. Claflin delivered her speech last evening in Irving Hall, in German. She appeared as a candidate of the German-American Progressive Association for Senatorial honours in the VIIIth Assembly District."

Sun, August 12th, 1871. New York City.

"The German-American Progressive Association turned out in full number at Irving Hall last night to listen to a political

22 *

speech in German by Miss Tennie C. Claflin, of the famous banking firm of Woodhull, Claflin & Co., and independent candidate for Congress in the Eighth District of this city. The hall was well filled with an attentive and appreciative audience, composed largely of the better class of German citizens, with their wives and daughters, with a liberal sprinkling of the American element.

"Miss Claflin appeared, smiling her acknowledgments of the vociferous cheers and deafening applause that greeted her. She was dressed in a dress of black organdie with a small figure in colours, made *en train*, and very plainly trimmed. Her hair, which she wears short, hung loose and bushy about her forehead and temples. She wore no jewellery or ornaments. As soon as the applause had subsided, she proceeded to speak in a clear, strong voice, using the German language, from which we translate her remarks as follows :

"MISS CLAFLIN'S SPEECH. ARE WOMEN CITIZENS ?—'The law under which I—and with me all women, in whose behalf I know that you are all interested—claim the rights of a citizen of the State of New York, reads as follows: Article first, section first, of the Fourteenth Amendment : "All persons born or naturalized in the United States, and subject to the jurisdiction thereof, are citizens of the United States and of the State wherein they reside."

"'I fulfil the necessary conditions. I was born in the United States, and am therefore a native citizen of the same, and subject to the jurisdiction thereof. Why, then, I ask you, should I not be allowed to vote ? And if I am allowed to vote, why may I not hold an office ? (Applause.)

"IS A WOMAN CAPABLE OF HOLDING OFFICE ?—' Do you believe that a woman, for no other reason than because she is a woman, must necessarily lack the energy to perform the duties of an office ? or do you believe that things could go worse in the administration of our national affairs than they now do ? Try the experiment merely of entrusting a woman with the performance of official duties, and if you find that your interests suffer by so doing, the power will still be retained by you to retrieve your mistake.

" ' But do not imagine that you can entirely ignore a movement which does not rest merely on the law, but which also brings into the contest the best and soundest cosmopolitan ideas.'

" WILL SHE BE ADMITTED IF ELECTED ?—' Neither need you entertain any apprehension that Congress will withhold my seat from me if I receive a majority of the votes. It is a part of my object to make this case a test; and there is, up to this date, no law which either forbids the people to elect a woman to an office, or which forbids her to accept it.

" ' Corruption and bribery, if not indeed foreign to the nature of women generally, are in any event foreign to my nature. And, without having to resort to means which are prevalent among politicians, who stuff the ballot-box and pay repeaters, I shall step into the arena as a candidate for the office of Representative of the Eighth District in Congress, commending myself entirely and exclusively to your favourable regards.'

" A PRESENTATION.—At the conclusion of the speech, the hall rang again with cheers and applause, in the midst of which Miss Claflin was presented with an elegant basket of flowers, arranged with exquisite taste, the initials ' T. C. C.' being formed in monogram in the centre, with ' M. C. 8th Dist.' around the outside. On receiving this beautiful token, which was understood to be the gift of her Wall Street friends, Miss Claflin retired from the stand.

" After listening to short speeches by Judge Reymert and Mr. Hugo Eloesser, the audience dispersed.

" THE CANDIDATE SERENADED.—At a later hour in the evening, the German admirers of Miss Claflin favoured her with a serenade at her palatial residence on Murray Hill. A full military band, one of the best in the city, was provided, and performed some choice selections of operatic airs. Miss Claflin appeared upon the balcony, and very briefly returned her thanks for the honour."

Globe, August 20th, 1871.

"A much later sensation in this class of journalism is the hebdomadal sheet bearing the names of Woodhull & Claflin, which started some fifteen months ago. Its tone, which from the first was startling and aggressive, made even a more unfavourable impression on the public than the establishment of the lady proprietors in their Broad Street office. The names of these two 'bold women' were on every tongue. Any gossip concerning them was eagerly grasped and turned to capital for the newspapers. But the sisters were prepared for all of this. They persisted in the even tenor of their way, with as unswerving will as would have been possible had they ridden the top wave of popularity. They wrote, they spoke, they acted with undaunted perseverance; and while people stood aghast, Woodhull & Claflin were cutting their granite way to future success. Last winter Mrs. Woodhull came before the public in an entirely new character. Not content with disseminating her views through the columns of her paper, she prepared her celebrated memorial and went to Washington to press the cause of woman on the basis of the Fourteenth and Fifteenth Amendments. Although a regularly organized society was then in convention assembled, many members of which repudiated all sympathy with Mrs. Woodhull, she seemed, nevertheless, to take both the ladies and the judiciary by storm, actually accomplishing more by this novel effort than could be claimed for any previous convention, besides winning for herself wide-spread favour.

"Women who had denounced her before, now took her hand in sincere friendship. Mrs. Hooker, Mrs. Davis, and many other well-known reformers, became at once her staunch supporters, while the sweet and gentle Lucretia Mott sent her greeting, saying, ' Victoria, my heart and home are ever open to thee.'

" Her paper continued daily to increase in circulation. It is now probably the most influential journal of its kind in the country. However it may be regarded elsewhere, in New York it is looked upon as a strong ally and a formidable adversary, and notwithstanding the prejudices that did exist and are still perceptible, it is universally admitted that *Woodhull & Claflin's Weekly* is destined to wield a powerful influence in the ultimate enfranchisement of women."—*Cincinnati Chronicle and Times.*

The Herald, September 19th, 1871. Cleveland (Ohio).

"About five thousand people assembled in the Rink to listen to the lecture of Victoria C. Woodhull, on Constitutional Equality.

" Her address occupied in its delivery fully one hour and a quarter ; was listened to with unbroken silence, save for occasional outbreaks of applause."

The Cleveland Plaindealer, September 19th, 1871. Cleveland (Ohio).

" A very large audience gathered in the Rink. Her manner is the very reverse of forward. She is unquestionably deeply in earnest and unflinching. She read her lecture, the elocution being faultless. Her voice is clear and musical."

Banner of Light, September 19th, 1871.

"Mrs. Woodhull was greeted with applause as she walked forward on the speaker's stand. In a calm and dignified manner she commenced reading her address. The large audience at once became silent, and gave a most respectful hearing to the earnest speaker.

" Mrs. Woodhull holds her manuscript in one hand, and in tones firm and at times musical, delivers her message to the people. We wish we could portray the scene in the Rink during Mrs. Woodhull's oration. It was a sight never to be forgotten to see the vast assemblage under the magic spell of the eloquent speaker—not of eloquence technically so-called by the schools, but that eloquence which comes from earnest conviction, wherein the look of the eye, the expression of the face, and the quiver of the voice all go to show that things superficial have been laid aside, and that the domains of earnestness, sincerity, and fidelity have been fully entered upon. Mrs. Woodhull may well feel proud of her effort in Cleveland. She came, she saw, she conquered. Prejudice melts before her genial presence ; scandal flees away into oblivion when (in her own impressive way she talks to you—you see the light ?; yes, the light of honour and truth shining in her eyes, and all who are friendly to those that have been friendless rejoice to know that Mrs. Victoria Woodhull is slowly but surely marching on to peace, harmony and prosperity."

Daily Times, October 10th, 1871. Brooklyn (N.Y.).

" The Masonic Hall was crowded last evening by a respectable and intelligent audience gathered to hear Mrs. Victoria C. Woodhull discuss the claims of women to franchise. . . Mrs. Woodhull spoke for nearly an hour and a half, and was loudly applauded at intervals."

Sun, October 25th, 1871. Baltimore (Md.)

" Mrs. Victoria C. Woodhull—candidate of the 'Equal Rights Party' for presidency of the United States, upon the great Political Issues—lectured at Masonic Temple."

Gazette, October 25th, 1871. Baltimore (Md.).

" MRS. VICTORIA C. WOODHULL.—This lady, who has become so prominent an advocate for woman's rights, and who more recently has been extensively advertised as a candidate for the next Presidency of the United States, delivered a lecture last night at Masonic Temple."

VICTORIA VICTA—VICTORIA C. WOODHULL AND TENNIE C. CLAFLIN AT THE POLLS IN THE CITY OF NEW YORK ON ELECTION DAY, NOV. 7TH. THEY PRESENT THEIR BALLOTS, BUT ARE DENIED THE EXERCISE OF THE ELECTIVE FRANCHISE.

VOTING.

New York Herald, November 8th, 1871.

OUR WOMEN POLITICIANS.

DESPERATE ATTEMPT OF DETERMINED FEMALES TO DROP A VOTE
—HEARTLESS CONDUCT OF TAMMANY INSPECTORS—VIC. AND
TENNIE WILL INVOKE THE LAW AND MAKE ROME HOWL.

"A new epoch is upon the unsophisticated citizen of New York.
Yesterday thirty-two unterrified, indomitable females attempted
to vote, but were refused the privilege by ungallant Tammany
democrats. Leading this formidable election innovation was
the intellectual Mrs. Victoria C. Woodhull, supported by the
piquant Miss Tennie C. Claflin, who advanced on the universal
suffrage question with the solidity of a Grecian phalanx and
the tread of a Roman legion. The line of battle was formed at
the headquarters of woman's rights, in Thirty-eighth Street,
where a solemn vow was registered, and each determined
female unsheathed her parasol and swore to vote in spite of
democratic denunciations and republican sneers. The elegant
drawing-room of Mrs. Woodhull at half-past two yesterday afternoon presented an animated appearance. A dozen intellectual
ladies had there congregated, and, to the accompaniment of
rustling silks, flashed words of wisdom from fluent lips. Nervous
but lily-white hands impatiently turned the leaves of ponderous
volumes, and in a flush of conscious pride the irresistible Tennie
read the following Fourteenth and Fifteenth Amendments :—

" 'All persons born or naturalized in the United States and subject to
the jurisdiction thereof are citizens of the United States and of the State
wherein they reside. No State shall make or enforce any law which shall
abridge the privileges or immunities of citizens of the United States. The
right of citizens of the United States to vote shall not be denied or abridged
by the United States, or by any State, on account of race, colour, or previous
condition of servitude.'

"The assembly thus satisfied themselves that the law was on their side, and, confident in their right, sallied forth and swept down on the astonished inspectors, who were immediately overwhelmed by a flood of legal lore and argument that would have convinced any but an unterrified democrat. The company on leaving the mansion threw out a skirmish line, but the field officers—Mrs. Woodhull, Miss Claflin, and Mrs. E. L. Daniels—deployed on No. 682 Sixth Avenue, the polling place of the Twenty-third district of the Twenty-first ward. Accompanying them as camp followers were several gentlemen who have earned a wide notoriety by the interest taken in the woman's rights movement. Behind the ballot box sat three vigilant inspectors, and when the beautiful would-be voters burst on their astonished gaze beards were stroked and coat-collars set in order. The usual preliminaries on the weather and other inconsequential subjects were entirely omitted, and Mrs. Woodhull, in the softest accents of womanly determination, stated that she had come there to exercise her privilege as a citizen of the United States to vote. The republican inspector held out his hand to take the bundle of reform tickets handed by the fair voter, but his democratic *confrères* objected and told her plumply that Tammany Hall had given them orders not to receive the votes of women. Indignation then sparkled from bright eyes, and the fair lady demanded if it was a crime to be a woman. She had registered and was therefore amenable to the law prohibiting illegal voting, but as nobody had arrested her she was not guilty of a misdemeanour, and therefore claimed the right to deposit her vote. The inspectors, however, were inexorable, and her persuasive eloquence fell on unappreciative ears. A crowd, however, soon collected and the little polling place was jammed by a couple of hundred quidnuncs who came to see how the 'new thing was going to work.' One sympathetic gentleman from Murray Hill lent the sisterhood much moral support by his advocacy of woman's right to vote. 'I have a

wife and family,' he said, 'and if I should be suddenly taken
away my property would be swept off by corrupt officials, and
they would have no power to stem the tide of political
dishonesty.' He wanted to see woman boldly enter the arena
and bring the refining influence of her sex to bear on the
political world. What may appear absurd to-day may assume
a serious aspect to-morrow, and the party espousing this
woman question will be the dominant one in the hereafter.
Mrs. Woodhull then delivered a long peroration on the science
of government, and Miss Tennie C. Claflin predicted that
republicanism would be the guiding star of progress, as it
had espoused woman's rights and was willing to allow the
fair sex all the privileges accorded to man. The inspector
wanted to know if she had come with a mandamus compelling
him to receive her vote, and receiving a negative reply,
regretted that he was acting under instructions and could
not receive it under any consideration. The ladies then
withdrew and retired to the mansion in Thirty-eighth Street,
where it was determined to commence a suit against the
inspectors for illegally preventing legitimate voters from
exercising the right of suffrage. Judge Reymert and Mr.
William M. Evarts are to be engaged as counsel, and this is
to be made a famous test question. The ladies are confident
that the right granted in Wyoming Territory and recently
in Michigan will be accorded in this State. A great deal of
enthusiasm and excitement are agitating the minds of these
petticoat politicians, and the fair candidate for the Presidency
is indefatigable in keeping the next live issue before the public
eye."

Times, November 8th, 1871. (New York City.)

THE RIGHT OF WOMEN TO VOTE.

A PROTEST FROM MRS. WOODHULL.

To the Editor of the "New York Times."

" I have been refused the right of voting by the Democratic inspectors of my district, the Republican dissenting and desiring to receive my vote. Under the election laws of the State either the inspectors are 'guilty of felony,' since they prevented a legal voter from voting, or I attempted to vote illegally, and either they or I shall be convicted of the crime.

"Article 2, section 1, of the State Constitution, provides: 'All male citizens, &c., &c., shall be entitled to vote.' Article 1, Section 1, provides : ' No member of this State shall be disfranchised or deprived of the right or privilege secured to any citizen, unless by the law of the land or the judgment of his peers.'

" I am a member of the State, and no law has been enacted to disfranchise or deprive me of any right or privilege secured to other citizens. Moreover, if a single citizen of the State of New York has the right to vote, every other citizen has the same right, with the exceptions referred to. The point involved can by no possible stretch be made to cover the right of the State to exclude women citizens of the State, since no law is better established than that a right secured by positive terms cannot be taken away by implication, and to take away the rights secured in positive terms by Article 1, section 1, of the Constitution, because Article 2, section 1, fails to provide for female citizens in terms, would be to take away such rights by implication. The Constitution of the United States is also equally clear in securing the right to vote to all persons. The Fourteenth Amendment, section 1, provides :—

" ' All persons born or naturalized in the United States, and subject to the jurisdiction thereof, are citizens of the United States and of the State wherein they reside. No State shall make or enforce any law which shall abridge the privileges and immunities of citizens of the United States.'

A PROTEST FROM VICTORIA C. WOODHULL.

" The right to vote is recognized as a citizen's right by the Fifteenth Amendment, as follows : ' The right of citizens of the United States to vote shall not be denied,' &c., &c. The right to vote, then, is possessed by citizens of the United States. Women are citizens, hence voters. But if there is any doubt about the right to vote being secured beyond the power of abridgment or denial by the Fourteenth Amendment in the provision which forbids the States to abridge the privileges of citizens of the United States upon the ground that [the right to vote is not included in privileges, I beg to submit that the Supreme Court of the United States has already settled that question. In delivering the opinion of the Court, Justice Bradley said :—

"' It is possible that those who framed the article were not themselves aware of the far-reaching character of its terms. Yet, if the amendment does, in fact, bear a broader meaning, and does extend its protecting shield over those who were never thought of when it was conceived and put in form, and does reach social evils which were never before prohibited by Constitutional enactments, it is to be presumed that the American people in giving it their *imprimatur*, understood what they were doing, and meant to decree what in fact they have decreed. The privileges and immunities secured by the original Constitution were only such as each State gave to its own citizens. . . But the Fourteenth Amendment prohibits any State from abridging the privileges or immunities of citizens of the United States, whether its own citizens or any other. It not merely requires equality of privileges, but it demands that the privileges and immunities of all citizens shall be absolutely unabridged and unimpaired. These privileges cannot be invaded without sapping the very foundation of republican government. A republican government is not merely a government of the people, but it is a free government. . . It was very ably contended on the part of the defendants that the Fourteenth Amendment was intended only to secure to all citizens equal capacities before the law. That was at first our view of it. But it does not so read. The language is : "No State shall abridge the privileges or immunities of citizens of the United States." What are the privileges or immunities of citizens of the United States ? Are they capacities merely ? Are they not also rights ? '

" The Supreme Court has, therefore, already decided that the privileges secured by the amendment are something more than equal civil rights ; in fact, that they include all political rights.

In an opinion delivered by Justice McKay he declares the law as follows :—

" ' All persons recognized by the Constitution as citizens of the State have equal legal and political rights, except as otherwise expressly declared.'

" Also, in the same opinion :—

" ' It is the settled and uniform sense of the word " citizen," when used in reference to the citizens of the separate States of the United States, and to their rights as such citizens, that it describes a person entitled to every right, *legal and political*, enjoyed by any person in that State, *unless there be some express exceptions made by positive law covering the particular persons whose rights are in question.*'

" Justice Washington makes the case still clearer when he says :—

" ' The privileges and immunities conceded by the Constitution of the United States to citizens in the several States are to be confined to those which in their nature are fundamental and belong of right to all free government. Such are the rights of protection of life and liberty, and to acquire and enjoy property, and to pay no higher impositions than other citizens, and to enjoy the electoral franchise, as regulated and established by the Constitution and laws of the State in which it is to be exercised.'

" If anyone should question what is involved by regulating and establishing the elective franchise, desiring to argue that it can be regulated and established out of existence, as in the present case of women, I call attention to the meaning of these words: To regulate is ' to put in order,' not to put out of existence; to establish is 'to make stable and firm,' not to nullify or withhold.

" Finally, the Act of Congress of May 31st, 1870, known as the ' Force Act,' to enforce the new amendments, makes it a penal offence, punishable by fine and imprisonment, for inspectors of elections to prevent citizens of the United States from voting, when they are properly registered and qualified.

" Much has been said in the daily Press about my claim being ' a farce,' by journals which persistently shut their columns to all rebutting arguments. I trust you may do your women readers the justice to publish this outline of the position by which it is claimed that women are legal voters under both the

State and Federal Constitutions. One-sided and dogmatic journalism is too common, and I shall hail the day when a free Press shall be inaugurated.

"VICTORIA C. WOODHULL.

"No. 44, Broad Street, *Tuesday, November 7th,* 1871."

The Press, November 10th, 1871. Philadelphia (Pa.).

"A large audience assembled to hear the noted defender of the Rights of Woman—Victoria C. Woodhull."

The Philadelphia Public Record, November 10th, 1871. Philadelphia (Pa.).

"Horticultural Hall last evening was filled, the audience being mostly ladies who had assembled there to hear Victoria C. Woodhull lecture on ' The True and the False, Socially.' Her brilliant oratory, fine impassioned eloquence, sweet-toned voice, dramatic powers, and graceful appearance fairly entranced the audience, the spell being frequently broken by enthusiastic demonstration."

Daily Times, November 15th, 1871. Hartford (Conn.).

"Mrs. Victoria C. Woodhull's lecture on ' Woman's Suffrage ' was delivered to a good audience at the Opera House last evening. It was well written, recapitulating the arguments of the Butler-Loughbridge pamphlet. It was a dignified, courteous speech in which all the arguments in favour of Woman's Suffrage, under the Sixteenth and Fifteenth Amendments, were brought together."

Popular Appeal, November 18th, 1871. Detroit (Mich.).

VICTORIA C. WOODHULL.

"This lady is announced to lecture on her favourite theme of equal rights for Women, at Young Men's Hall, on Saturday evening, 25th inst. We hope that no person will go to hear her from curiosity, but we do hope that every person who feels a

23 *

desire to form correct judgments either of persons or things, who
may feel an interest in the person or her theme, will attend, and
give her an attentive hearing, and her matter a candid consideration. There is probably no person in the country with
reference to whom opinions differ so widely as this same Mrs. Victoria C. Woodhull. Many persons and papers have committed the
mistake of seeking to put down the cause which she espouses,
with ridicule. On the other hand, many others find in these
very facts in her history the disciplinary experiences that have
evolved in her a soul-purity and spiritual illumination that make
her almost an angel of light. Between these wide differences
of opinion, there may be a golden mean. Her cause, moreover,
is one entitled to a respectful consideration, and it is alike
cowardly and unjust to seek to meet it with ridicule."

The Express, November 21st, 1871. Rochester (N.Y.).

THE SUFFRAGE.

" Victoria C. Woodhull lectured in Corinthian Hall before an
audience larger than is usual for lectures outside of the regular
course, and who came to hear the ablest advocate of Woman
Suffrage. She made a strong impression on the audience that
she was a woman of remarkable originality and power. It was
three times as large as the audience Robert Collyer called out,
and larger than Mrs. Livermore had, about the same time."

The Democrat and Chronicle, November 21st, 1871. Rochester (N.Y.).

" Her manner in private conversation is quick and nervous ;
her style of speaking in public seems very quiet and subdued,
but it may be expected at any moment that she may lose control
of herself and soar away into eloquence ; her voice is soft, clear,
and pleasant to listen to, at least in a public hall. There are
cadences in it that to an active imagination are suggestive of
the same story that is legible in her face. There can be but one
opinion as to the ability with which she advocates her principles.

Her public career has been short, and she has shown in it the skill and personal tact of a woman, and a manly courage bordering on audacity. Her brilliant qualities have won her many champions."

The Post, Providence (R.I.).

"Mrs. Woodhull is a speaker who possesses a very pleasing and impassioned delivery, giving to every sentence a just and appropriate emphasis and cadence, and sustaining the ear with a graceful variety of intonation. Her earnestness and eloquence of manner showed a fervid and enthusiastic interest in the subject-matter she was presenting."

The Whig, Troy (N.Y.).

"I know of no other public character with such a triumphant expression of impassioned thought."

Times, November 21st, 1871. New York City.

"One of the largest audiences ever collected together in a public hall in this city, assembled last night at Steinway Hall, on the occasion of a lecture by Mrs. Victoria C. Woodhull."

Tribune, November 21st, 1871. New York City.

"The Social Problem never had a bolder advocate than Mrs. Victoria C. Woodhull proved herself last night at Steinway Hall. The announcement that she would speak drew together a crowd such as Steinway Hall probably never before contained— a crowd which filled the house completely, seats, aisles, and galleries, for the name of Mrs. Victoria C. Woodhull, associated as it is with all that is startling in the sphere of social ideas, was a guarantee that the intellectual food sought for by many among the hundreds who heard her last night would certainly be forthcoming."

The World, November 21st, 1871. New York City.

" An overflowing audience crowded Steinway Hall in every part last evening, some of whom were cordially disappointed at the high moral ground and limited licence which the speaker's definition of Freedom would allow."

The Sun, November 21st, 1871. New York City.

" Steinway Hall was crowded last evening—boxes, floor, and galleries. The speaker was received with applause. She looked unusually well in her blue broadcloth. A tea-rose fastening her collar contrasted with her snowy neck and her light-brown hair now set back in Yankee style from her blushing face."

The Herald, November 21st, 1871. New York City.

" Last evening Mrs. Woodhull lectured to an audience of three thousand people. She had an inspired look. Her eyes burned with suppressed fire. She wore a fresh tea-rose, which enhanced the fairness of her skin, and combatted with the blushes on her cheeks for precedence."

Dispatch, December 2nd, 1871. Pittsburg (Pa.).

" Library Hall was crowded last night to hear Mrs. Victoria C. Woodhull, the most prominent woman of our time, discuss the Social Question."

1872.

The Post, January 6th, 1872. Boston (Mass.).

" The largest audience of the season gathered together, filling floor, balconies and side aisles, to hear the Lady Banker and Diplomatist."

The Herald, January 6th, 1872. Boston (Mass.).

" Music Hall was packed last night, to see Victoria . C. Woodhull, the inventor and expounder of so many advanced opinions on various subjects. Few of the audience expected to see in the lecturer what they did see—a small woman of frail figure, devoid of crinoline and all sorts of modern nonsense."

The Journal, January 6th, 1872. Boston (Mass.).

" Victoria C. Woodhull drew a large audience at the Music Hall. The famous lady is of medium height, rather slender, and rather careworn face."

The Advertiser, January 6th, 1872. Boston (Mass.).

" Something like 2500 persons gathered to hear Victoria C. Woodhull. The platform contained more people than have sat around a speaker on most occasions this winter. Everybody seemed to be animated with a desire to comprehend the personality of the bold proclaimer of what are known as social heresies."

The Commonwealth, January 6th, 1872. Boston (Mass.).

" A woman in her thirties, with well-formed features, bright, dark eyes, trim figure, modestly dressed, stood up in our Music Hall, on Wednesday evening last, before an audience filling the hall, many of them representative of the best thought of New England, and for an hour and a half with logical sequence and earnest voice discussed with the utmost plainness all the problems and relations of social and family intercourse. She was listened to with deference, encouraged with much applause, and retired with the verdict of all that she had spoken much truth."

The Republican, January 6th, 1872. Springfield (Mass.).

"Mrs. Victoria C. Woodhull spoke in the Music Hall last evening on the principles of Social Freedom, before a very intelligent and attentive audience. The house was packed. She stood before this critical and curious audience a surprise. They expected an absolutely defiant, utterly incomprehensible woman. She was perfectly comprehensible and perfectly womanly. She is magnetic, and one sees and understands the divinity that attracts all. Although a perfect law unto themselves, half of Boston will, any day, follow Victoria Woodhull as disciples of her faith."

Herald, January 12th, 1872. New York City.

WOMAN SUFFRAGE.

WASHINGTON, January 11th.

"Miss Anthony is proud that Victoria Woodhull presented her memorial before the Judiciary Committee, and the youth, beauty, and wealth of Mrs. Woodhull carried the day, and the grave legislators, 'even Ben Butler,' bowed before these combined attractions. No one made a leader of Mrs. Woodhull; *like all great leaders, she made herself."* . . .

Democrat, February 5th, 1872. Kansas City.

"On January 10th, before the Washington Congress at Lincoln Hall, Mrs. Victoria C. Woodhull delivered the ablest argument that has ever been made in favour of woman suffrage. When we say that the conclusion made upon her premises were as irresistible as any ever made by the great jurist Webster, Reverdy Johnson or Calhoun, we simply state the truth.

"She simply smashes Carpenter's logic as a boy would a mushroom by trampling upon it.

"The dunces at the Capitol, who imagine that because they were elected to the Senate, either through merit or bribery, they necessarily possess the intelligence to combat the doctrines advanced in favour of our political rights, have seen proper to differ from the ablest champion of her sex's rights.

"Every man and woman of the land possessing ordinary intelligence, is satisfied that if a citizen of the United States has a right to vote, all citizens have, unless for some reason they are expressly prevented. Women are citizens of the United States just as much as men.

"By what power and from what authority did man derive the right to vote?

"From the establishment of a form of government recognizing the citizenship of man. In other words, the men of this government made in, and incorporated into its fundamental law their rights, or rights which, in its formation, they assumed, belonged to them. Did they include women? We answer, Yes—not by the use of the word woman, but by the use of the word man.

"The rights of man are the rights of woman. They are inseparable in political communities, and in every instance where women are denied the same political privileges that men exercise, it is simply an usurpation by man, and a violation of every principle which enters into and underlies the foundation of this government.

"Women have the right to vote, practise the professions, sue and be sued, and the man or party that sets himself or itself up against this clear and plain right is simply kicking against the pricks of logic and coming events.

"By the amendment to the Constitution our liege rulers undertook to slip in the negroes alone. By these amendments Mrs. Victoria C. Woodhull claims that women are enfranchised. Her argument upon these provisions is not only clear and logical but eloquent and unanswerable."

Daily Chronicle, February 17th, 1872. Washington (D.C.).

" An audience composed, for the major part, of the representatives, and filling Lincoln Hall, were assembled there to hear Mrs. Victoria C. Woodhull's lecture. Her personal appearance was marked by an earnestness attractive to her audience, her voice was strong and sufficiently clear to be audible in all parts of the hall, although her enunciation was most rapid.

" The whole lecture was admirable in logical arrangement and force, clearly defining each point of argument, and combining all in strong conclusion; much epigram and a clear intelligence of subject pervaded and brightened the whole lecture, which was one of the best delivered here this winter."

The Washington Chronicle, February 17th, 1872. Washington (D.C.).

" An audience, composed for the major part of representatives of our most intelligent class of citizens, and filling the most distant portions of Lincoln Hall, was assembled there last night to hear Mrs. Victoria C. Woodhull lecture on ' The Impending Revolution.' "

The New York Herald, February 21st, 1872. New York City.

" Last evening the Academy of Music was crowded to overflowing with a fashionable audience of ladies and gentlemen. The aisles of the large auditorium were packed with ladies who were forced to stand. Irving Place was filled with a moving mass of people of both sexes. The proscenium boxes were many of them filled with the owners and their families and guests, who had come for the first time to hear Mrs. Victoria C. Woodhull. It can safely be concluded that there were as many people turned away last evening from the doors of the Academy as there were persons who found accommodation within the walls of the Temple of Music.

" Mrs. Woodhull read from notes slowly and with precision, and so distinctly that she was heard all over the Academy. There were but few interruptions last night, and when they occurred it was only to encourage her to proceed."

The Sun, February 21st, 1872. New York City.

" Mrs. Victoria C. Woodhull read her lecture, ' The Impending Revolution,' in the Academy last evening, to one of the largest assemblages ever seen in that hall.   An hour before the opening of the doors people began to congregate in Irving Place, and fifteen minutes before eight o'clock the multitude filled up the streets for three blocks each way.   Many were carried utterly off their feet, and so conveyed along with the surge into the vestibule.   The doorkeeper could scarcely take and separate the tickets.   She closed her lecture and walked off amidst immense thunders of applause.   She was literally covered with bouquets as she made her exit."

The World, February 21st, 1872.   New York City.

" The crowd which had gathered last evening at the Academy of Music to hear Mrs. Victoria C. Woodhull deliver her lecture on ' The Impending Revolution ' was immense."

The Star, February 21st, 1872.   New York City.

" The Academy of Music presented an unusual scene last evening, it being the occasion of a lecture delivered by the famous Mrs. Victoria C. Woodhull on ' The Impending Revolution.'   Thousands of people of both sexes gathered around the building in order to obtain admittance.

" At the conclusion of her remarks she was loudly cheered, and bouquets to any quantity were showered on the platform."

(Editorial.)

" Since the days of ' unpleasantness ' no such crowd has assembled in and around the Academy of Music as besieged that institution last night to hear Mrs. Victoria C. Woodhull.   Shortly after six o'clock a group collected in front of the main entrance, which by seven o'clock had grown into a crushing, swaying multitude. When the doors fell back a sea of humanity poured in with ever-increasing force, until the custodian of the Academy rushed up with terror in his looks and informed the Captain of Police that the building was tottering under its weight. The doors were slammed to as if by magic, and the crowd flowed backward."

The Cincinnati Commercial, May 10th, 1872.

" Somehow or other, Mrs. Woodhull as she stood there, dressed in plain black, with flushed face, gleaming eye, upraised arm, and quivering under the fire of her own rhapsody, reminded me of the great Rachel in some of those tragic or fervid passages in which the dominating powers of her nature and genius were displayed in their highest effect. She seemed at moments like one inspired, and the eloquence which poured from her lips in reckless torrents swept through the souls of the multitude in a way which caused them to burst every now and then with uproarious enthusiasm."

Evening Telegram, July 8th, 1872. Louisville (Ky.).

CANDIDATE FOR PRESIDENCY.

" The Hon. Samuel Cassey, ex-member of Congress from the Thirty-second district of Kentucky, arrived in this city yesterday, and declares that Kentucky would give Mrs. Victoria C. Woodhull twenty thousand majority over either Grant or Greeley."

Weekly Observer, July 13th, 1872. Belfast (Ohio).

THE COMING WOMAN.

" Among the candidates for the Presidency of the United States, if not the foremost, at least in some respects the most remarkable, is Mrs. Woodhull, of Wall Street, New York,

CONVENTION IN APOLLO HALL, NEW YORK. VICTORIA C. WOODHULL NOMINATED FOR PRESIDENT OF THE UNITED STATES.

Banker, Financier, Editor, and Advocate on many platforms of the Rights of Women. If multiplicity of offices entitle this lady to any consideration, she has undertaken the performance of a greater variety of duties than any member of the opposite sex has in general thought himself qualified to assume. Mrs. Woodhull brings the woman's question to the front, as only an American woman should have the bravery or the boldness to do; and as long as we are willing to make a woman a queen we cannot consistently deny her ability to be a president."

Times, October 28th, 1872. Chicago (Ill.).

"The Academy of Music was thronged to its utmost capacity to hear Mrs. Victoria C. Woodhull's lecture. Long before the hour at which it was announced the lecture would commence, all the seats had been sold, and a large placard was hoisted bearing the legend, 'Standing room only.'

"Mrs. Woodhull commencing in a low tone of voice, she warmed with her subject; enunciating some more than ordinary idea, she carried the audience by storm, being greeted with hearty cheers."

Tribune, October 28th, 1872. Chicago (Ill.).

"Mrs. Victoria C. Woodhull lectured last evening at the Academy of Music. The audience that gathered was the largest ever seen within its walls."

New York Herald, November, 1872. New York City.

WOODHULL AND CLAFLIN'S ARRESTS.

"During yesterday a great many visitors called upon the imprisoned sister-brokers and reformers at Ludlow Street Jail. Notwithstanding the influx of visitors, there was yet about the domicile of Mrs. Woodhull and Claflin a gloom that pervades all prisons which affected everybody with despondency. This feeling was not alleviated by the surroundings of the apartment of the sisters.

" The *Herald* reporter, on entering their cell last evening, discovered Mrs. Woodhull and Miss Claflin seated on a cot. Both the sisters expressed their willingness to suffer for what they conceive to be right. Their persecution, they declare, is the seed from which is to spring the perfect flower of a new religion of humanity."

Sunday Mercury, November 17th, 1872. New York City.

" Cell No. 11, now well known as the residence of Woodhull and Claflin, was a perfect camp meeting yesterday. On a small table was an appetizing dinner served for Mrs. Woodhull, who had eaten no breakfast. Just as Mrs. Woodhull began her dinner a woman entered and whispered ' your food is being poisoned,' and her appetite fled."

Chronicle, December 1st, 1872. Brooklyn (N.Y.).

" Yesterday morning Mrs. Victoria C. Woodhull and Miss Tennie C. Claflin, accompanied by two deputy sheriffs, were driven in a close carriage from the Ludlow Street Jail to the United States Attorney's office to meet their bondsmen, who, on the previous day, executed bonds in $16,000 each for the release of Mrs. Woodhull and Miss Claflin : they were there awaiting the decision of the District Attorney as to their capability to become sureties. In a short time the bondsmen were informed that they had been accepted.

" While the women-brokers were in the District Attorney's office, a gentleman stepped up to Mrs. Woodhull and told her that it was his duty to tell her that there was a conspiracy against her. He said that it was understood between certain officials and prosecuting parties that Mrs. Woodhull and Miss Claflin should be forced into Jefferson Market Prison, and, while there, the prison would be fired and they left to perish in the flames. He added that the parties referred to were determined to be rid of them at any cost. Mrs. Woodhull and Miss Claflin

THE ARREST

could barely credit the story, but the earnestness of the man, and the promise that, at an early day, he would tell all he knew of the plot, forced them to place credence in his story.

"The women-brokers then entered their coach, and an officer of the Jefferson Market Police Court stepped up to the door, and placing his hand on Miss Claflin's shoulder, said in a loud tone, 'Stop.' A gentleman hastened to the rescue, and pushing the officer aside, said, 'No, you don't. Mrs. Woodhull and Miss Claflin are still United States prisoners, and you cannot arrest them again,' as they have been warned of your infamous plot.

"The officer wilted. The women-brokers were then taken back to their old quarters in Ludlow Street Jail. To-morrow they will probably take their departure from that jail and procure bail in the other suits.

"The authorities seem determined to do their utmost, by placing every obstacle in their way, to prevent them from obtaining their freedom."

Herald, December 1st, 1872. New York City.

"Mesdames Woodhull and Claflin were taken again to-day from the County Jail to the Federal Building, preparatory to giving bail. They were accompanied by their counsel. Soon after their arrival they were conducted to the office of Commissioner Shields, where the bail-bonds were prepared. When the case was called,

"The counsel said they were prepared to give unexceptionable bail, but it would be useless for them to do so, as an officer of the Jefferson Market Court was outside in the hall, waiting to re-arrest them. He thought it would be better that his clients remain in the County Jail than to go to a cell in the Jefferson Market Prison. He had heard that the judge had been spirited away for the purpose of preventing the prisoners from being bailed.

"Mesdames Woodhull and Claflin were sent back to the County Jail."

24 *

Frank Leslie's Illustrated Newspaper, December 7th, 1872.

" But it happens that Mrs. Woodhull and Miss Claflin have been placed in a position to give them real consequence. They have been arrested by the United States' Government, and thrust into jail . . . Another thing which we dislike in the case is, that it has assumed too much the form of an ' *Inquisition.*' All the facts should have gone to the public. Woodhull & Claflin have a right to public opinion, and public opinion depends upon the press."

Vindicator, December 27th, 1872. Youngston (Ohio).

" The arrest and imprisonment of Mrs. Woodhull by the United States authorities is simply unwarrantable and outrageous, and should be denounced by every paper in the land. We know that in her arrest and imprisonment by Federal authority the freedom of the press has been wantonly assailed."

1873.

The Herald, January 6th, 1873 (Editorial). St. Joseph (Mo.).

"The most noted woman of America will lecture in the Opera House this evening. Her subject is 'Reformation or Revolution, which? or, Behind the Political and Social Scenes.' Mrs. Victoria C. Woodhull has a national reputation, and whatever may be said of her opinions upon the throbbing issues of the day, we have it from reliable gentlemen who have heard her elsewhere that she is the best lecturer now before the public. The Opera House should be crowded to hear her."

The Herald, January 7th, 1873. St. Joseph (Mo.).

"The lecture was one of the most vigorous, sensible, though radical protests against the shams of the nineteenth century ever listened to by a St. Joseph audience. Not one word was uttered to which every man and woman could not have listened to with propriety and profit."

"Mrs. Woodhull is a success. She is an excellent elocutionist, gesturing mainly with her eyes and head, occasionally stamping out a sentence and punctuating it with a nervous shake of the 'knowledge box'; and she tells more truth in one lecture than people are apt to hear in a lifetime elsewhere."

The Gazette, January 9th, 1873. St. Joseph (Mo.).

"The career of Victoria C. Woodhull is one of the most wonderful of this or any other century. Born, if we mistake not, in Ohio, she sought her way to fame and fortune, and became an earthquake in the religious, social, and financial circles of the metropolis of the nation. Think of her as you may, you cannot deny her power. A correspondent

writes from Kansas City: ' She does not express one gross
thought. She is not simply a " sensation," but is an earnest
woman—the finest speaker I ever heard. Our best ladies
attended her lectures here.' "

Times, January 9th, 1873. Seymour (Ind.).

" Mrs. Woodhull and Miss Claflin are out of jail, and have
recommenced the publication of *Woodhull & Claflin's Weekly.*
The number of the 28th will well repay perusal. That these
women have been shamefully persecuted admits of no doubt.
Every unprejudiced mind must admit the heroism with which
they began to unmask the immorality practised under the cloak
of religion so-called."

Republican, January 9th, 1873. Washington (D.C.).

" The United States Government, through the courts, has just
engaged in a business so small, contemptible, and dirty, as to
nearly, if not quite, obliterate its proud record of the last ten
years, and right here the courts have disgraced the Government.
The charge was preposterous, but the United States Commissioner held her and her sister in 8000 dols. bail each !
Knowing that she must be acquitted, the United States Grand
Jury rushed in and indicted her so as to prolong her
imprisonment.

" At the same time her paper was suppressed by main brute
force.

" Now, when it is remembered that these outrages were
all committed by United States officers in the name of the
Government, and in behalf of the person who refused to do
anything in his own behalf, we submit that the Government
has been disgraced, deeply disgraced, and that it is the duty of
the President and Congress to inquire into these high-handed
outrages and remove the stain from our proud record."

Evening Post, January 9th, 1873. New York City.

THE NAKED TRUTH

By William Cullen Bryant.

"Beautiful Truth once, in the days of yore,
   Put on the brave array
Which then the goddesses of Hellas wore,
   And issued to the day,
Robed in such sort, with graces so divine,
   That man, adoring, built to her a shrine.
The gods, indignant at the sight,
   Rose in defence of their invaded right.
Horror and infamy—they cried,
   'And Profanation!' and they came and went,
Pacing the ambrosial courts from side to side,
   Till a wild tumult filled the firmament.
Jove, to appease their fury, left the skies,
   And quickly stood before
The shrine of Truth, determined to chastise
   The sacrilege: he tore
From her the regal mantle which she wore,
   And stripped the robe away.
And flung to Falsehood's hand,
   Mantle and robe to serve for her array;
And gave to Truth this terrible command,
   'Be thou for ever naked from this day.'
And therefore, reader, let not Truth be blamed
   If evermore since then
She hides in corners humbled and ashamed,
   And rarely seen of men."

" 'Tis the 9th of January, 1873, and the posters on the dead walls of the city say Woodhull and the Naked Truth. Beecher and education are out to-night. From the palace and the prison they come to speak of God's knowledge and truth to man

The air is cold and biting; the chill of a Ludlow Street Jail shivers its way to the very marrow. Lies, in overcoats and rubbers, eagerly press up the Bowery; at the Junction of Fourth Avenue and the Bowery, greed and gain divide themselves. The sheep and goats pass on in opposite directions; some go to the preacher, some to the teacher. Ushers with bouquets, doubling and smiling, in wait for the preacher; ushers with locust clubs awaiting the teacher. Peter Cooper's monument is reached: humanity bless him. The Hall is lighted and the doors wide open for Woodhull and Claflin and free speech. A weak old man, but brave, saves New York from everlasting infamy and disgrace. Boston, blush and repent, and tell them the next time that they lie who say that the rebels of '76 are the last tyrants of '73. That you do not read revolutions backward and claim the inalienable wrongs of woman.

"An impatient and eager crowd of people surge up to the Institute door; some pass in, others turn back. I wonder at this retrograde move, and mentally exclaim—Is there a moral earthquake at the threshold even of Naked Truth! No; the people are braver and truer than their leaders: 'tis not in fear they turn away. The stratagem of religious persecution is at work; stalwart United States' marshals guard the door, with another arrest for Woodhull and Claflin; the seal of authority is on the writ. Now for the stripes and cross. The stars have fled the bunting of the nation, and sparkle on the breasts of a hundred policemen. Christian moral force exchanges the lion's skin for the fox's, and from the doorways of the Institution grins out upon free conscience, free press and free speech, with an old-time feudal sacerdotal leer. The Golden Rule is a policeman's club to-night, and Yankee Jesuitism whispers with bated breath: the end justifies the means.

"The marshals watch with lynx eyes for the coming of the woman of destiny. The sacrilegious act of exposing the animus of Mrs. Woodhull's persecutors must not, shall not take place,

and so the national police bid the people turn back : saying,
'There will be no lecture to-night; Mrs. Woodhull is to be
again arrested and flung into prison.'

"Hundreds turn away. Yet hundreds go in and, in a disappointed mood, sit staring at the vacant platform, patiently
watching for something, they know not what. Police to the
right of them, police to the left of them. A fearful display of
the dignity and strength of the Mosaic law. The ingenious
whisper, 'What does it all mean ; are they afraid of the people
or afraid of the truth ?' The display of the people's servants
in uniform is ridiculously out of place, a blind to hide the real
issue now pending before the people. The great want present
is not the reading of the Riot Act or the suspension of the
habeas corpus, but Woodhull! Woodhull! Woodhull! and the
arched ceiling of the Cooper Institute rings with the significant
command of three thousand voices in chorus: Victoria C.
Woodhull and the 'Naked Truth.'

"But to that great cry of want which goes up in noisy
demonstration from the impatient citizens no response comes
back, and thoughtful men and women who read the bitter lessons
of history aright grow still more indignant at this abridgment
of human rights, and muttered exclamations, such as Shame!
Outrage! Persecution! Inquisition! go the rounds of the
audience.

"The animus of this cowardly persecution seemed to be
thoroughly understood by all.

"The impotent and lame excuse of public morals was played
out, though Victoria was absent. Revolution had come ; and it
required all the manly efforts of the pious and severe-looking
poltroons in blue to keep within bounds the rapidly increasing
indignation.

"The clock fronting the now noisy throng shows past eight
o'clock. Three thousand befooled citizens, the approved of and
condemned of Paul, males and females, the enfranchised and

disenfranchised, are madly calling and stamping for Mrs. Woodhull. A United States marshal guards each door ready to arrest her if she dare attempt the trial. No one, not even her most intimate friends, know where she is.

"But see! here comes war in the garb of peace. A queer-looking old lady, tottering with age, and dressed in Quaker-grey, and close veiled, coal-scuttle bonnet of antique pattern, passes up the middle aisle to a front seat. The audience good-naturedly smile at this eccentric-looking female Rip Van Winkle. A few fashionables laugh outright at the absurdity of dressing so far behind the age, as if fossils were only to be found beneath coal-scuttle bonnets and cocked hats. The thought flashes through my mind—what if Naked Truth were muffled beneath Quaker-grey, and that the spirit of Ann Leigh masked the fiery and daring soul of Victoria C. Woodhull? But no, the nerve, the address, the heroism to outwit marshals waiting for her at every door, fifty policemen within, and as many without, from a persecuted and long-suffering woman almost hounded to death, were impossible.

"Twenty minutes past eight, and the shouting and stamping grows fast and furious. All is confusion, indignation and scorn, all but the veiled figure of the old Quaker lady in the front seat; that is calm, motionless, and at peace.

"A female form glides on the stage and essays to speak. We recognize a brave, true-hearted champion of truth. The noise dies out, and a perfect stillness takes its place; the proverbial pin might be heard to drop. She has just commenced to speak to apologize for the absence of Mrs. Woodhull. The motionless Quaker of the muffled face moves. She rises from her seat, and in the irresoluteness of old age, moves to the stairway of the platform, and slowly and deliberately ascending it, walks half way across the stage. A number smile at the serio-comic figure as it disappears behind one of the broad square pillars supporting the roof of the hall.

" In an impressive and eloquent manner she dilates upon this last outrage upon the rights and liberties of the people. To quote her own words : 'The enemies of free speech have another order of arrest for Mrs. Woodhull. She can't appear to-night, lest she be again thrown into an American Bastile. She has intercepted her enemies, however, so far as this : though they may shut out Mrs. Woodhull, they shall not prevent the delivery of the lecture, for she has deputed me to read to you "The Naked Truth ; or, the Situation Reviewed." The task, under the circumstances, is as painful to me as it is disappointing to you ; but the custodians of the law guard the doors of the Institute, and neither Mrs. Woodhull nor Miss Claflin can, no matter how much they may desire it, appear upon this platform to-night.'

" With the celerity of a flash of lightning the old Quaker lady dashed from behind the pillar. Old-age, coal-scuttle bonnet, and grey dress disappeared like magic. Had a thunderbolt fallen upon the audience, they could not have been any more surprised and astonished. There stood Victoria C. Woodhull, an overwhelming inspirational fire scintillating from her eyes and beaming from her face. The Quaker costume lay coiled at her feet, and, with her breast heaving with long-suppressed nervous emotion, her arms raised aloft in nervous excitement, her hair in graceful confusion, and the head thrown defiantly back like the head of Apollo Belvidere, she looked the personification of Liberty in Arms. Her voice rose in clear and piercing tones, like a song of love, blended with the war-cry of battle, and the pent-up forces of her soul rushed forth in an impetuous and irresistible torrent of burning, glowing words, thought, and voice, being full to repletion with the musical and magnetic energy of the Marseillaise. Her look and voice came unexpected and sudden as the lightning's scathe ; 'twas as ' fire to heather set,' igniting with an animated and undefined surprise each and every heart present. It was Otis in the fire of revolution ;

Garrison breaking the shackles of the slaves; Phillips in the alarm of labour; a Parker in the throes of religious despotism. The heroism, bravery, and truth of the woman swept with inspired credentials into all hearts; and, half in awe and admiration, the audience listened spell-bound to the great persecuted.

" Then the thunders came, peal after peal, of joyous applause in intense delight. The people saw nothing, knew nothing, wanted nothing then but Mrs. Woodhull, whose invincible courage and rare fidelity to truth had outwitted the enemies of free speech. Electrified into a fever of intense excitement and unbounded admiration, the audience greet each sentence as it falls from her lips with cheers and applause.

" Physical force, with the badge of authority on its breast, relaxed its austere look, dropped its club and gazed in rapt attention at the majesty of moral force in petticoats; the marshal forgot his writ of arrest; the thinker dropped the bigot; but Victoria had the floor, and falsehood, slander, and ignorance fainted to death in the grasp of eternal truth.

" For one hour and a half a tempest of startling truths in all their native loveliness and purity, fresh and dewy from the garden of Heaven, deluged the consciences of all present in the baptism of a higher faith than was ever dreamed of in the philosophy of Christian ethics.

" A great wrong done to this heroic soul stood at last revealed. and the cowardly, masterly inactivity of the public assumed the hideous proportions of moral cowardice and tacit guilt. Public complicity in this outrageous act of persecuting a brave and noble woman was felt to the core, and thrilled the audience with fearful forebodings and alarm at the imminent danger of threatening the life and perpetuity of free government. The right of free speech and a free press was seen to tremble in the balance, and that while cowards and fools laughed and jeered, this woman was battling alone for the liberties of the world.

From the deep draughts of common sense, delivered in that inimitable manner, the entranced listeners learned the dreadful, subtle secret of tyranny and persecution, and in the words of Franklin, 'Mokana stood revealed'—that most men, as well as most sects in religion, think themselves in possession of all truth, and that whenever others differ from them it is, so far, *error*.

"The lecturess made Persecution *versus* Prosecution show cause, and revealed the startling spectacle, in a so-called free country, of a single creed assuming moral censorship over the thought and speech of the American people, and sneaking through a false interpretation of the law into a ridiculous and absurd authority, at once treasonable and unconstitutional, and for the specific object of hushing up from the public ear those very offences in their teachers which they hypocritically condemn in others. Such a spectacle aroused memory from inaction. Again the fires of Smithfield illumined the night, and its ghostly shadow fell across the Cooper Institute. Once more the Christmas Eve log became the martyr's stake, and its burning crimson tongues licked out the life-blood of the champions and martyrs of truth again, as of old. New England gibbets creaked and groaned with the victims of sanctified ignorance. The revolution was a failure. The Constitution a mockery and a snare, and life, liberty, and the pursuit of happiness were swallowed up in religious intolerance, political persecution, and mental slavery. All this was seen, and more, and the arch-genius of individual liberty, the imprisoned, robbed, belied Victoria C. Woodhull loomed up before them in majestic proportions of heart and soul as the protecting spirit of American liberty, that, like Minerva from the brain of Jove, sprang from the people armed with truth to do battle for human rights.

" Strong men looked up to the little woman with the far-off look, and received her as a new revelation of womanhood, the prophetess of truth, the Messiah of politics, a weird, spiritual sibyl, infused with marvellous power to sway the souls of men and women to higher aims than fearing to face the Naked Truth.

"The man in blue was a policeman, again remembering his order of arrest, and with unusual and rare suavity of manner performed his duty by arresting Mrs. Woodhull.

"Too late. The much-dreaded Naked Truth had reached the public ear through the silver-tongued Woodhull, the brave. She is the superior strategist. The terrible syren has defeated you and charmed your cohorts and battalions to silence and inaction.

"The night of the 9th of January, 1873, passes into history, and the bravest and truest of her sex moves further up Calvary, from the rostrum to a prison."

The Gazette, January 10th, 1873. St. Joseph (Mo.).

"Say what you please of the subject of this article, she is a woman of power, and cannot be ignored. She 'will not down,' and the common-sense method would be to meet her squarely full in the face. All efforts to suppress her have proved abortive, and have only tended to increase her fame."

"The impression that all her ideas are concentrated in a lecture or two is entirely erroneous. She is not only ready at all times to defend herself against attack, but continually acts on the aggressive, ill-concealing the innate force that longs for expression. The intense activity of her brain is remarkable. She is a woman of culture and large experience."

Mercury, January 12th, 1873. New York City.

"For the *second, third, fourth, and fifth time* Mrs. Victoria C. Woodhull has been arrested, thrown into prison, and liberated on bail. If the charges be true, and can be maintained by proof, the proper way is to proceed to trial and convict her. But that 'this great Government of the mightiest Republic the world ever saw,' should repeat from day to day its sledge-hammer attacks upon these women, is, to say the least, unjust. It does not seem right, in any view that one can take of the matter, that the whole machinery of the Federal Government, with its courts and marshals, should be placed at the back of a man who has somehow or other chosen it for his private business to deprive this woman of her liberty."

Evening Journal, January 14th, 1873. Jersey City.

"On Mrs. Woodhull's arrest we must say that the course pursued toward her is unprecedented and oppressive as well as most unwise. If she had committed an offence against the law, let her be tried and punished, but why should annoying, underhanded, or cowardly methods of reaching her be adopted? The manner of her arrest at Cooper Institute was contemptible and cowardly. The means used to get up the new complaint against her were sneaking. Let us have no more of that sort of work."

Commercial Advertiser, January 14th, 1873. New York City.

"Why do the United States marshals continue to play with Woodhull and Claflin as a cat plays with a mouse. If they are to be prosecuted, let the suit be pressed; common fairness forbids that they should be persecuted. What is the secret of their treatment? The arrest, liberations, and re-arrest are a mockery of justice. In the name of personal freedom and personal responsibility we protest against further double-dealing in this case."

Weekly Record, January 15th, 1873. Aledo (Ill.).

"Mrs. Victoria C. Woodhull, recently discharged from custody, was again arrested on Thursday evening at the close of her lecture, and consigned to prison. The cause of the eighth arrest is not assigned. Is Mrs. Woodhull arrested for making and repeating those charges? If so, the parties who caused her arrest have made an egregious blunder. Her arrest and incarceration in prison will not confute the charges. On the contrary, as the case now stands, it looks as if Mrs. Woodhull had been imprisoned for daring to expose crimes committed by persons claiming to be oracles in religion and morality."

Record, January 16th, 1873. Dundee (N.Y.).

"Mrs. Victoria C. Woodhull and Miss Tennie C. Claflin, after having been incarcerated in Ludlow Street Jail four weeks, are now at large again on bail, and have issued another number of their paper of which we have received a copy. We look upon their treatment as unjust, impolitic, and cowardly."

Pioneer, January 18th, 1873. Houston (Mo.).

"These women, among the most intellectual, pure and true of our country, have been driven from pillar to post, and refused a place to rest their overtasked bodies and brains, and, at last, to add to their great sorrow and misfortune, and the further disgrace of the United States authorities, were cast into prison. And for what? for exposing the baseness of the pretenders of righteousness."

Republican, January 26th, 1873. Waverley (Iowa).

"Mrs. Woodhull is again incarcerated. We can only look upon her incarceration as persecution by those who are afraid of this fearless woman. 'Truth crushed to earth will rise again;' and yet, though at present plunged into a New York prison, she will yet triumph over her enemies. Unable to defend their position like men, they seek to cover up their characters by casting their accuser into prison.

"This is but a resurrection of the persecution that attended the advancement of ideas by fearless men when they were bound at the stake for their opinions. Shame upon such manhood."

VICTORIA C. WOODHULL AND TENNESSE CLAFLIN IN COUNCIL WITH THEIR LAWYER
IN LUDLOW STREET JAIL.

Independent Thinker, February, 1873.   Greenville (Ala.).

"Social revolution is a thing that takes place not once in a century, for social ideas of all others are the most difficult to change: yet nothing less than a social revolution in the United States has been inaugurated, and from the zeal with which it is being urged and the persecution that is heaped upon Mrs. Woodhull and Miss Claflin, if it does not ultimately prove triumphant neither its friends or its enemies will be to blame.

"Mrs. Victoria C. Woodhull is the most perfectly intellectual woman in all probability that now lives. Her intellect is vigorous, powerful, comprehensive, voluble, accomplished, and refined. Her motives have been rather misunderstood, misconstrued, or wilfully perverted. She is directing the splendid powers of a great mind and, perhaps, a greater amount of energy and individual effort than ever before proceeded from such a source. Demanding intellectual elevation of her sex, she asks for equality for woman with men before the law, and the same treatment at the hands of public opinion, that the male libertines and debauchees shall be degraded as well as female prostitutes. She demands nothing but justice at the hands of society and the Government.

"She had to be crushed at all hazards, and the paper that was being circulated broadcast over the country must be suppressed. She was indicted in eight different cases and required to give bail in $8000 dollars each. Friends were intimidated by threats from going upon her bonds, and those more intimately connected with her were also arrested on hatched-up charges and likewise thrown into prison. But in spite of all these trials, difficulties, and persecutions she is once more at large."

The Gazette, February 1st, 1873.   Davenport (Iowa.).

"She talked very plainly, told many truths, and advocated ideas which, if adopted, would spare woman a great deal of misery. She demanded that every house of prostitution be

25 *

abolished; she wanted women so pure that when they find a
fallen woman they will lift her to virtue. She said the idea of
becoming a mother is never looked upon with sanctity enough;
and just as soon as the mothers of the country commence to
think, prostitution will cease. All that she ever asked was that
the basis of marriage should be love—educate your daughters to
marry for love, and not for money or homes. She closed with
appeals to her hearers to make their boys and girls pure to start
with, so that their lives may be pure."

The Democrat, February 2nd, 1873 (Editorial). Davenport (Iowa).

"Mrs. Woodhull need look for no canting censure from us.
Whatever may be the general opinion of the influence of her
teachings, one thing is self-evident—she is terribly in earnest.
The iron has entered into her soul, and she pitilessly lays bare
the shams and shortcomings of society. The casual observer
who noticed the pale-faced woman, with no meretricious adorn-
ment, who stepped on to the platform in the Opera House on
Saturday night, warmed up with the remembrance and recital
of her wrongs. Who heard the throbbings of the mother's
heart, who saw the welling-up of a mother's tears, must be of
sterner stuff than mortals usually are if he or she denied her
sincerity. We venture to say that those, if any, who went to
gratify a libidinous disposition, were disappointed, and the
prurient prudes who anticipated a chance to advertise a blush,
felt that the scalpel of truth was dissecting their motives.
The entire absence of hesitancy, or, on the other hand, any
emphasized manner in the delivery of certain facts, put the
audience at their ease, and effectually silenced even those who
might be there to jeer. There was not one hiss or sign of disapprobation throughout the lecture; and, so far as we could
learn, not one person regretted having been present.

"She is a fearless, earnest woman, and until she says and
does more outrageous things on the platform than she did last

night, we see no reason to join in the pack who would hound her
to a prison or a suicide's grave. Let us have free speech on
every subject, and there is no doubt that the world will be better
for it."

The Herald, February 3rd, 1873 (Editorial). Dubuque (Iowa).

" There is nobody but knows that Victoria C. Woodhull
lectured in Dubuque last evening. She is a woman who has
been hooted and railed at *ad infinitum*, but has created more
stir, more sensation in our city than any man who ever
trod the dust of its streets, or any other celebrity who ever
trod the boards of the Athenæum. She is a woman of brains,
of eloquence, of elegance. She is a woman like herself and
nobody else. She is emphatically Victoria C. Woodhull to the
core—bold and defiant in her theories on the questions of the
day, unrelenting in declaring them, and speaks the nakedest and
most unadorned truth we have ever listened to from a public
speaker; but in no sense can Mrs. Woodhull be termed an
immodest woman, except it be in her bluntness in discussing
social topics. Her face, while possessing all the softness and
delicacy of expression which naturally belongs to a woman, is
also possessed of a breadth and contour indicative of masculine
vigour of mind. She has a perfect grace of oratory; every
gesture and attitude is refined and eloquently expressive, and
she sends forth her silvery-voiced sentences as though she had
the power of a hurricane behind her."

The Times, February 3rd, 1873 (Editorial). Dubuque (Iowa).

" The lecture was delivered to a crowded house. The
lecturer was given a most respectful hearing, and kept her
audience in rapt attention by her brilliant oratory and fine
impassioned delivery. If she were aiming for stage effect only,
she would be most successful, and could carry her audience

with her as she willed, entrancing them with her fervid, earnest eloquence, which we have rarely seen equalled and never surpassed in any speaker, and leading them her willing subjects."

The Reform Leader (Editorial). Oskaloosa (Iowa).

"She probed the politics of the country to the ‚bone, and presented a terrible picture of American degeneracy, alleging the basis thereof to be our social system. She is the most eloquent and powerful female orator we have ever heard, and advances sóme of the grandest and most humanitarian ideas ever uttered by mortal."

ACQUITTAL.
Sun, June 30th, 1873. New York City.

"Mrs. Woodhull and Miss Claflin were arrested some time ago, charged with offence against the United States, for a considerable number of days, and finally released on giving heavy bail.

"Their business is broken up, and they were put to much inconvenience and subjected to many indignities.

"The prosecution opens—it proceeds—it closes ; then what?

"Why, then, the learned Judge of the United States District Court, who presides at the trials, informs the accused that there is no occasion for them to introduce any evidence in their defence; *that no case has been proved against them;* and he instructs the jury to render a verdict of not guilty, which they immediately do without leaving their seats.

"For the wrong which has been done to these women, they have no redress. The injury is irremediable."

Evening Journal, June 30th, 1873. New York City.

"One more chapter in this most extraordinary case was concluded. Thursday Mrs. Woodhull and her sister were acquitted by the Judge of the United States Courts, who said that the

THE ACQUITTAL.

prosecution had no case. This is a righteous decision. The prosecution of Mrs. Woodhull was one of false pretences from the outset. She was most shamefully oppressed in the preliminary legal proceedings, both by demands for *excessive* bail and imprisonment."

Star, October 18th, 1873. New York City.

"Last night, Mrs. Victoria C. Woodhull lectured at Cooper Institute. Long before the hour announced for the commencement of the lecture the hall was completely packed, and a large portion of the audience were ladies. The aisles were crowded, and, in fact, every available spot in the hall was occupied.

"Mrs. Woodhull stepped to the front of the platform. The recent harrowing given her by the authorities has had a telling effect on her, and her health has been much impaired. On coming forward she was greeted with rounds of applause."

Herald, October 18th, 1873. New York City.

"At Cooper Institute last evening a crowd of at least 4000 people assembled to hear Mrs. Woodhull lecture (and between 4000 and 5000 on the outside). Before eight o'clock the aisles and entrances were completely filled. After that hour there was room nowhere in the hall for the numbers who came to hear the fair lecturess.

"Mrs. Woodhull and her sister were at the back of the stage. When Mrs. Woodhull advanced to the front she was greeted with tremendous applause."

The World, October 18th, 1873. New York City.

"The large hall of Cooper Institute was last evening filled to overflowing to hear Mrs. Woodhull."

Record, November 8th, 1873. Lynn (Mass.).

" The announcement that Mrs. Victoria C. Woodhull would speak in Odd Fellows' Hall on Tuesday evening last, attracted an audience respectable in character and number. That Mrs. Woodhull is gifted with remarkable talents, we think no one who listened to her on Tuesday evening will deny. Her manner of presenting her subject to her hearers is logical, thoroughly systematic, in many respects quite original, often electrifying, sometimes astounding, now soaring to lofty heights, then gracefully descending to plain unvarnished facts, sending a thrill of conviction home to the minds of the listeners; but it is when speaking without notes that she is most brilliant, and is best appreciated by the audience. She apparently never stands upon negative ground, every position taken in her arguments and conclusions indicating positiveness in a remarkable degree. Her intimate knowledge of the political status of the country is astonishing, and her manner of unmasking and exhibiting the corruption which is centreing in Washington, permeates throughout the length and breadth of our land, and is eating out the very vitals of true Republicanism, startles her audience; on those points no candid thinker and observer can gainsay the facts, that the views presented by her, Tuesday evening, on politics and finance were sound, clear, and explicit, and are worthy to rank among the ablest and most truthful expressions of master minds."

Journal of Commerce, November 15th, 1873. Detroit (Mich.).

" Mrs. Victoria Woodhull drew a fine audience at the Music Hall last evening. She is emphatically the best female lecturer of the day, and may well be called the 'Queen of the Rostrum.' She possesses that wonderful power of holding her audience, in some cases even against their will, securing that rapt attention in such a manner as must be gratifying to herself."

Evening News, November 15th, 1873. Detroit (Mich.).

" Mrs. Woodhull lectured at the Music Hall last night.

" Mrs. Woodhull came upon the platform at eight o'clock and began her lecture. . . . When she launched into her own manuscript, however, and uttered her own thoughts, her voice became clear, her eye brightened, and her whole manner was that of one rapt in the consciousness of a great duty to be performed. Whatever her enemies say, there is no room left to doubt her earnestness nor her great ability. In all the elements of oratory she is head of the rostrum."

Union, November 15th, 1873. Detroit (Mich.).

" Mrs. Woodhull delivered her lecture on Friday night to a respectable audience at the Music Hall. Her lecture was extremely able. We have never heard nor read such brilliant reviews of our financial troubles, the logic by which they were enforced was remarkable for its clearness and power. Mrs. Woodhull is a rapid speaker, and throws her soul — a soul that has felt very deeply too—into all she says."

Commercial, November 16th, 1873. Port Huron (Mich.).

" On Monday evening the people of this city will have an opportunity to see and hear the most eloquent woman of her time, and the most daring in the promulgation of her ideas and views. Mrs. Woodhull, of whom we have heard so much— whose utterances have shaken society to its foundation. There is no doubt of her ability to deliver a fine lecture. She is described by those who have seen and conversed with her to be a graceful woman, with refinement in her manner, and an intellectual face, which can glow with enthusiasm and deter- mination, or light up with the soft radiance of pathos and sympathy. Whatever may be the result of her labours, she unquestionably believes herself to be intrusted with a high and holy mission to bring happiness to the human race. She may be mistaken *or the world may be mistaken*. There have been people whose teachings were even more unpopular with the world than hers, while they lived, who after death were cherished by the children of their persecutors in affectionate remembrance. We would prefer not to be among the stone-throwers of this world."

Detroit Union, November 17th, 1878.

"A tremendous audience greeted Mrs. Woodhull at St. Andrew's Hall last night. Every inch of standing room was occupied. Her address consisted of a series of hits, some of them very pointed and some very powerful. She complained (very justly) of the fact that the editors of the morning papers all called on her to express their entire concurrence, personally, with her doctrines, and then either treated her with contempt or lied about her in their papers.

"She apologized for what she had said that might be construed into a lack of veneration for Christ. She was a religious woman, and revered Him and His doctrines. But she despised the hypocrites who had His name for ever on their lips but had none of His principles in their hearts. She said it was a disgrace to the city that Mayor Moffat had to speak of the number of prostitutes living there. They must be debauched and prostituted by men. *Men* must be their partners in guilt. She would say to the ladies of Detroit, batter down their doors. Say to them, 'Our husbands, our fathers, our brothers have debauched you; those who are near and dear to us have injured you. *Therefore* you are our sisters, and we will stand by you.' This, she said, would end prostitution. 'Your houses of ill-fame,' she said, 'are not maintained by your young men and boys, but by your fathers, husbands, and brothers.'

"She said she asked no man or woman about their past life. Her question was, How much of God have you left in you? What can you do now?

" There were a great many ladies present. Her conversation was very plain, but not in any sense gross. She said, ' To the pure all things are pure.' The most revolting thing in Nature is taken by the chemist, its elements analyzed and its purposes ascertained.

" But to the obscene mind everything is vulgar, because seen through vulgar eyes.

" After the lecture hundreds of men and women crowded round the stage to see and speak to her. One man claimed the attention of the audience to say it was the grandest thing seen during the Christian era. On the whole she was well pleased with her audience, and pleased them in return."

Evening News, November 17th, 1873. Detroit.

" Mrs. Woodhull addressed an immense audience at St. Andrew's Hall last evening. Hundreds were unable to gain admittance. Her speech was received with round after round of enthusiastic applause. Her language in regard to the sexual relations was plain, direct, and forcible, and the ladies in the audience, of which there were a large number, seemed, if outward indications can be taken as a criterion, to indorse her views fully and heartily. Her argument was that the sexual relations were the great basis of society, and by a sickening mock modesty, of which parents and preachers ought to be ashamed, the subject was hidden from the youth of the land, thus working incalculable evils to their minds and bodies."

Saturday Morning Journal, November 22nd, 1873.
Port Huron (Mich.).

" On Monday evening of this week Mrs. Victoria C. Woodhull delivered her famous lecture at the Opera House. A large and respectable audience greeted her, among whom we noticed his honour the Mayor.

" Although reading from manuscript Mrs. Woodhull spoke in a clear, distinct manner, with force and fervour, and at times rising to a degree of eloquence unsurpassed by any public speaker of her sex. She was logical and plain in her language. She handled her subjects without gloves, and in a manner that showed she was well informed upon the subject of finance and politics, and, besides, had peeped behind the scenes.

" She reviewed, in a masterly manner, the corruption of the present administration of our Government. In speaking of the corruption, venality, peculations, frauds, and swindling going on all over the country, she cut right and left, sparing none, and frequently calling forth applause.

" Mrs. Woodhull is a bold agitator, and no doubt, if her theories are correct, will accomplish a great deal towards bringing about a new order of things. The bold and fearless utterances of reformers may, for a time, be met with opposition, yet if their claims are just they will in good time be adopted.

"Mrs. Woodhull touched upon the social question, and certainly told some wholesome truths, which had their effect on a portion of her audience. In speaking on the question of prostitution, she said that there were laws for the punishment of female prostitutes, but she had failed to find any laws in relation to the male prostitutes. She claimed that the seducer should be condemned by society as well as the seduced, and thought it an outrage, a gross injustice to females, and a barbarous state of society that condemned an act in a woman, while applauding and courting men who were the real criminals. Her talk upon this subject was plain, but in nowise gross or offensive. To the pure she claims all things are pure, but to the obscene and vulgar all things are gross.

" The lecture created a sensation, and her discourse throughout was an able effort, and was listened to with marked attention by her audience."

Daily Democrat, November 23rd, 1873. Grand Rapids (Mich.).

" Luce's Hall was well filled last evening on the occasion of
Mrs. Woodhull's appearance, and among the audience we noticed
a great many ladies. The lecturer appears to excellent advantage, has a good voice, and handles the subject she undertakes
without gloves. By this we do not, by any means, wish to be
understood that she is vulgar, but, on the contrary, that she
attacks the Political, Industrial, and Social abuses of the day in
a fearless manner, and speaks her mind in regard to them in a
way not to be misunderstood. She commenced by saying
that it might appear presumptuous for a woman to appear
before an audience in which there were so many men, but that
she had found so much of which to complain that she could no
longer hold her peace. In speaking of the corruption in the
present Government, she said, ' When a Tammany Ring converts
millions of the public money to its own use, for charitable
purposes (?), and it is accounted of little significance ; when
hypocrisy sits enthroned in the most popular churches, and the
Christians, in a holy unity that was never known until now,
seek to establish a sectarian God, Christ, and Bible in the
organic law of the country, and are going to succeed; in a
word, when everything that is false, corrupt, damnable, runs
riot at the expense of the hard-working industrial masses, and
is considered too respectable to be inquired into by anybody
that comes out of a Nazareth ; when all these things are, is it
not time that change come ? Is it not time for this Babel
(which we call government, and which is growing so high as to
put its occupants beyond the reach of the people) to topple over,
and be buried in its own ruins ? '

" Mrs. Woodhull then proceeded to speak especially of the
wrongs of the present system of government, sorting them out
and condemning them in her own peculiar and forcible manner.
The social question was thoroughly ventilated, yet in a way

which could not be offensive to her hearers, although the
language used was very plain and to the point. The speaker
claimed that it was the province of every man and woman to
examine these questions; and to discuss them freely and fairly
was no more than their just right, taking no heed of the false
modesty of the day, which excluded them from general
conversation.

" On the whole, we were favourably impressed with the
lecture, although there were some deductions from facts stated
that we did not feel like believing true. This, however, is not
necessarily the opinion of all the audience, as we make no claim
that Mrs. Woodhull or any portion of her hearers are not as
well entitled to their opinions as we are to ours.

" There were many fundamental truths presented which we
could wish that the people at large were impressed with, and
we trust that all who can will attend the lecture to-night."

Eagle, November 24th, 1873. Grand Rapids (Mich.).

" On Sunday evening Mrs. Woodhull gave a lecture at Luce's
Hall on ' The Social Question.' On this occasion the hall was
literally crowded—seats, aisles, and every inch of standing-room,
doorway, and entrance-hall. Hundreds went away, unable to
gain admittance. We hardly need repeat that her doctrines on
this subject are the most liberal : Free-love in her sense;
which, however, does not mean promiscuousness, as many people
seem to insist that it should. The present system of legal
marriage is the object of her special attack, and she charges
upon the legal violations' of and outrages against love, committed under cover of legal matrimony, the major portion
of the unchasteness, and misery, and pollution existing outside
of it. It was in this lecture that she minced no words, but, as
she said, aimed to call things by their right names, and to hold
up to sight moral ulcers, inside and outside of the marriage

relation. The obscenity she charged was not in the subject, but in the bosoms of those who feared knowledge upon what she regarded as the most vital of all subjects, as affecting the welfare and the very life and health of all people.

"Mrs. Woodhull has a pleasant voice, and ordinarily speaks with deliberation, enunciating clearly and distinctly, and making herself heard by all in a large audience without any appearance of exhaustive or strained effort. She says : 'Wherever I find a social carbuncle I shall plunge my surgical knife of reform into it up to the hilt.' As it regards consequences personal to herself, she declares she never takes them into the account ; she may be shut up in prison, or even led to the stake, but she will not turn a hair's breadth to the right or left from the course marked out for her own conscience and the teachings of her guardian spirit. In a recent speech in Chicago, she said : 'I am charged with seeking notoriety, but who among you would accept my notoriety and pay a tithe of its costs to me ? Driven from my former beautiful home, reduced from affluence to want, my business broken up and destroyed, dragged from one jail to another, and in a short time I am again to be arraigned before the courts and stand trial for telling the truth. I have been smeared with the most opprobrious epithets and the vilest names, and stigmatized as a bawd and blackmailer. Now, until you are ready to accept my notoriety, with its conditions—to suffer what I have suffered and am yet to suffer—do not dare to impugn my motives. As to your approval or dissent, your applause or your curses, they have not a feather's weight with me ; I am set apart for a high and sacred duty, and I shall perform it without fear or favour.' "

Daily Democrat, November 25th, 1873.　Grand Rapids (Mich.).

"On Sunday evening Luce's Hall contained the largest audience that ever assembled to hear a lecturer in this city, while hundreds of the people, mostly ladies (for the men managed to crowd in somewhere) were obliged to go away. In fact there was fully enough went away to fill the hall up again. The speaker did as she had promised to do, call things by their right names, attacking in a fearless manner what she believed to be the abuses of the present social system. In her lecture on Sunday night, Mrs. Woodhull claimed that much of the misery and crime of the day was due to the present state of our marriage laws. She held that the discussion of these questions was eminently proper ; that it affected the health and welfare of all, and as such deserved the earnest attention of everyone. Hardly a place we visited yesterday that we did not hear this wonderful woman discussed.

" There is much good resulting from Mrs. Woodhull's lecture ; it sets people thinking whether she spoke the truth or not. If she did, then, says the thinker, Have I lived rightly ? If she didn't, her words perhaps induced him to go home and treat with greater consideration the family he believed to be his own eternally."

1874.

Herald, January 10th, 1874. St. Joseph (Mo.).

" Tootle's Opera House was well filled last night with citizens of St. Joseph and vicinity, who were attracted thither by the fame of the lecturer, Mrs. Victoria Woodhull. The audience was composed of our most solid and sensible citizens, every one of whom, we venture to assert, was most agreeably disappointed. Let us say, in the outset, that the lecture was one of the most vigorous, sensible protests against the shams of the nineteenth century ever listened to by a St. Joseph audience. Not a word was uttered during the hour and a half of Mrs. Woodhull's lecture that every man and woman in the nation could not have listened to with the utmost propriety and with undeniable profit.

" She earnestly entreated every woman to observe the old Greek motto ' Know Thyself ! '   She insisted that there must be truth and knowledge between mothers and their offspring, and thus would crime, prostitution, and misery be avoided. Her remarks on this topic were very forcible, and her strictures upon that false modesty or delicacy which prevents parents from preparing their children for the battle of life before them, were not only timely and truthful, but known to be so by every person there.

" Mrs. Woodhull tells more plain truth in one lecture than our citizens will be apt to hear elsewhere in a lifetime. Her lecture was pronounced by all who heard it one of the ablest and best which has ever been delivered here. We know many men and women were deterred from attending last evening lest she should say something which they would blush to hear. Mrs. Woodhull told the truth about such people. Only a weak mind blushes to hear the truth when uttered in decent English. The strong mind, the clear vigorous intellect looks nature squarely in the face and recognizes truth in something especially adapted to its wants."

26 *

The Gazette, January 10th, 1874. St. Joseph (Mo.).

" Yesterday we called on Mrs. Woodhull at the Pacific Hotel and were received by her in an easy and vivacious manner. Conversation turned upon national topics, and she manifested a perfect familiarity with every question of importance now agitating the American people. The impression quite frequently entertained that she has concentrated all her information and ideas in a lecture or two, and relies for reputation upon these studied efforts, is entirely erroneous. She is ready at all times to defend herself against attacks at any point. And not only that, but she constantly acts upon the aggressive, and, although she listens respectfully, she can ill-conceal the innate force that apparently longs for expression in words. The intense activity of her brain is remarkable. She is a woman of culture and large experience."

Daily Commercial, January 11th, 1874. Leavenworth (Kan.).

" Last evening, as announced, Mrs. Victoria Woodhull delivered a lecture at the Opera House. There was a very large audience indeed in attendance.

" The first part of the lecture dealt with the subject of political reform, and among what was said by the speaker, there was a great deal that might be highly commended.

" Mrs. Woodhull told a great many truths concerning the male prostitutes whom she insisted should be punished equally with the females, and concerning public men, whom she accused of being largely the supporters of bawds and of infamous houses."

Times, January 11th, 1874. Leavenworth (Kan.).

" The political part of her lecture was as nothing. When she struck the topic of social reform, throwing aside her manuscript she launched forth a perfect torrent of eloquent and impassioned words. Nothing can describe her terrible earnestness."

Leader, January 13th, 1874. Lincoln (Neb.).

"At Mrs. Woodhull's lecture last night there was a large audience at the Opera House.

"The great portion of the lecture was in relation to general politics. The latter part was a plea for the right and duty of the people to drop mock modesty, and look the social question fairly in the face, discussing at proper times and in a proper spirit. We are satisfied that Mrs. Woodhull made friends among the respectable people of Lincoln by her course last evening, and that she would be accorded a larger audience on another visit."

State Journal, January 13th, 1874. Lincoln (Neb.).

"Notwithstanding the severity of the weather there was a good audience at the Opera House last evening, to hear the famous Mrs. Victoria Woodhull lecture. The extremely cold weather, however, kept many ladies away, but there was withal a fair number of them present.

"The first portion of her speech was read from printed copy, but when she took up the social question she spoke entirely extempore. She gave utterance to some plain and startling truths.

"She was satisfied, after a century of trial, our government was a failure. She denied the right of men to legislate for her. She had no voice in making the laws, and, according to the Constitution, was therefore not answerable to them. She ridiculed the idea of going before the people like the other lady lecturers, asking for sixteenth amendment, &c.

"She attacked the heavy land-owners, railroads, and stock-brokers, and handled them without gloves.

"She then took up the social question, which she styled errors of omission, having special reference to the dependent classes, the women, children, maimed, insane, and idiotic.

"The present social system makes every woman dependent, and she called upon legislatures to see that women were supported, while they remained in that condition. Carry the theory out to its logical results. How many women, if they were not dependent, would be found in the haunts of vice and brothels of our cities?

"There is a false society. You erect and maintain a system, one of the legitimate fruits of which is crime, and then you punish the criminal.

"There is one hope still, which is that men and women will meet in solemn conclave and discuss the purity of the social question. If it was rightly understood, the prisons would not be filled. I have asked mothers with bad children if they wanted those children, and they would answer, ' No, Mrs. Woodhull ; I tried to murder them unborn.' There is no blushing. The men and women who stand pure before the people need not blush. Murder is stamped on more than one woman for neglecting to inform their children of their natural condition."

Republican, January 15th, 1874. Omaha (Neb.).

"The Academy of Music was filled last evening with all classes of our citizens to hear Mrs. Victoria Woodhull's lecture, which was full of enthusiasm and eloquence, and delivered in a very confident and spirited manner. She was very bitter against the present federal system, and often received loud encores, from which we concluded that her sentiments were endorsed.

"In speaking of the causes of dissatisfaction, she stated that negro slavery was not so great a cause for dissatisfaction then as are the more subtile slaveries now; that the latter should be abolished the same as the former. The corruptions, frauds, failures of the last two years are a sweeping condemnation of the system under which they have flourished.

"She charged upon the government that it was not republican in form, and that it was a failure because it has neither secured freedom (and by this she means the personal rights of individuals), maintained equality, nor administered justice to its citizens.

"At this point she took up the social question to a small extent, and spoke of woman's sexual ignorance. She said, in consequence of woman's non-fulfilment of the Greek motto 'Know thyself,' there was to-day not one healthy person living. That false society made it a matter of blush and shame for a mother to inform her children of their natural condition. 'Murder is stamped on more than one woman for this neglect.'

"She demanded that male prostitutes be punished equally with the female, asking, 'Who supports your houses of prostitution? It is not the young men—it is your dissatisfied husbands.' "

Daily Globe, January 16th, 1874.   Council Bluffs (Iowa).

"The announcement that Mrs. Victoria Woodhull, the great expounder of social reform, would deliver her celebrated lecture at Dohany Hall last evening, attracted thither as large an audience as the spacious Opera House could accommodate. The audience represented in a greater degree the intelligence, respectability, and 'upper-tendom' of the city than many had been led to anticipate. Jew and Gentile, believer and unbeliever, rich and poor, high and low, white and black, all were there; and the representatives of orthodoxy and heterodoxy, Grantism and anti-monopoly, sat with like complacency under the 'droppings of the sanctuary.'

"Rich in wit, logic, and pathos, strong in argument and pointed in application, her discourse was listened to with the closest and most respectful attention, and not unfrequently applauded. Warming up with her subject, with a flushed face, and in an earnest and caustic manner, she reviewed the present administration and arraigned it for its numerous crimes.

"Hypocrisy, cant, and boastful pretensions, were the subject at which her swiftest and most pointed shafts of ridicule were hurled. In her hands, irony, satire, and sarcasm are no mean weapons, and right nobly did she employ them in enforcement of what all were constrained to admit to be true.

"Earnestness of purpose and intensity of feeling characterized her lecture throughout, from the slowly pronounced preliminary with which she began, to the rapidly uttered and stirring sentences which marked its close. Her position, though not always of such a character as to meet with universal approbation, were in the main well taken and generally so tenable as to gain the tacit assent of those maintaining more conservative views. Nothing that she said was of such a nature as to cause the blush of shame to mantle the cheek of the veriest prude."

Detroit (Mich.), January 16th, 1874.

" DEAR MRS. WOODHULL,

"The high and holy mission which you are called upon to perform for the elevation and final emancipation of woman from fetters that enwrap and bind her in a bondage worse than slavery itself is worthy of you. And each day the world is made more bright and beautiful by the heaven-born inspiration which flows out upon it from your soul. I was born and reared in the log cabin of old theology, and never knew or comprehended that it was possible for any truth to exist outside of its narrow walks until some six months since I had a quickening of my perception by a new birth into the grand and noble realm of spiritual enlightenment. Since then my soul has lived daily in the fount of eternal truth, which has enabled me to see that you are performing work which you have been called upon to do,

'By those who love us now, as well
As ere they went above to dwell.'

"Aye, how pure and sweet is the love they manifest for us in bringing the glad tidings of redemption to our sisters who are groaning beneath the burdens of wrong that have been, and are daily, heaped upon them through ignorance and grossness on the part of their husbands !

> ' Our brother man, how blind is he
> To all the laws of God,
> When he refuses this to see,
> That love is cause of harmony,
> And not the tyrant's rod.'

" I have many experiencies I would like to give the world for its use while I was living in my theological cabin, but will not at present.

" Praying the angels will bless you in your work, and that the light of truth may dispel the darkness that envelopes the minds of many of our brothers and sisters, I am yours, for the universal emancipation of woman's soul and body,

" PEARL."

Republican, January 16th, 1874.   Council Bluffs (Iowa).

" She is a powerful speaker and fairly magnetizes her audience to an extent we have seldom witnessed."

Nonpareil, January 16th, 1874.   Council Bluffs (Iowa).

" She told more facts, at which none should blush, and none can deny, than we ever heard in so short a space of time. We believe it was the unanimous verdict last night, that ' Woodhull Lectures ' are racy, able, and profitable."

Journal of Commerce, January 17th, 1874.   Kansas City (Mo.).

" Last night the elements seemed to join in the universal strife which Mrs. Woodhull creates wherever she opens her lips in eloquent protest against the social, political, and religious wrongs which we all feel, but owing to wholesome fear seldom do ourselves the justice to acknowledge. We were glad to see a comparatively large number of ladies present. If, when a woman advances heterodox opinions, she does not at least gain the attention and respect of her own sex, she certainly stands a very poor chance to succeed. We can safely say that after the convincing exposition of the social theory given by Mrs. Victoria Woodhull last night, any woman with an idea can never say she rejected its principles for their lack of truth. The chief part of the lecture, however, was not devoted to her so-called 'hobby,' but was a masterly *exposé* of a fraudulent government and its miserable administrators. Mrs. Woodhull is a strong-minded woman, whose sincerity of intent and earnestness of purpose are only equalled by the unexampled patience by which she has borne persecution, seldom, if ever, endured by another woman.

"John Stuart Mill has said : 'I can tolerate everything else but every other man's intolerance.' There is decidedly too much intolerance of opinion in regard to 'Woodhullism.' It is unnatural and unjust to deny a hearing to one so terribly in earnest and so complete in her self-abnegation to her work as we know Mrs. Woodhull to be. As a speaker the latter is *extraordinaire*. With a melodious voice, expressive face, and graceful form, she combines a power of acting and incognition of presence which renders her irresistible. When carried forward in her impetuous delivery, she speaks like one inspired—by the good genius of a good work."

Programme, January 17th, 1874. Kansas City (Mo.).

" Eloquent, impassioned, speaking from the depths of a profound sincerity, she strikes a vein of sympathy in her audience which, on account of her deep strength and powerful interest, seems like the effect of magic to those dispossessed of that wonderful imagination wielded only by the divine right of truth. There is nothing dreamy, speculative, or far-fetched in Mrs. Woodhull's correct, outspoken views. With bold, trenchant emphasis, she cuts right and left amidst the miserable shams which society sustains and opinions have sanctioned as just. If there is one popular vice more to be deprecated than another, it is that affected false modesty which shrinks from the utterance of one's thoughts as they exist, plain and unvarnished in the imagination. There is but one name for truth the world over. It is what we are all struggling for, the *ultimatum*, the essence of all our judgments.

"How, then, can we attain it in the smallest degree, when we studiously, persistently deny its value in our speech and intercourse ?

"It is this incubus of modern times, this fear of *speaking* what what we *think*, which Victoria Woodhull combats with all the native strength and originality of her truth-loving spirit.

"It is a significant fact in her favour, when we hear it said on all sides, that men and women are afraid to go and hear her, for it only serves to show the tendency of all to gloss over the evils and corruptions in life, by shunning the open and direct means of extirpating them."

The Journal of Commerce, January 17th, 1874. Kansas City (Mo.).

"As a speaker, Mrs. Woodhull is *extraordinary*. With a melodious voice, expressive face, and graceful form, she combines a power which renders her irresistible."

Freeman, January 18th, 1874. Leavenworth (Kansas).

"Mrs. Woodhull delivered her lecture Sunday evening, January 11th. Her lecture has attracted so much criticism that it has been the general topic. It deals in the main with stubborn facts ; the propriety of a lady discussing such topics in public will undoubtedly be questioned by some, but the positions taken by the speaker are sound, and the arguments used seem to be incontrovertible. After seeing and hearing this noted woman, we are satisfied that the popular estimate of her does her much injustice. We found Mrs. Woodhull an accomplished and lady-like woman, honest in her convictions and terribly in earnest. Everyone who undertakes to do anything in conflict with the established notions of the public must expect to be abused, but we believe Mrs. Woodhull to be the best abused woman in the world. However, she is able to hoe her own row, and in her war upon the sins and shams of modern society, is doing a vast amount of good."

State Register, January 18th, 1874. Des Moines (Iowa).

" Curiosity has been on tiptoe ever since the announcement that Mrs. Woodhull would speak in Des Moines. Mrs. Woodhull came, has spoken, and promises to speak again. She insists that the newspapers won't tell what they actually think. There is one newspaper that she can't accuse of untruthfulness hereafter. We think that she is a woman with wonderful power of eloquence. She tells many truths, unpalatable doubtless, and unusual, but actual and disgraceful truths—not disgraceful to the speaker, but to the parties whose habits make them truths. She tells some startling things that she says are true. She is witty, logical, and an orator second to few in the land. The lecture was well worth hearing."

The State Journal, January 18th, 1874. Des Moines (Iowa).

" She is the most eloquent woman who ever addressed a Des Moines audience, and one of the most eloquent of all speakers."

Reform Leader, January 18th, 1874. Oskaloosa (Iowa).

" In her lecture in Des Moines, Iowa, January 17th, Mrs. Victoria Woodhull wiped out the prejudice against her, and put many to thinking about things upon which they have hitherto been indifferent. She probed the politics of the country to the bone, and presented a terrible picture of American degeneracy, alleging the basis thereof to be our social system. She is the most eloquent and powerful female orator we have ever heard, and advances some of the grandest and most humanitarian ideas ever uttered by mortal."

January 19th, 1874. St. Joseph (Mo.).

" Mrs. Woodhull took St. Joseph by storm. The St. Joseph *Daily Herald*, one of the most liberal papers in the United States, has no words too strong to use in her behalf. I send you an extract from the pen of a lady correspondent of that journal showing the effect of truth on prejudice.—Respectfully, C. F.

" Curiosity to see Mrs. Woodhull, whose name has been heralded throughout America and Europe, led me to the Opera House, Friday evening. I went expecting to be shocked : I went full of sympathy for my sex, that were almost becoming infamous through this notorious agent.

" I expected her to strike boldly at our *sanctum sanctorum*— the fireside influence; and she did strike. She disclosed to her breathless audience the ashes and vermin concealed by the artful ignorance of the mothers and the pleasure-loving sires.

" I expected to hear her denounce woman's virtue and ridicule her purity, and she did it, and for the first time in life I felt that there is a *pureness for a woman that is perfidy*. The mother who devotes her life to church and prayer-meeting, leaving her sons and daughters to wile away the hours in debauchery and falsehood, rather than take them by the hand and explain the mysteries of the life which they, ignorant alike of moral and physical laws, are converting into a burden to themselves and others, are practising a virtue that is *perfidious*. I expected her to denounce the churches, and she did denounce them. But she *did not* denounce the humble Jesus Christ, who, eighteen hundred years ago, supped with harlots, and was a brother to the greasy fisherman. She denounced the gilded representatives of to-day who are drinking, blindfold, their own life-blood. She cried out, *not against* the Jesus who said to the harlot ' go, and sin no more,' but bitterly she denounced the Jesus Christ of to-day who cries from our gilded pulpits and religious journals, ' away with this woman, for she has fallen,' *fallen from where and by whom ?* When a boarding-school is turned into a harem, she cries out, not against the arts of the seducer, but against the infamous modesty of the mother who could send a daughter into the world to fall a victim to her own ignorance. She cried out against the pastors because they were political leaders of an impolitic people, not because they were co-labourers with Christ.

" I went to hear hisses, and I heard them, but they were hurled at the head of the Government that sits cloaked with chaste garments, from the foot of which strides a cloven hoof. I went expecting to be mortified, to be made indignant; I left mortified to shame and indignant to disgust with a press so false and politic that but here and there can be found an editor who will write what he knows to be true.

" It is not ours to-day to spot her with indignation of our ignorance, while we may safely follow many of her teachings.

" I listened with anxiety for the utterance of a sentence that should brand her the unchaste woman the bilious press has pronounced her—*but I listened in vain.*—E. T. M."

State Journal, January 19th, 1874. Des Moines (Iowa).

" The Court House was filled at an early hour, on Saturday night, to hear Mrs. Victoria C. Woodhull, the woman about whom so much has been written and talked. From the first word that she uttered, all could see that she was in earnest in her work. To say that she is not eloquent in treating her subject would be exactly contrary to the truth. *She is the most eloquent woman that ever addressed a Des Moines audience, and one of the most eloquent of all speakers.*"

Daily Gate City, January 21st, 1874.   Keokuk (Iowa).

" Mrs. Victoria Woodhull delivered her lecture at the Opera House last evening.   She is an effective and eloquent speaker. The utterances were different from any that any of us have heard from the platform before, especially from a woman.   But swift sentence is simply to debar the just judgment which Mrs. Woodhull asks, and which she has a right to ask.   The truth is that much of her lecture was unexceptionable, containing stern, rigorous, forcible facts that American society may well give a hearing to."

Democrat, January 22nd, 1874.   Ottumwa (Iowa).

" Mrs. Victoria Woodhull spoke at Lewis' Opera House on Monday evening to an audience respectable in numbers and in character.   The audience was composed largely of the thinking portion of the community, which includes women as well as men, and young men as well as old ones.   The distinguished speaker had for her discussion the questions which came up naturally to the surface.   She displayed wonderful ability, tact, and oratory.   In discussing these questions she brings to her assistance some very weighty arguments which are joined together systematically, and when in a bulk they seem rather too ponderous for any of her enemies to assail.

" Her first appearance did not attract sympathy, but invited criticism.   She was all sarcasm ; and her playful advances bore in them the wonderful resemblance of a lion playing with its prey.   This, however, was only the overture to the divine play which she afterwards rendered.   As she warmed up on the subject, the hair thrown back over her majestic brow, her eyes sparkled with the inner consciousness of genius, and as her bright graceful form towered, the lips moved with the speed of a racehorse, and the sarcastic Mrs. Woodhull became transformed into the inspired priestess of a *new religion*.

"It was a success. The woman came into the hall the object of slander, the accursed of the ministry, the slandered object of a subsidized press; she came among her audience with scarcely *ten* sympathizers, and at the close of her speech she was the heroine, the idol of her worshippers. Victoria came. Victoria conquered."

Republican, January 22nd, 1874. Galesburg (Ill.).

"It rained on yesterday evening, as probably most of our readers know; in fact it poured. The circumstances, doubtless, prevented a large audience from assembling at the Opera House, to hear the lecture of the famous Mrs. Victoria Woodhull; she lectured nevertheless, and proclaimed her startling sentiments in no less startling language. Much that she said was true enough, and said in unexceptionable phraseology. This was particularly the fact in her advice to mothers, which would have proved a profitable lesson to *every* mother in Galesburg."

State Journal, January 26th, 1874. Springfield (Ill.).

"Though perhaps Mrs. Woodhull's audience at the Opera House was not so large last night as it would have been had she not been prevented by a railroad accident from fulfilling her engagement the previous evening, still there were few empty seats, and the audience was a most respectable one and very attentive.

"She is decidedly attractive in appearance, and in the delivery of her lecture was natural, perfectly self-possessed, and at times especially earnest. The opening part of her lecture was devoted to a discussion of the subject of political reform. She arraigned much of the hypocrisy of the day in terms severe and scathing, and her protest against latter-day shams, though terrific, was generally endorsed by her hearers. Discussing the social question, she advocated the observance of the oft-neglected Greek maxim, 'Know thyself.' She earnestly insisted upon the necessity of truth and knowledge between mothers and their offsprings, as calculated to prevent much of the crime, prostitution, and misery of the present day; and while earnestly protesting against prudery and the false modesty or delicacy which prevents parents from adequately preparing their children to meet and combat the trials of life, her remarks were none too forcible, but, on the contrary, timely; and so regarded by her auditors.

" Mrs. Woodhull told a great many truths concerning the male prostitutes, whom she insisted should be punished equally with the females, and this sentiment was vigorously applauded. To those who look at nature squarely in the face and are not averse to plain speaking on a subject of great importance, there was nothing said which anyone would blush to hear."

Magnet, January 27th, 1874. Decatur (Ill.).

" Mrs. Woodhull gave a lecture for an hour and forty minutes, at the Opera House, last evening to a fair and intelligent audience.

" She is a fearless, eloquent talker, and in this respect has no superior, or even an equal, in the American lecture field."

The Pantagraph, January 29th, 1874 (Editorial). Bloomington (Ill.).

" Mrs. Woodhull delivered her second lecture last evening. The subject was the social question, which she handled with that utter fearlessness, earnestness, and eloquence which characterized her first lecture. Most of her audience went to hear the marriage relation discussed as recognized by the law and the Christian world, and they heard it, and the attack was more fierce and the denunciation more bitter, perhaps, than they had ever dreamed the tongue of man or woman could pronounce.

27

410

Many of the audience expected to hear a woman degrade her sex, but we are pleased to say that those who did were very badly mistaken, for while she dealt with plain facts in unmistakable language, she used no expression that savoured of vulgarity or that could be so interpreted by any save the mind that gloats over degraded human nature. Victoria told more truth in each of her lectures here than we often hear condensed into a discourse of two hours.

"She tore aside the veil of mock modesty and sham, and revealed the skeletons that haunt the lives of millions, giving utterance to sentiments that the inmost soul of many a member of her audience declared to be the truth."

Gazette, February 1st, 1874. Davenport (Iowa).

"Mrs. Victoria Woodhull lectured in Hill's Opera House last evening.

"The first portion of her address was devoted to what she esteemed the evils of our government, its rottenness through corruption, and its oppression to the labouring masses. Mrs. Woodhull then took up the social question. She announced her opinions on the subject of matrimony—for one thing, that the sublimest office a woman can perform is to bear the image of God in reality. She talked very plainly, told many truths, and advocated ideas which, if adopted, would spare woman a great deal of misery. She demanded that male prostitutes shall be held as amenable to law as the female prostitutes. She demanded every house of prostitution be abolished; she wanted women so pure that when they find a fallen woman they will lift her up to virtue. She said that the idea of becoming a mother is something woman has never looked upon with enough sanctity; and just as soon as the mothers of the country commence to think, prostitution will cease. All she ever asked was that the basis of marriage should be *love*—educate your daughters to marry for love and not for money or homes. She closed with appeals to her hearers to make their boys and girls pure to start with, so that their lives may be pure.

"Her lecture was delivered with an earnestness that gave it eloquence, and held the audience in closest attention."

Democrat, February 2nd, 1874. Davenport (Iowa.).

"The basic foundation-stones of republican government are free speech and a free press; and we hold that it ill becomes the latter to make use of the privilege in attempting to suppress the former. Discussion of every topic, ventilation of the boldest and broadest views always do good. Truth is immortal and falsehood ephemeral, and if there be truth in her utterances, abuse will not kill their vital power; if they be wrong, let them be calmly and dispassionately met, discussed, and controverted. Much that she says is startling, some perhaps revolting, to half-educated men and women, but in the whole of her lecture on Sunday evening we failed to see blasphemy, obscenity, or lewdness, with which the press so frequently charge her. As Byron said in his apology for 'Cain,' it is impossible to make Lucifer talk like a respectable dissenting minister, and it is equally as impossible to 'prick the carbuncle of social evils' without saying something which may shock the fastidious.

"The lecture on Sunday evening was attended by a large respectable, and enthusiastic audience. Many ladies were present and we did not see anyone leave the hall, though her utterances on the social question were free and pointed; but we could not recognize any of that promiscuity, or abandonment, with which she is so liberally credited, and we feel certain that the most refined lady in the audience felt that there was more to admire than condemn in her references to the education of youth, the sanctity of conjugal union, and the brighter prospects,

27 *

for their own sex. There was not one hiss or sign of disapprobation throughout her whole lecture, which is the best commentary on the report of her obscenity; and, so far as we could learn, not one person regretted having been present.

Argus, February 2nd, 1874. Rock Island (Ill.).

" On Sunday evening Mrs. Woodhull made her second appearance in Davenport. She had the most respectful attention of the large audience present, which was composed of the so-called most respectable families of Davenport, as also a large number of our own citizens, all of whom acknowledged the strong hits at the defects of our social system by hearty applause.

" The germ of her whole lecture is in opposition to the present *legal* marriage, and she rakes the by-ways and slums of society for illustrations, and does not hesitate to enter *polite* circles for some of them. She finds her strongest arguments in the family circle—in the lack of confidence between man and wife, the custom of teaching children from youth to marry for money; and condemns the unwilling mother for filling our jails and penitentiaries, and giving to the street the rowdy and the blasphemous, also for neglecting the physical education of her young children just coming to manhood and womanhood. She illustrates these points with facts which are known to those who have had the opportunity of seeing much of the world and which cannot be disputed.

" And on this point she speaks with considerable feeling, using the strongest terms in condemning the ministers, the doctor, and the editor, as teachers of the people, for fearing to discuss these questions as they do exist—for mock modesty in avoiding subjects so vital to the life, health, and happiness of the human race.

" She breaks through all social restraints and takes the

broadest and most democratic position, and predicts a near future when there will be the same public discussion of these subjects, without even a blush mantling the cheek of the most circumspect listener, as is now held secretly.

" Such is in brief the subject of her much-talked-of lecture, as all she names exist right under the very shadow of the sanctuary, in the daily path of the pastor and in the daily practice of the physician, and in many family circles."

Herald, February 3rd, 1874.   Dubuque (Iowa).

" There is nobody but knows that Mrs. Victoria Woodhull lectured here last evening.   She is a woman who has been hooted and railed at *ad infinitum*, but has created more stir, more sensation in our city than any other celebrity who ever trod the boards of the Athenæum.   She is a woman of brains, of eloquence, of elegance.   She is a woman like herself and nobody else.   She is emphatically Mrs. Woodhull to the core— bold, defiant in her theories on the questions of the day, unrelenting in declaring them, and speaks the nakedest and most unadorned truth we have ever listened to from any speaker—but in no sense can Mrs. Woodhull be termed an immodest woman except it be in her bluntness in discussing social topics.   She is rather a handsome woman than otherwise. Her face, while possessing all the softness and delicacy of expression which naturally belongs to a woman, is also possessed of a breadth and force of contour indicative of masculine vigour of *mind*.   We shall not presume to give anything like a text of her lecture.   The rapidity of her enunciation precludes the chance of the reporter taking them with exactness ; and even if he did obtain a full text, it has none of the brilliant fire of inspiration which enchains the listener at the time of delivery. She has a perfect grace of oratory ; every gesture and attitude is refined and eloquently expressive, and she sends forth her silvery voiced sentences as though there was the power of a hurricane behind them."

Telegraph, February 3rd, 1874. Dubuque (Iowa).

" A large and fashionable audience, composed of the aristocratic ' ten ' and the demagogic ' hundred,' crowded the Athenæum last night to hear the celebrated lecturer, Mrs. Victoria Woodhull. She was simply dressed, in a neat black suit, and from the moment she made her appearance on the stage until she retired was listened to with attention and closely scanned by a discriminating audience. Mrs. Woodhull seems to be equally at home on every subject she touches upon, and as a successful lecturer she is undoubtedly queen of the rostrum. She is at times vehement, impassioned, and her fervid and burning words scathe and scorch like intermittent flashes of lightning. We have been agreeably surprised at hearing her speak, and have come away with the idea that she tells a great many home truths, not very palatable to those rings whom she so strongly denounces."

Times, February 3rd, 1874 (Editorial). Dubuque (Iowa).

"Mrs. Woodhull gave her promised lecture last evening in the Athenæum to a crowded house. The lecturer was given a most respectful hearing and kept her audience in rapt attention by her brilliant oratory and fine impassioned delivery, entrancing them with her fervid, earnest eloquence, which we have rarely seen equalled and never surpassed in any speaker, and leading them her willing subjects.

"The first part of her lecture was devoted to the political condition of the country. Then she took up the social question.

She said, 'Every wife should say to her husband, "Wherever you go I will go, for if it is not a fit place for a woman to come to, it is not a fit place for a man." Wherever you find the noblest women you find the purest men. A pretty compliment you pay your wife when you tell her she is too weak in moral power, that she cannot stand what you can without damaging her moral nature! The great demand of the age is for better men and women. But here comes a woman, ready to tell you out of the fulness of a mother's heart how to bring into this world better men and women, and you start back with horror! I do not urge that women be brought down to the level of impure men—*I do urge that men be brought up to the level of pure women.* I demand the same anathemas for the male prostitute as for the female prostitute. I want death and destruction to every house of prostitution in this country! There are considerably more than one million prostitutes. Those women come from somewhere. Every fifteen years one million virgin girls grow up into prostitutes. These are your daughters, mothers of America. A great deal has been said about the prevention and cure of prostitution; but little or nothing has been done toward accomplishing it. I will tell you how to accomplish it: send your daughters out into the world as peers of your sons; teach them that it is honourable for women to earn their living—and then give them a chance to do so.' Proceeding to describe what marriage *should* be, she claimed that to bear a child is the most sacred and honourable mission on earth. The pregnant woman is a co-worker with God in giving to the world an immortal being. Whoever makes so noble a deed a theme of vulgarity only proclaims the foulness of his own base nature. Mothers themselves are ashamed when they ought to be the proudest. They try to murder their children before birth, and then wonder why those children, when grown to be men, turn out murderers. Preachers turn all their attention to saving souls when they would be in much better business saving bodies."

February 7th, 1874. Janesville (Wis.).

"An audience of the most intelligent citizens greeted Mrs. Woodhull on Wednesday evening, February 4th.

"Mrs. Woodhull came forward, looking somewhat careworn and weary, and was received with applause. And for one hour and a half she held her audience spell-bound, save when the flow of earnest eloquence was interrupted by some keen point of satire upon the shams of the day, which elicited the applause of the entire audience.

"There was but one opinion the next day, and that was, ' She told truth, and everybody must admit it.'

"In company with a few friends we met Mrs. Woodhull at the hotel next morning, and had the pleasure of listening to her conversation on the important topics of the hour. It is here that one may obtain a view of the real ability of this lady. Every sentence she utters is a clear cut diamond, which strikes upon the ear like a prophecy or an oracle, carrying conviction with it.

"Long will we remember that interview, and the words of counsel and encouragement that were given us.

"Thanks, Mrs. Woodhull; and may the world soon learn that she whom it is slandering and persecuting is the angel that is rolling the stone from the door of the sepulchre of its purity and peace, that they may arise to glory to bless and save humanity. C. W. T."

Standard, February 12th, 1874. Northfield (Minn.).

"Mrs. Victoria Woodhull, the best-abused woman on the American continent, is to speak in St. Paul and Minneapolis this week. We say the best-abused woman, for the reason that her persecutions have chiefly been for the utterances that were truths. Yet because she struck boldly into their faces the rules of society established by Madam Grundy, she must be crucified for uttering them. All admit that she speaks truth, and yet it is such unwelcome truth that they do not wish to hear it.

"'Desperate diseases require desperate remedies,' and it is expected that the doctor's probe and lance will at times make the flesh shrink and quiver, and the patient sometimes scream in agony, and yet it is necessary that they be used in order to save the patient's life.

"Mrs. Woodhull is using the knife and the scalpel on the diseases that have made society but little better than 'rotten to the core,' and with a bold, unflinching hand, holds up the hypocritical cant of the day to the public gaze in all its hideous deformity. When people are willing to denounce error, even though advocated by the clergy, and accept truth even should Mrs. Woodhull preach it, the world will be better off than at present."

Pioneer, February 12th, 1874. St. Paul (Minn.).

"The well-known Mrs. Victoria Woodhull lectured here last evening, at the Opera House, to an audience that crowded the building from the footlights to the upper tier. The lecture was listened to with marked attention, and several parts of it were applauded with a good deal of earnestness. It was throughout bold, defiant, and all of it was delivered with glibness and confidence. It was not without its bitterness, especially when she was dealing with the shams of society, which she handled with a freedom that was never before indulged in by any speaker in this city.

" Mrs. Woodhull is of medium height, light complexion, with
blue eyes. Her face indicates great vigour of thought, she
has a broad high forehead, from which she occasionally pushes
back her heavy brown hair. As a speaker she irresistibly
attracts attention, both on account of the matter and the
manner, and one listens continually wondering what will come
next."

Pioneer, February 13th, 1874. St. Paul (Minn.).

" The second lecture at the Opera House by Mrs. Woodhull
was attended by another large audience, that filled the house
both upstairs and down. It was listened to with the closest
attention, and several portions of it were applauded with a
good deal of vehemence. The lecture was a terrible invective
throughout against what she considered to be shams of society.
The following is a very brief synopsis, *and a very brief one too.*
Mrs. Woodhull is full of the subject and speaks with great
rapidity and vehemence, and it is difficult at all times to catch
with accuracy what she says.

" At the beginning of her lecture Mrs. Woodhull spent some
time in expatiating on the peculiar and lackadaisical humours
of fashionable society on the subject of social reform, and said :
When I first started out I had no idea of the magnitude of the
fight I was enlisting in. I was mute with surprise at the
blind folly of society women, and their wanton caprice,
indolence, and carelessness on a subject of most vital importance to their happiness. I propose to throw off the mask
and discuss this subject openly and sincerely to a good purpose,
when I find that the homes of a proportion of our richest and
most influential, as well as the homes of the commoners, are full
of misery.

" Pass your Social Evils' Bill. Let us have an examination ;
but let us know about the men as well.

"What an idea this is of your women going round and praying at saloons to the keepers. If the mothers would make no more drunkards there would be no more trouble. When I was at Clinton Junction on my way here, I was stopped by a man who said he wanted to speak to me, and hoped I would not be offended. He exposed his breast to me, which was marked with a bottle. He said, 'When my mother was carrying me she went into a saloon and was seized with an unconquerable desire to drink.' She brought forth a drunkard. Let the mothers agree to breed no more drunkards and there will be no use for saloons. It is the women who make these drunkards.

"The day must come when the study of the laws and relations of the sexes be made a pure and holy thing if we would have better men and women. If a man stocking a farm should act with so little foresight and discretion as men and women do in making children, he would be called a fool.

"If a woman respects herself others will respect her. If any man speaks disrespectfully of any women it only shows the conditions of his home and surroundings. These questions cannot be dealt with without saying hard things. I complain that mothers do not explain to their children these matters. If they would have their children act right and be right, mothers should explain to them all about their bodies, and not allow them to be abused by secluded indulgence.

"In New York they have a foundling hospital. What does that fact suggest to you? Why it suggests just this. If a young lady becomes pregnant, she can go to this hospital, leave her child, and then go back to society again as respectable as ever. What a commentary on civilization and your religion.

"In the olden times we are told how they caught a young woman in the act of adultery. Now, what did they do with

that young woman ? Well, they took her to Jesus. He told
her to go, and sin no more. This is what they did with the
woman. *But what did they do with the man ?* They did not
bring him around. But if the stoning had commenced and he
had been there, she had no doubt this man would have been
the first to throw stones. She concluded by saying that when
women of the country are pure enough to speak on these matters
freely, you will find that this debauchery will cease, and
women will be purer and better. If mothers want healthy
children they must see to it that the children are started
right."

Leader, February 17th, 1874. Eau Claire (Wis.).

"Mrs. Victoria Woodhull appeared before the intelligent
portion of this city on February 13th. As usual, she was filled
with the spirit of inspiration, while her countenance beamed with
radiance of love for her suffering kind. For two hours she
held the crowded hall in rapt suspense as her electric flashes
lit up their mentalities as by a magic wand. That she spoke
as with a tongue of fire all could not help but realize who
listened to her soul-thrilling utterances as they fell like
pointed arrows from heaven's quiver into the thrilled hearts
of that awe-stricken assembly; for many who had gathered
there to blush and curse, ere she had fairly commenced, were
prepared to go forth to love and bless. But vain would it be
to undertake a portrayal of her perfections in oratory and
eloquence, for that also would require the perfection of the
perfect.

"Wherever she moves she causes vibrations of love and
purity to arise upon the sea of life that pass through and
around the spiritual universe, leaving this holy and benign
influence upon all the souls therein contained. Hence, it is in

this sense that she has been chosen by the gods as one of, if not the saviour of, this nineteenth century, of which after generations will sing, and to which they will look as the birthday of a world's emancipation from bondage. Therefore, her future as her past is to be glorious. She is destined to shine in the horizon of progress until reform is needed no more."

Monroe Co. Republican, February 20th, 1874. Sparta (Wis.).

"On Sunday evening last we listened to Mrs. Victoria Woodhull at the Opera House, La Crosse, upon the social question. Having heard and read so much of this distinguished woman, we improved the opportunity to hear her speak. Her audience, as on the preceding evening, was a large and intelligent one. Mrs. Woodhull appeared upon the stage promptly at eight o'clock, not the coarse and unprepossessing woman we had expected to see, *but emphatically the reverse.* Instead of what we expected came a small, well-formed, and modest appearing woman, with brown hair, fair complexion, and blue eyes, possessing an earnest and thoughtful look, but with little or none of the indications of eloquence and power she soon exhibited. She opened her subject with a quiet announcement, and then proceeded to a terrible arraignment of the crimes of men in high places, and launched with the force of a Hercules hot thunderbolts at the hypocrisies of priests, Churches, and law-makers.

"That she is telling truths is not to be denied, but that she is telling it far in advance of the readiness of the people to receive them and to act upon it is painfully evident to a majority of her audience. When warmed up with the harrowing recital of the wrongs of women, she seems to speak in the very glow of inspiration, and impresses her hearers with the unquestioned conviction that she can borrow at pleasure the thunderbolts of the gods and hurl them with unerring precision into the very citadel of our time-honoured and most sacred tradition. We most unhesitatingly applaud her courage, her eloquence, and her zeal."

Daily Herald, May 13th, 1874. Salt Lake City.

" MRS. WOODHULL'S LECTURE.—The theatre was crammed last evening, the audience embracing the most cultivated, learned and refined members of the best society, of both sexes, and from among the professions. The career of this lady is one of the most remarkable of this or any other age. Mrs. Woodhull on her appearance was greeted with a round of applause, which was repeated frequently during her lecture. At first she appeared modest, though not timid, reading from manuscript a severe censure on the government, the dishonest course of its officials, and the politics of the nation, sparing neither political party. But finally becoming warmed up in her subject, she cast aside her manuscript, and throwing her whole soul into what she was saying, poured into the ears of her spell-bound audience such a torrent of more than womanly eloquence as few ever heard from the tongue of either man or woman.

" Mrs. Woodhull has such an unenviable newspaper notoriety that her every expression is watched to see if it cannot be tortured into a bad meaning; but those who went there last evening expecting to hear words unwomanly fall from her lips were disappointed. Her lecture was characterized throughout with an earnestness of purpose highly commendable."

Daily Herald, May 14th, 1874. Salt Lake City.

"MRS. WOODHULL'S SECOND LECTURE.—The lecture of Mrs. Woodhull at the Institute last evening was well attended by a mixed assemblage of ladies and gentlemen.

"What she said was highly appreciated and frequently elicited loud applause, both for the eloquent manner of the delivery and the sentiments expressed. The intense activity of Mrs. Woodhull's brain, and the tragic strength and wonderful fluency with which she is endowed, are remarkable, while the amount of information and facts she has picked up are still more so. She is in earnest in the promulgation of her reform ideas."

News, May 19th, 1874. Gold Hill (Nev.).

"The lecture of Mrs. Woodhull last evening at Piper's Opera House, Virginia City, was well attended, the theatre being crowded in every part. Gold Hill certainly was pretty fully represented in that audience, and the dress circle contained a goodly proportion of ladies. Mrs. Woodhull has been written and abused into a national prominence. We have never seen the Opera House filled with a more interested and critical audience, seemingly disposed to hear and honestly judge of what this noted lady had to say. Mrs. Woodhull possesses a good appearance, a full clear voice, and a deeply earnest manner, which gives full force and weight to her words. Logical and pointed in her argument and applications, witty, playful, or pathetic at times, and again merging into the keenly sarcastic, she manages her subject with the most consummate skill and with striking effect. She handled the political, religious, and social status of the nation and society without gloves, making numerous telling points, which drew forth strong and repeated applause from her audience."

Evening Chronicle, May 19th, 1874. Virginia City (Nev.).

" MRS. WOODHULL'S LECTURE.—Piper's Opera House last evening was crowded with people who had assembled there to hear Mrs. Woodhull's lecture. They applauded the many telling truths made in the matter of corruption pervading high political, social, and governmental circles. Mrs. Woodhull is, without exception, the best lady-speaker ever heard on the Pacific Coast. She has a pleasant voice, enunciates clearly and distinctly, and she unmistakably is a logician of marked ability. Her readiness in repartee was very happily illustrated last evening, when interrupted by a disciple of John Barleycorn in the dress circle."

Common Sense, May 22nd, 1874. San Francisco (Cal.).

" MRS. WOODHULL IN VIRGINIA CITY.—The Opera House was packed last night to hear Mrs. Woodhull's lecture. Business men went in and paid a dollar for standing-room : they only wished to get a glimpse of this notable woman. Having seen her, they remained to hear what she had to say. Standstillism is not accordance with the world's creed. So these men, who stood until the last word was spoken, rushed to the office to secure seats for themselves and friends for to-night. And those who were shocked because Mrs. Woodhull, good Samaritan like, decided not to pass us by on either side, turned with the tide to hear the brave woman expound the new scriptures. Mrs. Woodhull, true to her promise, unmasked hypocrisy. She called political thieves, land swindlers, and corrupt Christians by their right names. She insisted upon civil service reform : she demanded purification of our legislation ; but she would begin these reforms in our homes—in the mother's heart. She is right, so the thinkers in the hall said. One grey-headed man remarked, on leaving the hall, ' The woman has told us God's eternal truth.' Another said, ' We all know the world is over-full of private as

well as public corruption ; but who expected to hear the facts
from a woman ? ' A certain class will honestly curse Mrs.
Woodhull, because they do not understand or recognize the
truths she tells nor comprehend the woman ; another class hate
her for letting the light into the dens where they hide themselves;
still another class sing hosanna and hail her as one sent from
heaven."

Common Sense, June 4th, 1874.   San Francisco (Cal.).

"Mrs. Victoria C. Woodhull, the apostle of social reform, spoke
in Platt's Hall last evening. Her opening discourse it was not
our privilege to hear; but judging from the report of many
sensible and truthful men and women who were there, it was
replete with facts. She is an earnest, outspoken woman, and
does not weaken her ideas by the use of unmeaning language.
She calls things by their right names; and consequently gives
offence to those who do not like to hear themselves characterized
truthfully. One of the purest women in this city, an old Quaker
lady, well-known to most of our readers here, could see nothing
evil in what Mrs. Woodhull said, while men whose vileness is
patent, ' blushed to the tops of their bald pates.' "

"*Second Lecture.*—On Tuesday evening the editor of this paper,
with his wife and two daughters, went to hear Mrs. Woodhull.
Never having met her, and judging of her only by newspaper
reports, we certainly were not prejudiced in her favour. She
said some bitter things against marriage as it is, *but not one
word against that true union of souls which alone constitutes
marriage*. She advocated free love; but in a sense so high
and language so pure that the very personification of chastity
could not *justly* find fault with it; and then she spoke of promiscuity ; but she called it death, and warned her listeners from
it as from the road to hell. There was not one word in her
lecture from beginning to end that the most innocent
28

might not safely hear, and judging from the applause of the
audience, her hearers fully sympathized and approved of all she
said. The galleries were mainly filled with ladies.

"Mrs. Woodhull proved herself in the only lecture we heard to
be the true friend of woman. Her teachings, as set forth in this
discourse, could not fail, rightly understood, to greatly benefit
and ennoble womankind."

Mercury, June 10th, 1874. San José (Cal.).

"The audience at the Opera House last night was respectable
both as to size and quality, there being present both gentlemen
and ladies who hold high positions in society. Mrs. Woodhull
was received with applause. She was plainly dressed in black,
with no attempt at ornament, her jewellery being sombre black,
even to her watch-guard. She has a fine presence, and is what
would be called a handsome woman by unprejudiced persons.

"A brief synopsis of her speech will be found elsewhere;
although no mere sketch can begin to do the subject justice.
That Mrs. Woodhull uttered many grand truths, no one that
heard her can deny; that she said many sharp things is also
certain. At times she was an incarnate Jove, scattering the
lightnings of fierce invective right and left; and again she
touched all hearts with a tender womanliness that moistened
every eye. She is intensely in earnest in all that she says, and
possesses a wonderful power over her audience."

Independent Californian, June 10th, 1874. San José (Cal.).

"We attended Mrs. Woodhull's lecture last evening. Of Mrs.
Woodhull's earnestness there is no question. We believe her
to be sincere and honest. She dives right into what she conceives
to be wrong, without regard for anybody's reverence for religion,
superstition, or anything else, with scathing invectives and
scalding vehemence, uprooting every vestige of evil from out-

growth of our social restrictions under existing institutions of marriage, &c. The sexual philosophy of love and marriage is a great, grave, and mighty subject; one on which depends human weal or woe. 'If you seriously talk the matter over before your marriage, you will never repent it afterward; for marriage is the most sacred relation that human beings can enter into; one that not only the purest love but the best motives and highest intelligence should mutually comprehend before accepting it.' "

Mercury, June 11th, 1874. San José (Cal.).

"A report of Mrs. Woodhull's second and last lecture, in this city appears in another column. Some who went to her lectures expecting to find food for ridicule, remained to become deeply interested, and came away enthusiastic."

Common Sense, June 20th, 1874. San Francisco (Cal.).

MRS. VICTORIA C. WOODHULL IN SAN JOSÉ.

"This noted lady appeared before a San José audience, giving two lectures, 'Reformation or Revolution, Which?' and 'Woman—the Wife and Mother.' Her audiences were composed of the best and most intelligent of our citizens, who listened with profound and respectful attention, frequently applauding her most radical utterances.

"*Mrs. Woodhull, unlike all reformers who have preceded her, descends from the world of effect, and grapples with the cause.* No pen can truthfully report her. The eloquence that she sometimes pours forth from her impassioned soul as she paints in vivid flashes the wrongs of her sex, startles her audience like the lurid lightning's glare across the gathering darkness of a coming storm. Again she seems to stand in awful majesty, hurling in vindictive torrents forged thunderbolts at the system that binds, fetters, and tortures both soul and mind. In

28 *

her appeals to the better natures of her hearers for respect and appreciation, for womanhood and motherhood, she stands forth in all the grandeur of transfigured womanhood, a very goddess of love and beauty. 'Tis then she wins all hearts and melts them to tears.

"It is the unanimous verdict of all who have heard her that she is sincere and terribly in earnest, however much they may differ with her in her theories. No lecturer has been more respectfully received in this city than was Mrs. Woodhull."

Chronicle, July 4th, 1874. San Francisco (Cal.).

" The announcement that Mrs. Woodhull would lecture drew a large audience to Platt's Hall last evening. The seats on the floor and in the gallery were all occupied, and a fringe of humanity extended entirely around the lower part of the hall. There was a large attendance of ladies present which monopolized all the best seats, thrusting into the background more modest but equally anxious manhood."

Common Sense, July 11th, 1874. San Francisco (Cal.).

"Mrs. Woodhull's oration drew a crowded house to Platt's Hall on Friday evening of last week. Every seat was occupied, and but few available inches left of standing-room. The audience was of the first character. Mrs. Woodhull was warmly greeted, and as soon as the hum of the immense multitude was stilled, and the first clear notes of her ringing voice sounded over the vast audience, the magnetism of this marvellous woman began to be felt; the proverbial pin might have been heard to drop; every eye was fixed upon her; every ear was strained to catch the smallest word that fell from the lips of this wonderful woman—who stood there plainly dressed in black, with a rose at her throat."

Daily Union, September 28th, 1874. New Haven (Conn.).

" The announcement that Mrs. Woodhull would deliver an address at Loomis Temple last evening on ' What is True and What is False Socially,' drew out, as might have been expected, a large audience bent upon listening to this noted woman. The hall was densely packed, and by eight o'clock standing-room was hardly attainable."

Bonny, October 1st, 1874. Portland (Me.).

" This famous lady addressed an audience of over a thousand people, in which the best intelligence of the place was represented, in the City Hall.

" Her friends here were pleased to see the close attention paid to her remarks, which occupied an hour and a half of rapid, graceful, and earnest delivery, compelling everyone to accord her the praise of being a most eloquent speaker as well as a refined and cultured lady. She handled her subject in a fearless manner, denouncing the false in most scathing terms, and portraying the true in the holiest and most beautiful language. She gave everyone something to think of, and we venture to assert that hundreds left the hall better men and women for having listened to this much-slandered but irrepressible woman, whose advice every mother will do well to reflect upon and put into practice.

" Prejudice against her died an easy death in her winning presence, and we prophesy that in the future Mrs. Woodhull will be a welcome and popular speaker whenever she chooses to return to Portland."

Argus, October 2nd, 1874. Portland (Me.).

" Last evening City Hall contained an audience numbering more than one thousand, including many ladies, to listen to the lecture of Mrs. Victoria C. Woodhull. Among the listeners were many of our prominent citizens."

Daily Public Opinion, October 10th, 1874. Trenton (N. J.).

" Contrary to the anticipations of many, her lecture was very well attended and well delivered, announcing many novel ideas as well as many of the soundest truths. It denounced the government as rotten to the core, the system false. The source of all this evil was attributed to the false social system of the day, which was stigmatized, with all the force at the speaker's command, as deleterious above everything else. She was frequently interrupted with applause."

Public Record, October 17th, 1874. Philadelphia (Penn.).

" Horticultural Hall, last evening, was filled, the audience being mostly ladies, who assembled there to hear Mrs. Woodhull's lecture. Her brilliant oratory, fine, impassioned eloquence, sweet-toned voice, dramatic powers, and graceful appearance fairly entranced the audience, the spell being frequently broken by enthusiastic demonstrations."

Inquirer, October 17th, 1874. Philadelphia (Penn.).

" Last evening Horticultural Hall was filled by a large audience assembled to listen to a lecture by Mrs. Victoria C. Woodhull, on the subject 'What is True and False Socially.'

" Her appearance on the platform was greeted with applause, and throughout the discourse she held the closest attention of her hearers.

" The speaker's easy flow of language and the earnestness with which she advocated her cause elicited frequent applause from the audience."

Star, October 17th, 1874. Philadelphia (Penn.).

" Mrs. Victoria C. Woodhull lectured in Horticultural Hall last evening to an immense audience."

Daily Eagle, October 21st, 1874. Reading (Pa.).

"Mrs. Woodhull, who is one of the most gifted and daring
women in America, will lecture at Mishler's Academy of Music,
this evening. This lady is the advanced guard of that coming
glorious army of women who will overthrow sin, shame, and
sorrow, and in their place plant virtue, innocence, and love—
always keeping in view the proud mission of woman, which is
to elevate, ennoble, and improve. This lady has been persecuted
and abused, hounded down by unrighteous laws ; but, like the
Persian fable of the rain-drop, the better she is known the
better is she to fill that place in the diadem, which is the brightest
and most dazzling page in Persian history. Everyone should
be present to-night."

American Weekly Tribune, October 25th, 1874. Reading (Pa.).

"Mrs. Victoria Woodhull lectured at the Academy of Music,
Wednesday and Thursday evenings. While she is a plain
speaker on plain subjects, she tells more truth in her way than
any other lecturer, without regard to sex, we have ever been
permitted to hear. While the masses may turn upon her course
and self with disdain openly, they are secretly planning in their
hearts how they may follow her. A mind crammed with
intellect, as is hers, cannot fail to make a lasting impression,
and every day the principles poured from her lips are gaining
more foothold. Condemn her who pleases, she is advocating a
cause which cannot be resisted, and which one day will not
only be respected and become popular, but be advocated from
every pulpit in the land, and cherished by all who can read aright
its principles."

Times and Dispatch, October 22nd, 1874. Reading (Pa.).

"Mrs. Woodhull, applying the scalpel of her oratory to the
pustular tumours of the social system with an unrelenting

purpose and a pitiless hand, moved her audience with her
eloquence as the magnet sways the needle, at the Academy of
Music last night.

"She did not say one word that brought the blush of shame to
any intelligent person's face. The best evidence of the fact
that she has something to say is the respectful attention paid
her last evening during a two hours' lecture. As she poured out
the story of her own wrongs and those of both sexes, she seemed
a modern Joan d'Arc."

Intelligencer, October 28th, 1874. Lancaster (Pa.).

"Mrs. Victoria C. Woodhull lectured on Friday evening in
Fulton Hall. She was plainly but elegantly dressed; she has a
tall and graceful figure, and moves with great ease upon the stage.
She has a broad brow and a very fine face. When flushed with
the excitement of speaking, it may fairly be called beautiful.
She is manifestly a woman of naturally very fine intellectual
powers, and displayed a degree of ability and force which we
were not prepared to see. The first part of her speech was well
and calmly delivered from notes which she held in her hand and
occasionally referred to; after twenty minutes or more, the
lady, warming up to her subject, soon began to pour forth
extemporaneously a succession of well-conceived, strongly
worded, and warmly delivered sentences. Some passages were
exceedingly eloquent and well constructed, and her language
well-chosen. In fact, the lecture was delivered throughout with
an earnestness and effect which showed the lecturer to be
possessed of high power."

1875.

Telegraph, January 9th, 1875. Newburgh (N.Y.).

" If there is a woman in this country who has been better abused than Mrs. Victoria C. Woodhull, the social agitator of this period, we would like to see her. She arrived in this city yesterday and gave a matinée lecture to women. In the evening she lectured to all.

" Mrs. Woodhull was received with great applause. She began her lecture by reading from manuscript, but gradually warming with her subject she placed the manuscript on the table, and spoke as she felt, citing numerous incidents in her extended career since she began the ' Social Crusade,' as proofs of the views she holds, and at times rose to enthusiasm in her denunciations of the ' rottenness and hypocrisy' of society as at present constituted.

" Her audience manifested their appreciation and approval of 'telling points by frequent and uproarious applause. Whatever they say of Mrs. Woodhull, they cannot deny her sincerity and a power of oratory possessed by but few men or women. There is an earnestness in her speech and something about this woman that is above sensationalism."

Pantagraph, January 20th, 1875. Bloomington (Ill.).

" The Opera House was filled. Mrs. Woodhull promptly began upon the work in hand, and from the first held her audience deeply interested.

" As one listens to Mrs. Woodhull no doubt can be entertained of a supreme belief on her part of the efficacy of her theories, and that she is sincere and honest in their advocacy. She possesses every quality that is required to form the orator. When under the fire of her own eloquence, her face lights up

with a beauty of the *spirituelle* order, which seems to place its
subject above the capacity for much that has been said about
her in the press. Her language is chaste, and her sentences
well formed, and they pour forth as if they came from an
inexhaustible fountain.

" But this is the prelude merely. She begins her speech in a
common-place way, and sticks to her notes until her feelings
come into sympathy with her subject, then the divinely gifted
powers of oratory burst forth in all their splendour as she treads
the platform with all the fury of an enraged tigress that has
lost her young, hurling defiance at their captors and challenging
them to the contest. Her words are barbed arrows, that go
home with unerring aim ; and when the strain closes, the
audience bursts forth in applause. As if appeased by the
offering, she becomes transformed, and now she pleads in tones
and words for her scheme for the better conditions for the
people, that are irresistible. And then from this, at a single
leap, she goes to ridicule or sarcasm, presenting her picture
in such a style that roars of laughter follow. And what makes
this all the more effective, is that it seems to flow without the
least effort on her part. She makes the audience believe what she
believes, feel what she feels, see what she sees. In these regards
she seems to be unapproachable."

Pantagraph, January 21st, 1875. Bloomington (Ill.).

" Last evening Mrs. Victoria Woodhull appeared for a second
lecture in Schroder's Opera House. The theme of her discourse
was the prophecy of St. Paul, ' The last enemy that shall be
destroyed is death.'

" She confined herself more strictly to her notes than upon
the previous evening, and spoke over an hour in a manner that
riveted the attention of her auditors to her thoughts and utterances. The solution of the prophecy, she thinks, will be

brought about by the observance of the laws of sexual relations, which she has so long advocated, and of which she is perhaps the most clearly defined exponent at the present day. She once more gave her views on the social and sexual problem in her characteristically fearless and candid manner, discussing the delicate topic, not as though she relished the task or admired the expression which the theme demanded, but as though she felt it her *duty* to speak as she did. No one can deny that a very large per cent. of all she said last evening was *truth*—startling, appalling, terrible truth."

Daily Herald, January 29th, 1875 (Editorial). St. Joseph (Mo.).

" MRS. VICTORIA WOODHULL'S LECTURE.—If Mrs. Woodhull did not lodge a few telling shots into the rickety hulk of fogeyism last night, then we do not know what sharpshooting is. The lecture was a fierce onslaught upon the lamentable ignorance which prevails in every household upon the laws of life and the governing principles of our most vital functions. She told the truth, and every man and woman present knew and felt that her words were true. When she declaimed against the prudery and false modesty which control the wives and mothers of to-day, her dramatic action and vehement impassioned oratory roused the audience to the highest pitch of enthusiasm. The modest and sanctimonious portion of the community lifts its hands in holy horror at the mere thought of a woman appearing before an audience in behalf of her sex; but these very self-same Pharisees feel in their hearts that there is need of exactly the social reformation which she demands."

Daily Herald, January 29th, 1875. St. Joseph (Mo.).

" A large, intelligent, and enthusiastic audience assembled in the Opera House last night to listen to the most remarkable woman of the age—one who has caused more commotion, called forth more criticism, excited more thought on vital matters, who has more inveterate enemies, and more enthusiastic friends, who has been more widely and badly abused, and had more honest, though flattering, encomiums in the same space of time than almost any other person, man or woman, who has ever lived. As an orator she stands unquestioned, even by her enemies, as the 'Queen of the Rostrum,' her brilliant perorations, uttered in the most highly dramatic and finely impassioned manner and rich-toned voice, fairly entrance the audience and carry conviction almost whether they will or no. She stands before her hearers a veritable impersonation of the words she utters. Nobody who sees her can doubt that she is not only in earnest, but honest in all she says ; indeed, her purposes seemed based upon a deep-seated religious enthusiasm.

"When to all this is added that she is an editor of a widely circulated paper, and an author of well-known reputation, her title as 'The most remarkable person of the age' is fully established. A little more than three years ago she flashed upon the country, and her work that she has done, to all which we have alluded, has been performed in this brief time.

"Last evening the members of the Joint Asylum Committee visited the Opera House and listened to the lecture of Mrs. Victoria C. Woodhull, after which they repaired to the Ladies' Ordinary of the Pacific, where a splendid banquet was tendered them by Senator Young and Representatives Bittinger. Several citizens were also present by invitation, among whom we recognized Mayor Hosea, Judge Grubb, Col. James N. Burnes, Calvin F. Burnes, Col. Koch, Major Hartwig, F. M. Tufts, James N. Burnes, junr., E. W. Fox, Mr. McGinnis, Dr. Catlett, C. B. Wilkinson.

"A novel feature of the entertainment—sitting at the table beside the President—was Mrs. Victoria C. Woodhull, who was specially invited by the managers and again sent for by the assembled company. Speeches were made in response to

calls. . . . At the close Col. Burnes paid an eloquent and
glowing tribute to *Pluck*, saying that we all admire that quality
in man or woman.

" He then directed his remarks to the lady present, and paid
her a compliment which only he can pay any man or woman, for
the exhibition of this virtue in so remarkable a degree as to
draw the intense fires of the fiercest opposition ever encountered
by a woman. At the close of his remarks, Mrs. Woodhull was
loudly called upon from all parts of the hall, and she arose and
delivered a fifteen-minute speech full of fire, eloquence, pathos,
and argument. She thanked the gallant presiding officer for
daring to say, in his invitation to her, that women were entitled
to sit at the council of men ; she was proud of the privilege of
listening to the speeches of men sent out by the State to
investigate the *result* of those fearful evils whose *causes* she had
been depicting publicly and so earnestly endeavouring to cure.
Her speech was the most keen, cutting, touching, and fascinating
argument, in favour of her side of the question which she spoke
to, we have ever heard."

Commercial, January 81st, 1875. Leavenworth (Kan.).

" Last night Mrs. Woodhull spoke at the Opera House to a
good audience—a gathering of intelligent people who wanted to
hear what Mrs. Woodhull had to say and how she said it. In
the dress-circle we noticed a large number of ladies who were
intensely interested in what the speaker had to offer. For over
an hour the audience was held by the eloquent words eloquently
spoken. Mrs. Woodhull was evidently in ill-health, but her
arguments were forcibly put and to the point."

Commonwealth, February 2nd, 1875. Topeka (Kan.).

" A much larger audience greeted this famous social iconoclast
at her second appearance last evening than on the occasion of
her first visit a year ago. Whatever may be said of Mrs. Woodhull,

her rhetorical talents are unquestioned, and she certainly does
not permit anyone in her audience to doze. Her remedy for
crime and her method of abolishing it may be comprehended in
the word ' Stirpiculture,' the improvement of the human race
by the application of the ' doctrine of natural selection' to the
human family. She repudiated the notion that free-love, as
she advocated it, meant *promiscuity*, and maintained that the
inevitable result would be to prevent promiscuity, which was the
curse of society now.

"All this was illustrated and enforced by eloquence and
earnestness, and many apt and telling hits. Her discourse
contained many unpalatable but not the less forcible truths."

Daily Times, February 14th, 1875.   Grand Rapids (Mich.).

"Mrs. Victoria C. Woodhull gave a splendid lecture before a
large audience at the Opera House last evening. The subject
was ' The Destiny of the Republic,' and was handled with rare
eloquence."

Democrat, February 14th, 1875.   Grand Rapids (Mich.).

" Last evening, at the Opera House, Mrs. Victoria Woodhull
gave her famous lecture, ' The Destiny of the Republic.' The
audience was as large as has greeted any lecturer this
season. Mrs. Woodhull's manner is graceful, and her enunciation is clear and distinct. Her lecture abounded in striking
effects."

Sentinel, February 19th, 1875.   Ionia (Mich.).

"Union Hall was filled on Wednesday evening to hear and
and see Mrs. Victoria C. Woodhull. ' The Destiny of the
Republic' is the title under which Mrs. Woodhull attacks the
institution of marriage, and this she does in such a manner that
the audience listens to an undisputed groundwork of facts

dressed in brilliant language. There is little doubt that she has been largely misrepresented in her character and life, and that she honestly believes and maintains her position in regard to social questions. In pointing to the imperfections, miseries, and crimes of life in so-called Christian countries, she does not overstate the truth. In declaiming upon the terrible condition of women in the marriage relation, facts sustain her only too often.

"She used perfectly plain language in discussing the delicate but important themes connected with the marriage relation, and no one could listen to her without being convinced of the great importance of more general information on these matters, and a stricter adherence to natural laws in all that relates to reproduction.

"There is very much in her lectures to challenge thoughtful attention, and she is capable of doing much good by her agitation of topics which are treated with too much prudishness by public teachers, and yet involve more than any other the moral and physical welfare of the race."

Republican, February 19th, 1875. Lansing (Mich.).

"MRS. WOODHULL'S LECTURE.—A good audience was in attendance at the Opera House last evening to listen to this eloquent woman. Mrs. Woodhull thinks the Republic in a bad condition, and, in fact, is no republic at all as long as the women are denied the right to vote, hold office, and receive the same pay for the same work as men do. When this desirable point is reached, she says the gallows and penitentiary will no longer cast their black shadows over the land; for women, enfranchised and free, will form harmonious unions, by which a better race will be developed. Mrs. Woodhull's oratorical powers held her audience throughout, and her remarks were frequently applauded."

Genesee Gazette, February 27th, 1875. Flint (Mich.).

" MRS. VICTORIA WOODHULL AT FENTON HALL.—Monday evening this famous lady lectured to a large audience of ladies and gentlemen on the ' Destiny of the Republic.' The disagreeable state of the weather, no doubt, prevented many from attending; nevertheless, the widespread fame of the speaker was sufficient to draw almost a crowded house. The lecture lasted two hours, and was listened to attentively, interrupted at times only by applause from her listeners. She is a rapid and eloquent speaker, is downright earnest in all she says, and says it in the plainest and most comprehensive manner. Her sentiments, of course, have their supporters and opposers; but it matters little to her what anyone thinks or says about her. She speaks her views fearlessly, believing that she is doing that which will eventually lead to the elevation of her sex in all duties of life which they are called to fill."

New York Times, July, 1875. New York City.

" Mrs. Elizabeth Cady Stanton says:—' Victoria Woodhull's acquaintance would be refining to any man. In her character and person there is never anything but refinement in word or movement. She has a beautiful face—the ideal of spirituality. Victoria Woodhull has done a work for Women that none of us could have done. She has faced and dared men to call her the names that make women shudder. She has risked and realized the sort of ignominy that would have paralyzed any of us who have longer been called strong-minded. Leaping into the brambles that were too high for us to see over them, she broke a path into their close and thorny interstices, with a stedfast faith that glorious principle would triumph at last over conspicuous ignominy, although her life might be sacrificed; and when, with a meteor's dash, she sank into a dismal swamp, we

could not lift her out of the mire nor buoy her through the
deadly waters. She will be as famous as she has been infamous,
made so by benighted or cowardly men and women. In the
annals of emancipation the name of Victoria Woodhull will
have its own high place as a deliverer.'"

Argus, August 21st, 1875. Albany (N.Y.).

"Mrs. Woodhull lectured at Martin's Opera House, last evening, upon the Bible mysteries. She based her reasonings upon
some texts of Scripture, which she read from the prophecies of
Daniel, the Revelation of St. John, and the history of Creation.
She assumed that the Garden of Eden was intended to mean
the human body, and that the temple of God was the same
thing."

Sunday Trojan, August 22nd, 1875. Troy (N.Y.).

"Mrs. Woodhull lectured at the Opera House last evening.
She read the introductory portion of her lecture from manuscript,
it being a succinct review of the principal points in the world's
history, social and political, down to the time. Upon concluding
the perusal of her manuscript she rolled it up, and addressed
the audience for about an hour, wielding the Damascus blade
of her eloquence with such force and fervour as to involuntarily
command rounds of applause. It is certain that Mrs. Woodhull
utters truths and advanced ideas worthy of consideration. She
considered the American people the culmination of the development of nations, and paid a high tribute to their superiority
over other races. The fearless and earnest manner in which
she discussed the sexual question enchained the closest attention.
Mrs. Woodhull presented a strong argument to prove that the
triumph of her doctrines would do away with prostitution and
crime, empty our jails and penitentiaries, and introduce a mil-

29

lennial era, insuring a lofty plane of moral, mental, and physical development. She believed that the process of evolution would eventually produce a perfect woman, possessing every virtue and worthy attribute of her sex, from whose progeny would spring a perfect race.

" In an impassioned outburst of eloquence, she charged the responsibility for the evils of intemperance and prostitution upon the mothers of our race, saying it was their duty to instruct their children in matters appertaining to their bodies, and not leave it for others to do."

Morning Whig, August 23rd, 1875. Troy (N.Y.).

" Mrs. Woodhull spoke at Griswold Opera House, on Saturday evening. The house was filled by an intelligent audience. Mrs. Woodhull's presence and graceful bearing instantly impressed the audience, and when the rich sweet tones of her voice were added, there was the most perfect quiet. She read a finely written synopsis of the proceedings of the human race out of the East to mingle in this western land. After reading for a short time she proceeded extempore. She next showed that in this country a new process has been set up, where all races, kindreds and tongues are being merged into one common race which will contain the different characteristics and qualities, physical, mental, and moral, of all the races. Such a race she concludes must be the perfect race, and that will establish a perfect social organization which will gradually spread over the earth, and take in all its people, and that they will ultimately become one people, having one government, one common interest and purposes.

" From this point she came back to her well-known theory that a perfect race can consist only of perfectly formed men and women, and declared that millennial period can never come until none but such people are born. Here is the vital point of all for which she contends. She showed that the human race can be improved by scientific propagation, and said that humanity ought to be the most important and worthy subject for investigation and improvement.

" She next showed that the misery, vice, and crime, with which the world is cursed, exists because the propagation of the race is carried on without any regard to the results to be obtained ; that the criminal and vicious classes were made so by their mothers during gestation, or by inherited characteristics from their parents. The capacity to commit a crime must exist in the individual before it can be called into action, and this capacity is an endowment for which the person possessing it is not responsible. The criminal classes recruited constantly from the children born of mothers who did not want them—in other words, from unwilling or undesired children. To rid the world of all these classes it only requires to place women in such position that they will never bear children except when they want them, and this is her whole right. She went on to say that what is required to produce none but good children cannot be instituted so long as women do not have the absolute control of their persons—their maternal functions. Every impression and thought, and especially every strong desire of the mother, has its effect upon her unborn child. Mothers do not realize this, however, and her opposers do not intend that she shall get their ear to awaken them to their terrible responsibilities in this regard."

Sunday Evening—Second Lecture.

" Last evening's lecture was an exposition of Mrs. Woodhull's understanding of revealed religion. She spoke from the texts : Daniel xii. 8 and 9, and Revelation x. 7.

" The Bible, Mrs. Woodhull thinks, is a book which is sealed to ordinary mortals. The curse that is put upon woman is :

'Thy desire shall be to thy husband; and he shall rule over thee.' All the sin in the world comes as the result of this curse, and the curse itself came as the result of a violation of the law of nature. . . . . . . 'Through education and knowledge on this subject she expects the strong carnal propensities to grow less and less, mankind to be physically improved and women especially, and the perils of maternity be removed, because the pollution of the body will be at an end.' "

" The human body she regards as the Temple of God, and the fall of Eve the subjection of woman to man. The garden of Eden is simply the human body. All the words relating to salvation refer to salvation of the body. 'Keep my saying, and ye shall never die,' refers to bodily life. The beginning and end of the Bible establish its unity, the first part speaking of the tree of life from which if Adam and Eve were not shut out they would eat and live for ever; and the last, of the tree of life, ' the leaves of which were for the healing of nations, and from which we are to get a pure river of water of life and die no more.' The perfection of living that the speaker wishes to see is to purify the stream of life; and woman, once the slave of man, *is to be redeemer of the race.*"

Free Press and Times, August 26th, 1875. Rutland (Vt.).

" Mrs. Woodhull lectured last night at the City Hall. Her lecture was listened to by a large and respectable audience, and the appreciation of the hearers was evinced by their frequent and hearty applause. Mrs. Woodhull is a very effective and eloquent speaker, and was listened to throughout with the closest attention."

Advertiser, August 31st, 1875. St. Albans (Vt.).

" Mrs. Woodhull delivered her lecture last night at Academy Hall to an audience respectable in numbers and above the average in intelligence. The lecture was a bold and fearless discussion of social problems, which are daily receiving more attention from thinking people of both sexes and all conditions in life, and the agitation and discussion of which are unquestionably steps in the path to a higher civilization. 'The veil of false shame is dropping away from before the eyes of the people, and they are learning in the school of bitter experiences that the social relation and the perpetuation of the race must receive pure, honest, and thoughtful attention, instead of having their discussion tabooed as inconsistent with modesty and morality.' Mrs. Woodhull tells an immense amount of plain truth, and truth that sadly needs telling, and her manner and words carry conviction of her deep earnestness and sincerity. There is no denying that our social system is seriously imperfect, and it is only by *free and fearless discussion that we can hope to find true solution of the problem*, and eventually attain to the highest perfection as a race mentally, morally, and physically, of which humanity is capable.

" The lecture was able, and the speaker eloquent, holding her audience perfectly to the close. Doubtless a great many ladies and lords of the creation desired to hear Mrs. Woodhull, but stayed away fearing it might not be 'proper' to go. It will be pleasant for these to know that an audience more than ordinarily intelligent and respectable applauded her to the echo when she told just why they stayed away, and said with perfect truth the pure in heart never think of fearing to be put to the blush by an honest discussion of questions which should command the respectful thought of all. We failed to note a word in her lecture which was in any sense unfit for a lady's ears, and we frankly say we think Mrs. Woodhull is doing a great good to her race in breaking the seals and opening the way which at last leads out of darkness and ignorance which cloud society, stunt the race physically and mentally, and clog the wheels of universal progress under the laws of God."

Dispatch, September 1st, 1875. Watertown (N.Y.).

"MRS. VICTORIA C. WOODHULL.—There was an intelligent audience at Washington Hall last night, to listen to the most remarkable woman of the age—one who has caused more commotion, called forth more criticism, excited more thought on vital matters, who has had more inveterate enemies, and been more widely and badly abused, and had more enthusiastic friends, and *honest* though flattering encomiums in the same space of time than any other person, man or woman, who ever lived. As an orator she stands unquestioned, even by her enemies, as the 'Queen of the Rostrum'; her brilliant perorations enforcing her most radical utterances, and uttered in the most highly dramatic and finely impassioned manner and rich toned voice, fairly entrance the audience, and carry conviction almost whether they will or no. She stands before her hearers a veritable impersonation of the words she utters; nobody who sees her can doubt that she is not only in earnest, but honest, in all she says; indeed, her purpose seems to be based upon a deep-seated religious enthusiasm.

"When to all of this is added that she is an editor of a widely circulated paper, and an author of well-known reputation, her title as 'the most remarkable person of the age' is fully established. A little more than four years ago she flashed upon the country, and her work that she has done, all to which we have alluded, has been performed in this brief time. A mind endowed by extraordinary talent in so many directions is a rare occurrence in this history of the world, and if she lives she will doubtless leave an impress upon the race which in extent at least will compare favourably with that of any who have lived before her."

Daily Times, September 1st, 1875. Watertown (N.Y.).

"Mrs. Victoria Woodhull lectured last night. First she read from manuscript, but the latter part of the lecture was spoken,

with only occasional references to it. She became more and
more impassioned as she proceeded, and her trenchant hits and
sarcasms, uttered with fine elocution, elicited frequent applause.
Mrs. Woodhull is one of the most eloquent and forcible speakers
who have appeared on the American platform ; and she is the
boldest of them all. More than this, she succeeds in impressing
most of her hearers with the idea that she is honest and convinced of the theories which she so ably advocates. She is
one of the most magnetic of speakers, and her manner is most
graceful and *apropos* to the words spoken."

Morning Herald, September 9th, 1875. Utica (N.Y.).

" The audience in the Opera House last evening, to hear
Mrs. Victoria C. Woodhull's lecture, were composed of an equal
number of ladies and gentlemen, and some of our most respectable citizens. The opening of the lecture was delivered from
notes, as it included numerous statistics. The peroration was
very fine, and there is no doubt that Mrs. Woodhull is the best
lady lecturer that has appeared at the Opera House. The
lecture contained many points worthy of serious consideration,
and nothing that could give offence to the most fastidious.
She certainly made a good impression upon her audience, and
gave many of her auditors new views in relation to the position
that she occupies upon the social question."

Democrat, September 13th, 1875. Binghamton (N.Y.).

"At the Academy of Music, last night, Mrs. Victoria C.
Woodhull spoke to a good house. The relation of the sexes is a
subject that cannot be easily discussed with full freedom without
offending the notions of the *ultra*-fastidious. Mrs. Woodhull,
however, managed with easy grace to impress her audience with
her views of the prime importance of the responsibilities of

parentage, and appealed with much earnestness to the mothers
of the land to educate themselves and children to the necessity
of a right start for the perfected man.

"Mrs. Woodhull is evidently an earnest woman and has
attested the courage of her convictions. A strain of sadness
hallows an earnest peroration and evokes sympathy for one who
has evidently suffered in the strange mischances of our social
life. We are sure the audience carried home a better opinion of
Mrs. Woodhull personally than they had formed, and a more
sober consideration of many of the problems of our social and
domestic life."

Daily Advertiser, September 14th, 1875. Elmira (N.Y.).

"MRS. VICTORIA C. WOODHULL.—An audience of goodly
number gathered last evening at Stancliff Hall to hear this
editor, author, and lecturer, who has probably been more talked
and written about than any other woman living. She has a
pleasing, attractive presence, and a voice that, in every instance,
measuring the sentiment to be uttered, fills it full of meaning,
force, and eloquence. As one said of her : ' A mind endowed by
extraordinary talent in so many directions is a rare occurrence
in the history of the world, and if she lives she will doubtless
leave an impress upon the race, which in extent, at least, will
compare favourably with that of any who have lived before
her.'

"Her lecture contained many sentiments to which there could
be found few who would not heartily subscribe as tending toward
the physical and moral advancement of the human race. Most of
them, however, were far in advance of present thought and
thinkers, and so, the world being hardly prepared for them, she
who gives them utterance is, by the masses, frowned upon and
severely criticized. The audience present manifested frequently
their approval of what she said by the heartiest applause."

Sentinel, September 14th, 1875. Rome (N.Y.).

"Mrs. Woodhull lectured here last Tuesday evening. All who heard her were pleasantly disappointed, and should she return here, as she promises to do, she will have a much larger audience. She is a forceful, eloquent speaker, and handles many questions, not so much discussed as they should be, with boldness hardly expected of a woman. At the same time she uses no indelicate words, no improper phrases. In all her lecture from the first to the last, while there was much food for thought, there was not one word to offend the most fastidious or to grieve the most sensitive. It is one of woman's rights to denounce what she believes to be wrong, and this right Mrs. Woodhull exercises in public without sacrificing her dignity. Indeed, we incline to the opinion that mankind would be happier if women delivered more public lectures and fewer curtain ones."

Daily Derrick, September 18th, 1875. Oil City (Pa.).

"Mrs. Woodhull made her first appearance in this city at the Opera House last evening, and lectured on 'The Principles of Finance, or Behind the Political Scenes.' She interested the audience greatly, and held them, from the beginning to the end, close observers of her words. She declared our system of government a failure, and that from its system grew its corruption. When she touched the social question she told plain truths."

Daily, September 20th, 1875. Parker City (Pa.).

"'The lecture to night' was in everybody's mouth, and as the time approached interest increased, and before opening the discourse a large audience had assembled, made up of a large portion of the best members Millerstown society affords. Ministers of the Gospel were there, and people of all ranks. It was acknowledged by everyone that no other speaker could,

under the circumstances, have commanded such order. Mrs.
Woodhull has an interesting presence, and commands the respect
of the audience on first appearance. As she proceeded with her
work before her, she grew more and more intense. No one
hearing her could doubt that she was not only in earnest but
honest in all she says, and in fact her purpose seems based upon
religious enthusiasm. While speaking she was a study for those
who have heard and read about her, and add to this fact that
she is the editress of a paper whose circulation is numbered by
thousands, and a person bearing a reputation enviable to some
while it is the cause of malice to others, her title as *the most
remarkable person of the age*, is fully established.

"During the progress of her lecture she was frequently
applauded, and as she proceeded in the part more closely relating
to the social question, the audience became more deeply interested. Here she gave a literary and rhetorical treat such as few
present had ever enjoyed. We thus speak of her as we saw her,
and as members of the press are in duty bound to do. She has
theories of her own, but one thing is certain, they are some
distance in advance of the age in which we live."

Daily Derrick, September 20th. 1875. Oil City (Pa.).

THEY WENT, SAW, AND WERE CONQUERED.

" Mrs. Woodhull's reception at the Opera House last week
was significant as an evidence of an under-current in regard to
social usages and political principles, which at least is sufficiently
powerful to restrain prejudice and permit a plain unvarnished
statement of the crying evils of both state and society upon a
public platform. The respectful hearing which Mrs. Woodhull
commanded, coming before an audience, as she did, who went
there out of pure curiosity, if no worse motive, expecting, no
doubt, to have their sense of propriety shocked, but submitting
thereto that their curiosity to hear this much-defamed woman
might be gratified.

"What was the object each went out to see? Everyone can answer for himself. *What they saw was a woman pure and simple, who came before them evidently inspired with a keen sense of the wrongs of humanity, and determined to devote every gift of mind, soul, and body with which her Creator had endowed her, to their redress. She seems to have put aside all thought of present honour, content to receive whatever obloquy or shame the world may see fit to bestow, repelling only when by doing so she may help on the cause she has so deeply at heart.* Yet we doubt not every word of sympathy and appreciation sinks deeply, and is sincerely treasured in this self-sacrificing soul who labours on, content to do her work and wait for a time, or eternity if need be, to prove her truth, and thus bring her reward.

"Strange as it may appear, that portion of her address which was devoted to the social relation or the relative position of the sexes, and the evils to society as a whole which grow out of the false relation now existing, commanded the sympathy and approval of the audience to a much greater extent than did her views upon finance and its kindred topics. Yet this was the great rock of offence which shipwrecked Mrs. Woodhull's reputation, and caused society to gather up its skirts lest the hem of its garments should be drabbled in the verge of the furthermost wave her going down had started. The old philosophical idea that a wave once started was never fully spent till its motion reached around the world seems to be true in the world of thought or morals. Do what we will we cannot escape these moral waves. If we gather up our garments they wash over our exposed feet, and there is no rock so high for us to stand upon but their momentum gathers force to reach it.

"It is no use for us to shut our eyes and say there is no wrong to be redressed. If we had no better proof of the existence of wrong, the very fact that Church, State, and Press have all cried out 'Down with this woman, her sentiments menace our peace!' would be sufficient to prove to the thinking mind that

there was a skeleton in their closets they feared to have exposed.
No idle cry of alarm at a fancied evil awakens such a vindictive
response as has been called forth by the voice of this heretofore
unknown, unpretending woman.

"Surely the cankering iron sunk deep into her soul ere it
wrung this piercing cry from the depths of her womanhood."

Daily Derrick, September 23rd, 1875. Oil City (Pa.).

"MRS. VICTORIA C. WOODHULL (second appearance).—Although
only four days have elapsed since Mrs. Woodhull lectured in
this city, the Opera House had a much larger audience last
evening. She had chosen for the subject, 'The True and False,
Socially,' and under this caption she made a fierce onslaught on
the lamentable ignorance which prevails in every household
upon the laws of life. She spoke many plain truths. As one
of her listeners said, 'She told more truths than I wanted to
hear.' When she spoke of the false modesty of many wives, or
drew the picture of the virtuous mother, her vehement, impassioned oratory drew loud applause from the audience."

Journal, September 29th, 1875. Racine (Wis.).

"Mrs. Woodhull appeared at Belle City Hall on Saturday
and Sunday evenings. Her subjects were well handled. Too
much that she discoursed of was true to the letter, as any cosmopolitan can testify. There are both truth and poetry in the
acts and speeches of Mrs. Victoria C. Woodhull. She portrays
vividly woman's duty, and at the same time mirrors man's
crimes, and places before the thinking mind nature in such a
shape that 'even the wayfaring man, though a fool,' may
comprehend it."

Telegraph, September 30th, 1875. Kenosha (Wis.).

"Mrs. Victoria C. Woodhull delivered a lecture last Monday
evening in Kimball Hall. Mrs. Woodhull spoke from eight

until half-past nine o'clock. About half of her lecture was read from manuscript, and the rest was the outpouring of the earnest, sincere heart of a mother. Her perorations were really fine, the eloquence of mind and soul completely devoted to the work before her, and in which she seems to be honestly and earnestly engaged."

(Editorial.)

"Mrs. Woodhull commenced her lecture by giving the oft-repeated quotation, 'Westward the star of empire takes its way.' She traced the onward march of this star, which carried civilization with it, from the extreme Orient to the extreme Occident—from its birthplace in India and China, millions of years before time, according to the Christian reckoning, westward through its many advances, till it made its last and gigantic stride across the heaving and rolling breast of the Atlantic to find resting-place in America. In all these ages past what people have died out—blotted out of existence by degeneration—unwritten histories of the Oriental ruins or mound-builders of this continent do not tell us.

"Then she launched boldly forth upon the tide of extemporaneous eloquence, hurling fierce invectives at the false modesty that will not let society discuss the basic questions of sociality. She said that the true virtue is intelligent discussion of these questions, and want of virtue is what is suppressing it. Mrs. Woodhull had been abused, hooted from one end of the land to another, because she thought that woman, as woman, should own her own body—(applause)—that she ought to say when she will become a mother, and when she will not. 'I do not believe in low ideas. Those who have low ideas are those who have not virtue enough to talk upon this subject without blushing, when there is no cause for blushes except their own want of virtue. Talk of Free Love—there is no other love but free love. God's love is free—it rains upon the good and bad alike—all love is free, and all else is enforced.

" ' When *men* are required to be as pure in heart and person as women, instead of being rich, society will be improved. When the young are taught the laws of life and taken into the heart and confidence of parents the world will become more virtuous. No one has loose ideas when discussing the ways of improving stock. In the fine art galleries of the old country where are statues of men and women true to nature, ladies and gentlemen pass along without blushing, because there is nothing to blush for. The people who dare not discuss these subjects are the vulgar, the impure, the ignorant, and the vile. All this vulgarity, impurity, ignorance and vice must be eradicated by the process of evolution, through discussion, virtuous habits, education, and intelligence.' "

Union, September 30th, 1875. Kenosha (Wis.).

" A fair audience came together in Kimball Hall, on Monday evening, to Mrs. Victoria C. Woodhull's lecture. It is her due to say that the lecture might have been heard without shame by every man, woman, and child in the city. She would have society mend many of its ways, eliminate the ignorance existing with regard to things of vital concern, and cure itself of the squeamishness which is but a covering for many phases of sin. The justness of her standard of masculine purity is as exacting as any standard of feminine purity now existing, and was apparent to all. The rearing of children she thought should be undertaken with a better sense of the responsibility and duties to be incurred. The ignorance of physiological laws, which is the cause of the world's miseries in the shape of idiotic and deformed progeny, the failure to discontinue procreation when organisms are unconditioned for bringing forth healthy children —these were the themes of the speaker's strongest condemna-

tion. The littlenesses, the narrow, contracted views and general
shortsightedness of her own sex she denounced with a bitterness
which in its line could not be surpassed. She is undoubtedly
on a worthy mission."

Argus, October 2nd, 1875. Racine (Wis.).

"Mrs. Woodhull lectured on Saturday evening at Belle City
Hall to a respectable audience. Not one in the house had
heard her before. The more timid portion had their misgivings as
to whether the lecture would be proper to hear, but we noticed
that from that class, many of whom are mothers as refined and
conscientious as Racine can boast, were the first to express their
approbation and applause in no unmistakable manner. 'Mrs.
Woodhull seemed at moments like one possessed, and the
eloquence which poured from her lips in reckless torrents swept
through the souls of the multitude in a way which caused them
to burst, every now and then, into uproarious enthusiasm.'
"Mrs. Woodhull will probably return here within a few weeks
or months, and we predict that Belle City will not be large
enough to hold her audience."

Lumberman, October 9th, 1875. Oconto (Wis.).

"This lady, now of American and European fame, lectured in
the Music Hall on the evenings of Saturday and Sunday last. Her
audiences on both evenings were good, composed of a number of
ladies, notwithstanding an under-current of ignorant influence
that was brought to bear to prevent such an attendance. In
treating her subject she made a fierce attack on the unpardon-
able ignorance which now prevails in relation to the laws of
life.
"In her peroration she, in affecting and eloquent terms,
referred to the persecution she had already endured, both from

the press and the public generally. We only judge her as she should be judged—as we saw, heard, and appreciated her. Were she the character that many would represent her to be in their jealous ignorance, even then her teaching should not be discarded. 'Do as they desire you, but not as they do,' is an old and oft-quoted lesson, and were every man and woman in the land to follow the teachings of Mrs. Victoria Woodhull, there would be more purity, more honesty, and more happiness in the land. She is a power, a power that talent and genius always is."

Citizen, October 12th, 1875. Beaver Dam (Wis.).

"Mrs. Woodhull lectured here Monday night. A great many people who would have liked to have seen and heard her stayed away because they have a wrong idea of its nature: from what they have read and heard they expected she would say things unfit for the ears of refinement. *Nothing could be further from the reality.* It is true she touched a great many delicate points, but she did it in such a manner that no one could take exceptions. And they were matters with which no one can become too familiar."

Inter-Ocean, October 16th, 1875. Chicago (Ill.).

"Mrs. Victoria C. Woodhull lectured at McCormick's Hall last evening on 'Social Evils, their Cause and Cure.' If the audience assembled because they believed and sympathized with her doctrines, and not from curiosity, Mrs. Woodhull ought certainly to feel flattered, for the following were not few. Every seat was filled and there was barely standing-room. Nor was the crowd composed of outcasts of society. Audiences not a whit more respectable and refined have gathered in the same all to hear Theodore Thomas and the most celebrated lights of the rostrum and concert-room. At least one-third of those present were ladies, and among their number were many who rank high in society and who are not noted as riders of hobbies.

" Among the gentlemen were ex-Governors, railway superintendents, and eminent divines. If they came and took their seats hesitatingly, fearing that they were to be seen in bad company, they were soon at their ease, for in every direction could be seen others of equal rank. Throughout the whole lecture the closest attention was paid to the speaker. The applause was frequent. Mrs. Woodhull's style of speaking is earnest, and such as to impress her auditors that she is convinced of the truth of all that she says."

Morning Courier, October]16th, 1875. Chicago (Ill.).

BRAVE MRS. WOODHULL.

" Mrs. Victoria C. Woodhull's address at McCormick's Hall last evening was listened to by an immense concourse of people. No seat was left unoccupied, and many persons were standing. The lecture can only be likened to a mountain torrent long pent up, which at last bursts its bounds and carries a fearful pressure upon everything in its course. Mrs. Woodhull, in the two hours of continued discourse, attacked in turn the Church, the Government, and the individual,—the first for its hypocrisy and pretensions, the second for its tyranny and usurpations, and the last for his follies and weaknesses."

The Chicago Tribune, October 16th, 1875. Chicago (Ill.).

" McCormick Hall was crowded to repletion last evening to hear Mrs. Woodhull lecture. The audience was largely composed of women. The lady appeared on the rostrum about a quarter-past eight o'clock, dressed in a plain black dress, white collar and cuffs, a bunch of roses on her breast being all the effort at ornamentation."

The Chicago Times, October 16th, 1875. Chicago (Ill.).

" Long before eight o'clock last evening the stairway leading
to McCormick's Hall was crowded with counter-currents of
humanity—the one flowing up delighted, the other pouring
down disgusted. The seats had all been taken at an early hour,
and many hundreds were compelled to forego the privilege of
listening to Victoria C. Woodhull."

Times, October 17th, 1875. Chicago (Ill.).

" On last evening Mrs. Victoria Woodhull appeared, for the
seventh time, before a Chicago audience for the discussion of
the social, moral, political questions with which she has so long
been identified. Such vast audiences as assembled on Friday
and Saturday evenings to listen to this priestess in the temple
of truth have never before been gathered together for a similar
purpose in the history of this city, and in point of intelligence,
respectability and numbers they were such as would have been
flattering to the feeling of any speaker in the land, however
distinguished and reputable.

" Mrs. Woodhull alluded to the flattering reception she had
received on the occasion of her present visit to Chicago, and
took opportunity to call the attention of her hearers to a few
points in her career which she deemed especially worthy of
notice. When she had commenced the advocacy of her doctrines
she said she had been thrust to the chilly borders of society by
a fierce and remorseless public opinion. She had not faltered in
her work on account of it. Herself and sister had been five years
in Broad Street, New York City, had made and lost fortunes.
They had been dragged through the filth and mire of a detestable
and rotten society. They had been plundered of their wealth by
those who proclaimed themselves their friends. She had
endured abuse, suffered contumely, outrage, and persecution,

until her soul was faint and her brain on fire. Still, she had
persevered, until now the misty vapours were rolling away and,
like Noah's dove, she had found a place to rest. She said her
ideas in regard to the relations of the sexes had been especially
perverted and misunderstood.

" Promiscuity in sexuality is simply the anarchical stage of
development wherein the passions rule supreme. When spirituality comes in and rescues the real man and woman from the
domain of the purely material, promiscuity is simply impossible.
As promiscuity is the analogue to anarchy, so is spirituality to
scientific selection and adjustment. I am fully persuaded that
the very highest unions are those that are monogamic, and that
these are perfect in proportion as they are lasting. Sexual
freedom means the abolition of prostitution, both in and out of
marriage ; means the emancipation of woman and her coming
into ownership and control of her body ; means the end of her
pecuniary dependence upon man, so that she may never, even
seemingly, have to procure whatever she may desire or need by
sexual favour; means the abrogation of forced pregnancy, of
ante-natal murder of undesired children ; means the birth of
loved and wished-for children, endowed by every inherited
virtue that the highest exaltation can confer at conception, by
every influence for good to be obtained during gestation, and by
the wisest guidance and instruction on to manhood industrially
and intellectually."

Daily News, October 19th, 1875. Aurora (Ill).

" There was an intelligent audience at the Opera House last
evening to hear Mrs. Victoria Woodhull, the most remarkable
woman of the age. She had chosen for her subject ' The True
and False, Socially,' and under this caption she exposed the
lamentable ignorance which prevails in every household upon
the laws of life. She spoke many plain truths, and many

excellent moral and practical sentiments. Her dramatic and tragic talent is irresistible. She is at all times interesting, and possesses those personal charms of beauty, form, and features, which are almost a necessary adjunct to the highest degree of talent, and an imposing appearance and a graceful manner, a full and pleasant voice, and an animated delivery. But, above all, she knows how to make the tritest truths ring with the freshness of impassioned oratory. Nobody who sees her can doubt that she is not only earnest but honest in all she says."

Leader, October 22nd, 1875. St. Charles (Ill.).

"We had the pleasure to listen to this remarkable lady last Monday evening at Aurora. We wish we had the room and the ability to give her lecture entire, for we know it contained many solid truths which could not fail to better all before whom it might be placed. But as it is impossible for us to do this, we shall simply speak of her as she impressed us, and as she is.

"Mrs. Woodhull is a reformer in every sense of the word, and that she is a thoroughly honest one, is shown in her deep earnestness, by every word and action. She spoke one hour and a half in Aurora the other evening, and not one word fell from her lips which the purest lady in the land might not have listened to with perfect propriety; ay, more, might not have listened with profit. The major part of her audience, numbering between four and five hundred, was composed of ladies, and we venture the assertion that not one regretted being present. Mrs. Woodhull is not only argumentative and forcible, but a wonderfully elegant and eloquent speaker. At times her language, action, and utterance are perfectly majestic. Indeed, we never before heard a speaker with such thorough command of all the accessories of perfect oratory. Our belief is, that she is a pure, noble-hearted woman engaged in what she, at least, believes to be a worthy cause. If you ever have an opportunity, readers, go and hear her, and then judge her. She made a friend of everyone who

heard her the other evening; and Aurora hasn't a house large
enough to accommodate the audience which will assemble to
hear her the next time she speaks in that city."

Star, October 22nd, 1875.   Logansport (Ind.).

"Mrs. Woodhull lectured at the Opera House last evening.
The audience was, in point of intelligence, as flattering an one
as ever greeted a lecturer in this city.   The speaker was listened
to with rapt attention, and now and then as she forced home
some unpleasant truths, was encouraged by bursts of applause.
Her tones are clear and penetrating, but her utterances are so
rapid that little room is afforded for the graces of elocution.   She
does not employ the aid of gestures until she warms up with the
earnestness of her thoughts, then she exhibits true oratorical
ability and dramatic skill.   Her style is always animated, rather
giving the impression that she has so much to say that she must
speak quickly and economize her time.

" She handled her subject, the social problem, without gloves,
presenting the shams, superficialities, and inconsistencies of the
present order of things in their true colours, tearing aside the
veil placed over them through false modesty."

Herald, October 23rd, 1875.   Aurora (Ill.).

" The auditorium of the Opera House was well filled on Monday evening by an audience of respectable and substantial citizens
assembled to hear Mrs. Woodhull lecture.   The speaker fully
sustained her claim to be one of the most eloquent orators of the
day.   Her deportment on the stage is modest and ladylike, her
language chaste, and her voice musical in the extreme.   The
discourse was full of passages that were delivered with a telling
earnestness, and rewarded with hearty applause.   Mrs. Woodhull
told a great many truths, but her remedy for the evils she
depicted was the spread of intelligence.   Mrs. Woodhull may
effect much good by rousing attention to the importance of the
subject mentioned."

Daily Journal, October 23rd, 1875. Lafayette (Ind.).

"The lecture of Mrs. Woodhull last night was listened to attentively by a respectable audience of ladies and gentlemen. The house was not 'filled to overflowing with men and boys drawn there by a vulgar curiosity,' *but by thoughtful men and women who heard with marked attention and applauded many of the statements made.* If anyone went there to find gratification for a prurient appetite they came away woefully disappointed. If Mrs. Woodhull is to be measured by what she says rather than by the idea popularly entertained of her, she must be set down as a woman with a vivid conception, Utopian though it may be, and to the advocacy of which a being-possessed devotion lends eloquence. Lafayette last night heard solid and substantial truths, perhaps unwelcome to some, but none the less truths relating to vital matters. When a truth is uttered it avails nothing to avoid its effects, let the source from which it comes be what it may. Mrs. Woodhull graphically depicts social evils, but whether the remedy summed up in a higher intelligence which she suggests will prove adequate, is a question that admits serious discussion. One thing is certain that the appeal she makes, and the diffusion of intelligence which she so earnestly urges, can be productive of nothing but good, although it may not prove a panacea. It may be just the thing to decry and denounce Mrs. Woodhull, but we can see nothing in her lecture to condemn, or which the most chaste and refined cannot unblushingly hear."

Leader, October 23rd, 1875. Lafayette (Ind.).

"Mrs. Woodhull has come and gone. Her lecture was listened to by a respectful and respectable audience, and were it to be repeated every nook and corner of the Opera House would be occupied."

463

Bee, October 23rd, 1875. Lafayette (Ind.).

"The lecture of Mrs. Woodhull at the Opera House drew out a fair audience of ladies and gentlemen. She spoke for an hour and a half. The audience was composed of intelligent, thinking people. Her words of truth were applauded. She uttered no word that could cause the virtuous mother to blush, and none will deny that if what she said was practised the world would be made up of better men and women. She made an earnest and eloquent appeal to mothers to get acquainted with their daughters and sons, and teach them to live in a God-like manner. There was nothing in her lecture to condemn, while there was much in it to commend, and we venture the prediction that if she were to return to this city and deliver the same lecture she would be greeted with the largest audience that ever assembled in the Opera House."

Gazette, October 25th, 1875. Terre Haute (Ind.).

" Mrs. Victoria C. Woodhull, who has been the most fearfully maligned, abused, hated and scorned woman in some localities and the most enthusiastically loved in others, of any public woman in America, lectured at Dowling Hall on Saturday night. Her subject, if not already known, might be easily guessed. It is the one subject in the advocacy of which she has consecrated her life. She has thrown her startling ideas into the abodes of sanctimonious piety, and frightened from their lurking-places the greatest hypocrites in the land. She is certainly in earnest, certainly imbued with Hercules' energy, and an unlimited confidence in the truth of her ideas. No one can fail to be impressed with her sincerity."

Daily News, October 28th, 1875. Fort Wayne (Ind.).

" Mrs. Victoria Woodhull lectured at the Opera House last evening. At an early hour the throng began to arrive, and by the time Mrs. Woodhull made her appearance on the stage (eight o'clock), the house was densely packed. The audience was a refined one; we doubt if Colerick's Opera House has ever contained an audience composed of a better class of people than assembled there last night to hear Mrs. Woodhull's lecture. She made her appearance neatly dressed in black, and at once began her discourse. Her voice trembled slightly at first; but as she warmed up on her subject, she displayed an impassioned oratory that drew the applause of the audience. She was very vehement and gave evidence of long study and patience in her mission of reform."

Gazette, October 28th, 1875. Fort Wayne (Ind.).

"The lecture of Mrs. Victoria C. Woodhull of last evening, at Colerick's Opera House, was well attended, and the audience was one of intelligence and respectability, such as any speaker might feel proud to address.

"Mrs. Woodhull speaks as one who firmly and emphatically believes in the truth and integrity of what she is saying. 'The True and the False Socially' was discussed with a degree of common sense and vigour, that was only exceeded by its purity and goodness of purpose. The audience could well afford to listen to Mrs. Woodhull."

Sentinel, October 28th, 1875. Fort Wayne (Ind.).

"The celebrated Mrs. Victoria Woodhull made her first appearance in Fort Wayne last evening at the Opera House. She delivered her lecture to a very fair and respectable audience; some of the best ladies in the city were there, and evidently did not regret going.

"Mrs. Woodhull's appearance is that of a superior woman mentally, and she has the art of clearly and forcibly expressing herself. She is not excelled by any female speaker who has preceded her in this city."

Daily Argus, November 3rd, 1875. Akron (O.).

"Solomon says, 'He that answereth a thing before he hears it, showeth himself a simpleton.'* This language will apply to that class of bigots who prejudge and condemn a person upon general hearsay without instituting a personal investigation. It is a scriptural as well as a philosophical doctrine, that we should 'prove all things and hold fast that which is good.' We make the observations in view of the lecture delivered by Mrs. Victoria C. Woodhull, in the Academy of Music, last night, which was listened to by a large and respectable audience.

"We wonder not that she is called 'Queen of the Rostrum,' when she holds her audience spellbound, apparently without an effort, from her first appearance upon the stage until she utters her last syllable. Possessed of a finely developed physique, standing erect, completely self-possessed, her large restless eyes peering in every individual face as though addressing each hearer in person, her own soul catching fire at the inspiration of her own words, and all the energies of her nature being roused up by the vast importance of her theme, she pours forth such a stream of eloquence—fervid, liquid, electric—as to compel even the admiration of her most malignant opposers.

"Her eulogy upon the person and character of Jesus, as an inspired teacher, and as an exemplar of every possible virtue, was the most beautiful in its wording and execution we ever listened to.

"But woe be the hypocrites and the *roués* who sit in her presence."

The Inquirer, November 7th, 1875. Cincinnati (Ohio).

"Cincinnati enjoyed a novelty last evening at Robinson's Opera House. Victoria C. Woodhull, the most generally known woman in America, appeared upon the stage of a lecture hall, and for two hours talked to two thousand people upon

* He that answereth a matter before he heareth it, it is folly and shame unto him.—Prov. xviii. 18.

some subjects that many men lack the moral courage to face publicly.

"The Opera House was crowded long before the curtain rose at eight o'clock. Every available seat found an occupant early, and the late-comers were forced either to find seats in chairs brought in, or, more unfortunate still, to stand. And the character of the audience was good—away above the average collections which usually fill our theatres during the run of a popular drama. The major part of it were men in the middle and maturer periods of life—men who came with an expectation that they were to hear something uttered by this wonderful woman which would furnish them with food for thought through many a day. They were not disappointed. One-fourth of the people in the house were ladies of the best families, too : ladies who were not too cowardly to come out to a public place and listen to a lecture which in their hearts they long since had a desire to hear. We venture to say that they went away well pleased with themselves at having had the 'grit' to go.

"The lecturer did not lose any time in useless courtesies of superfluous smiles. She advanced directly to the footlights and opened her mouth. From that instant till ten o'clock she kept up a constant flow of words. Her manner through it all was easy, her gestures graceful, her voice strong, her articulation perfect, and the expression of her face sometimes, when she got warmed up to her subject, grew almost spiritual.

"In this style of argument, improving as she went, and culminating in a grand climax of thought, the lecturer proceeded for two hours. Much of what she said was wildly applauded, and not a person left the hall until she had bowed herself from the stage at the close of the lecture."

Daily Inquirer, November 9th, 1875. Cincinnati (Ohio).

"Mrs. Woodhull delivered her second lecture, last night, to about eighteen hundred persons assembled in Robinson's Opera

House. Although her audience was not so large as it was on Saturday night, its tone was really good, there being many ladies present. Three of the proscenium boxes were occupied by families. The appearance of the stage was the same as on Saturday night, and the lecturer was dressed the same. There is nothing flashy in Mrs. Woodhull's attire; on the contrary, her dress is exceedingly plain, though neat. Not a piece of jewellery is visible anywhere on her person, not even a ring. But a woman with the fine figure and graceful manner of Mrs. Woodhull needs not the aid of fine clothes and glittering jewellery to show them off to advantage.

State Journal, November 10th, 1875. Columbus (Ohio).

" The parquette and dress circle of the Athenæum was filled last night by a quiet, attentive audience, about one-third of whom were ladies.

" Promptly at eight o'clock Mrs. Woodhull appeared at the back of the stage, and walking to about the centre, commenced her lecture. Our want of space forbids an extended abstract of the lecture, suffice it to say that the lecturess uses old-fashioned Saxon to express her ideas, dashes at naked truths without any by-play, and calling things by their right names. At times she grows terribly earnest, and fires off her words as if they were red-hot and unpleasant occupants of her mouth. 'I never heard anything like it.' "

The Ohio State Journal, November 10th, 1875. Columbus (Ohio).

"Mrs. Woodhull possesses a voice, an enunciation, and a manner that would have made her fortune upon the tragic stage. At times she grows terribly earnest. 'I never saw or heard of anything like it.' "

Representative, November 13th, 1875. Fox Lake (Wis.).

"There was quite a large attendance at Mrs. Woodhull's lecture on Tuesday evening. Judging from the frequent applause of the audience, her theory on the 'social question' was not offensive to their ideas of either morality or good breeding. On the contrary, we venture to say that none present could take the slightest exception to the propriety of her language, or to the soundness of her opinion upon the subject discussed. Of refined and graceful appearance, and eminently pleasing manner, she creates a favourable impression upon all, and her oratorical powers and intellectual abilities rank among the best speakers of the age."

Commercial, November 15th, 1875. Pittsburg (Pa.).

"Mrs. Victoria C. Woodhull lectured at the Academy of Music last night to a crowded house."

Daily Post, November 15th, 1875. Pittsburg (Pa.).

"Mrs. Woodhull delivered her lecture to an immense audience at the Academy of Music, last evening. The house was literally packed with an audience that seemed to hugely enjoy the lecture, judging from the enthusiastic applause."

The Dispatch, November 15th, 1875. Pittsburg (Pa.).

"Mrs. Victoria C. Woodhull appeared last night at the Academy of Music and delivered a lecture, to a crowded house, of an hour and a half in length. She spoke in a clear musical tone, and enforced her points with dramatic action, which made her manner impressive and earnest. On opening, she delivered as the text, the 16th, 17th, and 19th verses of the third chapter of First Corinthians.

"'Know ye not that *ye* are the temple of God, and that the spirit of God dwelleth in you? If any man defile the temple of God, him shall God destroy; for the temple of God is holy, which temple ye are. For the wisdom of this world is foolishness with God. For it is written, He taketh the wise in their own craftiness.'"

Th? Evening Leader, November 15th, 1875.   Pittsburg (Pa.).

" Those who went to hear Victoria Woodhull deliver a salacious lecture last night were disappointed; not only disappointed, but roundly rebuked. They only heard a woman of very marked ability, perhaps the most eloquent of all the women lecturers in the country, discourse on a very delicate subject with marvellous tact, and with not the remotest approach to impurity of word or thought, and tell the people plain truths which were good for them to hear from some source."

Daily Gazette, November 15th, 1875.   Steubenville (Ohio).

"The rain on Saturday evening prevented a large audience from gathering at the Hall, yet if Steubenville had been sifted for the express purpose of accomplishing such a result, it would not have been possible to present a more select or intellectual audience than assembled on that evening to hear Mrs. Woodhull."

Evening Standard, November 17th, 1875.   Wheeling (W. Va.).

" The first appearance of the celebrated Mrs. Victoria C. Woodhull in this city last night was the occasion for a large turn-out.

" Mrs. Woodhull opened her subject by referring to the westward march of the empire, beginning with the political greatness of the Egyptian people under Sesostris, succeeded successively by that of Persia and Media under Xerxes, and Romans under Cæsar. She then brought out the truth—the stern, undeniable truth—concerning the fathers, mothers, sons, and daughters of the land; attributing crime, disease, and misfortune in many forms to the want of purity of character among the people. She said ' that society did not have the candour or purity to consider or rebel against social evils, that it was fostered by the negligence and ignorance of parents, and the failure of society to demand the same purity from young men that is required from young women.'

"Mrs. Woodhull showed how the population of our Republic was composed of a union of people from all countries, and how this country was destined to be the most magnificent empire, and how necessary it was that social reform should find a place in the advancement of the nation.

"In the general introduction of her subject—that of the 'Social Evil'—the lecturer expressed herself in words of elegance and classic mould, and in so doing she became properly enthused for the very effort that formed the principal theme of the evening. She was opposed to promiscuity of intercourse between the sexes. She places the social question before those of religion, ethics, and education as much more important, because prevention is more important than cure. She regards the basic principles of life as the foundation for all happiness— the source of all, or nearly all, personal evils. She said, 'with reference to the marriage relation, that the civil paper that joins man and woman is of no consequence without love and affinity.' She expressed her belief that in a pure state between man and woman lay the fountain-head of human virtue and happiness. Or we may add, in words of a familiar couplet from Pope:

> "'The surest virtues thus from passions shoot,
>   With nature's vigour working at the root.'

"Men must no longer insult all womanhood by saying that freedom means the degradation of woman. Every woman knows that if she were free she would never bear an unwished-for child, nor think of murdering one before its birth. It is because she is not free that these prevail. It is the children who are conceived in enforced commerce, and those whom mothers fail to kill before their birth, who recruit the ranks of

the vicious and criminal classes. No child conceived in love
and born in hope was ever yet a criminal. Mothers may make
their children what they wish; but they make them, without
wishing, what they are. Mothers should remember this: no
person ever does an act with the capacity for which he or she
was not endowed from birth."

Daily Register, November 17th, 1875. Wheeling (W. Va.).

" For the first time a Wheeling audience had an opportunity
last night to hear this wonderful woman lecturer. She is in
all respects most wonderful, as she is also the best known
woman in America. Mrs. Woodhull impresses one that she is
honest in her convictions, and that she is intensely—nay, recklessly—wedded to, and eagerly and passionately advocates, her
cause. Her soul seems to catch fire at the inspiration of her
own words, and all the energies of her nature seemed roused up
by, to her, the vast importance of the theme. She is capable of
varying her subject to the circumstances with a remarkable
originality."

Times, November 18th, 1875. Canton (Ohio).

"Mrs. Victoria C. Woodhull lectured at the Opera House on
Wednesday evening. Her audience was an appreciative one,
composed extensively of ladies who went to hear the 'truth,'
and they heard it. Mrs. Woodhull is an excellent speaker, and
presents her argument in such an earnest manner that the most
ignorant can fully understand her meaning. She comes down to
solid facts, and endeavours to impress upon her audience the
necessity of raising children to lead pure and virtuous lives.
Mrs. Woodhull has been vilified and abused by both press and
public: if we understand her correctly it was because she told
truths, that all know are truths, but do not like to hear them.
We trust that Mrs. Woodhull will again visit us, and if she does,
we can safely assure her a jammed, crowded house."

Repository, November 19th, 1875. Canton.

"Mrs. Woodhull delivered her lecture at the Opera House on Wednesday evening to a large audience. The lecture was a peculiarly good one, and was delivered in good taste. Mrs. Woodhull is excellent, and her graces of elocution are such as to command the attention and secure the admiration of her audience. After the first half-hour she laid aside her notes, and for an hour poured forth a stream of oratory that was as remarkable for its substance as for its vehement and earnest delivery and extraordinary rapidity and power. She certainly enchained her audience throughout. There can be no doubt of her ability, nor that it is of a high order.

"That her views of social reform, so far as the general laws of procreation and of personal habits of both sexes are concerned, are the correct views we also believe. They are in accordance with the highest standards of science as expounded and admitted by the ablest scientists of the time."

Banner, November 19th, 1875. Mt. Vernon (Ohio.).

"Mrs. Woodhull lectured at Woodward Hall on Thursday evening. We have no doubt nearly every lady in Mt. Vernon was anxious to hear and see what she had to say; but conceiving that it would not be 'respectable' to be seen in the hall concluded to keep away. *They certainly missed a treat*, for instead of anything that would bring a tinge to the cheek of the most refined and sensitive lady, the lecturer championed the cause of woman, and in 'thoughts that breathe and words that burn' uttered great truths that mankind and womankind might profit by. Many have formed a wrong impression of Mrs. Woodhull. She utters nothing immoral or impure—nothing that would not grace any pulpit or rostrum in the land. And we venture to say if she visits Mt. Vernon again there is no hall in the city large enough to hold the audience that will turn out to hear her.

"She is the best female orator we have ever listened to. Her

voice is musical and clear, her enunciation full and distinct, her
gestures graceful and her elocution earnest and emphatic. She
has a wonderful command of language and never uses an
improper word to express her ideas."

Vindicator, November 19th, 1875. Youngstown (Ohio).

"Mrs. Victoria C. Woodhull delivered a lecture at the Opera
House in this city on Thursday night of last week, unlike anything
ever before heard by a Youngstown audience. The house was
well filled, and those who filled it were very attentive when they
were not enthusiastic, and very enthusiastic when they were not
attentive. The lecturer herself was sufficient to attract attention
by her transcendent eloquence and absolutely fearless and terribly
pointed style presenting what she believes to be the fundamental
truths of human existence and welfare. There is no mistaking
her inspired earnestness, nor is there any dodging of the points
of many of her assertions and statements. Her basic theory is
that the human race is at fault in its methods of procreation, and
to this she attributes the prevalent crime, insanity, idiocy,
drunkenness, and bodily ailments and deformities which afflict
mankind. She argued that love, left free to choose its mate,
would annihilate promiscuity as at present practised. She gave
startling facts and figures of the state of society in general, and
dwelt long and eloquently on the necessity of regenerating the
race to prevent retrogression into ignorance.

" We have not the space to give a proper review of her lecture,
but it is certain that it left a deep impression upon her audience,
both in regard to the matter involved and her sincerity in urging
its supreme importance. Such was the verdict of all who
remarked upon it after it was concluded, and we are sure if she
visits this place again she will command a much larger audience.

" She being terribly in earnest in trying to tell the truth and
do good, should be respected accordingly, and not be vilified
unheard."

31

(Editorial.)

"Mrs. Woodhull's lecture in the Opera House on Thursday evening of last week was well attended. Mrs. Woodhull is indeed the 'Queen of the Rostrum.' Her lecture was listened to with interest, and the large audience went away from the Opera House with something to think about."

Daily Sentinel, November 23rd, 1875. Indianapolis.

"Mrs. Victoria C. Woodhull was greeted last evening, at the Academy of Music, by a large and intelligent audience. Many of our best ladies and gentlemen went to hear what this 'persecuted,' but talented, genius had to say. . . . . As she warmed with her subject her excitement showed itself in a flushed face, which gave her a handsome and very young appearance. 'I don't want you to build a monument to my memory when I am gone, but I do beg you to let me, without calumny and persecution, build my own monument while I live. I would rather be cherished in the hearts of the people for the sake of the living truth than be rich in jewels and stocks; and it is in the hope that my plain, earnest language may lead some here present to be pure men and women. I now bid you good-night.' (Great applause.)"

Daily Journal, November 23rd, 1875. Indianapolis.

"Mrs. Woodhull's lecture at the Academy of Music last evening attracted an audience which, both in respectability and size, was not inferior to those which greet the distinguished stars of the theatrical or musical world.

"After the first fifteen minutes Mrs. Woodhull discarded her manuscript, and talked to the audience directly and forcibly. Her manner is peculiarly earnest. She spoke for anh our and a half; closing with a strong and glowing advocacy of her

much persecuted views, pleading forcibly for the recognition
and love of society, and finally bowing herself gracefully from
the stage amidst thunders of applause."

Courier, November 25th, 1875. Greenville (Ohio).

"This noble, gifted woman appeared at Odd Fellows' Hall last
evening, and for nearly two hours held a fascinated audience of
the most intelligent men and women ever assembled here spell-
bound, only interrupted by spontaneous bursts of applause. To
give any conception of the wonderfully eloquent appeal—(for it
was an appeal to the purest and highest in man and woman)—
we would have to give the lecture entire.

"We have seen what purports to be full reports of her lectures,
but none gave the slightest idea of the earnestness, purity, and
love for the human family, that we found while listening with
rapt attention to her oratorical powers. We could not take notes,
but sat and drank in the words of truth.

"The whole lecture was overflowing with the love of a mother's
heart, appealing to fathers, mothers, sons, and daughters for a
purer morality and closer interchange of thought, a commingling
as it were, in spirit, so that no impure thoughts and desires can
enter the holy temple of home.

"She departed but once from her loving appeal when she took
up the case of a minister who had attacked her from his pulpit
last Sunday, when she poured forth a flow of invective that
would, had he been there, caused him to wish the earth to open
and swallow him. She said, '1 was assailed from the pulpit by a
priestly debauchee (for no gentleman would attack a woman
behind her back)—and ignorant (for no intelligent person would
do so until they had heard)—a coward (for he dare not meet
a woman face to face, but throws a stone when her back is
turned)'—and in this strain continued for several minutes, with
the audience in hearty accord with her, as was manifested by
their frequent and hearty applause.

31 *

" To show how she held on the hearts of her hearers we note one fact, that not a single person retired till the last farewell words were uttered.

" At the conclusion of the lecture it was entertaining to listen to the remarks of the retiring throng—'wonderful'—'I would not have missed it for worlds'—'I hope I may live better for the truths I have heard to-night.' A prominent citizen remarked, 'I came prejudiced against her, and now think there was nothing said but what every man and woman in the world ought to hear.'"

Republican, November 27th, 1875. Meadville (Pa.).

" An audience about three times as large as we ever saw assembled in the Opera House to attend a lecture greeted Mrs. Woodhull last evening. That the lecture effectually disabused the minds of our citizens of the false ideas previously entertained of her, was clearly demonstrated by the breathless attention given her throughout the lecture, except when their admiration took the form of hearty and merited applause.

" Mrs. Woodhull although taking ground which few people publicly endorse, yet from the large audiences which attend her lectures, and the pressing invitations from lecture committees which pour in constantly from all parts of the country, lead her and many others to believe that the doctrines she advocates are gaining ground.

" We can only say it was truth, God's truth, and put in a way that could be understood. The social crimes were laid bare with a fearless hand; men and women shown to themselves in their passions, in a way very well calculated to make them recoil from the picture which they could not deny to be true to the life. During all this there was not a word spoken that could bring a blush to the cheek of any educated, pure-minded man or woman, and we feel that it is simple justice to say of this much-abused woman, that no man or woman can listen to her lecture without being made nobler and purer.

" We hope that Mrs. Woodhull may return at no distant day and repeat her lecture, when we earnestly hope that every mother in Meadville will hear her."

New York Mercury. From Corry (Pa.) Correspondent, under the date of November 30th, 1875.

" Mrs. Victoria C. Woodhull lectured on the 29th inst. to a good house, comprising many ladies, and some of the most intelligent citizens. The night was very stormy and the weather intensely cold, so that Mrs. Woodhull may regard the occasion which could draw out so large an audience on so inclement an evening as an especial ovation. She was repeatedly applauded during the lecture, and at its close."

Independent, December 1st, 1875. Massillon (Ohio).

" Mrs. Woodhull's lecture at the Opera House last Wednesday was attended by an intelligent audience, who were entertained for an hour and a half with one of the most interesting discourses ever delivered in Massillon. Mrs. Woodhull has an excellent voice and her delivery is attractive and pleasing, and the thoroughly attentive manner in which the audience listened to her speaks volumes in praise of her ability as a speaker. We unhesitatingly state that we would like to hear the lecture repeated."

Observer, December 2nd, 1875. Erie (Pa.).

" Mrs. Victoria Woodhull treated her views upon the social question in the Music Hall last evening. She spoke for an hour and a half, and drew applause from her hearers. Mrs. Woodhull is one of the best female speakers in the country.

" Mrs. Woodhull's idea seems to be that all unions between the sexes should be based on love. She denounced women who

marry for the mere sake of being married, or who sell themselves
for money, as worse than prostitutes. No children born out of
love, she said, would be perfect; the inmates of our insane
asylums and penitentiaries are the offsprings of those who had
no affection for each other.

"Mrs. Woodhull is an earnest woman, who believes she has a
mission to accomplish."

Standard, December 4th, 1875. Syracuse (N.Y.).

"Looking back two or three years ago to the audience which
greeted Mrs. Woodhull in Weiting Opera House, and then
looking in at Shakespeare Hall, which was filled by an audience
which listened with interest to the speaker, they evidently were
not all drawn by curiosity, if we may judge from the applause.

"Mrs. Woodhull, in a musical voice, read the following
text:—

"Know ye not that ye are the temple of God, and that the spirit of Go
dwelleth in you?'—1 Corinthians iii. 16.

"She held the close attention of her audience throughout,
proving herself a mistress of oratory, and many of her points
were strongly applauded."

Courier, December 4th, 1875. Syracuse (N.Y.).

"A Syracuse audience had an opportunity last evening in
Shakespeare Hall of hearing the remarkable Mrs. Victoria C.
Woodhull—the wonderful, the great Woodhull. The house was
filled with an intelligent audience of ladies and gentlemen, about
equally divided.

"She called attention to a statement in one of Herbert
Spencer's articles in a magazine, which she said was beyond
anything that she had ever said. It was this: 'It is a lamentable
truth that the troubles which respectable hard-working married
women undergo are more trying to the health and detrimental

to the looks than any of the harlot's career.' What a commentary is this on the so-called sacred institution of marriage from the pen of the acknowledged leader of the scientific and philosophic world. 'But, yet, I am denounced,' she said, 'because I am doing everything in my power to bring about a better state of things for this class of women.'

"But she is willing to wait for her justification. Indeed, she said it had already begun to come. Where three years ago there was never a word upon these subjects printed in the papers, scarcely an important paper or magazine can now be found in which it is not discussed in some form. Moreover, some of the oldest and the most popular papers and magazines are now advocating substantially the same thing that she advocates, the only difference being that they have not the moral courage yet to show how the desired results are to be obtained, while this is a task from which she never shrinks.

"Such was the general tenor of Mrs. Woodhull's lecture last night. She is an extraordinary woman, and there is a peculiar fascination in her intense emotional nature, her utter and reckless devotion to an idea, her eager and passionate advocacy of her cause. She at once showed a perfect familiarity with what she was talking about. Her manner was easy, her gestures graceful, her voice strong, her articulation perfect, and the expression of her face when she got warmed up to her subject grew spiritual. Nobody who sees her can doubt that she is not only in earnest but honest in all she says: indeed, her purpose seems to be based on a deep-seated religious enthusiasm. *If she should appear here again, as we hope she may, no hall would be too large for her.*"

Democrat and Chronicle, December 6th, 1875. Rochester (N.Y.).

"Corinthian Hall was filled last Saturday evening with a large attentive audience to hear Mrs. Victoria C. Woodhull. Shortly

after eight Mrs. Woodhull appeared before her audience plainly
arrayed in black dress with no ornaments. She excited the
interest of her hearers by her first sentence, and held their
undivided attention to the end.

"The press throughout the country commends Mrs. Woodhull's lectures, and speaks in the highest terms of her oratory."

Evening Express, December 6th, 1875. Rochester (N.Y.).

"Mrs. Victoria C. Woodhull lectured in Corinthian Hall last
Saturday evening. The hall was filled with an intelligent
audience. That Mrs. Woodhull is a woman of ability no one
will deny. Her 'persuasive eloquence' convinced her hearers
that she 'means business' in the reiteration of her social theories.
She is convinced that editors are becoming more intelligent,
high-minded, and unprejudiced. Her address occupied about
one hour and a half, and was listened to with the closest attention. She spoke rapidly, and appeared as if it was difficult to
keep pace with her thoughts. She took her text from
Corinthians:—

"'Know ye not that ye are the temple of God, and that the spirit of
God dwelleth in you?'"

Express, December 6th, 1875. Buffalo (N.Y.).

VICTORIA C. WOODHULL.

How She Has Fought Single-Handed Against the World.
The Weak Woman Whom They Would Once Have Stoned
now Reigns a Queen among Her Former Persecutors.

"To-morrow evening that most wonderful of wonderful women,
Victoria C. Woodhull, will deliver one of her characteristic
lectures in St. James's Hall, probably the last she will ever
deliver in this city, a fact much to be regretted by all. Years
ago, when she first gave expression to what was then considered
her very 'peculiar views,' the populace, untrained to the broad
comprehensive truths she uttered, stood ready to stone her
to death, and in their bigoted madness sought her life.

But now a change has come over the spirit of the world's dreams. Men and women of high intellectual attainments, social standing, and great wealth, grasp her by the hand glad to do her honour, happy to possess her friendship. When the news of her coming was flashed over the wires yesterday afternoon, a motley congregation of people gathered about the entrance of the Tifft House, eager to catch a glimpse of the woman who fought single-handed against, conquered, and transformed the world. Unlike in years gone by, they looked and wondered. There was no gritting of teeth, no clenching of fists, no shrinking aside and gathering up of garments lest sin should pass by contact, but instead, a true welcome! the enthusiasm of which was marked in the glistening eye and ruddy cheek. The woman against whom every hand was raised had merged in the queen, whom none were ashamed to reverence. In the history of this great world, among the names of the great, the glorious and good, there is not to be found one brighter than that which belongs to this very remarkable woman whose career has been one of the most wonderful that ever attended the life of any individual, and this, if there be no other reason, seems to be corroborative of her claims. The opposition that she has met and overcome, the persecutions that she has survived, and the calumnies outlived, all point to a wonderful character and prophesy a wonderful career. Had not some more than human power been present with her she would long since have sunk beneath the powers that have sought to crush her. The greatest wonder now among her opponents is that she is alive, while her friends begin to have almost equal faith with herself in her mission as set forth by her, from the fact that she exists, that she has survived what would have crushed any other person. At one time she had not only the whole power of the Church and the government arrayed against her and determined on her destruction, but their immense power was reinforced by the weight of the entire press of the country.

What individual is there living besides Victoria C. Woodhull who would ever have thought of contending against such an array as this? But she never quailed before them. On the contrary, in her darkest hours she defied them, and she has at last come off conqueror over all. A triumph such as this places her name at the very front rank of the great conquerors of the world. Standing alone, deserted by those who should have been her friend, despoiled of all her means by the rapacity of the Government officials, whose acts they well understood would be winked at in this case, and she, one weak woman, gave a whole nation— the great nation of the world—battle, and came off victorious, because she had faith in her mission and knew that she was right; and, moreover, because she knew that she had the hosts of heaven on her side, while she also knew that the hosts of hell were on the side of those with whom she was contending. Such is Victoria C. Woodhull.

"THE BEGINNING.—Her first public effort was a descent into Wall Street, where her appearance caused no less astonishment than did her doings carry consternation. It is said that ten thousand persons visited her office the day she opened in that locality, all of them intent to know what were the motives that impelled her to take such a step. They saw large and elegantly furnished offices, containing all the paraphernalia for conducting a large banking and brokerage business; but this was all. They saw not beneath the surface; they knew not that behind all this were the elements and the purpose to destroy 'the street,' so-called. They should have known, however, had they stopped to philosophize a little, that the coming among them—a coming into their well-guarded precincts—of a woman, causing such a commotion and summoning them all to do her homage, had a potent meaning for them either for good or evil; but it is probable that none thought so far or deep as that. At that time Wall Street was in its glory. Scheme after scheme, in which millions of money were made, was being constantly put upon the gullible and unsuspecting public. Sharp practices destitute of real talent, and shrewd management in which honour found no place, were at a premium there. All such flourished, and to the external view everything in the country was at the very height of its prosperity. Little did these soulless speculators know that the woman's real purpose in coming into Wall Street was to burst this gigantic bubble.

"But they were not long kept in suspense; for no sooner had she fairly established her banking-house and gotten that business well under way, then she began the publication of a weekly newspaper with the avowed intention of making public the rascalities that she had ferreted out, and before the year was spent she had exposed and demolished every fraudulent scheme that was then on foot among them. The denizens of that locality were thunderstricken. Everything against which her pen was levelled fell. Its blows were mightier than the sword. Down they went, one after another in rapid succession—Tweed rings, fraudulent railroad schemes, and the banking-houses both in this country and in Europe which were palming them off upon the people; life insurance companies reduced from forty for the whole country to nineteen; fire insurance companies crumbled; Swepson & Co.'s Great Southern Bond scheme fraud; Mexican claim swindles, all, all tumbled beneath the vigorous blows that this woman dealt them with the rapidity and precision of a gladiator, all of which may be still found standing on the pages of *Woodhull & Claflin's Weekly* in any of the public libraries.

"WOMAN SUFFRAGE.—Having set the ship of reform in financial things afloat, and gotten her well into the current, she next gave her attention to political and industrial reform. She seized the movement for Woman Suffrage within her powerful grasp, and raised it by a single effort from the quagmire of expediency, where it had languished for twenty years, into a question of Constitutional law, and obtained the approval of

the best Judge of Constitutional law in the country for her
position that the Constitution as it is gives woman the right to
the ballot, and the Government has had to arbitrarily reverse
all precedents, both of law and custom, regarding the meaning
of citizenship, to escape the force of her attack. By this act
she rose to the head of the woman movement, where she now
stands virtually, whether so admitted or not, and where she will
remain until the question shall be finally settled in her behalf.

"She next took hold of, and handled with the policy of a
master-mind, the subtle questions of political economy, involved
in the mooted and unmooted points of the labour problem. She
delivered speeches and wrote articles on finance, land, labour,
commerce (internal and external), on taxation, representation,
the tariff, public debt, banking, currency, and on many other
collateral questions, with such power and vigour that the
leaders in this special field of reform sought her assistance.
But they learned that her principles were altogether too broad,
and covered too wide a field for them to grapple with at that
time, while she could not—and did not—afford to drop any
part of her scheme for general reform for the sake of abetting
any special line of reform. It is amusing now to visit labour
conventions and hear the leaders discourse learnedly on the
subject that they heard from her in her saloon (where the
literati and the wisdom of not only this country but Europe
also were constantly represented), and regarded as impracticable
less than five years ago. Some of the leaders, however, acknowledged that it was on her remarkable and exhaustive speech on
'The Principles of Finance,' that they based the financial plans
in their platform. It is the same everywhere. All reforms, of
whatever kind, are now being removed by the inspirations
received, in one form or another, from this remarkably talented
woman. Being virtually the acknowledged leader of the several
movements that were to be combined and used to force the
Government to terms, in the spring of 1872 a convention of

'The Equal Rights Party' was called to construct a platform of principles, and to nominate candidates for the succession. Twenty-six States and four Territories were represented by over five hundred delegates, than whom a no more patriotic, earnest, and orderly set of people were ever assembled. At the close of a speech made the evening before the day fixed for making the nominations, the Convention, amid the wildest enthusiasm, nominated the speaker by acclamation for the first place on the ticket, and the name of Victoria C. Woodhull was given to the world as that of the first woman who had received a nomination by a public National Convention for the highest office in the gift of the people.

"She next turned her attention to the social world. Here she found more difficulty in getting herself before the country. The people were so wrapped up in their corrupt social habits, and had instituted such disparity of custom between the responsibility of the different sexes in social things (which disparity was one of the first things which she attacked), that, as if with one accord, they refused to listen—or rather, the press refused to take up the subject, and in place of doing so, set about berating her for disturbing the domestic peace and tranquillity, and representing the doctrines to be just precisely the reverse of what they were.

"It was said of her that she advocated demoralization, and was opposed to marriage. She retorted by denying the allegation, and quoting from her speeches to prove it, which, by the way, she had had printed purposely to meet such an emergency. In spite, however, of all she could say or do, the press refused to do anything save to berate and misrepresent her. Seeing this determination, she took a terrible resolve. She determined to turn their own batteries upon them, and to fight them with the weapons that they had put in her hands. In respect to the social problem, there has already been, in fact, a revolution. The entire sentiment of the country has undergone a change, and it is admitted by everybody now that there not only is such a question, but that it is one that demands the attention of all enlightened people.

" Thus, in three several directions and times, has Mrs. Woodhull moved the country to thought upon vital subjects—financial corruption, political dishonesty, and social demoralization. This is, indeed, a wonderful career. Either one of these movements should have occupied an ordinary lifetime, but this extraordinary mind has accomplished them all within the brief space of six years, and this, she says, is but the beginning of what remains still to be done.

" What a wealth of labour has been attached to her, and how perfect has been her accomplishment of the great and varied tasks set before her ! The mind seems too finite and weak to move a world, and yet it has been done by this woman. Springing from the old German families of the Hummels and Moyers, whose ancestors were of royal blood, she stands in birth the equal of the highest born, while the power of her subtle mind places her on a level with the intellectual levers that move the earth. It is indeed strange that she now exists. The persecution she and her sister have undergone would have crushed to the ground the whole army of reformers of which she is the representative head. She is the sun that is dispelling the clouds of doubt and uncertainty, and disclosing to the view of the vast multitude the truth radiant in its beauty, lovely in its perfection. And the end is not yet, for though she is seemingly standing on the highest pinnacle of fame, she sees beyond other fields to be gleaned of misunderstanding and dross of soul."

Commercial Advertiser, December 6th, 1875. Buffalo (N.Y.).

" Despite the rain, St. James's Hall was filled both upstairs and down last evening, the attraction being a lecture by Mrs. Victoria C. Woodhull. Among the audience were many staid and sober married men, who would, without doubt, have relished the lecture highly had it not been for the absence of their wives, whom they were compelled, through stress of weather, to leave at home. The lecture was one which very few women possess the peculiar ability to deliver. Nevertheless it was one which is entirely proper for everyone to hear; *indeed which everyone ought to be the better for hearing.*"

The Courier, December 6th, 1875. Buffalo (N.Y.).

"Victoria C. Woodhull lectured at St. James's Hall last evening on 'The True and False, Socially;' and, notwithstanding the very disagreeable weather, the hall was filled with a highly intelligent audience. With such audiences as that of last evening, through an entire season, it must be evident to the most casual observer that 'advanced ideas,' when advocated boldly, are sometimes pecuniarily profitable. Mrs. Woodhull has been roundly abused; but the American people are the most generous people in the world, and the feeling is gaining ground that she has been misrepresented, and has been made to suffer unnecessarily. Mrs. Woodhull has persuasive eloquence, a fiery energy, and an earnestness whose genuineness cannot be questioned. She is a woman of great ability, and states her views with singular clearness and force.

" Her appearance last evening, as she stepped upon the stage, was that of an intelligent woman, with a finely-chiselled face, an intellectual forehead, and a pair of eyes all her own. At first she delivered her argument in a sort of mechanical way, but as she proceeded with the discussion she grew earnest and impassioned. Her language took on the impetuosity of a mountain torrent, and her ideas chased each other with lightning feet. She indulged but little in rhetorical flourish, and flights of fancy she did not attempt. Her business was too serious for these things, and every movement seemed freighted with responsibility to her. She overflowed with her subject, and struggled bravely to keep pace with her thoughts. After the first quarter

of an hour it was a veritable oratorical storm, succeeding to a
sort of intellectual calm; and her plea with the world to think
as she did was as vehement and passionate as if doomsday were
at hand and the world was unregenerate. Her attitude and
bearing, and the rapid utterances of thought, feeling, indignation, pity, and despair were those of a rhapsodist; and the
sincerity of the woman was completely manifest. There was
nothing melodramatic about her manner; there were no pre-
meditated climaxes; no regular recurrence of finely-rounded
periods; no oratorical claptrap whatever. What she had to
say she said in her own way and with a spontaneity, eager
energy, and accuracy of emphasis really refreshing. She is a
social iconoclast, and tears down with a fury that seems born of
inspiration. We content ourselves with giving her credit for
honesty of purpose and oratorical talents unequalled by any
lady to whom we have ever listened. She was frequently
applauded with a will, and when she retired from the stage the
demonstration was as enthusiastic as any orator or actor could
desire."

The **Express**, December 6th, 1875 (Editorial). Buffalo (N.Y.).

" Among the most notable things of the season is the changed
tone with which Victoria C. Woodhull has been greeted by the
press of the West, where she has been lecturing. It would
seem as if they had got the idea that this woman is not as black
as she has been painted, and that she is entitled to be heard in
her own behalf, and on any legitimate topic of public discussion.
This change of front by the press, from denunciation to candid
criticism or cautious handling, has had its effect on the public
mind, if we may judge by the size and character of the
audiences Mrs. Woodhull has been gaining. Her present theme
relates to a subject that has been tabooed too much for the
good of the world; has been relegated to the physician's study

or reserved for the after-marriage detection; if learned at all by the young in time to be of any value to them, has been done surreptitiously, and made uselessly and wickedly a thing of shame and guilt. The developments of social unsoundness of the past few years have perhaps prepared thoughtful people to seek a remedy in freer discussion and better knowledge of the laws of life. This willingness has helped Mrs. Woodhull to her large and respectable audiences. Anyway she has had them. Her present movement towards the ascendant is one of the strangest turns in her fortunes."

Express, December 6th, 1875. Buffalo (N.Y.).

"St. James's Hall last evening received a large crowd to listen to the lecture of Mrs. Victoria Woodhull. The intelligent ladies predominated. She came upon the stage alone, and opened her lecture without any introduction. The audience saw in her a lady above the ordinary height, tastefully dressed in black. It was seen that she possessed a strong, intelligent face. Her ability as a speaker soon made itself manifest, and kept the uninterrupted attention of everyone from the beginning to the end of her discourse. She has a power of saying things with a crispness and force, and uttering delicate truths with originality, that is possessed by few public speakers. She speaks with an earnestness and sense of thorough conviction which rises to real eloquence. During her lecture she said that intelligence must come, or this race will die away. With intelligence morbidness, ignorance, and disease will be banished. She next spoke of the sacredness of woman in the gestative state, and of the homage which ought to be paid to her.

"There is a thing that Mrs. Woodhull talks about that we wish every man, woman, and child could have talked to them — that is the criminal neglect to educate the young properly in the physiological facts that all must certainly learn some time,

32

if not properly and purely, then improperly and vulgarly. Mrs. Woodhull's appeal to mothers to let the first light her boy or girl gets on this awful mystery of reproduction come from the sacred lamp of a mother's experience, a natural, a pure, a sacred education, instead of being made unnecessarily and stupidly a shame, to be learned secretly in the streets from those who lead by impure suggestions of knowledge to impure use of it—if all mothers could read, ponder, and act on Mrs. Woodhull's talks it would be well.

"We believe there is more freedom every year in the discussion of that view of the subject by scientific, medical, and secular journals, and by the clergy and the medical profession; so that proper knowledge is supplanting vicious knowledge, so that distinction between ignorance and virtue is becoming known, and that the theory that ignorance is the mother of purity as well as devotion is being largely rejected."

Daily Union, December 7th, 1875. Lockport.

"An audience of more than average size assembled in the Hodge Opera House last night to hear Mrs. Victoria C. Woodhull. She came upon the stage with the Bible in her right hand. She quoted her text:—

"'Know ye not that ye are the temple of God, and that the Spirit of God dwelleth in you?

"'If any man defile the temple of God, him shall God destroy; for the temple of God is holy, which temple ye are.'

"She commenced her lecture with a very cursory sketch of the rise and growth of civilization, which brought her quickly to what she considers the dead stand of the present day. There is not a perfect man or woman in America. Our homes are blighted, our firesides are desolated, our cemeteries are filled, our asylums and penitentiaries are crowded, all from the effect of evils which it is in the power of mothers and fathers to prevent by discarding false delicacy, and teaching their children what they will otherwise surely learn from others to their great harm. Let mothers learn physiological facts, which are now called 'vulgar,' and teach them to their children. Ministers may preach and pray for the coming reformation; but it will never come till they and all people go to work to teach scientific truths—till they let the soul alone and try and save the body."

Daily Journal, December 7th, 1875. Lockport (N.Y.).

"Notwithstanding the unfavourable weather last evening, Mrs. Victoria C. Woodhull was greeted by a good-sized audience at the Hodge Opera House, and was listened to with the closest attention for two hours. She prefaced her lecture with the following scriptural passage:—'Know *ye* not that *ye* are the temple of God, and that the Spirit of God dwelleth in you?'— Corinthians iii. 16. And from that time until the close she unrelentingly advanced her theories, astonishing her hearers at times with impassioned eloquence, and the determination with which she uttered her sentiments. During her remarks she said she fully realized the disadvantages under which she was compelled to labour in her great work of reform; but when mothers were brought to realize that they are responsible for nearly all crimes committed by their children, they will see where they have been at fault in not daring to say to their daughters that their bodies were their own; and in maintaining them as the temple of God, they will learn that to trust their sacred rights to the stronger sex is a great crime; they must throw off their false modesty, and instead of allowing their children to learn from the rabble, must themselves give the information so much needed, and teach them that intelligence regarding the ways of God in nature is at all times virtuous."

32 •

Republican, December 18th, 1875. Springfield (Mass.).

"For a Sunday-night audience Mrs. Victoria C. Woodhull met with a notable reception. The people filling the body of the hall were certainly intelligent and respectable. Mrs. Woodhull proved a pleasant disappointment to many. She was, of course, unmistakably earnest, honest, and serious.

"At Westfield, Saturday, Mrs. Woodhull was also met by a good audience, including several physicians, prominent church officers, clergymen, and several prominent citizens, nearly all accompanied by their wives."

Evening Gazette, December 16th, 1875. Worcester (Mass.).

"One of the events of the lecture season occurred last evening, in the appearance on the Mechanics' Hall platform of Mrs. Victoria C. Woodhull. She fully enlisted the sympathies of her audience, and at its close was heartily applauded. Many who attended the lecture went away with a much higher opinion of Mrs. Woodhull than they had formerly entertained."

Daily Press, December 16th, 1875. Worcester (Mass.).

"There was an attraction at Mechanics' Hall last evening, and that attraction was Mrs. Victoria C. Woodhull."

1876.

The Gazette, January, 1876. Washington (D.C.).

" Not the least remarkable of the revolutions wrought in the sentiments, feelings, and conduct of the people of this country, and in the tone of the public press, is that which has taken place in respect to Mrs. Victoria Woodhull, and the peculiar theories of which she is the especial and distinguished exponent.

" A few years since this lady was the object at which the poisoned arrows of slander, contumely, and scorn from a thousand quivers were directed. Every vile and disgraceful epithet within the vocabulary of our language was hurled at her devoted head. All that the ingenuity and malignity of the most unscrupulous could devise was done, not only to blacken and make infamous her private character, and drive her from the public rostrum, but to make her the one social outcast in whose behalf neither justice should be invoked nor respectful consideration be awarded.

" With a few honourable exceptions the entire press of the country lent itself to the ignoble work of abusing and maligning this lady, attributing to her sentiments she never expressed or avowed, theories she was never in affiliation with, and charging her with utterances which were a foul libel on every feeling of her heart. Trampling under foot every generous and manly feeling, losing sight of her claims upon them as a woman and mother to courteous and respectful treatment, the press everywhere, in its zeal to pander to a morbidly diseased public sentiment, left nothing undone to heap odium on her personal character, and make infamous her public teachings. Nor was this all. The power and authority of the Federal Government must needs be invoked to aid in the nefarious work of crushing this weak and defenceless woman, whose only offence was that

she had stripped away the mask, and revealed in all its hideous-
ness the sorrow and suffering, the mental and moral abasement
that permeated the social life of our people. She had probed the
outward seeming, and discovered the leprosy within; she had
torn from certain pampered social pets the hypocritical cloak that
concealed the deformity of their actual lives, and so the Government and press must rush to the rescue, and by abusing the
prerogatives of each, seek through defamation and abuse to
break the force of the truths uttered.

"Had the evils so boldly declared by Mrs. Woodhull to exist
been but the figment of a diseased brain, had it not been seen and
known of all men that her statements were true, had not both
men and women, in the privacy of their own homes, admitted
the absolute necessity for some radical change in our present
social system, there can be no doubt but that this lady, under
force of all the appliances used for her destruction, must have
been driven into an obscurity from which she could never again
have hoped to emerge.

"But what do we see? Mrs. Woodhull—who but a few years
ago was the target at which a thousand envenomed shafts were
aimed, against whom myriads of tongues were wagging and
myriads of pens scribbling, who was held up as a consummate
moral leper, against whom every man's voice and hand should be
raised, who could find only second-rate halls in which to be
allowed to declare what her views really were, and had these
most infamously distorted—is to-day admitted to be engaged in
a great and noble work. No longer shunned, her society is
sought by the best and purest in the land; and from being an
object of vituperation and abuse, she has become one of courteous
and respectful attention at the hands of all. No longer driven
into obscure garrets and out-of-the-way halls, she finds it
impossible to comply with one-twentieth of the invitations
received to lecture to the best audiences in the land. An end
has come to misrepresentation, too; and now the press every-

where discovers and shows eagerness to acquaint its readers with the views of this lady as declared by herself.

"This change, so creditable to the people and press of the country, cannot fail of being especially gratifying to Mrs. Woodhull. She has battled against the most tremendous odds, and won a signal triumph. Through contumely and scorn, through sadness, imprisonment and tears, through persecution almost unto death, she has never faltered, but with a courage and heroism born of a conscious rectitude of purpose, has devoted herself with singular fidelity to the work of regenerating her race, and lifting the fell incubus which has well-nigh crushed out all purity from the social life of our people.

"In the relentless storm of obloquy through which she has passed in the deepest gloom that has enveloped her steps, in the darkest night of desolation and misery that has come upon her life, this lady has never for one moment allowed her faith in a final vindication of her own character and the correctness of her principles to be shaken. And that vindication has come in the disposition everywhere manifested to admit that Mrs. Woodhull's advocacy of them in no sense derogates from her claim to recognition as a lady.

"It is a gigantic step forward in the direction of solving this vexed social problem when the best men and women in the land, admitting the necessity for its candid discussion, no longer malign those who devote themselves to that behalf—when there is a disposition to call things by their right names, and demand that the standard of moral excellence to which one class is required to measure up shall be that which the lives of all classes must be judged.

"With the advent of this new era, Mrs. Woodhull will fill altogether a different place in the estimation of the public from that which ignorance and malice have hitherto assigned her. From being denounced as the enemy of a wise, pure, and well-organized social system, she will be recognized as among the ablest of those who have striven to establish it; from being thought inimical to the sanctity of home, she will be looked on as pre-eminently the advocate of unions that shall be unto death, as the upbuilding of homes on whose altars will ever be enthroned a deathless and changeless love; and from the lips of those who have denounced and abused her will come forth blessings on her name.

> " Sow love and taste its fruitage pure ;
>   Sow grain and reap its harvest bright ;
> Sow sunbeams on the rock and moor,
>   And find a harvest-home of light."

Courier, January 4th, 1876. Newark (N.J.).

"Mrs. Woodhull was greeted at the Opera House last evening by an audience that was much larger than many that have attended some of the best theatrical performances there this winter. The ladies and gentlemen present were highly intelligent, and paid earnest attention to the lecture. When Mrs. Woodhull gradually warmed up she became truly eloquent, and seemed to glow with genuine inspiration."

Advertiser, January 4th, 1876. Newark (N.J.).

" Mrs. Woodhull lectured at the Opera House last evening on those social problems of life of which she is a prominent exponent and advocate. She speaks rapidly and earnestly without special effort at rhetorical effect, and in a tone of voice which is at all times clear and distinct. Her audience was respectable in number, and those present were orderly, attentive, and frequently enthusiastic."

Journal, January 4th, 1876. Newark (N.J.).

" A good-sized audience greeted Mrs. Woodhull in the Opera House last evening.

" Many who had not seen Mrs. Woodhull before, and had only judged of her personal appearance from the caricatures

on the bill-boards and in the shop windows, were agreeably
surprised to find her a very handsome woman, with pleasing,
and not stagey manners, which immediately won the favour of
the audience."

Register, January 4th, 1876. Newark (N.J.).

"Mrs. Victoria C. Woodhull lectured at the Opera House
last evening, and was welcomed by a large, certainly respectable and highly intelligent audience composed of ladies and
gentlemen, who paid deep attention to her argument. Mrs.
Woodhull is one of the most eloquent we have ever heard."

Herald, January 4th, 1876. Elizabeth (N.J.).

"The damp, rainy, and in every way disagreeable weather
accompanying the fog, which enshrouded the fair city of Elizabeth, and its scarcely less fair suburbs, on Friday evening, was
not reassuring to the hundreds who had anticipated a rare treat
at the lecture to be given at Library Hall by Mrs. Woodhull,
and a premonition of probable wet feet and possible colds
in the head deterred many from attending. But no considera-
tions of hygiene are supposed to afford any excuse for the non-
attendance of the lecturer, and accordingly Mrs. Woodhull,
having travelled in defiance of the weather authorities, appeared
promptly at the hour of eight; where her eyes met those of an
audience composed of people of high intellectual culture and
refinement, and of the best possible standing in society. The
audience consisted largely of ladies.

"Launching at once into her lecture she was soon found to
be a brilliant and eloquent speaker, with a real genuine earnestness rare among lecturers. It is quite evident, however much
others may differ with her, that Mrs. Woodhull believes what
she says, and is in earnest in her efforts to bring about results
which she conceives to be for the world's good. She is certainly

honest. Both her manner and her language were refined and ladylike, and in the discussion of subjects generally looked upon as too delicate for ordinary conversation, she struck that happy means where her language was forcible without being in any way coarse or vulgar. Her views as to what children should and should not learn from their parents were excellent, and she corrected many gross misapprehensions as to the doctrine she teaches. Her lecture was listened to most attentively, and should she, at some future time, consent to appear again before an audience in this city, she will be greeted by a full house."

Evening Journal, January 6th, 1876. Jersey City (N.J.).

"The advent of Mrs. Victoria C. Woodhull occurred last night in Kepler Hall in presence of a respectable audience, one-third of whom were ladies, and all of whom fine people. Precisely at eight o'clock she walked upon the platform and opened her discourse. Her lecture last night was one that every man and woman in the land should hear, for it was fruitful of good and comprised a well-chosen discussion upon the social relations between parents and children, and between men and women. At first she was dispassionate to coldness; but when she warmed up she hurled lightnings of cogent truths and eloquent appeals for humanity.

"Her lecture began with a learned dissertation upon the advance of civilization, during which she said that without constant renewals by immigration the people of this land would become extinct, because of the systems which have so long obtained here have produced a social condition inimical to the advancement of the race and conducive to its final extinction.

"In concluding, Mrs. Woodhull said: 'No one who has not passed through the fiery furnace of affliction and adversity and become emancipated from public opinion could stand the load of opprobrium that I have been forced to carry. I sometimes grow weary under its weight and sigh for rest, but my duty to my *sex* spurs me on. Therefore I want your sympathy, your sustaining love to go on with me and bless me ; and when I leave you for other fields of labour and stand upon other rostrums, fearing that I may not be able to do my duty, I want to feel the yearnings of your hearts following me with prayers that my efforts may be blessed. I want tho blessing of these fathers, the affection of these sons, the benediction of these mothers, and the prayers of these daughters to follow me everywhere, to give me strength to endure the labour, courage to speak the truth, and a continued faith that right will finally triumph.' "

Evening Argus, January 6th, 1876. Jersey City (N.J.).

"Mrs. Victoria C. Woodhull delivered her long-expected lecture at Kepler Hall last night before an intelligent audience, among whom could be discerned a number of prominent officials and citizens with their wives. About eight o'clock Mrs. Woodhull appeared. She looked like an earnest, sincere woman, and evidently believed in the somewhat startling views she set forth. Mrs. Woodhull's favourite views on the marriage relation and the duties of parents to their children were listened to with marked attention throughout, and the frequent hits she made brought loud applause.

"Mrs. Woodhull began by reading from the Bible, and then launched into what she called the theory of social evolution by which human races are to be harmoniously blended and man and woman made perfect. Mrs. Woodhull said she meant to go on advocating these reforms until they should bear fruit."

Times, January 8th, 1876. Jersey City (N.J.).

"Mrs. Victoria C. Woodhull was at Kepler Hall on Wednesday evening, and was listened to by an intelligent, appreciative audience. At the conclusion of the lecture it was amusing to listen to the remarks of the retiring throng : 'Splendid.'

'Wonderful.' 'I would not have missed it for any money.' 'I hope these truths will do us all good.' "

The National Republican, January 11th, 1876. Washington (D.C.).

"Mrs. Victoria C. Woodhull should, and does probably, feel proud of the audience which greeted her last night at Ford's Opera House, to listen to her lecture, 'The Human Body, the Temple of God.' The spacious edifice was crowded with both ladies and gentlemen, many of the latter representing official and prominent business circles, and by all was the most respectful attention given to the utterances of the great reformer.

"The portion of her lecture in which she referred to herself was in perfect good taste, for, after enduring all the obloquy cast upon her, and suffering in prison for opinion's sake, she certainly had a right to congratulate both herself and her audience on the fact that she had lived down her persecutors, and had drawn together as respectful auditors so large and intelligent an assemblage in the National Capital.

"During the evening she was complimented by the presentation of a basket of beautiful flowers, and at the conclusion of the lecture she was so enthusiastically applauded as to reappear and bow her acknowledgments."

The Chronicle, January 11th, 1876. Washington (D.C.).

"As large an audience as ever assembled to listen to a lecture in this city gathered in Ford's Opera House last night to hear Mrs. Victoria Woodhull. The audience was also an eminently intelligent one, comprising a large number of most respectable ladies—old and young. The lecture was frequently interrupted by applause, which was specially hearty at the close, and at one point a large and handsome bouquet was presented to her."

Morning News, January 11th, 1876. Washington (D.C.).

"Mrs. Victoria C. Woodhull delivered her popular lecture at

Ford's Opera House last night to a large audience. Mrs. Woodhull's appearance on the stage was greeted with applause."

The Telegram, January 11th, 1876. Washington (D.C.).

"Ford's Opera House was packed full last evening with an
appreciative audience, the preponderance of which were intelligent and refined ladies, to hear the celebrated lecturer, Mrs.
Victoria C. Woodhull, discourse plainly upon the startling and
ugly facts of which our social fabric is composed. The lecturer
received an ovation worthy of the cause she has espoused, and
for which she has been so *bitterly* persecuted. She was
repeatedly applauded by the vast audience and brought before
the curtain upon the termination of her lecture."

Daily Critic, January 11th, 1876. Washington (D.C.).

"Last evening Mrs. Victoria C. Woodhull lectured at Ford's
Opera House to a large and appreciative audience, and were she
to repeat her lecture one week hence Ford's Opera House would
not furnish seats for those who would then desire to gain
admission.

"The lecture was listened to with rapt attention, and it was
the desire of nearly everyone present that he or she should have
the privilege at an early day of again sitting under the pleasant
voice of Mrs. Woodhull to hear some of her wholesome truths.

Mirror, January 18th, 1876. Carlisle (Pa.).

"A good audience assembled in Rheem's Hall last night to
hear Mrs. Victoria C. Woodhull discuss the 'Theory of Life,
Socially.' Promptly at eight o'clock Mrs. Woodhull stepped
upon the stage and opened her lecture by reciting from the
sacred writ the passage upon which her theory is based, and at
once entered upon the consideration of her subject with a spirit
and earnestness which won the closest attention of her audience.

Many of her passages were peculiarly forcible, and throughout the lecture was deeply interesting, thoroughly chaste, logical, and eloquent. Our space is too limited to permit even a brief report of the line of argument, or a comprehensive idea of this lecturer's faith, assertion, proofs, or theories, but this we must say: throughout the lecture was such as any pure, intelligent mind could safely listen to and highly appreciate, if not for faith in its teachings, at least for its eloquence, earnestness, and manner of delivery. Mrs. Woodhull will have no trouble in obtaining a full house should she lecture here again."

Herald, January 20th, 1876. Carlisle (Pa.).

"MRS. VICTORIA C. WOODHULL'S LECTURE.—This lady lectured in Rheem's Hall on Monday evening. The evening was wet and disagreeable; a fair audience was present, however.

"Mrs. Woodhull appeared and commenced her lecture, which continued for an hour and a half. In justice to this lady we are constrained to say that we went to the hall prejudiced against her, but we freely acknowledge that we have never listened to a lecture that abounded with so many solid, substantial truths and so replete with instruction. We wished, as we heard this lady, gifted with much more than ordinary descriptive powers, that every husband and wife, as well as every parent, in the place, had been present, for we feel sure they would have benefitted by the lecture. Her ideas, many of them new, contained startling truths, worth the consideration of every well-wisher of his race. Mrs. Woodhull is a graceful and gifted orator, clothing her subject in chaste and beautiful language. Should she visit Carlisle again she would have a crowded house."

The Tribune, January 22nd, 1876. Johnstown (Pa.).

" The lecture delivered by Mrs. Woodhull in the Opera House last night was thoroughly enjoyed by the ladies and gentlemen present. She is a rapid, yet clear and distinct, talker, and possesses a richly modulated voice, which is exceedingly pleasing to the listener. There were many home truths spoken last evening by this lady in such an impressive manner as to touch the hearts of her audience, and the close attention with which her discourse of an hour and a quarter was received showed that it was highly appreciated by all present."

The Democrat, January 22nd, 1876. Johnstown (Pa.).

"Mrs. Victoria C. Woodhull delivered her lecture on the 'True and False, Socially,' in the Opera House on Friday evening last. There was a great crowd out to hear her—high-toned, appreciative listeners. Mrs. Woodhull, in personal appearance, is far handsomer than any other lady we have ever heard on the rostrum—graceful and feminine in all her movements and positions. There is nothing masculine about her voice and gestures, but everything denotes the sweet-voiced, cultivated lady. She spoke about one hour and a quarter, and the very close attention given her by the audience was an evidence that she was interesting and entertaining. The lecture surpassed the expectations of the public, and was a rare treat, being one of the most elegantly delivered lectures ever heard in our town."

News, January 26th, 1876. Ashtabula (Ohio).

"Mrs. Victoria C. Woodhull's lecture at Smith's Opera House last Monday evening was, in many respects, a remarkable one. The hall was well filled with a good representation of the best classes of citizens. Perhaps one-half of those present were ladies. Mrs. Woodhull came before her audience very plainly dressed, advanced to the centre of the stage, and there stood, with neither desk nor manuscript before her, holding in her hand only a pocket-Bible, from which she read several texts. The entire audience listened throughout with the most perfect attention, interrupted only by applause at the sharp hits or telling passages of the address. Mrs. Woodhull is unquestionably a woman of genius, a fine and very impressive speaker and apparently talks from a full heart without hesitation because she has something to say and is vitally in earnest—at times moving some, at least, of her hearers, whom we know of, even to tears. The lecture was, indeed, a remarkable one ; much of it vastly true and equally important, in substance apparently very different from what the audience must have expected. It was an earnest appeal for the purity of the body. Its effects, as a whole, must have been good ; and we feel sure, if she had been announced to lecture again the next evening the hall would have been filled to its utmost capacity."

Voice and Echo, January 29th, 1876. Johnstown (Pa.).

"Mrs. Victoria C. Woodhull delivered her famous lecture on ' The True and False, Socially,' at the Opera House on Friday evening of last week to a select and appreciative audience. From the beginning to the close she entranced her listeners with the most eloquent, rhetorical, and convincing speech that has ever been delivered in our city. As the truths, like pearls, fell from her lips they were eagerly caught up by her admiring hearers and digested intellectually, and the praise given her since will testify that her eloquent display was never excelled by Phillips, a Choate, or any other person. Would that all the mothers and daughters in our city could have left the *false* at home and heard the truths fall from the lips of one of their own sex. She certainly has the moral courage to disseminate such facts as none dare dispute. When she visits us again we are confident of an overflowing house greeting the appearance of the ' Queen of the Rostrum.' "

Tribune, January 29th, 1876. Kokomo (Ind.).

" Several days ago all seats in the Opera House were engaged to hear Mrs. Woodhull, who lectured last night. The audience

was composed of our most intelligent, refined people. Everywhere Mrs. Woodhull is greeted with the same audiences of
respectable, honest-thinking people. It may be idle curiosity
that brings them out to listen to her ; but no matter what the
attraction is, they go to hear the only woman in America who
dares to attack the social evil sin in the plain way that she
does. Mrs. Woodhull may justly be proud of her Kokomo
audience, for it was such an one as rarely congregates to hear a
lecture. There was a large number of most respectable ladies,
old and young. She spoke about an hour and a half, and closed
with an earnest appeal to the people of Kokomo to give their
sympathy and moral support in the crusade which she is waging
for the elevation of the race and of her sex. The lecture was
frequently interrupted by applause, which was especially hearty
at the close."

The Globe-Democrat, February 2nd, 1876. St. Louis (Mo.).

" If, among the large audience of ladies and gentlemen who
were present at Armory Hall last evening to hear Victoria C.
Woodhull lecture, any went with the expectation of hearing
anything advanced by that lady that was either immodest or
licentious, they must have left the hall disappointed in that
respect, but much better informed on some matters than they
were before they entered it.

" Mrs. Woodhull appeared on the platform attired in a very
plain, dark-coloured dress, and spoke with great animation for
about two hours. Her utterance is very rapid, but distinct;
her language forcible, and her gestures appropriate and effective.
Everything she does, both in utterance and action, seems to be
spontaneous. She never hesitates for a word, and her strong,
vigorous thoughts are clothed in the most appropriate language.
Unlike most fluent speakers, she deals but little in imagery,
and her efforts have no attempt at rhetorical embellishments ;
and yet she is an orator of great ability. In the treatment of

her subject she goes straight to the point under consideration
for the time, and says what she has to say in vigorous Saxon
and then passes on. Her strength as a speaker is in her
earnestness. Her audience at once become *en rapport* with
her, for they feel that they have before them a woman who is
in 'dead earnest,' and that the words which are falling from
her lips are not the mere coinage of a mental process, but they
are thoughts coming straight from her heart, earnestly uttered,
because earnestly felt.

" 'Now, when I speak of marriage, I wish it to be distinctly
understood that I mean that ideal marriage against which all
human shafts may beat in vain. I mean that marriage of which
it may be said of its subject truly, "They have been joined
together by God, and no man can put them asunder"; I mean
that marriage to which, when once entered upon, there can
never come a desire to depart from it; I mean that marriage
which is so sacred, so pure, so holy, so chaste, that there cannot,
by any manner of means, be even so much as a single dis-
sentient cause between its two equal factors; I mean that
marriage in which the two opposite representatives—the
positive and the negative elements—of the race come into a
perfectly blended and perfectly acting one-whole person; that
marriage which requires that this perfect one shall be a unit
in all the affairs and dispensations of life;—in short, I mean
that marriage into which for any foreign element to even so
much as cast a shadow must necessarily deface its divinity and
its sanctity, its oneness and its beauty! Marriage is regarded
as a too frivolous matter—is rushed into and out of in a haste
that shows an utter ignorance or else a total disregard of its
responsibilities, as if it were an institution specially designed
for the benefit of the selfish wishes and passions of the sexes.
But to look at marriage in this light is not to see it at all in
that of the public good, or, ultimately, in that of individual
happiness. Marriages that are based upon selfishness or passion

can never result in anything save misery to all concerned. I am opposed to improper marriages only—to marriages that bring unhappiness to the married and misery to their fruits; and such as do this, had I the power, I would prohibit. I would guard the door by which this state is entered with all the vigilance with which the young mother watches her first-born, darling babe. I would have no one enter its precincts save on bended knee and prayerful heart, as if approaching the throne of God; as if to enter there were, more than any other way, to give one's self to the service of God. So strictly would I guard it that none who should enter could ever wish to retrace their steps. I would make divorce an unknown thing by abolishing imprudent and ill-assorted marriages. I would make the stigma so great that woman should find it impossible to confront the world in a marriage for a home, for position, or for any other reason save love alone; and I would have her who would sell her person to be degraded in marriage to be culpable, as guilty, as impure at heart, as she is held to be who sells it otherwise. I would put every influence of the community against impure relations and selfish purposes, in whatever form they may exist, and encourage honour, purity, virtue, and chastity. *I would take away from marriage the idea that it legally conveys the control of the person of the wife to the husband;* and I would make her as much its guardian against improper use as she is supposed to be in maidenhood. It should be her own, sacredly, never to be desecrated by any unwelcome touch. I would make enforced commerce as much a crime in marriage as it is now out of it, and unwilling child-bearing a double crime. I would have man so honour woman that an impure or improper thought or self-desire, other than a wish to bless her, could never enter in his heart.'

" The lecture was listened to by the large audience, a large proportion of whom were ladies, with rapt attention, and the speaker was frequently interrupted by loud applause.

508

"While Mrs. Woodhull, in dealing with a subject which is
generally ignored in the pulpit and on the platform, calls a spade
a spade, there was nothing that fell from her lips which could
justly shock the sensibilities of the most refined. On the contrary, there was around it an elevated, moral, and even religious
tone. The subject is one that is demanding the attention of all
who are interested in social ethics, and who is there that is not
interested in a matter that so vitally affects the general welfare
of humanity? Her views are in advance of the day in which
she lives, but there were but few, if any, present last evening who
could differ from her, and even if they did they derived an
intellectual pleasure in listening to the keen, clear, earnest
thinker, who thoroughly believes in the mission she is advocating.
They heard some plain truths, it is true, some of which came
home to them, but they were told by a fearless woman, who has
an abiding faith in the old motto, *Veritas prevalebit.*"

The Globe-Democrat, February 2nd, 1876 (Editorial).

St. Louis (Mo.).

"Mrs. Woodhull's experience, as a woman, has been the
most remarkable of any on the American or European continent.
Subjected to the scorn and contumely of a very large class of
respectable people, she has always associated with the most learned
savants of both hemispheres, and enjoyed, to a wonderful degree,
their esteem and admiration. No ordinary woman could have
sustained herself under the circumstances which have surrounded
Mrs. Woodhull. Adverse fate at times seems to have buried her
almost out of sight; but she has come through all her perilous
trials unscathed. Unlike any woman orator in the country she
speaks entirely extemporaneously. She has neither manuscript
nor notes, but goes upon the stage with a simple skeleton upon
which she builds her literary structure. As an idea marches by

she clothes it in the language of the moment and lets it go. In a certain sense she is an emotional speaker, and yet not mistaken of those accurate and practical modes of expression common to a trained orator. Her ideas upon the social question will doubtless contain some new thoughts, but we are assured that they possess no element which cannot claim the approval of the good Christian. On this point Mrs. Woodhull's friends claim that she has been grossly misrepresented, and that she has never yet given expression to a theory not in consonance with social purity and Christian integrity. Certainly her published lectures contain nothing a fine lady could hesitate to repeat. Her manners are cultured and refined, and possess that poetical movement which is always a marked attribute of the true gentlewoman. Her countenance possesses great intellectuality and purity of expression; her conversation is exceedingly brilliant and chaste, and strikingly indicative of a woman of cultivation and character."

Journal, February 2nd, 1876. St. Louis (Mo.).

"Mrs. Victoria C. Woodhull lectured last evening in Armory Hall upon ' The True and False, Socially.' A large audience was present, representing in character the best element of the St. Louis social world, a large proportion being intelligent ladies, proving that the strictures of the press throughout the country on this irrepressible and unconquerable woman have had the effect to enhance the public interest in the social theories she advances. Mrs. Woodhull's elocution is almost faultless, her voice at times ringing out full and clear as she promulgates some grand ideas, and again sinking into a whisper, every syllable distinct and clear as if it were a thing hewn out of marble.

"At the conclusion of her lecture Mrs. Woodhull held an informal reception in the room adjoining the hall, and a large number of ladies and gentlemen shook hands with and congratulated the great social reformer."

Dispatch, February 3rd, 1876. Kokomo (Ind.).

"One of the largest and most highly educated lecture-
audiences of the season filled the Opera House on last Friday
night to hear Mrs. Victoria C. Woodhull deliver her celebrated
lecture—'The True and False, Socially.' It was noticeable
that the audience was about equally composed of the male and
female elements. Prejudice and mock-modesty, doubtless, deterred a few delectable individuals from enjoying one of the
ablest lectures ever delivered in this city. Promptly at eight
o'clock Mrs. Woodhull stepped before the footlights and began
her lecture. For two hours she poured hot shots into the shoddy
ramparts of a diseased and debauched moral and social fabric.
As she progressed in her lecture her face flushed with inspiration, and her whole being was aglow with the enthusiasm and
sentiments of her topic. She piled fact upon fact, argument
upon argument, in a rapid flow of impassioned eloquence. She
drove home many wholesome facts that the world affects to
disbelieve, but knows full well. She denied free-love as the
world understands the term. Her free-love, she said, was the
free-love of God to the world. She said she had been traduced,
vilified, misrepresented, and imprisoned for maintaining the
right. To the world that had hated her and tried to crush her
she now offers her bleeding heart in love. She said that those
who knew her in a false light should yet know her as she is;
those who hated her should yet love her; and the world that
refused to listen to her story should yet accept her truths, and
become reformed from social and moral degradation. Mrs.
Woodhull's lecture was able and full of truths. Those who
went to hear a coarse woman were happily disappointed. Mrs.
Woodhull is a handsome, unostentatious, honest-appearing woman
of wide learning and great depth of mind. She talks as a
mother who knows the joys and sorrows of maternity, as a
woman who has suffered much for her principles, as a repre-

sentative of her sex who is boldly breasting public opinion for
the promulgation of a great social reformation. She has made
many friends in Kokomo, and removed a false prejudice that
had long been entertained against her. All who heard her
pronounce her lecture a grand, masterly effort."

Daily American, February 5th, 1876. Nashville (Tenn.).

" As had been anticipated, the Opera House was packed last
night with an audience eager to hear Mrs. Victoria C. Woodhull
lecture on ' The Human Body the Temple of God.' Dress
circle and parquette were jammed, and the galleries were better
filled than was ever before witnessed in that Thespian temple.
The audience was composed of the more intelligent and cultivated
citizens of the community, the ladies present being the wives and
daughters of business and professional men. After the lecture
Mrs. Woodhull received several letters, couched in the most
complimentary terms, and specially asking that she might deliver
another lecture, but she finds it necessary to leave for New
Orleans to-day."

Evening Mail, February 5th, 1876. Nashville (Tenn.).

" The lecture of Mrs. Victoria C. Woodhull at the Opera House
last night, on ' The Human Body the Temple of God,' attracted
a respectable and appreciative audience. The best of order
prevailed during the evening, and the audience seemed to be
deeply interested."

Avalanche, February 8th, 1876. Memphis (Tenn.).

" Many gentlemen and ladies who heard Mrs. Woodhull's
lecture at Memphis Theatre, on Sunday night, were so well
pleased that a petition was circulated yesterday, requesting her
to repeat the lecture, and a number of signatures had been
obtained before it was discovered that Mrs. Woodhull had left
for Nashville on the early train."

The Appeal, February 8th, 1876. Memphis (Tenn.).

"On Sunday night one of the largest and most thoroughly representative audiences ever gathered in the theatre assembled to hear Victoria C. Woodhull. By eight o'clock every seat was occupied. The bench and the bar, the press and the medical profession, as well as the mercantile, the mechanical, and the labouring classes, were fully and ably represented, and the faces of all present indicated, especially after the fair lecturess made her appearance, a very tension of interest. Mrs. Woodhull entered upon the work before her without introduction or preliminary—indeed, almost abruptly. This, however, was pardonable in view of the visible effect her appearance worked, and when it is remembered that she had hardly opened her mouth ere her mastery, so to speak, was confessed. At first her words came slowly, deliberately—indeed, nervously; but once fairly launched upon her theme, the flow of ideas and words was steady and rapid, both occasionally merging into periods as startling, as eloquent, and beautiful as any ever delivered by the best orators of our language. At times she reached the loftiest flight of forensic effort, and roused her audience from the repose of a death-like stillness to most enthusiastic applause. Every point she made was caught by the audience, and was greeted as it deserved. Five or six times this applause was delivered with unusual fervour, and with an enthusiasm that surprised even those most favourably inclined towards the lecturer, who so nobly contended for her sex; and at the close, when, after what seemed vain efforts on her part to take her leave, she finally bade adieu, the most deafening and prolonged shouts recalled her again and again to receive the warm and generous plaudits of those who had listened with pleasure and profit to one of the most logical and able lectures ever delivered in Memphis upon any subject—if not the ablest. She answered every call, until at last, breaking through all form and ceremony, hundreds, both old and young, stepped upon the stage and

personally congratulated her upon her success, each one giving
assurances of satisfaction and gratification. Among these were
many ladies, and most conspicuous of all the young men—
gentlemen of position and culture—some of whom, failing of
opportunity on the stage, followed her to the hotel, and through
the medium of ordinary introduction expressed to her the most
unbounded gratitude for the instruction given them."

Constitution, February 10th, 1876. Atlanta (Ga.).

" Shortly after eight o'clock Mrs. Woodhull walked upon the
stage in a home-like way. She is a lady of commanding presence, fine carriage, good features, and an expression full of force
and intellectual energy. She has persuasive eloquence, fiery
energy, and an earnestness whose genuineness cannot be questioned. She is a woman of great ability, and states her views
with singular clearness and force. She was frequently applauded
with a will, and when she retired from the stage the demonstration was as enthusiastic as any orator or actor could desire."

Herald, February 10th, 1876. Atlanta (Ga.).

" A fair audience assembled at the Opera House last night to
hear the lecture of Mrs. Woodhull. When she appeared upon
the stage we saw a handsome woman, handsomely dressed.

" There was a quiver in her voice that betokened at first
thought a dash of diffidence and timidity. As the lecture proceeded, it seemed to be more like a tremor of tears in the pleading
of a woman for a place in the hearts of the people, one who had
suffered, one who had deep feelings of philanthropy and
affection, and who did not wish to be cast out from the affections
of her kind. The concluding portion of her lecture, in which
this feeling was stated, was of a moving and melting character.
Her picture of her trials, her separation from her daughter, and
that daughter's brave answer of love and loyalty, of the scene in
prison where, kneeling in prayer, she felt that she had had a

revelation of the future love of the people, and her appeal for that love, was eloquent and touching.

"The central idea was a reform of dissolute lives—the necessity existing for this in every corner of the land established by unvarying statistics. The method of reform suggested was to teach the child by fathers and mothers, specially by mothers, that the body is the temple of God. In doing this we must be true to nature, state facts just as they exist in nature, give all children information in regard to all matters pertaining to nature, the origin of life, the necessity of purity, the result of criminal indulgence, without the false modesty which too generally prevails.

"The sacredness of motherhood was a prominent idea in the lecture. The mother reproduced in the son, was a favourite thought urged with great force and beauty. No one could hear the appeal for purity in connection with that holy name and tie without an obeisance of reverence, perhaps a memory of tears.

"She maintained that reverence for the Bible was a cardinal point in her faith, and insisted that by some admission or in some form such a reverence was universal.

"There was nothing which would have been considered vulgar or improper in a scientific lecture from a physiological, medical professor to young men. The truth stated as to the prevalence of prostitution and its evil effects were undeniable, the ground taken against it, both in males and females, among married and unmarried, only such as any moral man and woman could take.

"There were, here and there, fine touches of humour, but the humour without the sting of sarcasm—it taunted without wounding. There were sallies of wit, bursts of eloquence, in words and act, brilliant passages of genuine oratory. As we have stated, the pathos of the lecture touched its every part as with gentle and quivering light, whose tremulous plea fell upon the heart already influenced by argument and aroused by appeal."

The New Orleans Times, February 11th, 1876. Memphis Tenn.).

Letter from Mrs. E. A. MERRIWETHER.

"MY DEAR E.—Yours of February 7 received. I would have replied, but Mrs. Woodhull has driven everything else for the nonce away. She is *grand!* she is *great!* she is *good!* She has wonderfully improved since I heard her in '72; *then* she was at bay with the world, and threw her gauntlet down and dared it to battle. The battle has been waged, the most unequal battle ever fought on earth.

"On one side the church, the press, the prejudiced world; on the other, a woman! And a woman has whipped the trio! Never was so tremendous a revolution! I will send you the *Appeal* with its plaudits. The theatre was crowded from pit to dome; she held them spellbound for two hours. I saw men and women weep, so passionate are her pleadings for the downcast. Those who did not hear her are crazy to hear her. If you see her beg her to give us one more lecture.—Yours, E. A. MERRIWETHER."

Herald, February 18th, 1876 (Editorial). Atlanta (Ga.).

"MRS. WOODHULL'S LECTURE.—The idea running through Mrs. Woodhull's lecture at De Give's Opera House last night made a powerful impression on the very respectable audience of intelligent gentlemen and ladies who heard her. The difficulty connected with the lecture was the reconciliation of the subject with feminine delineation of it.

"A scientific professor discussing the theory, that she elaborated before a college of students, would seem a very fit advocate of her views. And certainly if the lecture had been delivered by such a person before such an audience, its utterances would have been and must have been pronounced strikingly philosophical, full of well-considered reflection, and worthy of careful thought.

" The difficulty of accustoming one's self to the discussion of the delicate theme by a woman before a mixed audience of both sexes is hard to get over. *That over*, the impartial critic must own that Mrs. Woodhull spoke a deal of prominent truth, and grappled with live problems in a strong manner.

" Mrs. Woodhull grappled with the great social problems of human procreation, and to check the progress of disease and vice. She dealt largely in statistics of crime and sickness in illustration of her views. She contended that the production of a nobler race of people depended upon an intelligent understanding of the great laws of nature and a conformity to those laws. There was no mincing of words in her lecture in the portrayal of disagreeable things. She proved herself the possessor of a strong intellect, with unusual powers of fluent and forcible expression. She showed herself well posted upon statistics of human experience.

" We again repeat that had her lecture been heard from a professor in the curriculum of the university, we are frank to say, it would have been deemed orthodox and correct. Coming from a handsome woman on the rostrum before a social audience, it kept a Southern hearer in a sort of a whirl of revolutionary protest, due to the very audacious innovation upon deep-rooted prejudices."

Daily Picayune, February 21st, 1876. New Orleans (La.).

" Last night Mrs. Victoria C. Woodhull made her first appearance before a New Orleans audience at St. Patrick's Hall. Owing to a fire which occurred across the street, and the impediment offered for some time, the audience was not as large as it would otherwise doubtless have been. Notwithstanding this, there must have been some fifteen hundred persons present, about two hundred of whom were ladies—young, middle-aged, and old. It was decidedly an intellectual audience.

" At 8.15 Mrs. Woodhull stepped upon the platform, and her

appearance was the signal for a unanimous burst of applause. After a few words of an introductory character, she gave out the text of the discourse.

" Text from 1 Corinthians iii. 16-17 :

" ' Know ye not that ye are the temple of God, and that the Spirit of God dwelleth in you?

" ' If any man defile the temple of God, him shall God destroy; for the temple of God is holy, which temple ye are.'

" In her lecture she first treated of the ethnical constitution of Americans, and the result to ensue from the merging of many nationalities into one. She then proceeded to elaborate upon those themes of social interest developed in her interview with the Picayune reporter last Wednesday, first stating her opinion of the world, and its practices at the present day, then treating of the duties of parents towards their children, the conditions on which marriage should be contracted, wherein she would exact an equal amount of purity from both the contracting parties.

" Her speech was very rapid, but distinct, and every word was well rounded and articulated. Her gestures were few and easy, and her face would betimes light up with that fiery energy which sparkled in her eyes. The interruptions were few, for the audience paid rapt attention throughout, and only at times would they break out into applause, which, when they did, was unanimous and ' long drawn out.'

" At 9.30 Mrs. Woodhull retired from the platform laden with offerings of flowers, and amid a general expression of enthusiasm."

Republican, February 21st, 1876. New Orleans (La.).

" This lady has succeeded in attracting a good deal of interest in the minds of all classes of thinking citizens. Aside from the novelty of seeing a woman on the rostrum, or appearing before a New Orleans public as the champion of an idea or the witness of great truths, there is a sort of magnetic charm in the perfectly easy manners, the earnestness bordering on enthusiasm, and the great self-possession of this remarkable lady who fills the public eye.

" She holds up a mirror in which very many of the poor struggling integers of humanity see anything but complimentary reflections of themselves. We may admit her facts to be true, and address ourselves to the inquiry, Is her proposed remedy — the intelligence of women—adequate for the great evil ? And to pursue it further, is the high condition of intelligence which she demands for all mothers in America, for the whole world in fact, feasible or even possible ? None who heard her on Sunday night at St. Patrick's Hall can doubt she is thoroughly a good womanly woman, with a heart full of love for her species, and a most intelligent appreciation of everything that is beautiful in human love and a true religion of the heart.

" She speaks with great fluency and apparently with ease. It is next to impossible for a skilful stenographer to keep up with her, though the gist of her remarks is easy to retain in the memory."

Bulletin, February 22nd, 1876. New Orleans (La.).

" Notwithstanding the fact that a fire occurred opposite St. Patrick's Hall, Sunday night, just before the hour advertised for the opening of Mrs. Woodhull's lecture, a large and respectable audience attended to listen to the progressive views of that lady. Not only gentlemen attended, but the fair sex was well represented, fully one-fourth of the crowd being ladies.

" After some little delay, on account of the fire, Mrs. Victoria Woodhull entered, and taking a position near the centre of the stage, read her text.

" In her exordium she called the attention of her hearers to the fact that neither in written history nor tradition has the conduct and action of the human race been such as to leave upon the mind of an impartial reader the impression that any

people ever gave evidence that the body was regarded in a light
as sacred as the book of Divine inspiration intended.

" Following this, Mrs. Woodhull, with much power and grace
of diction, alluded to many interesting questions of society,
being frequently interrupted by the applause of her listeners.

" She leaves for Galveston this morning, where she intends
to lecture also."

News, February 28th, 1876.   Galveston (Texas).

" The announcement that Mrs. Victoria C. Woodhull was to
lecture in this city was sufficient to set everyone agog, and
develop the greatest amount of curiosity and comment.

" Sunday evening, the appointed time for the first appearance
of this distinguished lady, the Opera House was completely
filled in the parquette and parquette circle, while numbers were
obliged to seek seats in the circle in the second tier.

" Promptly at eight o'clock the curtain rolled up, disclosing
the set-drawing-room scene, and immediately thereafter Mrs.
Woodhull made her appearance, having in her hand a small
morocco-bound copy of the New Testament.

" Beginning in a low, earnest tone, Mrs. Woodhull gradually
became infused with her subject, until her words rang out like
hailstones on a roof, and carrying her audience along with her,
she won repeated and hearty applause as the telling point was
made. At the conclusion of the lecture a large number of the
gentlemen who had ladies with them took them on the stage,
and were introduced to Mrs. Woodhull, thanking her for the
fearless manner in which she spoke her convictions, and for the
new light she had thrown on them."

The Age, March 2nd, 1876.   Houston (Texas).

" There was a large audience of ladies and gentlemen at the
Opera House last night, to listen to the discourse of Mrs.
Woodhull upon social science. She came upon the stage with

a Bible in her hand, and dressed in an elegant velvet costume, which set off to great advantage her commanding figure. She took her usual text from first Corinthians, and began speaking in a low, nervous, and exceedingly rapid manner upon the ethnological phase of the world. Gliding out of this, her voice, gathering in strength, broke forth into periods of great oratorical power, freighted with magnetism of earnestness and depth of feeling which captivated her auditory, and bore it along with her to the close of her remarks. She denounced marriages of convenience as the gravest sins against God and nature. She sanctifies the human body as being the 'temple of God,' which no man or woman should dare profane. She urged that man should be as pure as woman; that young men should have the same moral test applied to them when seeking marriage as is now applied to young women. She depicted the duties and responsibilities of maternity, and portrayed its sacredness in colours of astounding impressiveness.

"She spoke on in the same nervous, rapid manner for more than an hour and a half, without pausing for the applause which ever and anon broke forth spontaneously from the audience in response to her telling hits. We rarely ever beheld an assemblage of any kind so completely under the influence of a speaker. Men and ladies were to be seen brushing the tears from their eyes as the pathos of this strange woman went home to their hearts, linking them together in that chain of common sympathy whose weird spell no individual present could successfully resist if they would. Many of the most thoughtful, intelligeı ' and prominent citizens of Houston were present to hear Mrs. Woodhull, and the unanimous voice of these attested that they discovered nothing to condemn in what she said, but on the contrary, much to commend.

"At the close of the lecture a lady advanced along the dress-circle and threw a bouquet upon the stage, which thoroughly interpreted the feeling of the entire auditory. Instead of leaving the Opera House, as is usual when an entertainment closes, the crowd seemed inclined to move towards the stage, and many did so, to be introduced to Mrs. Woodhull. If we had been told that such a scene as was there witnessed could have been possible in a Southern city, with Mrs. Woodhull as the central figure, we would have failed to realize it. It was wonderful, overwhelming, and astonishing to the last degree, and actual presence was necessary to fully appreciate it."

News, March 7th, 1876. Galveston (Texas).

"Mrs. Woodhull's lecture last evening drew a much larger house than on the occasion of its first delivery, and the proportion of ladies was much greater, and the greatest interest was manifested throughout the lecture, many of the ladies remaining, after it was over, to be introduced to Mrs. Woodhull. As a whole the lecture appeared to give *even* more satisfaction than her first appearance in this city."

The Daily Statesman, March 9th, 1876. Dallas (Texas).

"It is a great pity that every mother, father, daughter, and son in Austin, able to think reasonably, could not have been present last night to listen to the lecture of Mrs. Woodhull. It was a moral discourse, surpassing anything related to it that has ever been delivered in this city. If the world could think and act as she taught, man would become so ennobled as indeed to make of him the 'Temple of God.' She would teach man to be pure, and she believes the way for the world to become purified and man ennobled is for the mothers of the earth to cultivate the acquaintance of their children, to make them their confidants, and to teach them from childhood their true origin and the dangers that await them in society. And this is the great social question, about which, through ignorance, she has been anathematized. She would lift mankind into a higher sphere, out of which there would come a noble aspiration which

34

would purify the races of the earth. She claims that mankind should never become enchained by ignorance and vice, and that daughters should be reared to protect themselves against marriage contracts with men not as pure as themselves. Her discourse was elegant and pure, and she held her audience so enchained that the ending of it was met with universal regret. She will lecture again to-night, by special request, her proposed theme being ' Woman's Curse,' and we express the belief that there was not a husband or son who listened to her through her discourse last night who is not anxious to have the wife or mother to hear her."

The Statesman, March 10th, 1876. Austin (Texas).

" Mrs. Woodhull's second lecture at the Opera House last night was more largely attended than the first; fully one-half were ladies of the *élite* of Austin. In the most thrilling, glowing sentences she depicted the thraldom of woman, owing, as she claims, to the sense of false modesty which prevails; and exhorted the women, as mothers, to emancipate themselves, to rise to a true sense of their dignity, and to endeavour to rear a ' race of gods and goddesses.' She hails with joy the approaching millennium of free discussion, through the medium of the press, of truths which have heretofore remained as a sealed book. The auditors were held spellbound by her simple, unaffected eloquence, and bursts of applause were frequent, demonstrating the fact that her words carried conviction to the hearts of the hearers."

The Statesman, March 11th, 1876. Austin (Texas).

" Mrs. Woodhull was called back to Giddings by a committee of gentlemen and ladies who. being so well pleased with the first lecture, tendered her an ovation which should cause her to feel proud of the conquest won. She leaves the Lone Star State for her home in New York City, laden with laurels nobly battled for and cheerfully given. Mrs. W. is accompanied on her southern tour by her beautiful and talented sister and mother, the appearance of the latter of whom is that of a courtly lady."

The **Herald**, March 16th, 1876. Dallas (Texas).

" There was a large number in attendance at the theatre last
night. Mrs. Woodhull came before them, held her listeners
enthralled by her powers of oratory, by her beauty, by her
finished address, by the statements of undeniable truths that
struck conviction to the heart of every intelligent person within
the sound of her voice. What she said may have grated harshly on
the ears of some; but it was because the knife of facts and figures
cut away the diseased cancer of ignorance or wilful blindness
that has been eating into our hearts, and as yet no physician has
been found skilful or daring enough to probe the fester to the
bottom. We wish that every mother in our city could have
heard her last night, listened to her as with a mother's love, a
mother's experience, and the deep feeling that must be felt by
every true mother, plead in piteous tones for the more perfect
enlightenment of the rising generations. Her heart was in her
voice, and deep down into the sanctum of every breast sank the
barbed arrow of self-condemnation as they listened to her words,
and felt that she too plainly exposed the injury and neglect our
children sustain from those who love them best through a false
delicacy. Many gentlemen were there who are thankful that
they embraced the opportunity to hear, and who emphatically
stated that if she would remain another night, they would be
only too glad to have their wives, mothers and sisters attend.
There were men there, too, who went out of a prurient curiosity,
expecting to hear that which would pander to their depraved
tastes; but we will venture to assert that those same men left
the hall feeling that they had received a just and merited rebuke,
and who will hereafter speak of the lady who addressed them
last night in far different terms than what they did previously.
Mrs. Woodhull has done a great work here. She has dropped
good seed that will fall on fertile ground and bring forth the
perfect fruit. And wherever she goes, and in whatever city she

visits, she will receive no more hearty welcome than in Dallas, should she ever return here."

The Waller County Courier, March 16th, 1876. Hempstead (Texas).

" The lady whose name heads this article lectured last Sunday evening to one of the largest and most respectable audiences ever assembled in the city of Hempstead to hear a lecture on any subject."

The Stylus, Monthly Magazine, April, 1876. Austin (Texas).

" On the 8th and 9th ultimo our State capital was thrown out of the usual and monotonous groove of apathy and lassitude by entertaining as its guest the famous and renowned Mrs. Victoria C. Woodhull. Upon two consecutive nights she lectured in the Opera House before large and respectful audiences of ladies and gentlemen. The subjects of discourses were ' The True and False, Socially,' and ' Woman's Curse.'

" No uneasiness or embarrassment was visible in her features when she first appeared before her audience, and the same coolness and self-possession was maintained throughout the evening. Without any introduction whatever, she began to speak, and not many minutes had passed before the telling truths of her discourse were greeted with long and continued applause. Every eye in the audience seemed riveted upon her, and every ear seemed to be chained to the very rock of attention.

" Judging from her lectures, we have no hesitancy in saying that she is mistress of one of the finest and most powerful intellects with which in modern years nature has endowed womankind ; and again the beautiful and poetical ideas that were contained in almost every sentence, portrayed that she was also gifted with rare and brilliant fancy. Her diction is classical, limpid, and musical—arising at times to such a degree of eloquence and pathos, that it borders on the very edge of sublimity. But the greatest and most laudable virtue of her lecture is that she speaks truth—truth that finds an echo and a sanction in every generous and unprejudiced heart.

" But, in conclusion, without averring that we accept and endorse her doctrines, we will suggest the idea, that if every divine in the land would preach with her fervour and feeling, and throw aside all ' Mock Modesty,' while occupying the sacred pulpit, that not many years would elapse before the world would be rejoicing in the twilight haze of the sinless era of the great millenium."

Argus, April 7th, 1876. Brooklyn (N.Y.).

" Mrs. Victoria C. Woodhull stepped upon the stage of the Academy of Music last evening, with a morocco bound copy of the Bible in her hand, and read in the presence of fully twelve hundred people these words :

" ' Know ye not that ye are the temple of God, and that the spirit of God dwelleth in you ?

" ' If any man defile the temple of God, him shall God destroy; for the temple of God is holy, which temple ye are.'

" Mrs. Woodhull was frequently applauded."

New York Daily Sun, Friday, April 14th, 1876.

WOODHULL AND BEECHER.

VICTORIA CLAIMS THAT SHE IS BEING PERSECUTED—THE GREAT SCANDAL.

To the Editor of The Sun,—Sir, With surprise I have read your statement of the Beecher-Woodhull persecution, and the hot blood of indignation was roused in me to find the same spirit that prompted that persecution continued by the *Sun* in its reference to, and insinuations about me. To judge of "Woodhull" by your article it could be imagined that she might be, and probably is, something below which there is nothing. I had thought that the day for this sort of stuff was past. But let me glean the subtle stabs, the dark hints and blind insinuations from the article, of which no hold can be obtained to show what they mean, but which, nevertheless, are envenomed barbs well

35

calculated to pierce the remaining shreds of reputation which the outspoken persecution to which you refer had left us:

"To appreciate the atrocity of this persecution, it is not necessary to commit the mind to any sympathy for the woman personally; it is not even necessary to dispossess the mind of prejudice against or contempt for her opinions and deeds. * * * It enabled them to inaugurate a persecution cowardly and cruel, almost without parallel, and which would have been recognised immediately as such, had the victim been other than she was. * * * To form this estimate impartially it is necessary to imagine Plymouth Church, Noah Davis, A. Comstock, and the rest, combining to crush some person who is not a Woodhull."

Prejudice and contempt for her opinions and deeds! What opinions? What deeds? Does the *Sun* mean the opinions that she has been represented to hold by the press in its misrepresentations of her and them, or those which she really holds and which the press, after having misstated them, has refused upon proper occasion to state them correctly? Does the *Sun* mean the deeds which it has been insinuated by the press that she has committed, spread broadcast over the land to poison the people against her, or those which constitute her real life? Are they the imaginary figments of envenomed brains, pumped up into the public mind to help on the very persecution that the *Sun* criticises, or the actual experiences of the woman's life? What opinions? I repeat. My own opinions, set forth by myself before the two hundred or more audiences whom I have addressed in the last eight months, have been universally endorsed. Is it these opinions that, in the estimation of the *Sun*, entitle me to public contempt, or are they not rather those which the press has endeavoured to foist upon the public as mine, but which I utterly repudiate and reject, and which the *Sun* should know that I repudiate and reject, because it has had the opportunity to know? Let my opinions be properly and fairly presented to any audience that can be gathered from the most conservative circles of any society, and they will be endorsed. Why, then, should the *Sun* present them to the public as something to merit contempt?

And the same for her deeds. I repeat: What deeds? We have been traced from our cradles through every place in which we have ever resided, to our prisons, by detectives paid without stint by friends of Mr. Beecher, to fasten some single deed upon us that might be brought into court to be put in evidence against us, and they failed to find a blemish even. All the vile insinuations of dark deeds and darker lives, when traced vanished into thin air in the mouths of their inventors. After passing such a crucial ordeal as this, is it not time that we should cease to be pursued by the press, after the fashion of the *Sun's* article? It seems so to me. But if it do not to the press, why do they not rummage the mass of filth, and from its vile depth exhume some one fact to substantiate the insinuation of deeds that merit contempt?

But again: "Had the victim been other than what she was;" "to crush some person who is not a Woodhull." Worse and worse, and wherefore? The muddle into which the *Sun* has fallen about her opinions and deeds has caused it to reverse the facts in this case. It was because the victim was a Woodhull, was a Claflin, who possessed the sympathy and had the assistance of some of the best and noblest people in the world, who knew us, and who extended their sympathy and assistance because they knew us to be just what we were, that we were not convicted and railroaded to Sing Sing in ten days, according to the original programme. It was the strong hands and the strong support of these people, whose names it is not necessary to parade to the world, and their knowledge of the purity of our lives, the honesty of our motives, and the intentions of our movements, that defeated the infamous conspiracy. Had any part of the foul things that have been paraded before the world about us had any foundation in fact, there would have been no hope for us; and the *Sun*, if it have any conception of the spirit of the persecution, knows it well enough. It was because no part of them was true that we were not and could not be crushed;

35 *

and, for the same reason, our complete vindication is a question of time only.

But beyond all this, the proceedings that were instituted against us would never have been possible had it not been for the course of the press for six months previous to the publication of the *exposé*. For a year or more before that publication many, if not most, of the editorial offices in this city were in possession of the facts therein set forth; but no hint even ever found its way into any of the papers that Mr. Beecher was other than he should be. From the very day, however, that it became known to the press that I was also in possession of the same facts, and it was surmised that I might make them public, I became the target at which were shot off every ridiculous, improbable, and impossible shaft of vituperative abuse.

Had not the press thus prepared the way for outrage that was perpetrated upon us in the name of the law, Noah Davis would never have dared to issue the warrant for our arrest, nor his assistant to shamelessly declare, in open court, that the outrage was perpetrated because it was "well worth the while of the United States to vindicate the reputation of a revered citizen" by such an infamy. As the *Sun* says, "it was a persecution without parallel," and being so, is it to be supposed that the Church could have made use of the machinery of the courts as it did, unless the court officials were well assured that the press would wink at the outrages; aye, more, that it would receive its support and countenance? Nor were they mistaken, since the farcical proceedings by which we were committed to jail without a hearing were fully reported by the press, even to the very words of the District Attorney about vindicating the revered citizen, without a word of adverse comment. Hence, I say, that let the responsibility of Mr. Beecher and the time-serving officials be as great as it may for their part in the persecutions, that of the press is still greater for having first made it possible.

The press of the West and South, where I have been lecturing during the greater part of the season, upon hearing the statement of my theories, and the defence of my course, acknowledged that, following the lead of the New York press, they had done me a great wrong, and they did what they could to repair the injury. Instead of misrepresenting my opinions, and sending reporters to my lectures instructed, as were some at a recent lecture of mine in this city, " to make no report unless there should be a row," they gave honest representations of what I said. When the New York press shall do this tardy justice to a woman upon whom it has made it possible for the world to lay heavy hands, the bugaboo about " her opinions and deeds " will be exploded. This will come at last, though it may, perhaps, be delayed until I am passed away. But I have a fair daughter just budding into womanhood, to whom I wish to leave an untarnished name. It is for her sake, much more than for my own, that I pray for life and strength to pursue the lies with which my reputation has been blackened into every town and hamlet of the country where they have penetrated, and wisdom sufficient to catch and crush the foul things, so that their venom shall not embitter her future.

VICTORIA C. WOODHULL.

New York City,
April 10th, 1876.

Press, April 17th, 1876.   Providence (R.I.).

" Mrs. Victoria C. Woodhull appeared at the Opera House last evening, and delivered her lecture on ' The Human Body the Temple of God,' before a very large audience.

" The curtain rose at 8 o'clock.   Mrs. Woodhull soon entered by the rear entrance, walking to the footlights, looking intently at an open Bible, which she carried in her hand.   After standing for a moment she read two passages from second Corinthians as a sort of text.   At first she was slow in her delivery, but soon she warmed with her subject.

"Of the lecture itself much might be said. It was an exposition of the extreme views held by the lady on the social question. Her ideas have truth and justice on their side, particularly those referring to an equal condemnation of excesses of both sexes. The lady made a favourable impression and liberal applause greeted the passages which could not fail of stirring every pure heart.

"Should Mrs. Woodhull visit this city again she would be sure of a crowded house. She is surely as eloquent and enthusiastic a lecturer as adorns the public rostrum."

"Providence, R.I., U.S.A.

"Dearest Victoria,

"Sweet, loving, beautiful, as your two letters have been to me, I can only say just a word in reply, and that is, you stand in my heart foremost among the living. I have never for a moment felt like wrapping you in cere cloth and burying you out of sight. I have been with you in prison, in bondage, and in sickness. My heart yearns over you with more than a mother's tenderness, but I am a helpless invalid, waiting for my hour of departure; then, when I have laid aside the worn body, then I shall be near to help you; till then let me have rest. Believe in me, believe that I never betrayed a trust, never was false to a friend, and that at times truth is dearer to me than aught else in this life, but there are times when silence is all there is for me. My heart turns to you with tender, longing love. I remember you in the bitter Gethsemane in Philadelphia; then I saw that you must tread the wine-press alone. From the other side I shall see you at the moment of transfiguration. You must not publish this till I have passed beyond the veil, for I cannot enter in controversy and cannot endure letters.

"Lovingly yours,
"Paulina Wright Davis.

"I long for your loving words."

[This letter was written to Mrs. Woodhull a few months

before the death of Mrs. Davis, it having been reported by malicious people that Mrs. Davis ignored Mrs. Woodhull.]

New York Herald, May 6th, 1876. New York City.

"MRS.VICTORIA C.WOODHULL'S LECTURE.—The large hall of the Cooper Institute was filled last evening with a very respectable audience, assembled to hear Mrs. Woodhull.

"Mrs. Woodhull read several verses from the third chapter of Genesis, containing God's promise to woman that her seed should crush the head of the serpent. She said that redemption from the ills that affect humanity must come from woman, and that in order that they may fit themselves for their mission they should study the marital question in all its details and responsibilities. She denounced the practice of rearing girls for the matrimonial market, and insisted on woman's right to claim from her husband the same purity he expected from her. The mother should be the teacher of her family and the confessor of her child; and, in order to do this properly, should imitate the purity of the Virgin Mary. Here Mrs. Woodhull turned to a small statue of the Virgin, which was placed on a pedestal in the centre of the stage, and with much force called on all present, both male and female, to cherish and cultivate purity, and there would be no use for penitentiaries and prisons, no necessity for hanging men for murder, for murder would soon cease to exist; and thus intelligent mothers knowing their duties would bring forth virtuous children, and by that means cause vice to vanish from the world, and crush the head of the serpent. Mrs. Woodhull was frequently and loudly applauded."

New York Sun, May 6th, 1876. New York City.

"Mrs. Victoria C. Woodhull had a large audience in the Cooper Institute Hall last evening."

Register, May 20th, 1876. Newark (N.J.).

"Last evening Mrs. Woodhull lectured at Library Hall on a topic that is nearest to her heart. Mrs. Woodhull appeared in a dress of black cashmere, trimmed with silk, and no ornaments except a creamy-hearted rose at her throat. She stood there, and, with her great womanly heart, pleads for the elevation of all womankind. She has an easy, graceful action, a free and unembarrassed delivery, and her words are uttered with an earnestness which rivets the attention of the audience to the close. Such is her earnestness and the magic of her presence that there are scarcely any who come to hear prepared to condemn, that they do not go away deeply impressed by her words and captivated by her manners. There is no levity in Mrs. Woodhull's lecture. It is full of fire and enthusiasm, and even the coldest moralist or critic cannot help feeling that the woman is fully impressed with a generous belief in her 'mission' and feels all that she utters. Her words are a direct unequivocal arraignment of the abuses of society, marriage, the birth and training of children, and all the relations of our social life. She does not pause to express her meaning in indirect phrase, being apparently in too much earnest to select her language; and yet, listening to her address, the auditor cannot find aught to disapprove, either in the ideas or the words used. All through the lecture the closest attention was paid the speaker, and several times her remarks were heartly applauded.

"The lecture was concluded about half-past nine o'clock, and Mrs. Woodhull upon retiring was recalled upon the stage by the applause of the audience."

May 20th, 1876. Newark (N.J.).

"Mrs. Woodhull lectured at Library Hall last evening to an appreciative audience. Mrs. Woodhull declared that it was useless to discuss suffrage until the women of this country had raised up a better race of men. She was bold, as usual, in proclaiming the cause of insanity and crime, and said that if she could get the ears of the women of this country, in twenty-five years there would not be an insane asylum nor an incarcerated person in the land. She dwelt upon facts, and such facts as would be well for the mothers of this country to consider."

Sunday Sun, Brooklyn, N.Y., June, 1876.
WOODHULL AND CLAFLIN.
An Interview with the Ladies at their Home.
How they Speak and Act—A Talk with their Aged Parents.

"The most interesting hours which your correspondent passed in the Empire City were spent last evening at the home of the great female agitators, Victoria C. Woodhull and Tennie C. Claflin. Persons who know these ladies but through the straight-laced, narrow-minded and prejudiced channels of what is called society, have no just or true perception of their real worth or standing. A very few years ago it was considered indecent for females to advocate any cause, no matter how high or holy, before the public, but in the present century the old order of things changes with a wonderful rapidity. Now, women of culture and intellect are seen in the pulpit, are heard at the bar, are greeted on the rostrum, and the public are naturally interested in knowing something of the private lives of those who have displayed the nerve and bravery required to put themselves forward as the advocates of the rights of their sex in defiance of old prejudices.

"The reader who has but casually heard of Mrs. Woodhull or Miss Claflin may be inclined to form an extremely false and unjust idea relative to their lives and principles. The ladies have selected a peculiarly quaint and appropriate portion of the city for their residence. They live at 127, East Tenth Street, within one door of the church where the remains of the late merchant prince, A. T. Stewart, repose. In the immediate vicinity the descendents of the old Knickerbocker families reside. The families of the Stuyvesants, Kimballs, Fishes, and many others of their type, are here permanent fixtures. The neighbourhood is quiet and aristocratic, the place in fact to call forth and develop the strongest impulses of the soul, the spot where broad ideas and great principles love to germinate and ripen.

"Your correspondent had some difficulty in obtaining an audience with the ladies. They have recently returned from a lecturing tour through the Southern cities where they received a perfect ovation, being unable to attend to one half of the demands made on their brain and physical endurance. As a consequence, they require rest, and are averse to receiving visitors, but your correspondent was fortunate enough to gain admittance. Their residence is furnished in palatial style ; expense appears to have been entirely disregarded—the carpetings, the paintings, the ornaments, are all that art and taste could desire.

" The house is occupied by Miss Claflin, Mrs. Woodhull and her two children, and the aged parents of the ladies. Mr. Claflin, their father, is now four-score years, and is still hale and hearty. He stands six feet high and bears a commanding and dignified personal appearance. Some years ago he retired from the practice of the law. While at the bar he commanded universal respect both on account of his clear and learned views on abstruse legal matters and because of the honourable manner in which he carried himself through his professional career. As a boy, he was the most promising of the family, and as a man, he won the respect of all who knew him. In his prime he was the bosom friend and counsellor of Governor Snyder, of Pennsylvania, and of many of the most prominent men in the State. He was tendered many political positions, which he invariably declined, preferring the serenity of private life. Mr. Claflin's opinion was respected as the decision of a court, and lawyers and litigants considered a case won or lost as he might decide it to be strong or weak. In private life he was a model. He refrained from the use of stimulants of all kinds. He was an affectionate and exemplary father. His one vice, if vice it may be called, was a fondness for fast horses. His great anxiety appeared to be for the training and education of his children, so as to enable them, if it became necessary, to fight the battle of life on their own account. That his work was successful and great in results the remarkable history of his children demonstrates.

535

"If Mr. Claflin was an extraordinary man, his estimable wife may be considered more extraordinary. It is stated that a mother feels the pangs of her children. Who does not know what pangs these children have endured? For publishing the truth they have been scoffed at, been defamed, been belied, been cast into prison, have endured sufferings which must be felt to be known. All these sufferings the mother endured, and it is a miracle that she escaped through the ordeal alive. But God appears to bestow unusual powers of endurance on those of His servants whom He has appointed to special destinies. This lady bore ten children, and in speaking of them to the writer the aged mother was very much affected. She spoke of her children as the pride of her life; said she wanted all her children, and prayed at the time of her marriage that she would have a peculiar family, zealous of good works. In her early life Mrs. Claflin was a Methodist; latterly she has become a member of the Roman Catholic Church. She was always a strictly religious woman. She states that during the sixty years of her married life she never had an unpleasant word with her husband, and, indeed, it would be a difficult matter to find a family that have the evidences of union and happiness and of perfect accord more strongly marked than those now residing at No. 127, East Tenth Street. It is but natural that those ladies should revere such a mother; and that they do so is evidenced by the fact that they take her along wherever they go. In the last few years she has travelled an amazing distance—has been to Europe, and has several times traversed the length and breadth of the United States. In fact, she cannot endure separation from her favourite daughters, Victoria and Tennie.

The Claflin family are descended on the maternal side from the old German family of the Hummels, whose ancestors were of royal blood. Mr. Claflin himself comes from one of the oldest and most aristocratic houses in England. Branches of the family are to be found in almost every part of the United States; and wherever met they display a rare amount of ability,

and always appear as moral and high-spirited citizens. No
better commendation can be given to the family than to state
the fact that no one of their ancestry was ever a drunkard, a
prostitute, a convict, or a pauper; and in this degenerate age
this is a most remarkable matter, and can only be accounted for
by presuming that the purity and dignity of their blood was
sufficient to counterbalance all adverse influences and to enable
them to steer an honourable and independent course.

"Having gleaned the facts above narrated from a general
conversation with the ladies, the question of their business
career was next referred to, and the main points gathered from
the interview are given below. And here I will state that the
writer of this was the first newspaper correspondent who ever
published an interview with these remarkable women in the
year 1870. This was some months prior to the opening of their
banking house on Broad Street. Since then no one need to be
told what a world of suffering they have endured; what a flood
of falsehood and calumny was heaped on their devoted heads; how
the members of a wealthy Church, and the emissaries of an association calling itself Christian, have sought to trample them into
the dust, and brand them as felons, but time is the greatest
adjuster of human affairs. To-day the Mesdames Woodhull and
Claflin seem as young and as active as when your correspondent
first met them. They are welcomed and applauded whenever
they appear in public, while their persecutors stand in a very
awkward position before the country.

"Never before have women taken up and maintained their
own cause with such boldness and power, and it may be long
before the like is again witnessed. They reverted in a feeling
and impassioned manner to the difficulties that had been thrown
in their way, and recounted the battles they had fought in
vindication of the rights of their sex. The following are some
of the points they dwell on. They started many years ago to
combat the prejudice that existed against women receiving the
same compensation as men for the same labour, and they

preached the doctrine that men should be bound by the same rules of morality in their lives as women. Everybody now accepts that doctrine as sound, and for advocating this truth their reward was scoffs and persecution. A woman of ordinary nerve would have shrunk from the ordeal and sunk away from view under this outrageous treatment. But Victoria and Tennie have proved that their nerves are made of steel, and can give blows as well as receive them. They believed they had a right to speculate in the stock market. They did so, and opened a banking house, where they did a large and successful business. This was the first and only bank ever conducted by women. Having proved their ability in the Stock Exchange, they next started a newspaper, which was ably managed, and the pungency of their articles created many sensations throughout the country. Mrs. Woodhull believing in the right of her sex to vote and hold office, ran for the Presidency of the United States in 1872, and was well supported. It is stated that the ladies are now perfecting another novel and striking enterprize, of which the country will be made aware before long. To enable them to recuperate and work the matter up, the publication of their *Weekly* is temporarily suspended, and a trip to the Old World was advised by their physician.

" It is needless to state that wealthy women of their boldness and originality are not labouring and preaching merely for money. They have a higher and purer motive, the teaching and the elevation of the sex, and in their labours to that end have expended fortunes. They feel impelled to pursue their career while they breathe, rather than lead a life of ease and quiet, as they could well afford to do. There is something that excites one's admiration in the heroic manner they conduct the warfare. They go on their way as a dart from a bow. Their sayings are misrepresented. They regard this not. They labour on steadily regardless of the opinion of thoughtless and malicious enemies. The experience of Mrs. Woodhull has been the most remarkable of any on the American or European Continents. Subjected to

the scorn and contumely of a very large class of respectable
people, she has always associated with the most learned savants
of both hemispheres, and enjoyed to a wonderful degree their
esteem and admiration. No ordinary woman could have
sustained herself under the circumstances which have surrounded Mrs. Woodhull. Adverse fate, at times, seemed to
have almost buried her out of sight, but she has come through
all her perils unscathed.

"Prison gates and persecution do not cool the ardour of those
women. They appear to be dead, but reappear in their
writings and teachings more eloquent than before. Their
maligners tremble as though a sword of fire gleamed before
their eyes. In a free country, under a free government, never
before was man or woman so ruthlessly assailed for giving
expression to just and healthful doctrines. But this is only a
repetition of the old Bible truth, referred to by the Redeemer
where He encourages His followers, saying : 'They have
persecuted Me, they will persecute you also.' Expose the
naked deformity and the vile corruption of modern fashionable
society, then society will turn on you and strike you to the
earth if within its power. That those ladies have survived the
fierce contest and are still living, happy and prosperous, is a
proof that the God of nature has sustained them. The royal
blood of their ancestors and their fine personal physique have
borne them through the contest. The movement, which began
with a gloomy air around, will end in brilliancy, and the names
of the leading spirits who steered the vessel through the storm
will be remembered long after their mortal remains are consigned to Mother Earth.

—————

"Many of the noblest men and women of the country now
came forward in her support. The poet, William Cullen
Bryant, addressed a touching sonnet to her. The venerable
lady, Lucretia Mott, embraced her in the midst of a public
enthusiasm. The well-known Mrs. Stanton declared, 'I have

worked thirty years for woman suffrage, now I am made to feel
that woman suffrage is but the vestibule of woman's emancipation. Victoria Woodhull had done a work for women that
none of us could have done.' And Mrs. Isabella Beecher
Hooker, sister of the Rev. H. Ward Beecher, said : 'Mrs.
Woodhull has, with her prostrate body, bridged a chasm over
which womanhood shall walk to freedom.' "

The Item, July 7th, 1876. Philadelphia.

A MODERN JOAN OF ARC.

MRS. VICTORIA WOODHULL'S WONDERFUL WORK FOR REFORM.
EVENTFUL LIFE OF A REMARKABLE WOMAN—UNDAUNTED BY
SNEERS OR DUNGEONS—AN ILLUSTRATION OF PLUCK AND
PERSEVERANCE.

"All movements in each of the departments of an organized
human society have special inspiration ; have some special
person around whom cluster the various facts to which they
owe their advancement, and from whom, more than any
other, proceed the steps by which they advance. Nor does
the fact that others than this special one come into a movement
to add to its momentum, perhaps to introduce new departures,
affect the truth of this statement.

"But this fact, which is common to all movements among
people, is especially marked in the Woman's Movement in this
country, for among the galaxy of great and good and noble
women, to each of whom it owes something, there stands one
name prominent as having given to it both impulse and character. It is altogether improbable that Luther was the one who
first conceived the idea of opposition to Papal rule over the
conscience ; nor was Garrison the first to raise his voice against
the existence of slavery. Before Luther hundreds of hearts
had rebelled against the power of Rome, and before Garrison
thousands had felt the wrongs of those who toiled in slavery
beneath the burning heat of 'The Sunny South'; nevertheless it was Luther who raised that opposition into an organized

the scorn and contumely of a very large class of respectable
people, she has always associated with the most learned savants
of both hemispheres, and enjoyed to a wonderful degree their
esteem and admiration. No ordinary woman could have
sustained herself under the circumstances which have surrounded Mrs. Woodhull. Adverse fate, at times, seemed to
have almost buried her out of sight, but she has come through
all her perils unscathed.

"Prison gates and persecution do not cool the ardour of those
women. They appear to be dead, but reappear in their
writings and teachings more eloquent than before. Their
maligners tremble as though a sword of fire gleamed before
their eyes. In a free country, under a free government, never
before was man or woman so ruthlessly assailed for giving
expression to just and healthful doctrines. But this is only a
repetition of the old Bible truth, referred to by the Redeemer
where He encourages His followers, saying : 'They have
persecuted Me, they will persecute you also.' Expose the
naked deformity and the vile corruption of modern fashionable
society, then society will turn on you and strike you to the
earth if within its power. That those ladies have survived the
fierce contest and are still living, happy and prosperous, is a
proof that the God of nature has sustained them. The royal
blood of their ancestors and their fine personal physique have
borne them through the contest. The movement, which began
with a gloomy air around, will end in brilliancy, and the names
of the leading spirits who steered the vessel through the storm
will be remembered long after their mortal remains are consigned to Mother Earth.

"Many of the noblest men and women of the country now
came forward in her support. The poet, William Cullen
Bryant, addressed a touching sonnet to her. The venerable
lady, Lucretia Mott, embraced her in the midst of a public
enthusiasm. The well-known Mrs. Stanton declared, ' I have

others engaged for years in agitating the subject; true, that they
were earnest, honest, able women who were doing this; but
their labour was the guerilla warfare that did not even indicate
where the decisive battle was to be fought, and they were most
unjustly looked upon as a set of restless women, who, being
unsatisfied with their condition, resorted to this agitation as a
means of public notoriety, and as an outlet for their unrest and
domestic discontent.

" Let their labour be, however, regarded in the most favourable light, it was purely negative in its methods and purposes.
They went about it as if what they wanted was a favour which
those in power might be induced by their pleading to con-
descendingly bestow upon them. It was a privilege that they
asked at the hands of their legal masters, which they might or
might not grant them, and be consistent either way.

" To be sure they pleaded the benefits that would result from
the introduction of the woman element into politics; but this
part of their method was a disadvantage rather than otherwise,
since the politicians to whom they pleaded knew well enough
the truth of what they said, and for this very reason discoun-
tenanced the movement. They did not want a moral element in
politics to operate against their corrupt purposes and plans.
They knew that a Credit Mobilier was impossible in a Congress
composed partly of women, and so the pleadings of the women
had no effect upon them, other than to make them still more
determined not to grant what they were asked to do.

" But with the advent of Victoria C. Woodhull all this
changed. She bearded the lion in his den; she armed herself
with the Constitution, with the plain language of the organic
law of the country, and went to the National Capital, and
demanded what was hers by right. Her memorial, which was
introduced into the Senate by Mr. Harris of Louisiana, and into
the House of Representatives by Mr. Julian of Indiana, on
December 21st, 1870, fell like a clap of thunder, not only upon

36

Congress, but upon the whole country. By its audacious boldness, not less than by its logical statement of the law, it chal-
lenged and commanded the attention of the political and
journalistic world, and through them that of all the people at
large. Here was a new departure; a new and entirely unheard-
of proposition, made by a new and almost unknown champion of
the cause, who sprung herself and her reading of the Constitution
upon the country without any preliminary notice whatever.
Disdaining the slow and tedious methods of going before the
people, to urge them to action, she pounced upon Congress, and
almost wrested from it an admission of the legality of her
claim.

"Congress saw danger to Man's usurpation of the government
in this new champion for her sex, saw not only a woman but a
statesman and orator, capable of both comprehending and
defending Constitutional law, saw not a woman tearfully pleading
to be admitted to political equality upon the argument that it
would be a moral benefit to the country, but one who knew that
she had a right to be a political equal with man, and with
courage to face the highest legislative tribunal in the country
with her demand, and to call the government that withheld it
an usurpation. So unexpected an attack from such an unexpected quarter, and made in such a novel and unique manner,
with the dash of the woman combined with the diplomatic discrimination of the wiliest man, disconcerted the Congressmen,
and, scarcely knowing what they did, her memorial was not
objected to by anybody, and was referred to the Judiciary
Committee. Had there been any intimation of what was going
to be sprung upon them they would have been prepared to
quietly dispose of the whole business, but coming as it did,
they were surprised into doing just what the memorialist desired.
By this brilliant piece of strategy on the part of Mrs. Woodhull,
the movement of woman suffrage was lifted up from the plane
of special pleadings of expediency into a question of constitu-

tional law, where it will remain until it shall occupy her place in legislative halls, side by side with her brother, Man.

"Nor did Mrs. Woodhull's strategy begin and end with the simple introduction of her memorial into Congress. Upon the morning of its introduction, each Congressman found upon his desk a neatly printed copy of the memorial, together with a statement of the principal reasons for the claim, which reasons will stand for ever as the most concise as well as complete argument that can be offered for it. As was foreseen by Mrs. Woodhull, these brief documents were copied into the press all over the country on account of their novelty and originality, and thus by a movement, which for brilliancy of conception and successful carrying out will compare favourably with any ever made in any quarter for any purpose, the proposition, that Woman, under the Constitution, is entitled to the ballot, in a day became a national question, having a country-wide reputation, and with it the name of Victoria C. Woodhull rose at once into the ascendant in the Woman movement, in which position time and history will make it only the more prominent.

"But she did not let the movement sleep in the committee-room. She plied the members of the Judiciary Committee, and found several of them whom she compelled to acknowledge that her claim was right, and that it could not be successfully combated for any length of time; while General Butler of Massachusetts, and Judge Loughridge, of Iowa, felt the question to be of sufficient importance to demand a thorough consideration, and they prepared an elaborate and exhaustive report upon it, which will stand for all time a monument to their comprehensive judgment of constitutional law, as well as to the nonpartisan character of their statesmanship. It is not too much to say that their argument was unanswerable, that it never was answered, and that it can never be answered. Not only did General Butler thus cast his powerful influence upon this new

36 *

view of the subject, but he appeared upon the rostrum when Mrs. Woodhull delivered her first public address upon it, and fortified her argument by many legal propositions.

"Up to this time Mrs. Woodhull had never been identified with the Suffrage movement, and was barely known to the women who were engaged in its agitation. And here again her diplomacy appears in strong contrast to the usual woman method, for she so arranged the introduction of her memorial into Congress that it fell upon the eve of the Convention of the National Woman's Suffrage Association in Washington. As she anticipated, her brilliant movement captured the Convention, and the Association at once adopted her view of the Constitution, and invited her to a prominent place in its deliberations; and from that time she was regarded, by the women themselves, as the Joan of Arc of the movement.

"Besides all this she was rich, and did not hesitate to use her resources to forward anything she took in hand. The majority and the minority reports of the Judiciary Committee she had printed, and together with her memorial and argument she spread broadcast over the country. It is said that she expended not less than $10,000 in this propaganda alone, during the winter and spring of 1870-71, while her paper, *Woodhull & Claflin's Weekly*, almost wholly devoted to the subject, was to be found in every editor's room and in all public places throughout the country, as well as wherever in the world the English language is read. It is not to be wondered at that her accession to the ranks of the Suffragists was hailed with delight by those who regarded the National Association with favour, nor that it was received with dismay and vituperative abuse by the leaders of the American wing of the movement. But in spite of all the opposition that has been made to her view of the Constitution, it has come to be accepted by the best legal talent of the country as the law, and upon general principles it may be admitted that from the moment it acquired the national reputation spoken of above,

it was virtually conceded to be the law, although it may require
some further time to have it so recognized by the government
and to have the law take practical effect. It is, however, an
open question whether, if Mrs. Woodhull's plans could have all
been carried out, women would not have now been enjoying their
right to vote. But jealousies and divisions sprang up among
the advocates, which for a time defeated her. She conceived
the idea of organizing a great party, of consolidating into one
movement all the factions of reform movements in the country,
and of thus gaining the balance of power and of forcing one of
the great political parties into adopting her measures. She
even went so far as to draft a new Constitution which was an
embodiment of her political, industrial, and social views. But
the leaders of the various movements which she sought to bring
together, saw in her a rival of their ambitions, and, rather than
succeed with her, they chose at least present failure by themselves.

"This, however, did not deter Mrs. Woodhull from carrying
forward her propaganda after her own methods. She left the
movements, in which she had been interested, to struggle by
themselves as best they might, and for their principles to take
deeper root in the minds of the people, while she stumped the
country from Maine to California, and from Minnesota to Texas,
thrusting into public attention the principles that lie back of all
reform movements, and commanding the respect of all by her
earnestness of purpose, her brilliant oratory, and her comprehensive intellect.

"Without controversy, her campaign of last season, beginning
August 18th, at Albany, N.Y., and ending in Texas, was the
most brilliant ever accorded to any orator, and has marked a
revolution in the minds of the people regarding her real social
views. With one accord the press has been unanimous in her
behalf, and she now stands before the country, not as the avowed
advocate of social degradation, as she had been supposed to be,

but as the priestess of a new and higher order of purity and chastity than the world had ever before conceived of as possible; as the incarnation of womanly virtue, dignity, and capacity, and as such she is being enshrined in the hearts of a class of people who will eventually accord her the position to which she legitimately belongs.

"A striking result of her labours will be found in the Cincinnati Platform. The Republican Convention asserts as a Republican doctrine that the just powers of a government are derived from the consent of the governed, and that the honest demands of Women should be treated with respectful consideration, which is admitting the whole question of equal suffrage. This party has been actually driven to this position. For not only has Mrs. Woodhull been the Joan of Arc of the Woman movement, but she has been its Cervantes also, and has compelled the 'male usurpers' of the Government, by the keenness of her sarcasm, by the bitterness of her ridicule and by the cutting satire of her wit, after her logic and arguments were exhausted without the desired result, to admit in their declarations of principles that which they must soon enact in law. And this is all there remains to be done to fully invest Woman with her constitutional rights and prerogatives, and to crown with complete success the movements so brilliantly and auspiciously inaugurated in Congress in January, 1871.

"And then, should such a consummation react upon her, who has been its inspiration? In the natural order of events, there can be no mistaking what her future position will be. She is a natural born leader, possessing all the attributes to command all the capacities to govern, all the traits to attract, and besides she is a regal woman, having the bearing and presence of a queen among women. To all this she adds a spotless life and a devotion to truth and principles that never can be swerved by any inducement. With such a record of labour as she has,

with this character to give it strength and adding the lustre of
virtue to the whole, no power under Heaven can prevent her
being borne by the hearts of the people to the nation's pedestal
of honour by a triumphant acclamation such as this country has
never witnessed since it bestowed its highest gift upon the
Father of his Country, an acclamation that would pronounce its
subject to be the saviour of her sex, and as such the greatest
benefactor of the race of modern time, for Woman is the Mother
—the Architect of Humanity."

The Times, September 12th, 1876. Hamilton (Canada).

" Last evening, at the Mechanics' Hall, Victoria C. Woodhull
made her first appearance in Canada as a lecturer. There was a
respectable audience, who listened to the lecturer with marked
attention. Mrs. Woodhull is a lady of prepossessing appearance ; she is very eloquent, and her delivery is excellent.
Mrs. Woodhull treats in a masterly manner the social vices
and humbugs of the day, and her advice to mothers is well
worthy of consideration. At the commencement of the lecture,
one could not imagine that the quiet-looking woman who was
speaking in such subdued tones, could become so thoroughly
enrapt in her subject as to rise to the extremity of passion and
bring down the house with enthusiasm. But such is the case,
and on several occasions last evening, when her hits were
hardest, she was loudly applauded. The lecture, as we said
before, was an excellent one, and many who went last night
prejudiced against Mrs. Woodhull left the hall with a totally
different opinion, and should she lecture in Hamilton again, we
are sure she will have densely crowded houses."

Daily Herald, October 2nd, 1876. Boston (Mass.).

" Paine-Memorial Hall last evening was filled to overflowing
by people of both sexes, while hundreds were turned away unable

to find admittance. Tickets during the hour previous to the opening sold for one dollar and upwards, and they were purchased without question. An analysis of the audience showed some of the brightest lights of Boston society, women no less than men, attracted thither to see and study the woman who for four years has been the subject of the keenest criticism. About five minutes before eight o'clock Mrs. Woodhull appeared upon the platform from a side room, where she had been waiting with her mother, and was greeted with enthusiastic and long-continued applause. Her hair was loosely dressed, and during her delivery (which was highly dramatic and sometimes painfully emotional), often found its way over her brow and face, and was frequently brushed back impetuously to repeat its wayward pranks ere she had removed her hand. Holding a Bible in her hand, she began her lecture by quoting from Corinthians iii. 16-17, to show that the human body, her subject, was the temple of God. The lecture was the most striking one ever delivered in Boston, and was listened to with the utmost attention and with frequent applause. In chaste and refined language the lecturer dissected the marital relations, and probably told more truth in one short hour than has yet been heard in Boston. A full report will be found in another column."

Boston Herald, October 2nd, 1876.

EXTRACTS FROM LECTURE.

"The Boston Theatre, last evening, was filled to overflowing with people of both sexes. An analysis of the audience showed some of the brightest lights of Boston society. About five minutes before eight o'clock, Mrs. Woodhull appeared upon the platform from a side room, where she had been waiting with her mother, and was greeted with enthusiastic and long-continued applause. Holding a Bible in her hand, she began her lecture by quoting from Corinthians iii. 16, 17, to show that the human body, her subject, was the temple of God. She said there were hundreds of thousands of women all over the country now waiting in quiet, painful, agonizing watchfulness for society to recognize her true needs in her great and pitiful extremity. 'My only desire is to bring the world to look upon the frightful evils now fast spreading their pernicious influence, their incalculably bad example everywhere abroad over this beautiful world of nature and of God, and I have been denied a hearing. For four years the halls of Boston have been closed to me, but I know that the time is near when every mother, realizing her position, and every father informing himself as to his, will no longer allow Mrs. Woodhull to sue in vain for admittance. The time is near when our best people will view this question I discuss in its proper light; will convince themselves that it must be settled before any advancement can be made in the condition of society. The time is coming when everyone of any intelligence will see that there is nothing vulgar save ignorance. (Loud applause.) When this is thoroughly understood there will be no more opposition to freedom of speech. If there is any gentleman in this place to-night who thinks this is not a fit entertainment to which to bring his wife or daughter, he had better leave at once, for every place that is fit for him is fit for either his wife or child.' (Applause.) Speaking of her recent visit to Europe, and alluding to the Paris Louvre, and the large number of paintings and sculpture on exhibition there, Mrs. Woodhull said the sight brought a blush to none save the countenances of ignorant women. The vulgarity was not in the pictures nor in the sculpture, she said, but in the minds of the observers. She would teach the young woman of the country her true position, and what belongs to her as a woman, and the rights she has to guard and the privileges she has to insist upon. She would teach the young man of the world what every mother should teach her boy, to respect every other mother's daughter. 'I demand the same purity of the man who asks the woman's hand in marriage that is demanded of her. Society, if forced to admit the truth, would acknowledge, as women in society have acknowledged to me, that if women asked the same purity of men that these ask of women, there would be fewer marriages.' The speaker here pictured the horrible agony that racks a woman's breast who lives to follow her child to the gallows, and spoke of the crowded state of our prisons and houses of refuge. She said : 'I ask of every mother never to bear a child that can by any possibility fill a criminal cell or an idiot room. I ask that our mothers understand in all its importance this mighty problem; I ask that the ignorance which now hides it from her vision be at once and for ever dissipated, even though it exposes the truth in all its horrible and ghastly realism. You patronize horse trots and cattle shows; you discuss publicly, and have it reported in the newspapers, how to raise Durham bulls, and how to create fine stallions, and how to graft the good elements of one animal into those of another, and nobody remarks it; but if the poor mother, torn by conflicting emotions, racked with an agony none but a mother can conceive or realize, cries out in despair, "In the name of God, tell me how to create my child; tell me, in order that I shall not bear an idiot or a criminal," everyone would hold up their hands in holy horror. "Oh! she's vulgar; don't go near her," they would say. Who that boasts an acquaintance with the matter, will dare deny the fact, that one-half of our young men are dying of disease, induced by ignorance of the axiom " Know thyself;" seven-tenths of our girls arrive at maternity unfit, totally and entirely unfit, for the functions of a woman and a mother. The evil began and perhaps reached fruition at a boarding-school. We inquire, " Is this so ?" and receive the answer, "Yes, but don't speak of it," and thus it goes on. How many intelligent parents in this audience to-night dare tell their children the truth about the first question that a child thinks of asking?' The speaker then pictured a child asking its mother the question, 'Who made me?' and being told to 'Hush, and never talk so again,' how that child learns the fact upon the street, and acts upon it secretly, and learns to conceal its knowledge from the parent who taught it concealment. She then drew another picture of the child's receiving the information it sought, from a holy woman, a pure mother—'*Who made you, darling?* Mamma carried you under her heart days, weeks, and weary months, and at last went into the Garden of Gethsemane to bear you into the world. Now, my precious child, you can see why mamma loves you so; why she would give her life to save yours'—and basing its whole after-life and the current of its thoughts and actions on that frank avowal; she said, in conclusion, that child would never commit an act of which it would not dare tell its mother, because its mother had rendered concealment unnecessary and out of the question. When you understand this mighty problem of proper generation, all the mock modesty you have hitherto felt will die within you, and to this understanding the ideas Mrs. Woodhull have put forth will lead. The medical world says that one-half of our children do not reach the age of five years, and the reason is plainly apparent to any who understand the problem of proper generation. Not one in a thousand women is fit to become a mother, and the number of men fit to become fathers is still less. People call me a Free-Lover. The first place I ever heard the word free-love mentioned was in a Methodist church. The minister was holding one of those protracted meetings, and telling everybody to come forward to the mourner's bench where the love of God was free to all. There for the first time the idea that this was true struck me to fruition.

God is love, and love is God. Who dare tell me, to-night, that the love of God is not as free to me as to you? On the one side is pure, undefiled love; on the other is abominable enforced lust. I appeal for the former, and my appeal has closed the halls of Boston to me for four years. Your abominable lust I abhor, and God's intelligent love I adore.' (Applause.) Speaking again of a mother's influence, she said, ' how can a boy with the pleading, imploring face of his lady mother before him boldly and calmly meditate crime? The very face of such a mother checks all incentive to crime. Mothers of Boston, she said, become the teachers of your own families; become the confessor of your boy, and make it impossible for him ever to become reckless and unmanly. To-night, if I had the power, I would make it impossible—I would make it a crime for men and women to marry ignorant of parental responsibility. They have no right to marry and people these abominable institutions, for it is almost entirely from such sources that the recruits to these places come from. I want our people to recognize the divinity of marriage in its broadest and its deepest sense. I hold that when two people come together they ought to understand the responsibilities of marriage. When our mothers teach their sons the responsibility of creating a human being, and when they teach their daughters the great responsibility of maternity, you will have your son saying, "Mother, dare I marry?" and your daughter saying, "Mother, I do not know that I am worthy of marriage." (Applause.) A mother should proceed with the enthusiasm and the conception of her subject that an artist possesses. Besides her pride in her production as a mother, she should have an æsthetic feeling of satisfaction with the completeness and the thoroughness of the result she produces.' The speaker then drew a portrait of the common errands of mammas at the watering-places to dispose of their daughters in as business-like a manner as possible.

'I know hundreds of women,' said the speaker, 'who are in
sympathy, in strong sympathy with the views I advance,
who cannot render practical assistance because they would
forfeit the respect of society and their kindred. But what
do I suffer in this respect while fighting the terrible fight?
Oh, God! how few there are who have a just conception of
what agony I have endured. People who are afraid of losing
their respectability usually have none to lose. The woman
who cannot listen to a discussion of the great question of
proper generation, ought not to be allowed to become a
mother.' Resuming the discussion of the subject of the
human body as the temple of God, she said: 'This great truth,
for which I am pleading and giving up my life, must be
settled before any further advancement can be made. As
long as the mothers of America read the statement in the
daily papers unblushingly that one thousand criminals had
descended from one Margaret, surely I have nothing to fear
in the discussion of this question, save the ignorance that
makes such a statement possible. Our mothers will not teach
their children what they should, above all others, acquire
perfect knowledge of. Women are responsible for almost all
the misery and evil that accurse the country to-day.' The
speaker then described the many and peculiar influences to
which the woman subjects the child during the period of
gestation. Why close your halls to Mrs. Woodhull, and
oppose her errand to strip the veil which hides from the
people the engulfing dangers that surround them? 'I have
only to wait; the future will redress the wrongs that have
been done me. In my soul I have no ill-feeling for anyone
who has ever uttered a harsh or vulgar word about me.
During the four years you have persecuted me I have taken
my children and walked the streets of New York seeking for
admittance here, admittance there, with my little girl's arms
about my neck. I have suffered as no mother ever suffered

before, and it is because I have suffered so deeply that I am here to-night to put forth my claim. It will be granted, if not for the woman, but for the principle. You cannot crush me in the future any more than you have crushed me in the past: you cannot heap any more indignities upon my head; time will right me, and the near future establish my principles.' She closed her address at ten o'clock. Her thanks to the audience were interrupted by long-continued applause."

The Boston Times, October 22nd, 1876. Boston.

VICTORIA C. WOODHULL

HER FAREWELL LECTURE, "THE REVIEW OF A CENTURY; OR,
THE FRUIT OF FIVE THOUSAND YEARS."

"Victoria C. Woodhull leaves this country shortly for Europe, and has prepared a new lecture, which will be her farewell utterance. It is full of instruction, and presents new social ideas in a fresh and thoroughly effective manner. It is entitled 'The Review of a Century; or, The Fruit of Five Thousand Years.'"

Daily Globe, October 23rd, 1876. Boston (Mass.).

"Mrs. Woodhull has spoken in this city. The Boston Theatre was crowded; and, from the beginning to the close of her discourse, which occupied an hour and twenty minutes in delivery, the closest and most respectful attention was given her. At forty-nine minutes past seven she walked upon the platform, much after the manner of the late Charlotte Cushman in Queen Elizabeth, with haughty mien and measured tread, with a copy of the Bible in her hands. She was attired in a brown silk, tasteful and becoming, with lace at the throat and at the cuffs, and with a single rose upon her breast. She looked imposing and handsome, and her dramatic action at once captivated the audience. The lecture itself was probably one of the most remarkable ever delivered in Boston, and the many truths told last night will long be remembered by the hearers. Mrs. Woodhull met with frequent applause, and her lecture was warmly commended."

Daily Advertiser, October 23rd, 1876. Boston (Mass.).

"Victoria C. Woodhull lectured last evening in the Boston Theatre on ' The Human Body the Temple of God.' The theatre was filled to overflowing with an audience comparing favourably, on the whole, in point of respectability and intelligence, with the audience of a popular entertainment, including the proportion of ladies usual in such entertainments. The majority were evidently in general sympathy with the speaker. Mrs. Woodhull appeared on the platform, without introduction, tastefully attired. a rose at the throat being the nearest approach to ornament in the costume. She walked upon the platform carrying an open Bible in her hands, and the first words she uttered were the passages in the New Testament wherein the body is spoken of as the temple of God. Her manner was prepossessing, and her tone of the greatest earnestness. As a lecturer her style is intensely dramatic, and indeed her whole effort was one piece of acting, worthy of some of our most prominent stage favourites, and calculated to impress even the most determined opponents of her views. This was especially noticeable towards the close, when in pleading for a fair, impartial judgment of herself and her views, her language and movements became in the highest degree impassioned. Her lecture was interrupted by the presentation of a floral device, representing a broken anchor, and again at the close, a little child, dressed in white, ascended the platform and crowned her with a floral wreath. There was much eloquence and poetry in her language, and she retired amid hearty applause.

"It was a most remarkable lecture, delivered by the most remarkable woman in America."

Daily Journal, October 23rd, 1876 (Editorial). Boston (Mass.).

"Boston Theatre was crowded last night to its utmost capacity, by the best people of Boston, to hear Victoria C. Woodhull's new and startling lecture, entitled 'The Human Body the Temple of God.' Although the lecture was not advertised to commence till eight, there was not a seat or even standing room at half-past seven. At this time as high as two or three dollars were offered for admission, without avail. The lecture itself was one of the most startling expositions of the marriage relations ever heard, all in the most chaste, proper, and refined language. The lecturer was listened to with profound attention and frequently met with the most rapturous applause. A full report of the lecture will be found in another column."

Public Record, November 7th, 1876. Philadelphia.

"Concert Hall was filled last evening with intelligent ladies and gentlemen, who had assembled there to hear a lecture by Victoria C. Woodhull, the subject being 'The Human Body the Temple of God' (1 Cor. iii. 16, 17). Promptly at eight o'clock the curtain was raised, and Mrs. Woodhull, with an open Bible in her hand, advanced to the footlights and read the above-quoted text from Corinthians. She spoke one hour and thirty-five minutes, was dramatic at times and eloquent, and received rounds of applause.

"After concluding the lecture, the applause was continued until she acknowledged the compliment three times, by appearing before the curtain."

The Times, November 7th, 1876. Philadelphia (Pa.).

"The announcement that Victoria C. Woodhull would lecture last night was sufficient to fill Concert Hall with an audience of intelligence and respectability. One-third of those present were ladies. Occupying front seats were prominent residents of the city. Mrs. Woodhull's appearance was the signal for prolonged applause. The greater part of Mrs. Woodhull's lecture was taken up in showing that crime and misery result from the improper and vicious education of the young. Her utterances were greeted with applause, and at the close of her speech she was brought before the curtain three times."

The Item, November 7th, 1876. Philadelphia (Pa.).

" Alas! for a great woman born before her time! Noble, pure, eloquent, and independent, Victoria C. Woodhull has, with all the ardour and all the sacrificing devotedness of a noble woman's heart, given her life and her grand grasping mind to the espousal of her sex's cause, and, through that cause, the cause of all humanity.

" Ill-understood, prejudice has hurled its avalanches at her, at times nearly crushing her; and ingratitude is her only recompense for her noble and devoted work.

" Her flaming words find receptive ears; her grand principles of goodness, love, and piety command journalistic protection. The *Item* considers it one of the loftiest duties of its mission to announce to the public the true character of this much-defamed, good woman.

" Last evening was the occasion of her Star Lecture to a Philadelphia audience, at the Concert Hall. The house was crowded. The audience was composed chiefly of ladies.

" At a little after eight the curtain rose. In a moment Mrs. Woodhull appeared. A woman, beautiful, majestic, magnetic, with a face brimming over with emotive eloquence, and an eye full of keen intelligence. She came upon the stage Bible in hand, and with a self-possessed action.

" Mrs. Woodhull began by portraying, in words that burned with fire and struck home into every heart, the utter baseness, selfishness, and corruption that permeated society.

" In one sense society had uplifted its head to a peak of

37

civilization. Yet, at the same time, it was rotting away at the roots. Other civilizations had rotted and died, and this modern one, of which we are so proud, would also die and be swept from all remembrance, unless we could stop in our course, check the rot in the root, and cure our civilization of its threatened terrible disease.

"As a panacea for the disease of modern civilization, Mrs. Woodhull offered woman's influence. It was woman that made the criminals, for women were the mothers of the criminals, and had neglected to bring them up as good men. It was woman, and woman alone, that could save humanity; for in her lay the power to check all evil tendencies in infancy, and imbue her children with great and glorious principles of stedfastness in righteousness.

"Mrs. Woodhull concluded with such emotive power and eloquence that no one's eyes among her audience but were moist.

"Her words cannot be reflected in a printed column. No one can describe her speech and manners, and the magnetic influence with which she entrances her audience. She must be seen and heard to be appreciated.

"Oh! that her voice might reach every mother's heart; that it might encourage the faltering and reclaim the wicked.

"Victoria C. Woodhull is one of the greatest, one of the best, one of the purest of women."

Press, November 7th, 1876. Philadelphia (Pa.).

"Sunday night lectures in public halls, and on secular subjects, are a rarity in Philadelphia, and to the presence of such a notable woman as Mrs. Victoria Woodhull the crowded audience which last evening assembled in Concert Hall was due. Long before the doors were opened it was evident that the audience would be large. The crowd surged in a continuous stream, and by eight o'clock there were no vacant seats in the hall. It was an audience of decided respectability. A liberal

sprinkling of the theatrical profession ; it was generally such a
crowd as one sees in the better-class place of amusement. Of
elegant carriage, and with a fine intellectual face, she was
en rapport with the audience at once. Taking up a Bible, she
began in a well-modulated voice. She spoke in a strong, earnest
manner, commending the purity of life, and deprecating the
evils of modern society. She condemned the two great parties
of the country for corruption, venality, and profligacy, and fore-
told a bloody revolution in this continent unless a thorough
reconstruction of the present system took place. Storms of
applause greeted even the most radical expressions. After
speaking for an hour and twenty minutes, Mrs. Woodhull
concluded. She was brought three times before the curtain by
the long-continued applause. At the conclusion, a number of
ladies and gentlemen remained to pay their respects to the lady,
and to congratulate her on the evident success of her lecture."

1877.

Commercial Advertiser, January 7th, 1877. New York City.

" The interior of the building was literally jammed, and a dense throng outside, who could not gain an entrance, choked up Irving Place, and poured over into Fourteenth Street, and there they stood for more than an hour, until the close of the ' lecture.' In speaking of this strange scene, a morning journal says that it was a crowd of ten thousand persons, composed of ' rich and high-toned, elegantly-dressed ladies of acknowledged respectability, bankers, brokers, merchants, ministers, doctors— in fact, all professions were largely represented.' "

The New York Sun, January 7th, 1877. New York City.

" Chickering Hall was crowded last evening—boxes, floor, and galleries."

The New York Tribune, January 7th, 1877. New York City.

" The social problem never had a better advocate than Victoria C. Woodhull proved herself to be last evening. The announcement that she would speak drew together a crowd such as the Academy of Music never before contained ; a crowd which filled the hall completely—seats, aisles, and galleries."

Free Press, June 15th, 1877. London (Canada).

" MRS. WOODHULL'S LECTURE.—Those who heard her address were forcibly struck with the boldness and eloquence with which she dealt with the various questions of social reform which are attracting attention the world over. Topics that are tabooed in general society, that the clergy avoid, and physicians ignore, as she alleges, from the motive of self-interest, but which she asserts ought in reality to be the basis of every woman's edu cation. Mrs. Woodhull launched into with a directness and vigour of tact and argument which were suggestive of powerful con viction on her part, and of chaste and noble inspiration. For the practice of the *roué*, and the false sentiment which excused notorious unchastity on the one side while making purity a first condition on the other, she expressed her utmost abhorrence; she believed the influence of mothers, properly and intelligently exerted, to be equal to the complete physical and moral regeneration of the world; and the fulfilment of the natural conditions within their reach would result in a race of gods, in place of monsters and mental and moral pigmies which make up so large a proportion of mankind. There was nothing in her discourse inconsistent with a pure philosophy, or which might not be heard with advantage by those who, through false shame, continue in ignorance, and are prevented from investigating the truth of nature. At the close she was greeted with prolonged applause."

The Mail, June 22nd, 1877. Toronto (Canada).

" Victoria Claflin Woodhull ; a lady whose career has been as singular as any heroine's in a romance ; whose ability is of a rare and whose character of the rarest type ; whose personal sufferings are of themselves a whole drama of pathos ; whose position as a representative of her sex in the greatest reform of modern times, renders her an object of peculiar interest to her fellow-citizens.

" The malice of enemies, together with her bold opinion on social questions, have combined to give her reputation a stain. But no slander ever fell on any human soul with greater injustice. A more unsullied woman does not walk the earth. She carries in her very face the fair legend of a character kept pure by a sacred fire within, whose chief ambition is finally to present herself at the supreme tribunal 'spotless, and without wrinkle, or blemish, or any such thing.'

" The lady from her birth up has been the common property of the American public. She has defied slander and bitter persecution in the cause of humanity. To understand this great intellectual woman, we cannot do better than detail for our readers a brief sketch of her extraordinary career.

" Mrs. Woodhull as the zealous advocate of the cause of liberty and humanity has had many bitter persecutions to contend against ; indeed, to such an excess have they been carried, that it is truly wonderful how the lady has successfully, single-handed, combated them with triumph and honour to herself and admirers.

" There can be no doubt but that the career of this remarkable woman has been one of the most wonderful that ever attended the life of any individual. The opposition she has met and overcome, the persecutions that she has survived, and the calumnies outlived, all point to a wonderful character, and prophesy an extraordinary career.

" Had not some more than human power been present with her, she would long since have sunk beneath the forces that have sought to crush her. The greatest wonder now among her opponents is that she is alive, from the fact that she has survived what would have crushed any other person. At one time she had not only the whole of the Church and the Government arrayed against her, and determined on her destruction, but their immense power was enforced by the weight of the country.

" But she never faltered ; in her darkest hour her faith in her destiny sustained her.

" In her case the old miracle is enacted anew—the faith which removes mountains. A soul set on edge is a conquering weapon in the battle of life. Such, and of Damascus temper, is hers.

" In 1870, she founded a bank and published a journal. These two events at once gave her a world-wide celebrity.

" Aft r this movement she entered the world of politics, and by her hard-working, conscientious exposure of some of the most grievous errors and acts on record, she did more good for the American nation than half our greatest statesmen combined, the memorable document now known in history as 'The Memorial of Victoria C. Woodhull'—a petition addressed to Congress, claiming under the 14th and 15th amendment the right of women, as of other, citizens of the United States, 'to vote in the States wherein they reside'—asking, moreover, that the State of New York, of which she was a citizen, should be restrained by Federal authority from preventing the exercise of this constitutional right, is enrolled in history as the second declaration of Independence, and the lady herself from whose brain the strange document had sprung, like Minerva from the head of Jove, took the novel demand to Washington, where, after a few days of laughing from the shallow-minded. and of neglect from the indifferent, it suddenly burst upon the Federal Capital like a storm, and then spanned it like a rainbow. She went before the Judiciary Committee, and delivered an argument in support of her claim to the franchise under the new amendments, which some who heard it pronounced as one of the ablest efforts which they have ever heard on any subject. She caught the listening ears of Senator Carpenter, General Butler, Judge Woodward, George W. Julien, General Ashley, Judge Loughridge, and other able statesmen in Congress, and harnessed these gentlemen as steeds to her chariot. Such was the force of her appeal that the whole city rushed together to hear it, like the Athenians to the market-place when Demosthenes stood in his own and not a borrowed clay. A great audience, one of the finest ever gathered in the capital, assembled to hear her defend her thesis in the first public speech of her life.

"Assisted by staunch and able women, whom she swiftly persuaded into accepting this construction of the Constitution, she succeeded, after her petition was denied by a majority of the Judiciary Committee, in a minority report in its favour, signed jointly by General Benjamin F. Butler, of Massachusetts, and Judge Loughridge. To have obtained this report from

General Butler, the ablest head in the House of Representatives, was sufficient to entitle the brave lady to an enrolment in the political history of her country.

"Next we find this wonderfully gifted woman on the lecture platform, when she delivered masterly and inspired orations on politics, finance, and the most abstruse problems in political economy. The master minds of ¦America went to hear her with avidity, and were in most instances so struck with the depth of her acumen and judgment in the matters she lectured on, that they were forced to express their admiration in public, and some have said that if Demosthenes could arise and speak English, he could hardly excel the fierce light and heat of some of the sentences which have been heard from this singular woman in her glowing hours.

"In the spring of 1872 the United States advocates of political equality, anxious to render practical their views, having duly constructed a platform of principles, nominated Mrs. Victoria C. Woodhull as a candidate for the presidency. Thus the 'Equal Rights Party,' represented by twenty-six States and four territories, and over five hundred delegates in solemn National Convention, brought forward a woman for the highest office in the gift of the people to bestow.

"At the close of a speech made the evening before the day fixed for making the nominations, the Convention, amid the wildest enthusiasm, nominated the speaker by acclamation for the first place on the ticket, and the name of Victoria C. Woodhull was given to the world as that of the first woman who had received a nomination by a public National Convention.

"After her recent nomination to the Presidency she sent to the committee a letter, marked with superior dignity and moral weight; a beautiful piece of English not unworthy of Macaulay. 'I ought not to pass unnoticed,' she says, 'your courteous and gracious allusion to what you deem the favouring omen of my name.'

" 'It is true that a Victoria rules the great rival nation opposite to us on the other shore of the Atlantic; it is true, also, that in its clear etymology the name signifies victory! and the victory for the right is what we are bent on securing. It is again true, also, that to some minds there is a consonant harmony between the idea and the word, so that its euphonious utterance seems to their imaginations to be itself a genius of success. However this may be, I have sometimes imagined that there is, perhaps, something providential and prophetic in the fact that my parents were prompted to confer on me a name which forbids the very thought of failure; and, as the great Napoleon believed in the star of his destiny, you will at least excuse me, and charge it to the credulity of the woman, if I believe in the fatality of triumph as somehow inhering in my name.'

" In conversation, until she is somewhat warmed with earnestness, she halts as if her mind were elsewhere, but the moment she brings all her faculties to her lips for the full utterance of her message, whether it be of persuasion or indignation, she is a very orator for eloquence—pouring forth her sentences like a mountain stream, sweeping everything that frets its flood.

" 'Difficulties,' says Emerson, 'exist to be surmounted.' This might be the motto of her life. Prescient of the grandeur of her destiny, she goes forth with a resistless energy to accomplish it.

" She believes that intellectual power has its fountains in inspiration. And once when I put her to the searching question, 'What is the greatest truth that has ever been expressed in words?' she thrilled her listeners with the sudden answer, 'Blessed are the pure in heart, for they shall see God.'

" Let me say that I know of no person against whom there are more prejudices, nor anyone who more quickly disarms them. This strange faculty is the most powerful of her powers. She shoots a word like a sudden sunbeam through the thickest

mist of people's doubts and accusations, and clears the sky in a
moment. Questioned by some committee or delegation who
have come to her with idle tales against a busy life, I have seen
her swiftly gather together all the stones which they have cast,
put them like the miner's quartz into the furnace, melt them
with fierce and fervent heat, bring out of them the purest gold
stamp, thereon her image and subscription, as if she were
sovereign of the realms, and then (as the marvel of it all)
receive the sworn allegiance of the whole company on the spot.
At one of her public meetings, when the chair (as she hoped)
would be occupied by Lucretia Mott, this venerable woman has
been persuaded to decline this responsibility, but afterwards
stepped forward on the platform and lovingly kissed the young
speaker in presence of the multitude. To see her is to respect
her—to know her is to vindicate her. She possesses the
magnificent energies which make her a heroine of history. In
conclusion, amid all the rush of her active life, she believes with
Wordsworth, that—

> " ' The gods approve the depth and not
> The tumult of the soul.'

" So, whether buffeted by criticism, or defamed by slander,
she carries herself in that religious peace which, through all
turbulence, is 'a measureless content.' When apparently about
to be struck down she gathers unseen strength, and goes forward
conquering and to conquer."

Globe, June 29th, 1877.   Toronto (Canada).

" Mrs. Victoria C. Woodhull lectured to a large audience in
the Royal Opera House on Tuesday evening. She proved
herself to be one of the most able platform speakers ever heard
in Toronto, and completely knocked down the barriers of prejudice with which her name has been surrounded. Her handling
of the social question was delicate, but searching and convincing,
and the noble sentiments with which her lecture teemed

were rapturously applauded by her hearers. She has made many friends in this city, who will be pleased to hear of her return, if even for one night."

The Detroit Post, July 2nd, 1877 (Editorial).

" Mrs. Woodhull will deliver at Whitney's Opera House to-morrow evening her famous lecture, 'The Human Body the Temple of God.' This lecture has been delivered by Mrs. Woodhull in all the large cities of the east to immense audiences composed of the thinking people of each community. In Boston her audience numbered over four thousand persons. A decided change has come over the papers of the country in the last two years in their treatment of this remarkable woman. It was natural that the subjects she discussed should startle people, and the shock manifested itself in the press by tirades of abuse, which was more indecent even than the sentiments and utterances they falsely ascribed to their object. Since then, however, thousands in all parts of the country have heard Mrs. Woodhull for themselves, and have learned for themselves that she discusses questions of vital importance to the happiness of the human race with as much purity as eloquence of expression and with strong, if not invulnerable, logic. Whether people sympathize or not with her remedies, they have ceased to deny the existence of the disease, and the press, taking its tone from the change, now announces her advent and criticizes her utterances at least in respectful language."

1880.

VICTORIA WOODHULL.
WHY SHE CAME TO AMERICA AND RETURNED TO ENGLAND.

A DEFENCE OF TWO WOMEN WHO HAVE BEEN CHARGED WITH
MANY OFFENCES—THE VICTIMS OF SLANDER AND CIRCUMSTANCES.

[CORRESPONDENCE OF THE MORNING CALL.]

CHICAGO, Dec. 21.—A gentleman who has just arrived in this
city from New York, is very indignant over the manner in
which Victoria C. Woodhull and her sister has been treated
by a portion of the newspaper press of this country since their
recent arrival from England. One of the leading papers of this
city published in a letter from one of its regular New York
correspondents a pen picture of the return of Mrs. Woodhull and
her sister, Miss Claflin, their aged mother, and Mrs. Woodhull's
daughter, Zula Maud, and described the sisters as " two middle-
aged women, outré in costume, with the sharp, eager look of the
adventurous females that they are," and referred to their mother
as " an old woman so withered and brown and wrinkled that she
looked like one of the hickory nut dolls you find at country fairs."
The gentleman to whom I have referred said to your correspondent that it was, perhaps, needless for him to say that the writer
of the letter was a woman. "When a woman is to be covered with
mud, who but a woman would begin the deluge?" continued he,
"and a woman, too, who should not forget the old saying,
'Those living in glass houses should not throw stones.' She
goes on to speak of Mrs. Woodhull's daughter as Zula Maud
Woodhull Blood, and refers to the 'variable fortune of the
Woodhull and Claflin family,' after a muddled mess over matters
connecting Mrs. Woodhull and Miss Claflin with

THE LATE COMMODORE VANDERBILT,
A subject about which she evidently knew nothing, she closes

another paragraph with the highly important information that Mr. Wm. H. Vanderbilt, the Commodore's son, hurried Mrs. Woodhull and Miss Claflin to England by being very 'generous' to them. It is not my purpose or desire to attack a woman, but when the facts about Mrs. Woodhull and Miss Claflin's departure for England and their return to America would be just as interesting as misstatements, I might wonder that they were written at all if I did not know that the author was a woman, soured and embittered against the world, and who depends upon her imagination for her facts. And I ask in all fairness whether it is not high time that Mrs. Woodhull and Miss Claflin should be submitted to newspaper readers in a truthful manner? Enough has been said falsely against them to have driven them to the madhouse or the grave, and that they are able to move about in their senses is marvellous to me. I could tell you enough to fill columns of the *Call*, and it would be merely a plain statement of facts, which, if written by Charles Reade or Wilkie Collins, would outshine in seeming romance all that they have ever written. I am fully aware that the man who fights for a man—and especially a woman—who has been spat upon, traduced, and all but murdered by public opinion, has a herculean task before him. I am aware, also, that it may be said that he is a hireling, and was paid to do this kind of work; but in my own heart I know that this is not true, and that is enough for me. I am not engaged in painting black into white, or in transforming ordinary mortals into angels. Having personal knowledge of much of the public and private life of Mrs. Woodhull, I feel it a duty incumbent upon me whenever I have opportunity to

DEMAND THAT SHE SHALL HAVE FAIR PLAY.

"I will briefly tell you, then, why Mrs. Woodhull and Miss Claflin went to England, why they returned, and why they go back to England again. If it is worth the while of any newspaper to print anything about them, it is certainly proper that facts should be stated. Mrs. Woodhull's entrée into public life was at a time when she was recognized as a representative of Commodore Vanderbilt in Broad Street, New York. She saw a stalwart squad of women battling for suffrage at the National Capital. Defeat stared them in the face. She went to Washington and with all the energy which she, as a bright, business women, possessed, worked for them in their almost hopeless cause. She spent her own money liberally, and succeeded in having a minority report on her memorial presented by General Benjamin F. Butler to Congress. This was indeed a great victory, and Mrs. Elizabeth Cady Stanton, in the public prints, said of her: 'In the annals of history the name of Victoria C. Woodhull will have its own high place as a deliverer.' But jealous, spiteful women were then as now, and soon Mrs. Woodhull found that all that devilish ingenuity could invent against her name and fame was heralded in the world, and the work of her destruction was begun by the very persons who should have been her friends—idle, gossiping, and malicious women. Her unfortunate marriage with Colonel Blood, the views promulgated by him and Stephen Pearl Andrews in *Woodhull & Claflin's Weekly*, ground her deeper into the mire. But her heart rebelled against the views with which they associated her name. The combination of circumstances that surrounded her forced her to take the platform to defend herself. Everybody's hand seemed raised against her. Protestations from her were in vain. Andrews and Blood skulked for protection under her name. She was incarcerated in jail, and the officers who administer what they are pleased to call the law in New York,

DRAGGED HER DOWN DEEPER

In her misery until life was indeed almost unbearable. She went to California, and returned to New York, but the followers of Andrews and Blood were at her heels with their imprecations wherever she went. And she was a woman without a country and without a home. She went with her sister, her children and her aged parents to England, to live away from those who were determined that she should have no place in America wherein to lay her head in peace. William H. Vanderbilt had no more to do with her departure than did the youngest child in San Francisco. True, his bluff old father, it was never denied, intended to make provision in his will for her and her sister. In England she found warm-hearted, generous friends, who sympathized with her in her troubles, and who welcomed her among them. An era of peace and happiness was before her. The rest which she had long desired seemed at last within her control. Of course she was forced to do something to make a living for herself and children, and she took the platform again. It is no stretch of the imagination to say that no more learned or more aristocratic audiences ever assembled to hear a public speaker than were the audiences that greeted her. She became engaged to be married to a wealthy and accomplished English gentleman. But this was too much for the scandal-mongers of her native land to bear. Again they filled their carts with mud, and sent them this time across the ocean.

THE MARRIAGE ENGAGEMENT

Was postponed, and the once proud and haughty woman who had begun to realize that she was to have a happy home in a foreign land, found herself cast down and humiliated. Some of the would-be-murderers overleaped their ambition, however, and instead of accomplishing their object were rejected and spurned by the English people, and she found greater sympathy than ever before in English hearts. She came with her sister, Miss Claflin, their mother, and Zula Maud Woodhull, to this country in the Gallia, which arrived at New York on the 25th of November, 1880. And, by the way, it may be as well to say that Zula Maud Woodhull is Mrs. Woodhull's only daughter, and that her father was Dr. Woodhull, and not Col. Blood, from whom Mrs. Woodhull was divorced over five years ago.

"Mrs. Woodhull's object in coming to this country was to seek for justice, and to command that the abuse which was being heaped upon her should cease. Unfortunately she came when her health was shattered. She was no longer the strong, defiant woman as of old, and she reckoned without her health. Even in this condition she was not free from the mud-slingers, and they went to work again with a will. With her whole life saddened, the helpless condition of a grown-up son, and the taunts of evil-minded men and women, it was no wonder that she felt that life was scarcely worth the struggle. Her friends—those who never faltered in their devotion to her when she was over-whelmed with trouble—urged her to return to her home in England, there to remain until her health would permit her to come back to America and grapple with those who find sweet consolation in hounding a woman. On last Saturday she and her sister, their mother and Zula Maud, sailed in the White Star steamer Britannic for England. Mrs. Woodhull and Miss Claflin departed as they came,

QUIET, MODEST-LOOKING WOMEN,

In neat attire, not 'outré in costume, with the slap-dash air of the strong-minded,' but with constitutions undermined through sorrow and sickness, and with hearts so heavy with suffering that the very stones would have cried out for mercy could they have read them. In England they have a home that they can enjoy should the monsters of both sexes in this country not invade it. This is the sad and truthful story of their arrival in this country and their departure for England, and he or she who can find anything in it to create merriment is better fitted for a deeper and warmer climate than this. In saying this much I feel that I have done the duty of a man who knows whereof he speaks, and upon the statements made I stand fearing no truthful contradiction."

The gentleman having lived in California, said that he believed

many there would be glad to see Mrs. Woodhull set right before
the public in THE CALL.

The New Haven Union, December 30th, 1880.

DEFENCE OF MRS. WOODHULL

FROM THE ATTACKS OF WOMEN CORRESPONDENTS.

Special Correspondence THE NEW HAVEN UNION.

" NEW YORK, December 28th.—It may be thought wondrous
strange by some that a woman who has seen much of public
life, and whose private life has been at times wretched, indeed,
would be the last person in the world who would attack another
woman who has been a public speaker and who has known
what it is in its deepest significance to be humbled in private
life, and the wonder would be increased in some minds, no
doubt, should it be known that the former had really no substantial reason for assaulting the latter. But to those who have
been tossed about like a football, and to those especially in the
newspaper world, there is nothing remarkable about it. The
old saying, 'Those who live in glass houses should not throw
stones,' is too often forgotten by the women correspondents of
this country, and I have a recent instance in point which cannot
but be interesting to newspaper readers in general. Five years
ago Mrs. Victoria C. Woodhull decided to make her home in
England, or in some foreign land, so as to be far from the
scenes where her life was made almost unendurable by a pack
of men and women who seemed determined to for ever persecute
her. It is scarcely necessary to say that the industrious men
and women who were thus disposed towards her were of a class
that had previously professed the greatest admiration for her.
She had been led into endless trouble, it was evident, by the
man who, as her husband (Colonel James H. Blood), should
have shielded her.

" Stephen Pearl Andrews and others wrote for *Woodhull*

and Claflin's Weekly. The world at large was given to understand that these articles were written or dictated by Mrs. Woodhull, when the fact was that she had no more to do with writing or inspiring them than one of the great elms in the Green of your city. The story of her troubles is a long and sad one. What might have been a happy life was almost blasted. On every side she met with opposition when she attempted to make herself heard in her own defence, and at length she took her family with her to England, and after hard work in the lecture field there, where she was successful pecuniarily and socially, she established herself in a comfortable home. She found firm and devoted friends among the better class of the English people, and the prospect of a peaceful life to the end seemed assured. But the old gang of persecutors were not idle. They began to flood the Kingdom with their attacks upon her, and sought to create the impression that she dared not return to America. When the fact became known that she was engaged to be married to a wealthy and accomplished English gentleman her enemies here raved and wrote, and this gentleman was soon in possession of some of the choicest morsels of their literary efforts. Sick in mind and sick in body she ventured across the ocean a few weeks ago with the avowed purpose of meeting her defamers face to face, and compelling them to prove what they said of her or be for ever silent. She came without warning, and began the preparation of her plans of action. Her health was greatly impaired, more through sorrow than sickness, and she soon found herself unequal to the task.

"Scarcely had she landed in America before the veteran 'women correspondents' went to work with that fiendish delight so characteristic of some of them, and Mrs. Woodhull was pictured in anything but pleasant colours. I shall refer to but one of this class. Some years ago Mary H. Burnham, over the initials 'M. H. B.,' wrote from this city letters to a St.

Louis newspaper that gave her a national reputation, and created for her, especially in Missouri, many warm admirers. The gossip of the day was served up by her in the most piquant and refreshing style, and was widely copied into other newspapers. On the lecture platform in St. Louis she was heartily welcomed, and what she said was applauded or laughed at in a delightful manner. Her success as a lecturer in ‼ that State was apparent from the start. She had a husband who became troublesome. The swift wagging tongue of scandal began its work, and unpleasant stories flew in all directions with alarming rapidity. Mrs. Burnham's popularity began to fade, her troubles increased, and with more respect for her feelings than she has shown for a defenceless woman, the details are not now repeated. The second troublesome husband was also disposed of, however, and Mrs. Burnham married Stephen Fiske, the journalist and theatrical manager. Mrs. Burnham dropped out of existence as a newspaper correspondent for the St. Louis newspaper, and her friends disappeared as rapidly as they had come to her in the days of her glory. At length, after a long season of silence, she returned to the old business of stringing out newspaper gossip by the yard, and a short time ago began writing regularly from this city to the Chicago *Tribune* over the initials ‘M. H. F.’ Soon after Mrs. Fiske resumed this pleasant occupation Mrs. Woodhull arrived in this country, and Mrs. Fiske snapped at her with the eagerness of a starving dog after a bone. She served Mrs. Woodhull up to the Chicago people in her old time manner, and made so many outrageous misstatements that the *Tribune* corrected some of them. Mrs. Woodhull came here not to seek notoriety, as was charged by this correspondent among others, but to demand that her slanderers should cease their diabolical work. As I have mentioned here her health alone prevented her from carrying out her intention of calling them to account. On the 17th inst. she sailed in the Brittanic for England, and arrived

38 *

at her home in London. I give these facts to show how much injustice has been done to a terribly persecuted woman by women, and to ask of women correspondents generally whether it is possible that a deeply wronged woman cannot have justice done her by those of her own sex.

Chicago Tribune, December 23rd, 1880.

MRS. WOODHULL.

WHAT A NEW YORK JOURNALIST HAS TO SAY OF HER ARRIVAL IN AMERICA.

" The return of Mrs. Victoria Woodhull and her sister to New York after an absence of five years in England has called forth many items of gossip in the newspapers, and whether they were written unwittingly or maliciously have caused them much anxiety. A gentleman widely and favourably known is at present in this city, and yesterday said to a TRIBUNE reporter that, believing in fair play for everybody, the traduced as well as the glorified, he desired to correct some of the erroneous impressions which these items of gossip have created both here and elsewhere. And," continued the New-Yorker, " it is no wonder that Mrs. Woodhull feels that her countrymen and women should call a halt in this matter of needlessly torturing her. She with her only daughter Zula Maud, whose father was Dr. Woodhull, and not Col. Blood, from whom Mrs. Woodhull was divorced over five years ago, her aged mother, now in her 80th year, and her sister, Miss Claflin, arrived at New York in the Gallia on the 25th ult., desiring to see their native land once more, and their relatives and those of their friends who never wavered in their devotion to them in the darkest hours of their trials in New York. A pack of ~olves of both sexes, it seems, have found sweet consolation in continuing, with renewed vigour, the labour they loved so well—that of biting at them through the newspapers. Some of the

articles have, of course, been written unwittingly, or the
writers have relied upon their imaginations for their facts. I
saw a paragraph in a Hartford newspaper the other day, among
a half-column of alleged humourous items, setting forth that
the public would no doubt be grieved to learn that Miss Claflin's
health was precarious. The fact is that during much of her
stay in England and since her return to America she has been
so ill that her life was despaired of by those near and dear to
her. Fun has been poked at her mother because she is old
and wrinkled. That is true, she has endured much sorrow.
The sufferings of her daughters have been her sufferings.
Mrs. Woodhull's aged father, her son, whose mental faculties
were impaired from his birth, and whose condition is a helpless
one, and one of her sisters remained in England.

"One of the correspondents in writing of the arrival of
Mrs. Woodhull and Miss Claflin, says that they were 'outré in
costume, with the slap-dash air of the strong-minded.' Nothing
could be more unfair and untrue than this description of
them. They came neatly and becomingly attired, and
were as modest and unpretentious in their demeanour as
any lady. They had suffered much in sickness and in sorrow,
their health was impaired, and their hearts were heavy.
They were not poor in purse, were not adventurers, and
did not come here to add to their fortunes. When the
abuse that was once so familiar to their ears, and which
had nearly driven them to the madhouse or to the grave, was
heard again by them they felt that they should demand a hearing, and attempt to silence their defamers. But they reckoned
without their health, and their physicians and friends urged
them not to undertake just now the great task which they
began to plan, and to return across the ocean, and wait until
such time as they may recover their health. In a few days
they will again be in their English home. They ask no
favours, but simply demand that when anything shall be

said of them the truth shall be stated. Mrs. Woodhull is not made of stone, as some may imagine; she has a heart that is as warm and tender for her children as that of any woman in the land, but she has been driven almost to frenzy through the wanton attacks of women. Those who remember her on the platform as a defiant, or vivacious woman, and who now recall her as such, have little knowledge of the deep misery which she endured. When she first entered public life she was in well-to-do circumstances. She saw a small band of women at the National Capital struggling to secure the right of suffrage for their sex. She was then a bright, business woman, who had made much money in speculations in Wall Street. She went to Washington, poured out her money lavishly, and worked with remarkable energy for the little band. She accomplished more than them all, as Mrs. Elizabeth Cady Stanton publicly acknowledged, in securing the presentation through Gen. Benjamin F. Butler of the minority report upon her memorial to Congress. How was she rewarded ? All that fiendish ingenuity could invent to her discredit was poured out upon her by jealous women, and this was the beginning of the troubles which she has encountered to this very hour.

" Her unfortunate marriage to Col. James H. Blood, the doctrines promulgated in *Woodhull & Claflin's Weekly,* and Stephen Pearl Andrews and others to which they attached her name, added greatly to her misfortunes. She was dragged to prison and made to suffer when they were the guilty parties. She took the platform in her own defence, and attempted to stay the terrible wave of public opinion against her, but it was too late. Angered and embittered Blood and Andrews and their satellites hounded her wherever she went, and thus she had the bad and the good arrayed against her. On every side the cry seemed to be ' Down with her !' At length she went to England to seek a home, and took her family with her. There she met a generous sympathetic people, and she was heartily welcomed by them. She went on the lecture platform there, and addressed audiences than which none more intelligent or aristocratic ever assembled to hear a public speaker in England. She profited pecuniarily by these lectures, and established herself in a comfortable home which is still there awaiting her return. The avalanche of filth which skulking tormentors in New York, Boston, and elsewhere at once swept down upon her. The fact began to dawn upon her that unless she fought back she would soon be without a home and without a country. Mr. William H. Vanderbilt had no more to do with her departure for England than a child unborn, although it has been published far and wide that he gave her and her sister handsome sums of money to quit this country at the time the old Commodore's will was contested before the Surrogate in New York. One woman in New York, not unknown to fame as a newspaper writer and public lecturer, while in England last year became so abusive of Mrs. Woodhull that she was tabooed from society, and Mrs. Woodhull was more heartily welcomed in English homes than ever before. It would be useless for me to attempt to speak of all the slings and slurs at Mrs. Woodhull except in a general way, and I can only say that in my opinion there should be an end to it all. Mrs. Woodhull asks nothing but justice at the hands of newspaper writers ; and why is she not entitled to it as much as any other woman who has been in public life? I have faith enough in the journalists of this country to believe that they will treat her fairly when they understand her position. Those who say that she is an adventurer or seeking after notoriety do not know whereof they speak. In conclusion, I may say that I am glad of the opportunity to say a good word for the least understood and most abused woman in America."

ENGLISH NOTICES.

National Reformer, March, 1871. London (Eng.).

WOODHULL AND CLAFLIN'S WEEKLY.

" We note this journal specially, as a vigorous specimen of women's journalism. It is owned and edited by Mrs. Victoria C. Woodhull and Miss Tennie C. Claflin ; and Mesdames the editors, with force and fearlessness, make their journal refreshing. It attacks the huge Commercial, Railroad, Bank, and Insurance swindles, not simply with hard words, but with real argument and strong facts. Pushing forward the woman's question, it does so with pleasant freshness, chronicling daily acts of talent, courage, devotion, and endurance on the part of women."

The Nottingham Daily Express, September 5th, 1877.

"Last night a large audience assembled at the Mechanics' Hall, to hear a lecture announced by Mrs. Victoria C. Woodhull, an American lady. The audience was highly respectable, many of our local dignitaries being present, principally ladies. Mrs. Woodhull walked slowly upon the platform, having in her hand an open Bible, from which she read, ' Know ye not that ye are the temple of God, and that the spirit of God dwells in you ? If any man defile the temple of God, him shall God destroy; for the temple of God is holy, which temple ye are ' (1 Cor. iii. 16, 17). The lecture was delivered with great earnestness, and in an impressive and dignified manner. Upon retiring from the platform Mrs. Woodhull was cordially applauded."

The Nottingham Guardian, September 5th, 1877.

" Mrs. Victoria C. Woodhull, a lady whose lectures have been received throughout America with a quite exceptional display of interest and enthusiasm, made her first appearance in this country at the Mechanics' Hall last night. There was a very large attendance. Mrs. Woodhull appealed in the most impassioned and fearless language to her audience to awaken the responsibilities of life, and especially of maternity. She contended that the child too often gathers from ignorant and vicious companions knowledge which ought to be imparted by a loving, intelligent mother, and urged fathers and mothers to lose not a moment in making themselves 'acquainted with' their children. Mrs. Woodhull's address lasted for about two hours, and she manifestly made a deep impression on her audience, both by the vigour of her language, the courage of her illustrations, the earnestness of her manner, and, above all, the force and freshness of her eloquence. Mrs. Woodhull is unquestionably a great orator; and it is not difficult to understand how she has gained so remarkable a hold upon the people of her own country."

The Nottingham Journal, September 5th, 1877.

"Mrs. Victoria Claflin Woodhull, the American lecturer, made her first appearance in England last night. The hall was filled with a large, intelligent, respectable, and attentive audience. The lecture was given with great animation and oratorical effect, being frequently applauded."

The Liverpool Post, September 28th, 1877.

"Last evening Mrs. Victoria Claflin Woodhull lectured in the Concert Hall, which was filled by an audience of high standing in life, with eloquence. The lady concluded amidst prolonged applause."

The Liverpool Mercury, September 28th, 1877.

"Mrs. Victoria Woodhull, the famous American female orator, appeared last evening before a Liverpool audience, and delivered an address upon 'The Human Body the Temple of God.' There was a large attendance. Stepping on the stage and gracefully acknowledging the plaudits with which she was received, she took for her 'text' some verses from the Epistle to the Corinthians. Those who from prurient motives imagined that they were to hear something *outré* went away disappointed. With impassioned eloquence she reviewed the present state of society, and with dramatic action pointed out the weals and woes of a debauched nation. Her peroration was passionately delivered, and she retired with all the action with which a successful actress would acknowledge the enthusiasm of an admiring audience."

The Liverpool Albion, September 28th, 1877.

"Heralded by an American reputation and an European celebrity, Mrs. Victoria C. Woodhull appeared at the Concert Hall. The great orator was favoured with a large and sympathetic audience, to whom she discoursed for considerably more than an hour on the subject, ' The Human Body the Temple of God.' Expectation respecting the appearance and demeanour of the lady had been wound up to a high pitch, and certainly if piquancy in both is a charm, expectation was not disappointed. Mrs. Woodhull came upon the platform unaccompanied, but with more than the ordinary self-possession of a woman of the world. Mrs. Woodhull was well calculated to give a favourable first impression, and certainly the audience were so impressed. Nor, apart from the matter of her discourse, was the impression lost. She is certainly a splendid actress, and an orator of rare power. She has taken up a novel line. Its burden was that if all the mothers in the world would rise to a sense of their responsibilities, and act accordingly, the condition of human nature would immediately undergo a vast improvement."

"**Manchester**, October 16th, 1877.

" MADAM,

" I trust you will not think me very presumptuous if I address a few words to you on the subject of your Monday night lecture in the Free Trade Hall.

" I went to see you, I confess, principally from curiosity,

knowing but little of your former life—but little of your gallant struggles in America for the grandest of all causes—the cause which has for its object a great moral revolution. I came away from the Free Trade Hall that night with new and nobler ideas, and I hope new and nobler objects in view.

"To say that your delivery and eloquence were splendid, your powers of intonation and endurance marvellous, and your words convincing, or to say that had you gone on the stage you would have been the greatest actress in the world, would be but to reiterate truths which have been showered on you already; but I will say this, that if every mother were a Mrs. Woodhull, we might pull down nine-tenths of our prisons. Would that I could help you in your glorious work.

"I write to you to let you know that there was one, and, if I mistake not, many more in that room that night who heartily admired and humbly reverenced you and your grand moral courage. I also write to you to beg the great favour of your autograph, which if I get I shall always prize, and to ask you if you would be so kind as to let me know, in some spare moment, where to obtain your books, journals, &c., and if your Monday's lecture will be published. I trust it will. I have no right to ask you to do this—but the right of a mighty admiration of your character—if that be a right at all.

"Go on, Madam, in your noble cause, and rest assured, that although it may be in the dim future, perhaps twenty, perhaps fifty, perhaps one hundred years hence, your name will be reverenced and worshipped all over the Christian world as no other woman's name has been. Go on, Madam, as you have begun, for although the rain of slander may descend, the floods of obloquy come, and the winds of misconception arise, still your cause, either on this side the Atlantic or in America, will never die, for it is founded upon a rock, and that rock is—Christ. May you conquer here as you have conquered in America. With many apologies for the length to which I have been carried, and with all respect,

"Believe me, Madam,

"Your obedient servant,

"E. E. M."

"St. Stephen's Church, Westminster,
December 13th, 1877.

" DEAR MADAM,

" While that deeply interesting, so much needed, and most impressive lecture delivered by you last night is fresh on my mind, permit me, as a fellow-worker in the same great cause of evangelization, to share a few thoughts with you.

"The cause you advocate is a glorious one, and demands, as you say, the 'moral support' of the country. God bless the results of your mission! The only apology I can offer for writing what I do is that the work is a blessed one, and we are both co-workers for one and the same end.

" A word in conclusion. Pray take what I have written as coming from one who wishes you and your cause every success. I return to my own sphere of work—teeming with every vice—fortified and encouraged by your lecture, and desirous of benefiting my own audiences by the remarks I have had the privilege of hearing from your lips.

" I have the honour to be, dear Madam,

"Yours faithfully, Rev. B——, M.A."

Christian Union, February 13th, 1880. London.

MRS. VICTORIA CLAFLIN WOODHULL.

" Mrs. Victoria Claflin Woodhull, during this term of enforced repose, has been sought out by the noblest and highest-minded men and women of this country, and nothing but their kind and generous sympathy could have enabled her to recover so far from the effects of the fiery persecution and misrepre-

sentation heaped upon her by her enemies. Far removed
from the arena of that excitement, they have been able to
form a just and unbiassed estimate of the real qualities of
this extraordinary woman, and they find in her nothing but
the most pure-minded, self-denying philanthropy, her sole
ambition being the amelioration of the sufferings of her
fellow-creatures. Mrs. Woodhull insists with all the power
of her impassioned eloquence upon the evil results to the
world of interested and ill-considered marriages, and shows
what improvement would be effected in society if the sanctity
of marriage were better understood and sacredly respected.
She believes that woman's loving influence is to be the great
regenerator of the human race, and that she, under Divine
guidance, has a mission to instruct and prepare her sex for
the mighty responsibilities which rest upon them. Those
who enjoyed the high privilege of hearing Mrs. Woodhull at
St. James's Hall will ever remember how the audience was
held spell-bound by her fervid and impressive eloquence, and
her reward was that parents, sons, and daughters looked to
her afterwards to bless her for thus calling to their most
serious attention matters so important to their temporal and
eternal welfare. She has always been, even from her very
infancy, a most diligent and prayerful student of the Scriptures,
and as if by inspiration she has been able to make clear and
explain many of the hidden mysteries of the sacred writings,
in a most likely and convincing manner, and her work is
destined to be a lanthorn of light to those who seek for
enlightenment on these most vital and moral subjects.
That a woman who has devoted her whole life to doing
angels' work should have been so maligned and persecuted,
even up to the gates of justice, where alone she received a
verdict of blameless, is one of those marvels which the pages
of history only can explain, and which show that all those
who have fought for a good cause, from Saints and Martyrs

downwards, have had to pass through their Gethsemane of
mental suffering too exquisite for human utterance. She has
passed through her Gethsemane, and when she returns to
her native land her people will vie with each other to make
reparation for the cruel injuries they have done to the noblest-
minded and most self-sacrificing of women, whose only fault
was that she loved them too well."

Advertiser, August 12th, 1882. London.

WOMAN'S EMANCIPATION.

"Many women are struggling for women's franchise, and
think that when women, who must pay taxes if they are house-
holders, can vote they will gain their freedom.

"Mrs. Victoria Claflin Woodhull has, of all women who have
stood up for women's rights, struck the key-note, and in asserting women's rights has shown plainly, clearly, purely, forcibly,
what are women's wrongs; and until these are fully understood
and remedied never will, not only women, but all the human race
have their rights. So long as marriage is simply the expedient
to provide a shelter and food and necessaries of life, so long will
man (God's image) continue to create murderers, idiots, drunkards, thieves, and scoundrels, and prisons flourish, mad-houses
be built, asylums needed, Marwoods paid, and gallows erected;
but once let the holy teachings of Mrs. Woodhull be understood,
and marriage will be the thing of choice, not of necessity. The
procreation of children will be understood in its holiest condition.
Why call such knowledge impure, vulgar, and a shame to utter,
when not a spot in all this world, where stock is required and
raised, but men will discuss, try, and by every possible means
seek to improve the race, and why? That by careful study the
coffers may be better filled; yet yearly are thousands of helpless
suffering children born into this beautiful world to drag out a
miserable existence, some too hopelessly miserable in their condition even to realize that they live; we meet everywhere the

lame, the halt, the blind, the deformed, the idiot, and we need homes for these, and prisons for those born with sense, but impregnated with the parents' sins. God help and God enlighten those who so desecrate God's Holy Temple.

"Mrs. Woodhull would have none enter upon the holiest of all relations—marriage—save in a devout spirit; the divorces would cease, suffering would pass away, beauty, health, and enjoyment would be everywhere, and sad sights of suffering humanity would no longer meet our view."

MISCELLANEA.

MISCELLANEA.

[*From the* **Westminster Times,** *January* 11*th,* 1890.]

Long has base and vile calumny fallen like a continuous torrent on two noble heads and brave hearts, those of Mrs. Victoria C. Woodhull (Mrs. John Biddulph Martin) and her sister Tennessee Claflin (Lady Cook). Long have they suffered this terrible ordeal without a murmur, with an angelic patience. Still calumny continues to pour forth its torrent of bitterness.

Will nothing stop it ? Yes. The last drop makes the cup overflow.

A few weeks ago these ladies have again been violently attacked by American newspapers.

The following was published January 29th, 1881, at which time all the persons mentioned were alive :—

For years the famous Beecher article cast a dark shadow over the names of Victoria C. Woodhull and Tennessee Claflin. It will be remembered that Mr. Stephen Pearl Andrews, when arrested with all the staff of the paper, including Mrs. Woodhull and her sister, emphatically denied having had anything to do with it, and on this declaration was released. Three years after Mrs. Woodhull and her sister had been acquitted, the long and exciting trial, in which Mr. Tilton sued Henry Ward-Beecher for the seduction of his wife, at last, but unexpectedly brought out the truth. Stephen Pearl Andrews, having then nothing to fear, avowed with exulting pride the authorship of the objectionable parts of the article. It was afterwards proven that Andrews, so as to leave behind no trace of evidence against himself, had waited in the composing-room till the article was set up, and then had taken away his MS. article with him.

"It is necessary to state that at the time the 'Beecher Article' appeared Mrs. Woodhull was on a Western lecturing tour. The very night the paper went to press, she delivered an address at the Academy of Music, Chicago."

As may be seen in the foregoing re-published cuttings from the American Press, Mrs. Victoria C. Woodhull and Tennessee Claflin have suffered a martyrdom for a good and just cause. They have been made to drink the cup of sufferings to the dregs. Everything has been attempted to crush them to the earth. No torture has been forgotten.

Nobody can imagine half the *tricks* employed to attain this end. Out of some thousands we select the following specimens, which were published in the *New York Herald*, December 14th, 1886 :—

" One day, in 1872, when Mrs. Victoria C. Woodhull-Martin and her sister were passing Delmonico's, in Broad Street, on their way to their office, a man was boasting to several gentlemen that he had passed the evening before at their house on Murray Hill and remained until two o'clock. His conversation was all that was required to ruin and destroy any woman's character. He was saying he knew both her and her sister well, and was on the most intimate terms with them. At that moment a gentleman who knew them turned and asked him if he knew the two ladies who were just passing. Looking at them he said, 'No, I never saw them before. Who are they?' Then this gentleman told him, 'They are the two ladies you have been talking about, and every word that you have just said is a falsehood. My wife, son and myself dined with Mrs. Woodhull last night and spent the evening with her. Now, if you will go with me and repeat the same story to those ladies I will give you $1000.' But when he was confronted with his lies he fled from the place.

"On Mrs. Woodhull and her sister's first lecture tour through the South Atlanta (Ga.), when they arrived at an hotel they were told that two women had just been there representing themselves to be Victoria C. Woodhull and Tennie C. Claflin, and that they had conducted themselves in such a manner that the landlord had been obliged to put them out.

"There was a case of two Woodhull sisters (I doubt if their real name was Woodhull) for inveigling an old gentleman out of a large amount of money; they escaped to England. At that time Mrs. Victoria C. Woodhull was married and settled in London and knew nothing about it until she was asked if it was true that she had run away with this man's money from America. It might also be stated here that Mrs. Victoria C. Woodhull and Miss Tennesse Claflin could not have been the 'Woodhull sisters' for their maiden name was 'the Claflin sisters.'

"When she was crossing in the 'Gallia' a judge's wife turned to her and said, 'Do you know that Victoria Woodhull and her sister are on board?' 'Indeed?' 'Yes,' she went on, 'I know them; they are dressed in men's clothes.' The judge's wife said this not knowing that she was talking to Victoria C. Woodhull herself. It was afterwards published in a great many American papers that Mrs. Woodhull and sister arrived per steamer 'Gallia' dressed in men's clothes."

Even in London the impersonators have carried on their schemes.

"A friend of Mrs. Victoria C. Woodhull told her that a certain

American lady in ¡London was circulating the most terrible scandal about her. She called upon that lady to test the truth of this rumour, and asked her if she could give Mrs. Woodhull's address. She answered she could not do that, for Mrs. Woodhull was driven out of London over a year ago. Mrs. Victoria C. Woodhull then asked her if she knew Mrs. Woodhull. She said that she was well acquainted with her, and then entertained her for half an hour with the most atrocious calumnies about this lady. After she had finished Mrs. Victoria C. Woodhull rose to thank her for her information, telling her who she was. She then fell on her knees and begged Mrs. Woodhull not to prosecute her, as she was controlled by the evil one to talk so about a person she had never seen and really knew nothing about."

Soon after Mrs. Victoria C. Woodhull arrived in England, she received the following letter from one of the most eminent English writers, Mr. Charles Reade :—

"19, ALBERT GATE, KENSINGTON,
Feb. 14, 1878.

DEAR MRS. WOODHULL,
        A woman called here the other day in my absence, and at first represented herself as Mrs. Woodhull; but afterwards said she was not Mrs. Woodhull, but an agent, who wanted a dramatic piece from me. It seems to me there are people about you making rather free with your name. So I send you this.

Need I say that I pay no attention to any communications that are not in your own handwriting.

Yours very truly,

C. READE."

Here is another instance of defamation, published on January 29th, 1881, in the *Woodhull and Claflin Journal.*

Copies containing this paragraph were sent to every news-paper in the world :—

"One S. S. Jones, of the Chicago *Religio-Philosophical Journal*, endeavoured to pollute public morals by a contemptible production, framed on the lines of the Treat Pamphlet. Mrs. Woodhull subsequently went to Chicago in order to prosecute this man for libel. She had to remain in the city some days before she could procure the obnoxious and obscene pamphlet, which she finally obtained through the kindly intervention of an English journalist. This gentleman accompanied Mrs. Woodhull to the Grand Jury Room, where an indictment was at once obtained. On the very day that Jones had to come up for trial, he was shot by an injured husband whose wife he had seduced. Death was instantaneous, as he had received two bullets in his head. The Chicago leading daily journals (in 1877), in their description of the tragedy, headed the article ʻ Mrs. Woodhull Avenged.' Certain it is that a Nemesis often pursues the evil-doer, even before Justice lays firm hold of him."

* * * * * *

"We understand that her husband, from whom Mrs. Woodhull had obtained a divorce (in 1876), has recently been engaged in sending round letters, wherein he stoutly protests against the imputations which were once cast upon his former wife's honour. Such communications, we further ascertain, are couched in terms of endearment. As an act of reparation, such a course may be justifiable. But how comes it that at the time when a malicious, obscene, and scurrilous pamphlet defaming Mrs. Woodhull and her sister was hawked about the streets of New York City in 1874 and 1875, that he remained a silent spectator of the event? Upon what principle did he refrain from taking legal action against Treat, the vile, mendacious vendor and reputed author of such an outrageous publication? An outcast from society endeavours to make a living at the expense of a woman's reputation, and the injured lady herself has to go before a Grand Jury, and obtain an indictment against the miscreant whom the Court for the Trial of Criminal Offences finally acquits on the ground of insanity. Treat, it is true, was legally restrained from vending any more of his dirty ware, and the police destroyed his stock-in-trade. But this was no adequate satisfaction for the evil effected. Something lies in the background respecting so abominable an occurrence. It is not improbable that all the circumstances of the case may leak out some day, and that before long, when he, who should have been his wife's protector, may yet be proven to have been not only the author, but the person who actually furnished the money for the obnoxious publication.

"Not satisfied with calumniating Mrs. Woodhull in America, her former husband pursued his cowardly work in England. One day (in 1877) the agent that organised Mrs. Woodhull's lectures in London, brought her the same obscene pamphlet that was previously circulated in America. It was bearing her divorced husband's undeniable writing."

Mr. Martin and Sir Francis Cook are determined now to do everything in their power to stop this continuous persecution.

Rewards have already been offered as will be seen by the following paragraphs, that have been published in different papers, from which we have copied them.

———

The first appeared in 1878, in the London *Times* and in other dailies. It runs thus :—

"Mrs. Victoria C. Woodhull, being again compelled to commence libel suits against Americans who are constantly circulating malicious slanders, offers a REWARD OF FIFTY POUNDS for every letter that contains enough libel to enable her to proceed criminally and civilly, and Five Pounds will be given to any and every person who will give information that can be proceeded with legally against persons who are circulating these foul stories by word of mouth."

Here is an appeal, published in the *Woodhull and Claflin's Journal,* in its number of the 29th January, 1881. Copies of this number were sent to every publication in the world, and over one million copies to private people. It reads :—

" We have long been the victim of most unrighteous slander, which no power of ours has been as yet fully adequate to suppress. We now call upon our friends and the whole Press of *the world* to aid us in unearthing those vile traducers who wanton with our good name, which, though nothing to them, is to us our all, dearer than life itself. Whoever has aught to say against us let him come forward and say it, or else for ever hold his peace. If any one living can point to any corrupt or un-womanly action of our life, now is the time for him to disclose what he has to say. Then we could proceed criminally against the parties, as our object is to right our reputation and not to recover damages by taking civil process.—V. C. W."

The article mentioning the second reward appeared in the New York daily *Sun,* June 9th, 1889. It says :—

" I have been asked by Sir Francis Cook to contradict certain false statements concerning his private life which have been printed in America and which have caused him great annoyance. These statements are to the effect that a separation is pending between himself and his wife, Lady Cook, formerly Miss Tennessee Claflin. Sir Francis declares that nothing could be further from his mind or that of his wife's than the thought of a separation. He also denies most emphatically that his children have ever, as alleged, sought to bring about a separation. So unfilial a course, Sir Francis declares, would be impossible on the part of his children, apart from the question of their own interest, which would make it absolutely suicidal to offend Sir Francis, whose very large fortune is unencumbered by entail and entirely at his own disposal. So confident is Sir Francis that his children are guiltless of any such undutiful conduct that he declares he will give 50,000 dols. to anyone in America or elsewhere who will prove to him that either of his two sons or daughter or other relatives had employed detectives, as has been reported, to obtain such information as would make it possible for them to separate Lady Cook from her husband. Sir Francis, who was about cabling to America offering this reward when I chanced to see him to-day, may be relied upon to pay it to anyone who can fulfil the conditions under which it is offered. It is hoped that the circulation of these statements concerning Sir Francis will not be persisted in, for the malice which lies at the bottom would certainly be dispelled on acquaintance with them."

By the step which Mrs. Woodhull has taken thus tardily at the insistance of her friends the world has now for the first time the opportunity of forming a just and proper estimate of her character and qualities.

It has seen her in her brilliant phase, when she held spell-bound the largest audiences in all parts of the States (from 1870 to 1877), enunciating her splendid doctrines in the cause of suffering humanity.

It has seen her bowed low, almost unto death.

It will now witness her rise surely and rapidly to take that place in the affections of her people which for some time past has been so cruelly denied to her, and history will furnish no finer example of nobility and self-sacrifice in woman than the name of Victoria Woodhull.

It may be asked, Why did not Mrs. Woodhull take this mode of vindication at an earlier period, seeing that she had the power of clearing herself at once of all the calumny which had been heaped upon her? The answer is, that she arrived in this country (Aug., 1877) in an almost dying condition, that she has remained in London (England) ever since, and it is only quite recently that she has sufficiently recovered to undertake any exciting work.

The following article appeared January 29th, 1881, and was republished by a great many American papers :—

Our motive for publishing the annexed article is urgent, inasmuch as we have been bitterly reproached by our English friends for not having denounced our vilifiers, and proceeded against them criminally, previous to our coming to England. That we have done so, the following article is sufficient evidence. This article, we think it well to add, was reproduced in many leading daily journals of the United States. Having preferred the restoration of our good name, we were sufficiently satisfied, not caring for money damages, or wishing to display what might be construed as vindictive feeling by having recourse to legal process. We feel it our duty to assert, that when once the editors of the various papers found they were in the wrong, and that our explanations were satisfactory, they afforded such amends as lay in their power.—V. C. W.

Editorial of the Cincinnati Daily Enquirer.

Cincinnati (Ohio), July 27, 1876.—We have a startling card this morning from that very remarkable woman, Victoria

C. Woodhull. A New York letter, which we published the
other day, contained some inaccuracies which Mrs. W.
has undertaken to correct. In doing so, she has brought
out some facts concerning her life, habits, attainments, &c.,
which will be fresh to the public. Mrs. Woodhull says that
she has ordered her attorneys to procure six copies of the
Enquirer containing the matter complained of, properly
identified. This would lead the public to believe that a lot
of lawyers were about to be favoured with a big job, but
we have Mrs. Woodhull's assurance that the publication of
her card will be accepted as full reparation for the damage done.

From the CINCINNATI DAILY ENQUIRER.

NEW YORK, July 27, 1876.—From all over the country, papers
are pouring in containing a wickedly false and maliciously
libellous article against me, which is credited to the Cincinnati
Enquirer. I have not yet seen that paper, but have ordered my
attorneys to procure half a dozen from your office, properly
identified. I did not intend to make any reply to this malignant
attack until I should have them; but the injury I have already
suffered urges me to wait no longer, and the hot blood of indignation coursing in my veins as each fresh repetition comes will
not allow me to wait. What makes me more indignant, and the
article all the more viciously malicious, is that it was brought to
me before it was sent for publication, at which time I pronounced
it utterly false, and informed the person who brought it that I
should procure indictments against everybody who should have
anything to do with its publication. Thus the *Enquirer* was
warned of its character, and has no excuse. It has defied me by
the publication. It deserves to be made responsible to the
extent to which responsibility can be carried, both by indictment
and civil suit for damages.

Under the aggravating circumstances I am not certain
whether I ought to write at all; whether at the outset I

ought not, as much for the relations that such an outrage
bears to the community as to myself, to begin at the other
end. The press has fallen into a too common practice
of publishing libels one day only to retract them the
next to escape their consequences, which has made it a
reproach to the American people and a byword to the other
nations. I was thunderstricken to learn that the *Enquirer*,
which I had uniformly found a most honourably-conducted
paper, could be inveigled by a New York correspondent into the
publication of an article which, to say nothing about its dozen
libels, has all the ear-marks of a writer for the vilest police-sheet
in the country. The low and vulgar conception evident in every
sentence ought to debar a paper that would publish it from
admission into any family. And I was puzzled to know why
the *Enquirer*, of all other papers in the country, should have
now given this exhibit of malice against me when it had been so
courteous previously. When I lectured in Robinson's Opera
House last January, the *Enquirer* gave the best reports of my
lectures, as well as the most flattering personal comments of any
of the city papers.

Shame on the *Enquirer*, to thus ruthlessly pursue a woman,
who through every form of opposition, and, self-made, has
commanded such comments in its columns. Shame! Place
these remarks side by side with this article as an exponent of
its animus, and how much of it would stand for truth! Look at
it as I may, I can see nothing but malice in it. It is a string of
sentences, each one of which, save two, is barbed with a lie.
Never was there such a mass of venom in so small a space.
It must have been prepared revengefully, probably by some
one who had sought and failed to blackmail me to suppress some
such article. Such wanton maligning; such persistent following
of anybody by the press; of long-since exploded falsehoods, first
in one and then another of the outside papers by correspondents,
who live upon the price for suppressions of their damaging

articles, failing to obtain which they have them published, should receive severe chastisement.

"Living with one who was recognised as her husband!" Why shouldn't I have lived with my husband? and why shouldn't he be recognised as such, when we were married in Dayton, Ohio, regularly and properly by a Presbyterian minister, the Rev. Mr. Thomas, in 1866, the certificate of which, it is well known, I produced in the courts during our trials here in 1872 and 1873 ? Then, why these sneaking insinuations, unless it be to carry the idea that my life has been irregular ?

But how can I undo the damage? I never can. A lie travels where the truth can never follow it, and so much faster that the truth can never catch it. I shall have unnumbered papers sent me that contain the lies; but I shall never hear of their refutation. Among the thousands before whom I have appeared this article will excite contempt for the papers that have published it, as I have already occasion to know. They understand the meaning of such articles, and are drawn the nearer to me by them ; but it is among the millions upon whom, as a public speaker, I depend to make my audiences, in the places where I have never been, where the damage will be done.

Perhaps the *Enquirer* does not know that during our trials in the courts, paid agents in the Beecher interest traced us from our cradle up, to fasten some deed upon us that might be shown in court to our disadvantage, and failed to find a blemish even. All the vile insinuations vanish into thin air in the lying lips of their inventors.

VICTORIA C. WOODHULL.

HOW SCANDALS ARE SPREAD.

MRS. CLARA B. WARNER. Stated by herself to have belonged in a good position in Elizabeth, New Jersey—but now poor and ashamed to live in her own country from her husband having been a ruined man through Mrs. J. B. Martin and her sister Lady Cook at the time they lived in 23rd Street, New York—where he went first from curiosity to see them, then to his ruin and her sorrow. He became in every sense a ruined man and she could not bear her children to know their father's disgrace. She cried, and showed an extract from an American paper, not very severe to the best of my memory, but which she kept against them, and said she had mislaid another, a longer and a stronger article. She Mrs. Warner was a ruined woman, and a disgraced wife—through Victoria C. Woodhull and Tennie C. Claflin.

This statement was made at 27, Norfolk Street, Strand, in the spring of 1889, before Mrs. ——, and I think Mrs. —— was present.

The above is but a small part of the net woven to hurt innocent women by false and garbled statement got up from wicked minds to use false statements and to weave them into tales to hurt two who have never raised a finger to injure those who reviled them the bitterest. Thank God the clouds are clearing and the day has come when all their enemies will be crushed, for I have known them twenty years and never saw two *such* noble self-sacrificing women ; and my experience in the world, with professional, literary, and press people, has shown me how vile can be the harm done by want of thought as well as by intention in *one* weak moment. I even hurt them, but God forgive me. I was tempted by a cruel, designing, wicked man who showed the soft paw to deal a deadly blow and to make me the instrument. I mean Mr. —— who sent for me to do his dirty *dictated* work. I little knew what would follow, and never discerned his deep vindictive motive to strike Victoria C. Woodhull the greatest of Reformers, and her ever constant co-worker, Tennie C. Claflin—for to my knowledge *they* had never injured him—what ever tempted him to hatch such a vile conspiracy, perhaps to throw on others the reflex of his own life—a good man never could have divined so infamous a plot, but compensation has an inevitable law and he will reap as he has sown.

M. M. SCHÖNBERG.

January 18th, 1890.

MEMORANDUM.

WENT with Victoria to the Temperance Hospital in the Hampstead Road; asked the Lady-Superintendent for Mrs. Warner and found her in the ward. Were shown into the Board-room. Had a long conversation.

She did not ask our names or reason of our calling, but told her story with the utmost readiness. Was of Elizabeth, New Jersey, U.S.A., and had been happily married, but her husband (dead these ten years) had become unfaithful to her, had gone after other women. He became infatuated about Mrs. Woodhull, used to rave about her eloquence; no one could escape her influence, she was the "Psychology of New York." Her drawing-room was frequented by the best men of New York, Washington, and Boston.

Had never seen Mrs. Woodhull herself; had been brought up in strict Puritan ideas, would not trust herself in the presence of such a woman, thought she should have become a "demon" had she found herself in the presence of Victoria Woodhull.

Mr. Warner went constantly to Mrs. Woodhull's house, used to go every week, it might have been every day. Could not distinctly assert criminal intimacy, but knew they had been closeted together for four or five hours. Mr. Warner had described the parlour, and the pattern of the carpet. He had

seen Tennie Claflin sitting on the carpet, "in a kind of seance."
He had spent his money and her's (Mrs. Warner's) on the two
sisters.

Mrs. Woodhull had attacked Henry Ward Beecher, whom
Mrs. Warner believed to be innocent. Beecher had not seduced
Mrs. Tilton, but Mrs. Woodhull had ruined Tilton, and in fact
half the men in New York City and Brooklyn.

It was in 1876-1879 that this intimacy of Mr. Warner's arose,
it might have begun in 1874.

Believed that Mrs. Woodhull was now married and in
London; could not remember her husband's name, but pitied
him and his family. Could not understand how he could have
been induced to marry Mrs. Woodhull, supposed it was her great
power to infatuate.

Thought that such a woman as Mrs. Woodhull was hardly fit
to live. Victoria asked her what she should think of a woman
who made such charges without just cause against another woman?
Mrs. Warner thought that hanging would be too good for her.

Victoria then said, "I am Victoria Woodhull Martin. Every
word you have uttered is a lie; I have never known
Mr. Warner even by name, and he has never been in my house.
You have traded in London on this infamous story to elicit
sympathy and to get money. It is through just such wretches
as you that my name has been blackened in London and
America." I then read to her Miss Schönberg's statement.
The rest of the interview was a series of prevarications on the
part of Mrs. Warner, she attempting to deny or alter all her
previous statements.

She now said that she had not called on Victoria Woodhull
in New York, or proved the truth of Mr. Warner's statements,
because she did not know her address; that the "closeting"
was with Miss Claflin; that in all that she had said she
was only repeating what her husband had told her; &c. I
asked her if her husband had told her that he was spending his

money on Mrs. Woodhull or her sister? I asked her whether she was still prepared to take the word of her husband, who on her own showing had deceived her in act, against what she was now told. In the end she signed a sort of retraction. I told her that it did not matter what she signed, as the matter would not end in that room.

JOHN B. MARTIN.

January 18th, 1890.

For the first time in my life I have seen Mrs. Victoria C. Woodhull, and from all I have been previously informed of her from sources outside, I have undoubtedly been misinformed, and greatly regret any injustice which I may have done her when pressed by Mrs. ——— and Miss Schönberg at their private interview in Norfolk Street, Strand, to state what I had heard in New York both from my husband and his great friend. Having never known or seen her in New York or elsewhere, I have fully credited my husband's statement of his intimacy with Miss Claflin in New York City.

Upon seeing and talking with Mrs. V. W. Martin I do not credit any of the stories with which I have been deluded by persons who evidently have envied her power and marvellously beautiful spirit, and will gladly refute any impression that may have gone forth in any manner to disparage her in the slightest. After meeting Mrs. Woodhull Martin I consider her to be infinitely above any such conduct or behaviour as my husband and friends reported to me.

C. B. WARNER.

January 18th, 1890.

HOW PRESS LIBELS ARE WRITTEN.

FROM the bottom of my heart I regret that ever tempted in a weak moment I complied with that wicked wish of Mr. —— to write an article at·once spicy and telling about Mrs. J. B. Martin (Victoria C. Woodhull) and Lady Cook (Tennie C. Claflin). From beginning to end it was wicked, and I was made the tool of a conspiracy of wicked men to crush two women. The article referred to is practically mine, and headed—Two Sirens of New York: it appeared in the New York Morning Journal, May 9th, 1886.

The first article I gave Mr. —— he said was not *strong* enough, and gave me his suggestions to carry out, from, as he said to me, what he had heard lately at a dinner when their names were mentioned. The article was most infamous, false, and a lie; but his wicked tongue and fair speech gained a wicked advantage over me.

Afterwards Mrs. —— sent me first her card and then a painted New Year's card and a request to call first at an hotel near the Temple Chambers. At that place I saw her when she told me she had heard from Mr. —— that I could introduce her to just the people she wanted to see, Mrs. J. B. Martin, &c. I not falling into her wishes was called by her suspicious. The next time and only one at that place Mr. —— came in and did not know me; when I spoke to him Mrs. —— spoke to him outside her door, and came back with many excuses and apologies for his treatment of me, but said he was most peculiar, and had been her lawyer, but also her cause of much sorrow, etc.

Then she sent for me to lunch at —— and told me how upset she had been the previous week by Miss —— three days with her in hysterics abusing her for having Mr. —— to dine with her and

40 *

visit her,—and how ruined she was by his having compromised her, and that he had forbidden her to visit or to see Mrs. J. B. Martin or Lady Cook. To the latter she had she said written for a request to visit Sir Francis Cook's gallery at Richmond and had never received any reply.

Then she came up to me at Whiteley's and asked me why I had not been to see her (this was just before last Christmas) and why did I induce her to commit herself by visiting Mrs. J. B. Martin where she knew she had talked too much, and that I must do her a favor, get Brete Hart to call upon her—and gave me a bunch of violets.

In giving this my written statement of facts I do it with deep sorrow that ever word or action of mine no matter how tempted was done to injure these two women who deserve no such accusations.

M. M. SCHÖNBERG.

January 18th, 1890.

HOW SLANDERS ARE ORIGINATED.

WHEN in October, 1885, I claimed a year's salary from Mrs. John Biddulph Martin, and made an application for assistance to the Universal Beneficent Society on the ground that I could not obtain what was due to me from Mrs. Martin under an agreement; and when I subsequently renewed the claim through Mrs. Grey, of 8, Thicket Road, Upper Norwood, I knew that I had no claim on either Mr. and Mrs. Martin, or Sir Francis and Lady Cook. I was then as at other times the tool through circumstances of bad, wicked men who had hatched the plot to destroy if possible the grand destiny of two noble women. There has been all over the United States and England a plot beyond human credibility to ruin these ladies. I was chosen as the fittest strongest tool to strike a death blow. Such lies and inventions were not confined to London but spread like wild-fire all over the United States, and then when both these women were quietly settled in their English homes, the scorpions of jealousy and envy could not exist save by demon plots.

I would do all to undo the wicked lies designed by vile men to use me as their fittest tool to strike a death blow. Would I could undo my actions, if deep sorrow and heartfelt regret can plead I claim pardon on that score at their hands. My blows were hard and to the point—and meant to kill, but thank God they failed in the deep wicked designs of the men who hatched that plot, and had been at it for years striking in the dark at every opportunity that presented itself. No chance was lost to strike Victoria C. Woodhull and Tennie C. Claflin at every occasion where their names were mentioned, whether in drawing rooms, dining rooms, clubs, or balls, or hotels, or even business places—always lies hatched against them by wicked tongues.

M. M. SCHÖNBERG.

January 22nd, 1890.

WHAT WAS HER CRIME?

NEVER since the lowly Nazarene wrestled with his fate in that lone agony of the garden has mortal been so recklessly misjudged in doctrine or in deed, and so utterly deserted as is Victoria C. Woodhull; but never did grander instrument than she respond to the sweet touch of angel hands. At last, however, driven by wilful and persistent misrepresentation and brutal persecution, her outraged woman's heart bursts forth with its overburdened agony for its miseries, and not less for those of an unthinking world. She came to it with the love of a mother, the pity of an angel in her heart for its condition, her prescient soul filled with the destiny of unborn generations, to pour the healing balm into the wounds of the present, so that those who follow may be blessed thereby. She gave herself without reserve, devoting every energy of her body and intuition of her soul, giving all. She saw the people decaying, dying; death laying its icy hand on every family to claim its own, and vice and crime, the fruits of ignorance, casting blight everywhere. Her inspirations grasped the causes of this misery—the wild delirium of the human passions—and she depicted the desolation that follows in their trail in true but tragic colours.

But her path has been one long struggle up the heights of Calvary, bearing the cross of deprivation and opprobrium, which became heavier and sharper as she approached the summit. At every step a poisoned dagger tore her body; another outrage pierced her heart. Javelins of hate and fury, or else of envy or of malice, were thrust into her until not a spot upon her body but is transfixed by them; not a sympathy of her heart but what is wounded. Her life has been defamed; her reputation torn in tatters; her motives foully impugned; her statements egregiously perverted. The more unselfishly she devoted herself, the more bitterly has she been followed. No place except a dungeon has been deemed bad enough for her. If she were permitted to hire a house for shelter for herself, her aged parents and dependent children, she had to pay five thousand dollars for what others would have had for two; if she lodged at an hotel she has been charged hundreds where others paid but fifties; if she rented a hall in which to lecture, some cities have exacted four and six hundred dollars, for which others paid but one-fourth these sums, and then as if these extortions were not odious enough they were followed by denying the desired privileges altogether, city officials combining to prevent her lectures in halls for which she had already paid the enormous charges; turned from house and home; driven from hotel to hotel; the doors of even common boarding-houses closed in her face, until wandering in the streets of New York at midnight with her children, she applied in vain from hotel to hotel for a single night's lodging, and finally compelled in the small hours of the morning to resort to her office to seek repose upon its floor, for months unable to obtain a better place; her child shut out of school, or, if admitted under an assumed name, until her real name was discovered to the school, paying two thousand dollars for what others had for four hundred—a tax of hundreds per cent. levied upon her very name in everything, and all this for months before the publication of the Beecher scandal. Indeed, as soon as she attacked the evils in society, and showed the trail of the serpent in its core, and that the miseries of the race there have their source, this same society turned upon her and did its best to slay her. It was determined that its misdeeds should not be investigated, and it revenged itself upon her who wished only to save it from itself.

Besides the general persecution, she has had special ones to drain the scanty means that the others left her. The victim of a conspiracy between the Church and State, she was shut up in prison to stop her paper and her pen; dragged from the rostrum to the dungeon to close her mouth; put under excessive bail to keep her there; paying thousands of dollars to extricate herself; her office, trunks, papers, in the meantime ransacked and rifled; new prisons opening to receive her as fast as old ones closed behind her; her bail tampered with; induced to give her up when finally she had escaped from the last of their resorts; schemes devised while in duress to take her life, but defended against them all by the watchfulness of guardian angels, who assured her every day she should be rescued from the foul designs, but not without damaging her thousands upon thousands of dollars in her paper, destroying all her other business totally, and casting an obloquy upon her name, which she has not yet escaped. Let all these things be put together, and who will not wonder that she lives?

When the prison loomed before her, and the church was seeking to destroy her, and calumny had plaited its crown of thorns, when not a whilom friend stood by, why wonder that the agony of her Gethsemane should have well-nigh cheated it of its victim ?

Three times, indeed, during these fiery trials did this woman's weary feet stray to the grateful cool of the mystic river. 'Twas a heart-crushed wife and mother bursting the shackles of ignorance and prejudice, and going down to death burdened by their weight, but the mighty impulse of a million prayers appealing to angels stayed her footsteps, and would not permit her to cross over, but sent her back to her work unfinished. Was it simply the strain of her own toil that so well-nigh snapped the chords of life ?

Why should she have thus been called to tread the thorny road leaving her tracks blood-stained behind her ? Why have her sufferings been prolonged a thousand times beyond the bitterness of death ? Why the cross, the crown of thorns, the spear, the nails of crucifixion ? Surely these have not been for nothing. It is only through great trials that great truths are born, and those who cannot endure the former cannot bear the latter. It was for this that Jesus suffered, and it is for this that the persecutions of this age have been directed against this martyr-woman.

She has endured all this and still she lives, her nearest friends only surmising a portion of what she has suffered. Under all, she struggled to maintain herself and cause, going often in the greatest destitution, without even the necessary clothes and food for the comfort of herself and family, devoting every dollar from her paper and her lectures that was needed to keep that paper and her principles before the world. To be sure she has lectured and to crowded houses, and this has been thought to be a source of unlimited means for her; but the extortions to which she has been obliged to submit; the blackmailing from certain quarters

to which she has been subject; the prices of the keys of gold with
which she has had to open the doors of halls in each of the large
cities, spending in many instances, no matter how much they
were, double her receipts; obliged to keep up a large expense so
that her invalid boy might have a home in her absence; compelled
to take her daughter on her trips because no one could have her
at any price save under an assumed name (her sisters' families
even could not receive her, for her presence, as well as that of
her mother, caused their ejection from their homes, and destroyed
their means of living)—none of these things are considered in
such conclusion. No tongue can tell the extremities to which
this hunted woman has been driven by ignorance and prejudice;
nor the costs to them who have dared to countenance or shelter
her. Daily and nightly on bended knees, with streaming eyes
and breaking heart, she asks, how long, oh Lord, how long shall
this continue? The only wonder is that she has been able to
stand at all. Besides, she has been compelled to flood the
country in advance on her routes, with the favourable notices of
the press (which she never fails to win), to break down the
prejudice and prepare the way to be heard. Thousands of dollars
have been used in this way, and if they had not been, she could
never have kept herself before the country, nor carried on the
work. In all this, no pen can picture the distress to which she
has been reduced. The stones in the streets over which she
has travelled in her agony, would have cried out against her
persecutors could they have spoken of what was passing over
them.

Now, WHAT WAS HER CRIME?—What the offence for which all
these maledictions have been showered upon her? Intelligent
parentage has been the central fact of all her discussion, accompanied only with the demand for such conditions for woman as
will permit her, as God's own architect, to become a perfect
artist in the masterwork of creating His images; that woman
shall require the same chastity of man that he requires of her;

that the ruling passion, the demon lust, shall be subject to intelligence, and no longer riot barbarously, at the expense of womanhood, realizing that, when she shall become properly informed about the sanctity of maternity, she will crush this monster lust beneath her heel. She has asked for nothing more; she will be content with nothing less. And this is her crime. Who can bring against her any other?

Every mission has its aim, and that to which this woman has been appointed is the solution of the great mystery which the Bible itself declares to be sealed up within its pages—the key to unlock the tomb, and give the power to triumph over death, accomplishing immortality in the flesh and the resurrection. This mighty problem launched upon the world, made her the centre of such anxiety and expectancy that she was overpowered by the influence which tended to defeat the very purpose of her life, and to find relief she had to divorce herself both in body and in mind from the world; from everything, and turn the attention of the people in a new direction. For several months she has been compelled to refrain from contact with the world, and has only gone before it when compelled to do so. Taking advantage of this, interested persons have set false and malicious rumours afloat, and these rumours have penetrated to those who have a deep interest in the cause and saddened them. But she had to be free; the public mind had to be diverted from her so that the great problem of which she is pregnant might have its birth. Subject to this momentous truth, with her heart, soul and mind centered in the solution of this mystery, she is physically unable to encounter the world and struggle with it as has been her custom. Where once she could lecture every night, she is now incapable of doing so more than once a week, and even then at the peril of her life, or at the expense of days of prostration in which the development of the truths with which she is in travail is wholly checked.

Isolated in the heart of this great city, this weary woman sits

crushed by the persecutions that have, at last, made her home-
less, penniless, with none of the necessaries, to say nothing of
the comforts of life ; ground almost to death beneath the iron
heel under which she has been trampled so relentlessly ;
bowed in sorrow to see the world ignoring the balm she has to
offer it, and by permitting her to be crushed, crushing the great
truth which she was sent to discover to it, but still as earnest,
eager, devoted to that truth, as if the world had strewn her path
with roses rather than with thorns. The great mystery of which
she speaks has been made known to her, and under the right
conditions she can demonstrate it to the world. Under these
circumstances I make this appeal to the public for the assistance
that she needs to enable her to gestate this truth till its full time
is come. She cannot give up without this one more effort to
bear to the world the greatest, grandest, most stupendous fact
of all the ages—the fact which is to be the culmination of
creation—its last struggle to attain perfection for the race ; the
fulfilment of the prophecy of St. Paul, who said : "The last
enemy that shall be destroyed is death." The Bible declares
this fact o'er and o'er again ; the Christian world believes it.
"The time of the end," as declared by Daniel and re-affirmed by
St. John, which is the salvation spoken of by Christ when He
said "*He that believeth on Me shall never die,*" is near. General
indications show it, and special revelations prove it.

It is right, nay, it is a duty, to frankly state her situation and
seek the necessary aid to carry on this work, especially since
she is unable to secure it, as she had hoped to herself, by
lecturing. Her sensitive organization, strung up to the intensest
pitch by the tremendous import of her work, cannot encounter
the influences of public audiences. Their conditions appeal so
to her sympathies that she cannot restrain them, and they push
her on irresistibly to exertions beyond her strength, and she
retires from the rostrum with every nerve unstrung to fall into
the arms of friends who struggle for hours to keep the breath

of life in her, and followed by days of prostration, which she is now suffering from recent exertions in New York, Boston, Philadelphia, and other places. Thus it is impossible for her to fill the numerous engagements now offering. She must return to the printing press to reach the people. Hundreds of pages of manuscript, freighted with living truths, born since the suspension of *The Weekly*, wait for the printer, while the people, finding the loss of that paper not replaced by any other, demand its re-issue.

Drunkenness, licentiousness, debauchery, misery, hate and envy—vices under which the world moans with anguish, and from which it is sinking to decay and darkness (the very heavens draped in mourning for their effects) would flee before the dawning light of these life-giving truths for which the world cannot hope to look in any other direction. Everybody, save this woman, avoids this issue, is afraid to grapple with the monster publicly ; but she, overburdened with its import, and the desire to give it to the world, sits under its ban, deprived by its persecutions of the power to pour it out. She needs the assistance of the suffering people, and they require what she has got to give them, and cannot afford to leave her *hors-de-combat*. She needs a home in which to find repose and peace upon which the full realization of the truth depends, and in which she can receive those who seek it. Besides, her life hangs by a brittle thread dependent on relief to stem the tide of persecutions.

There are thousands of anxious hearts and willing hands ready to sustain her in this work, but the busy tongue of malice, the evil whisperings of hate and the terrible libels published by the press and people, knowing them to be false and monstrous, or not caring so they ruined her, have hid her from their sight, and she has no way to pierce the veil and reach their hearts save by this means ; thousands who are waiting for the truth believing it is soon to come. It is to these thousands that she addresses this communication, and to whom she reaffirms her undying devotion to this cause, denying any and all rumours that even cast a colour of faltering on her course; or a shadow of recreancy to the principles on which she stands, representative before the world, and which form the great drama, in which she has played, and will still play, the tragic part, and which constitute both the stage and the religion of her life, never to be deserted for any other until God himself shall ring down the curtain or reset the scenes.

Let those who find an interest in this, remember, that she has expended a princely fortune in this work, and besides giving all, also suffered all, and in remembering lend to God of this abundance, to help her to stem the tide, against which she is near to succumbing, and go on to a glorious culmination. Moreover, those who regard with wise and cool deliberation, the anarchy and confusion upon the brink of which this country now stands trembling, before finally falling into it; the famines and pestilences in divers places, and the wars and rumours of wars sounding through the world, will see the time approaching which Jesus said would precede the judgment day and resurrection, and will cast themselves loose from the institutions tottering with decay, to rally round the new that shall replace them when they shall fall; and thus inaugurate the new religion.

All communications should be addressed to Victoria Claflin Woodhull,* and remittances made to her in post-office orders, registered letters, drafts to her order (in no case sending money loose in letters, for such letters never reach her, forcing her to believe that her mail has been tampered with for years), to . . . . . or by express, which will receive immediate and proper acknowledgment.

TENNIE C. CLAFLIN.

New York City, *November 27th*, 1876.

---

* [Now Mrs. John Biddulph Martin] 17, Hyde Park Gate, London, Eng.; and 142, West 70th Street, N.Y. City, U.S.A.—*February 24th*, 1890.

Philip, king of Macedon, discovered great moderation even when he was spoken to in shocking and injurious terms. At the close of an audience which he gave to some Athenian Ambassadors, who had come to complain of some act of hostility, he asked whether he could do them any service.

"The greatest service thou couldst do us," said Demochares, "would be to hang thyself." Philip, though he perceived all the persons present were highly offended at these words, answered with the utmost calmness of temper, "Go, tell your superiors that those who dare make use of insolent language are more haughty and less peaceably inclined than those who can forgive them."

Julius Cæsar was not more eminent for his valour in overcoming his enemies than for his humane efforts in reconciling and attaching them to his dominion. In the battle of Pharsalia he rode to and fro, calling out vehemently, "Spare, spare the citizens!" Nor were any killed, but such as obstinately refuse to accept life. After the battle he gave every man on his own side leave to save any of the opposite from the list of proscription; and at no long time after he issued an edict, permitting all whom he had not yet pardoned, to return in peace to Italy, to enjoy their estates and honours. It was a common saying of Cæsar that no music was so charming to his ears as the requests of his friends and the supplications of those in want of his assistance.

Aristippus and Æschines having quarrelled, Aristippus came to his opponent, and said, "Æschines, shall we be friends?" "Yes," he replied, "with all my heart." "But remember," said Aristippus, "that I, being older than you, do make the first motion." "Yes," replied Æschines, "and therefore I conclude that you are the worthiest man, for I began the strife and you began the peace."

Antigonus, king of Syria, during one of his campaigns, one day overheard some of his soldiers reviling him behind his tent; but instead of summoning them to appear and answer for their contumely, and exercising his authority in their punishment, he barely drew aside the curtain of his tent, and said, "*Gentlemen, just remove to a greater distance, for your king hears you.*"

CPSIA information can be obtained
at www.ICGtesting.com
Printed in the USA
LVHW091007060121
675862LV00016B/46